SOCIAL STRUCTURE AND NETWORK ANALYSIS

SAGE FOCUS EDITIONS

social structure and network analysis

edited by
Peter V. Marsden
and **Nan Lin**

SAGE PUBLICATIONS
Beverly Hills / London / New Delhi

For information address:

SAGE Publications, Inc.
275 South Beverly Drive
Beverly Hills, California 90212

SAGE Publications India Pvt. Ltd.
C-236 Defence Colony
New Delhi 110 024, India

SAGE Publications Ltd
28 Banner Street
London EC1Y 8QE, England

Printed in the United States of America

Library of Congress Cataloging in Publication Data

Main entry under title:

Social structure and network analysis.

(Sage focus editions ; 57)
Bibliography: p.
1. Social structure—Addresses, essays, lectures. I. Marsden, Peter V. II. Lin, Nan.
HM131.S612 1982 305 82-10564
ISBN 0-8039-1888-7
ISBN 0-8039-1889-5 (pbk.)

FIRST PRINTING

Contents

Preface

The papers assembled in this collection reflect the content of the Albany Conference on Contributions of Networks Analysis to Structural Sociology, held at the State University of New York at Albany on April 3-4, 1981. This conference was called to draw together a group of researchers active in the study of social networks to discuss theoretical and substantive issues in structural sociology. Its premise was that there is more to network analysis than a new set of techniques for gathering and analyzing data; the network approach offers a natural method for bringing a *structural* viewpoint to bear on social science problems and for giving operational meaning to relational concepts. As such, it offers opportunities for making new contributions to established fields of social science knowledge. The focus of the conference was on the current state of and potential for such contributions.

We hope that the chapters herein will be of interest to those who have followed the development of network analysis and are interested in its capability to explain social behavior. We also think the book will provide an introduction to current substantive and theoretical developments and problems (as distinct from methodological ones) to those curious about the intellectual activity and excitement the approach has generated.

As editors of the collection and participants in the Albany Conference, we have numerous debts to record here. The conference was conceived by a planning committee composed of Nan Lin, Ronald S. Burt, Richard D. Alba, and Steve Rytina. Funding for the conference and the travel expenses of all participants was provided by several subunits of the State University of New York at Albany: the Department of Sociology (Nan Lin, Chair), the Vice President's Office for Research (Warren Ilchman, Vice President), and the College of Social and Behavioral Sciences (John Webb, Dean). Conference arrangements were smoothly coordinated by Peggi Patterson of the Department of Sociology of the State University of New York at Albany, and we are grateful to the following persons in that department for their assistance in the conduct of the conference and its associated social functions: Richard H. Hall, Paul Meadows (faculty), Linda Schroll (staff), and Carolyn Beeker, Mary Dumin, Kevin Fitzpatrick, Steve Light, Michael Lindsey, and Mary Woelfel (graduate students). We appreciate the commentary that James S. Coleman provided on some of the papers presented at the conference. The staff of the Department of Sociology at the University of North Carolina at Chapel Hill, including Ophelia Andrew, Bruce Geyer, Janet Jones, Marsha Jones, Carol Pickard, and Anna K. Tyndall, has been of invaluable assistance in the preparation of the final manuscript. Finally, Karen E. Campbell, Mary Ellen Marsden, and Catherine R. Zimmer assisted in proofreading.

Peter V. Marsden
Chapel Hill, NC

Nan Lin
Albany, NY

Introduction

If *social structure* is not the single most important concept in sociology, and in social science more generally, it is certainly one of a very small number of central concepts. The premise that behaviors or actions are interpretable only in relation to the positions of actors in social structure underlies much social scientific inquiry. There is at present, however, limited consensus on the meaning of the term "social structure." Some diverse views of the concept are presented in a collection edited by Blau (1975). Blau (1981) discusses different perspectives on the concept, seeking commonalities in these treatments. Often the concept of social structure is used as little more than a metaphor; frequently, even when the use of the concept is nonmetaphorical, efforts to apply it have been highly indirect on an operational level, attempting to measure social structure as reflected in individual attributes or in contextual variables given by group memberships.

Over the past two decades, however, and particularly during the 1970s, an approach to studying social structure known as *network analysis* has developed. Defining social structure as "a persisting pattern of social relationships among social positions" (Laumann, 1966), this approach focuses attention on relationships between actors rather than on attributes of actors or their group memberships. The distinctive features of the approach are its effort to deal explicitly and directly with the concept of social structure and its attempts to construct falsifiable models and methods for describing social structure and answering questions about its causes and consequences. Some recent review articles on network analysis are by Burt (1980c), Alba (1981), and Wellman (1982a).

Of course, the study of social networks did not begin in the last two decades; among the precursors of recent developments are Moreno's (1934) sociometry in school classrooms, numerous experimental studies of communication patterns in small groups (such as Bavelas, 1950), and observational studies in urban anthropology, in both developed and less developed countries (such as Bott, 1971; Boissevain and Mitchell, 1973).

Nonetheless, the 1970s witnessed the development of a self-consciousness among network analysts that does not appear to have been present prior to that time. By the end of the decade, in fact, some sociologists of science were inclined to view the social network approach as a new paradigm in social science and to regard network analysis as a new specialty area within sociology. Certainly, there were many organizational signs of the increased intellectual activity in the area. These include the founding of an interdisciplinary organization, the International Network for Social Network Analysis (INSNA), with its newsletter, *Connections*; the establishment of a new journal, *Social Networks*; the routine inclusion of one or more sessions devoted to social networks on the program for the Annual Meetings of the American Sociological Association; and the organization of numerous interdisciplinary conferences drawing together network analysts from diverse academic and nonacademic settings.

These organizational developments have provided some coherence to the study of social networks and may have contributed to the rapidity with which the diverse analytic approaches now available have been created. The developments are signs of an encouraging vitality, and they signal the possibility of sustained and cumulative work on a relational conception of social structure. Many persons involved in the study of social networks, however, find it appealing less as a specialty area in its own right than as a general orientation capable of capturing and giving operational meaning to concepts present in existing theories of social structure. These scholars are attracted to the study of networks because they think that such an orientation can lead to new contributions in established specialties and fields of inquiry, such as social stratification, urban sociology, the sociology of mental health, political sociology, or the sociology of formal organizations. The network orientation offers new approaches to describing and studying social structure and to dealing with complex problems of integrating levels of analysis: the manner in which individual actions create social structure; the manner in which social structure, once created, constrains individual and collective action; or the manner in which attitudes and behaviors of actors are determined by the social context in which action takes place.

The chapters in this collection are concerned with current and potential contributions of the network orientation to substantive fields in social science; they do not, for the most part, focus on the considerable methodological advances made in the area (but see Burt, 1980c; Burt and Minor, 1982). We should emphasize, however, that these are not merely "applied" studies; use of a network approach poses themes that are present in existing fields in new ways. It causes an analyst, for instance, to think differently about the manner in which social positions are defined or about the interplay between social structure and individual action. Most of the chapters are based on presentations made at the April 1981 Albany Conference on Contributions of Networks Analysis to Structural Sociology, which was called to focus the attention of network analysts on theoretical and substantive issues.

The chapters in Part I center on the study of social structure. The authors are concerned with issues in the areas of social stratification and urban sociology. In Part II, attention shifts to the consequences of social networks; here the authors address problems in social stratification, the sociology of science, the sociology of mental health, and political sociology. Part III contains chapters that are jointly concerned with social networks and purposive action. Substantively dealing with questions in the areas of political sociology and the sociology of formal organizations, the authors address issues having to do with the creation of relationships and social structures and with the use of social networks as resources by actors embedded within them. Finally, Part IV contains commentaries on the foregoing studies, provided by two eminent structural sociologists familiar with the network orientation, though not closely identified with network analysis as a specialty. These commentaries assess the status of and prospects for network analysis as a coherent approach to studying social structure.

I.

Network Studies of Social Structure

The four chapters in this section illustrate the diversity among network analysts, both in analytic approaches to the study of social structure and in substantive concerns. The effort to represent structure as a persisting pattern of social relations involves several subtasks: Rules of inclusion for actors and types of social relations must be specified; social positions into which actors are mapped must be identified; and regularities in the relationships linking incumbents of these social positions must be analyzed and characterized. With suitable representations of social structural features in hand, analysts are prepared to address questions concerning correlates or underlying causes of social structure. The authors of the following four chapters deal with one or more of these aspects of the analysis of social structure.

Breiger's chapter focuses on the identification of social positions as applied to social mobility studies. Drawing on his earlier work on the mapping of actors into structurally equivalent blocks or positions (White et al., 1976; Breiger, 1979, 1981c), he argues that the fundamental units of analysis for social mobility research should be social classes consisting of occupations that are structurally equivalent in a well-defined sense. In this context, Breiger argues that occupations are structurally equivalent if they satisfy a criterion of internal homogeneity defined by mobility relations. He outlines statistical methods for assessing the extent to which a proposed aggregation of occupations into social classes satisfies his internal homogeneity criterion as well as some other criteria that have been proposed. He illustrates the approach with a classic set of data on mobility in Great Britain. This discussion is followed by a brief note by Goodman concerning Breiger's homogeneity criterion and alternative criteria, which, in turn, is followed by Breiger's response. Elsewhere, Breiger (1981b) proceeds to characterize the pattern of mobility relations among social classes identified by the methods given here.

Moore and Alba are concerned with correlates of cohesion in elites. This, a second topic in the area of social stratification, has received substantial attention from network analysts because social relations, both overlapping memberships in formally recognized groups (such as corporate boards of directors and social clubs) and intimate interpersonal relations (such as friendship and intermarriage), are a presumed basis of elite unity. Here, Moore and Alba analyze data from the 1971-1972 American Leadership Study, centering their analysis on the class and status origins of persons identified as members of the American elite by this study. In addition to examining the extent to which the origins of elite members are representative of the American population, Moore and Alba explore the degree to which these background characteristics are associated with differentiation within the elite, conceived in terms of both group memberships and informal discussion relationships.

The network approach has been of special importance in the study of the urban community, in large part because it is well suited to test the implications of theories of social change which suggested that industrialization and bureaucratization were to create a mass society marked by the atomization of individuals and the withering away of informal relations of friendship, neighboring, and helping or support. Wellman's chapter reviews the work on community structure done by network analysts, which has shown that this image of "Community Lost" is incorrect. Wellman gives special attention to two studies, done by his research group, of informal relationships in the Toronto borough of East York. These studies examine the "personal communities" or "egocentric networks" (Mitchell, 1969) of urbanites, rather than attempting to portray the social structure of the community as a whole.

Rytina studies urban areas, too, but his concerns are quite different from Wellman's. Rytina adopts a macroscopic perspective, taking populous U.S. standard metropolitan statistical areas as his units of analysis. Drawing on Blau's (1977a, 1977b) macrostructural theory of social structure, Rytina examines effects of size distributions and proportions on levels of intergroup contact, indexed by intermarriage. He analyzes intermarriage levels by race, education, and mother tongue, finding that the heterogeneity of an urban area is associated with increased intermarriage and therefore with social integration in Blau's sense.

Though the chapters in this section do not exhaustively cover the range of approaches to the study of social structure taken by network analysts, they do illustrate several of those approaches. They are suggestive of the utility of the social network orientation within a number of substantive fields in social science. They also set the stage for the chapters in Part II, which are concerned with assessing the impact of structural features on individual outcomes.

1

A Structural Analysis of Occupational Mobility

RONALD L. BREIGER

One of the most promising developments within contemporary sociology is the bringing to bear of structural approaches on the study of social mobility and stratification. Sorokin (1927) set the agenda by insisting that mobility and stratification are *paired* concepts requiring *mutual* articulation, each meaningless without the other. Research findings and the development of explicit models mark the substantial progress attained by addressing this agenda within a variety of structural perspectives.[1]

In a review of several approaches, Fararo (1973: 488) concludes that "one of the most significant [outstanding] problems in mobility research is the representation of the 'space' within which positions exist, and within which social units exhibit movement from position to position. . . . This problem specializes to the definition of strata or classes." Definitions of strata and classes abound in sociological theory; however, progress in relating them to data on occupational mobility has been slight. Hope (1981c) remarks that,

> as actually practised, the analysis of class mobility is certainly less theoretical than analysis of vertical mobility, since a fair amount of theoretical work has gone into the specification of a vertical dimension, whereas theory does not even tell us how many classes exist,

AUTHOR'S NOTE: Financial support under grant SES80-08658 from the National Science Foundation is gratefully acknowledged.

much less how they should be constituted. Class analysis presupposes a theory of class measurement, which sociologists have simply not attempted to construct.

This chapter presents a conceptualization of social classes that provides models for the analysis of mobility tables. Mobility and class structure are treated as dual concepts, each requiring consideration of the other in its conceptualization and analysis. A specific analytical framework (Breiger, 1981b) is reviewed, and a new application is provided. Additionally, the chapter offers a perspective for consideration of the recent elaborations, extensions, and research applications of the framework (Breiger, 1981a; Goodman, 1981; Holland and Leinhardt, 1981; Hope, 1981b; Yamaguchi, 1982); in particular, the elaboration of Goodman (1981) is addressed in some detail.

Social Mobility and Social Structure

The two essential ideas that I employ are those of *boundary* and *pattern.* A fundamental contribution of structural sociology (see, for example, the discussion in Blau, 1981) is the definition of social structure as consisting of observable, bounded units that are able to sustain a self-consistent pattern of relations among themselves. This emphasis on self-consistency leads immediately to a structural definition of social classes–a definition that is distinct from the many other usages of the term that are widespread today (see Haller and Hodge, 1981; Pappi, 1981).

This perspective on social class, although it has remained largely outside the realm of quantitative mobility studies, is hardly novel. Six decades ago Max Weber developed an elaborate typology of classes, but he reserved the term "social class" for bounded units arising from the aggregation of mobility flows. A social class, in Weber's sense, is defined by the criterion of a common pattern of mobility chances, either within individual careers or across the generations (Weber, 1922/1978: 302). In the absence of this concept of *social* class, the analyst would confront an endless multiplicity of class situations. But for Weber a structure of social classes exists only when mobility chances of individuals within the classes cluster in such a way as to create a common nexus of social interchange (see, for example, Giddens, 1973: 43-49).

There is no shortage of hypotheses concerning social classes conceived as aggregates of occupational and industrial categories. To grasp the range of hypotheses, and the corresponding opportunities both for theoretical development and empirical research, consider just three contrasting claims.

For Thorstein Veblen (1904), the identification of social classes by reference to *occupational* categories was still a relatively recent phenomenon. "Leaving aside the archaic vocations of war, politics, fashion, and religion," Veblen cast the fundamental class boundary as the distinction between "pecuniary or business employments," on the one hand, and "industrial or mechanical employments," on the other.

> In earlier times, and indeed until an uncertain point in the nineteenth century, such a distinction . . . would not to any great extent have coincided with a difference between occupations. But gradually . . . there has supervened a . . . class of men [who] have taken over the work of purchase and sale and of husbanding a store of accumulated values. . . . [T]he distinction between pecuniary and industrial activities or employments has come to coincide more and more nearly with a difference between occupations [Veblen, 1904: 149-50].

As an example of a social class hypothesis formulated with direct reference to typical mobility chances, consider Weber's (1922/1978: 305) postulation of four social classes: the working class as a whole, the petty bourgeoisie, the propertyless intelligentsia and specialists ("technicians, various kinds of white-collar employees, civil servants"), and "the classes privileged through property and education."

A hypothesis of social classes formulated "to estimate the size of the working class according to Poulantzas' criteria" also raises questions about the class homogeneity of mobility chances. Thus, consider as a third example Wright's (1978: 54) cross-classification of occupation (white-collar against blue-collar) by type of sector ("productive" sectors including, for example, agriculture, construction, and manufacturing; "unproductive" sectors including finance, insurance, and government, among others).

A large number of other social class hypotheses might have been adduced (see, for example, Breiger, 1981b: 591-595, which is confined to a variety of claims formulated for the aggregation of a single seventeen-category occupational classification). The fact that most of these claims are mutually incompatible should have provided a clear challenge to analysts of mobility tables. Instead, researchers have persisted in treating such hypotheses as *exogenous* to the development of their formal models.

Within my framework, classes are observable units of analysis hypothesized to explain the detailed mobility from each occupational origin to each destination. This approach is "structural" in that it requires the aggregation of occupational categories so as to induce a homogeneity of mobility exchanges within each aggregate and between each pair of aggregates; in this way, the aggregates ("classes") and their relational structure provide the fundamental units for the mobility table. Thus, mobility and class structure are dual concepts, each requiring consideration of the other in its conceptualization and analysis.

This view of class structure departs from the imagery underlying most theories of social class, but I argue that the departure is advantageous. Veblen, for example, and writers on the so-called new working class, such as Gorz (1968), postulate inclusion of certain salaried professional and technical workers within the working class as it is traditionally defined (with reference to manual occupations). To the extent that this claim explains detailed occupational mobility by my criterion, it provides a testable hypothesis *within* the framework of this chapter. But this activity is quite distinct from assessing the principle underlying (for example) Veblen's theory, namely: that the engineer and technician are devoted to improving the practices of production, while the finance capitalist and the manager restrict production in order to maintain profit (Bell, 1973: 150). Any theory that postulates criteria other than mobility in its definitions of classes cannot be assessed in its own terms by my approach. The goal here is the further development of a *particular* theory of social class as "the totality of those class situations within which individual and generational mobility is easy and typical," with class situations treated as "typical probabilit[ies] of . . . gaining a position in life" (Weber, 1922/1978: 302). The resulting framework also allows assessment of other criteria of class definition (including consideration of work relations and relations of production). Specifically, the degree to which the postulated classes induce a homogeneous structure of macrosocial mobility may be assessed empirically.

Quantitative studies of the mobility table have tended to emphasize mobility *patterns* at the expense of the underlying stratification of class *boundaries.* Sorokin's (1927: 381) critique of this emphasis, formulated a half-century ago, continues to retain its force.

> It goes without saying that our epoch is a period of intensive social mobility. . . . At the present moment the Western peoples remind one of a pot of boiling water in which the water particles move up and down, to and fro, with great rapidity. To this is due the illusion that our present societies are as though not stratified, in spite of the fact that they are actually stratified. . . . Great mobility, with its intensive transposition of the individuals, makes such an

illusion natural and inevitable. So much for a general introduction to the subject. Now consider the facts.

Substantive Results and a New Application

Breiger (1981b) reexamined seventeen-category mobility tables from the studies of Blau and Duncan (1967) and Featherman and Hauser (1978). For these American data, the following statements may be made:

(1) A specific eight-class partition of categories, applied to 1962 data on intergenerational mobility to first job, explains the detailed mobility between occupational categories in a manner that will be made more precise later in this section.
(2) These eight classes appear robust across the period 1962-1973 in that they also account for detailed mobility to first job when applied to the 1973 data.
(3) These comparisons at two points in time for mobility to *first* job were matched when the same eight-class hypothesis was applied to separate tables reporting intergenerational mobility to *current* job in 1962 and in 1973.
(4) Six additional social class hypotheses were investigated; however, each of these hypotheses was rejected when applied to each of the four tables (twenty-four additional tests).
(5) The eight-class hypothesis did *not* explain mobility *within* the career (either 1962 or 1973 data on mobility from first job to "current" job); it specializes to the seventeen-category tables of intergenerational mobility and takes no account of "scheduled" mobility within career trajectories (Spilerman, 1977; Rosenbaum, 1979, 1981).
(6) Yamaguchi (1982), analyzing 1973 data on men aged 25-64 in the employed civilian labor force, reports that 92 percent of the between-group variance of respondents' educational attainments (measured in years of education) for the seventeen occupational categories is retained when the categories are aggregated to the eight social classes of findings (1-3 and 5 above); in this sense, "occupations within each social class are homogeneous regarding the average educational attainment of sons" (Yamaguchi, 1982).

This framework for mobility table analysis has recently received substantial additional elaboration by Goodman (1981), although he (1981: 615) is unduly pessimistic about its applicability to the "classic" British mobility data of Glass (1954). I will therefore demonstrate its applicability to the British data in this section and address several aspects of Goodman's elaboration in the following section.

The 1949 British data of Glass and his colleagues are presented in the upper panel of Table 1.1 as they appear in Miller (1960: 71; this table is also given in Duncan, 1979: 795, and in Goodman, 1981: 613). The category labels are: (1) professional and high administrative; (2) managerial and executive; (3) inspectional, supervisory, and other nonmanual (high grade); (4) inspectional, supervisory, and other nonmanual (low grade); (5) routine grades of nonmanual; (6) skilled manual; (7) semiskilled manual; and (8) unskilled manual (Miller, 1960: 71; Duncan, 1979: 794; Clogg, 1981: 845).

I will now provide a test of the claim that these eight categories may be aggregated into three classes that result from two hypothesized class boundaries: the division between manual and nonmanual occupations, and the division of nonmanual occupations into a salaried middle class and a less autonomous class of lower-echelon administrative and clerical personnel. Given the high degree of aggregation present in the eight initial categories of Table 1.1, this hypothesis is consistent with a variety of others that have more substantive relevance (reviewed in Breiger, 1981b: 591-595) and therefore does not allow a discrimination among them. However, the problem of extreme a priori aggregation and other challenges to the capacity of these data to yield substantive insight (reviewed in the concluding paragraph of this section) loom no larger in the present analysis than in other recent analyses of these data (Clogg, 1981; Duncan, 1979; Goodman, 1979, 1981; Hauser, 1979: 444-450). By hypothesis, then, Class I is composed of categories 1, 2, and 3; Class II of categories 4 and 5; and Class III of categories 6, 7, and 8.

My approach can be introduced by contrasting it with the one followed by Glass and his colleagues. These pioneering researchers (see also Rogoff, 1953/1979: 32) devised an idealized model of an open social structure, one in which no boundaries exist to the "fluidity" of mobility among structural locations. In this model of "perfect mobility," known more widely as the model of independence (Duncan, 1979: 796) or null association (Goodman, 1981: 647), "every member of society has an equal chance of reaching a particular status category" (Mukherjee and Hall, 1954: 225) in a sense that is specified by the model.

This idealized vision of "perfect mobility" actually characterizes the occupational structure of no known society. When applied to the data of Table 1.1, for example, the independence model yields a likelihood ratio chi-square value of 954.49, leaving 49 degrees of freedom; this model

TABLE 1.1 British Mobility Table, 1949

A. Data

Father's Occupation	*Son's Occupation*							
	1	2	3	4	5	6	7	8
1	50	19	26	8	7	11	6	2
2	16	40	34	18	11	20	8	3
3	12	35	65	66	35	88	23	21
4	11	20	58	110	40	183	64	32
5	2	8	12	23	25	46	28	12
6	12	28	102	162	90	554	230	177
7	0	6	19	40	21	158	143	71
8	0	3	14	32	15	126	91	106

B. Fitted Counts from Model of Table 1.2, Line 1

Father's Occupation	*Son's Occupation*							
	1	2	3	4	5	6	7	8
1	50	21.2	23.8	9.5	5.5	12.4	3.9	2.7
2	13.8	40	36.2	18.4	10.6	20.3	6.3	4.4
3	14.2	32.8	65	64.1	36.9	86.3	26.8	18.9
4	10.4	22.5	56.1	110	40	175.0	70.3	33.6
5	2.6	5.5	13.9	23	25	54.0	21.7	10.4
6	9.3	28.6	104.2	163.8	88.2	554	234.3	172.7
7	1.6	5.0	18.3	39.7	21.4	153.7	143	75.3
8	1.1	3.4	12.5	30.6	16.5	130.3	86.7	106

DATA SOURCE: Miller (1960: 71). In panel b, cells fitted exactly under the model are reported as integers.

positing the absence of structural barriers to mobility is rejected as a characterization of the British data.

Confronted by the stark manifestation of social structure, researchers have followed two broad strategies of mobility table analysis. One strategy, pursued over many decades, has involved retaining "perfect mobility" and recasting the data merely as a collection of deviations from this null model; this approach is unrewarding in principle (as shown in Blau and Duncan, 1967: 93-97; Tyree, 1973; Hauser, 1979: 428). The second strategy has entailed the search for *new* models that might actually characterize the observed data. The development of log-linear models for the mobility table (see, in particular, Goodman, 1972, 1979; Bishop et al., 1975) has been motivated primarily by efforts to understand the phenomenon reflected in the title of Duncan's (1979) paper: "How Destination Depends on Origin in the Occupational Mobility Table."

In contrast, I stipulate that occupational destination depends on origin *only* when the structure of classes is *ignored* by the analyst. "Classes" are those features of the social structure that allow perfect mobility actually to prevail, simultaneously, within each subtable defined by a partition of occupations into classes. The goal is to elaborate social structure as an exhaustive set of regions, each of which exhibits homogeneity internally.

With reference to the British data and the three-class hypothesis of this chapter, consider mobility from Class I to Class III: cells (1,6), (1,7), (1,8), (2,6), (2,7), (2,8), (3,6), (3,7), and (3,8) of Table 1.1. The "perfect mobility" model applied to this 3 X 3 subtable actually characterizes these data (yielding a likelihood ratio chi-square statistic of 3.18 on 4 degrees of freedom). Thus, occupational destination *within* Class III is independent of occupational origin for respondents beginning life *within* Class I.

For my model to hold, such internal homogeneity must characterize *each* of the nine subtables resulting from the hypothesized three-class partition; this is what is meant by a "global mobility regime" (Breiger, 1981b: 584). The sum of degrees of freedom left by these nine applications is 25, and the sum of the nine chi-square values thus obtained is 147.96 (reported in line 4 of Table 1.2; see Appendix A of Breiger, 1981b, for equivalent formulations of the model). This model does not characterize the Table 1.1 data.

Consider now the fact that fifty-six cells of Table 1.1 report observed counts of mobility *between* occupational categories, while the remaining eight cells (those on the main diagonal of Table 1.1) offer more ambiguous information: They confound counts of respondents whose job titles are identical with their fathers' and counts of respondents who have exhibited mobility to different jobs *within* the same category. A modification of the model of the preceding paragraph is to fit these eight "occupational inheritance" cells exactly and to postulate independence among the remaining cells within each subtable (compare Goodman, 1969, 1972). In the case of six subtables of Table 1.1 (those containing none of the eight "occupational inheritance" cells), application of this modified procedure yields chi-square values and degrees of freedom identical to those obtained in the application of the preceding paragraph. In the case of two subtables (namely, those reporting mobility within Class I and within Class III), different values are obtained which reflect the hypothesis of independence for off-diagonal cells within each subtable. The ninth subtable (reporting mobility within Class II) consists of just two rows and two columns; the hypothesis of independence for off-diagonal cells therefore fits the off-

TABLE 1.2 Components of Internal Homogeneity for the Three-Class Hypothesis of This Chapter (Model 2 in Breiger, 1981b)

Component	*df*	*Likelihood Ratio Chi Square*
1. Internal homogeneity, diagonal omitted	18	19.17
2. Internal homogeneity and occupational inheritance, Class II	1	10.22
3. Occupational inheritance, Classes I and III	6	118.57
4. Internal homogeneity, all cells estimated directly	25	147.96

diagonal cells of this subtable exactly (leaving no degrees of freedom and yielding a chi-square contribution of zero).

Summing the nine chi-square values for the model just described yields an overall chi-square value of 19.17, leaving 18 degrees of freedom (reported on line 1 of Table 1.2). This model therefore maintains fidelity to the detailed cell frequencies. Fitted counts resulting from this model of internal homogeneity (with diagonal cells fitted exactly; line 1 of Table 1.2) are reported in the lower panel of Table 1.1.

This successful application of the internal homogeneity model to the 1949 British data requires a cautionary note. Serious challenges have been raised concerning the validity of the data (Payne et al., 1977), which exhibit a variety of features that are markedly atypical of other mobility tables (Hauser, 1979: 446; Hope, 1981a: 150-159; Payne et al., 1977). Hauser (1978: 932) observes that "these data are no longer of great substantive interest, but they have been so thoroughly analyzed by students of mobility that they have become a standard set of observations against which each new model or method is calibrated." Indeed, during the last three years no fewer than six major research applications have had partial recourse to these very possibly flawed but nonetheless "classic" data. One convenience of the British data (but a convenience that has been exploited inappropriately, as I clearly believe) is the extreme amount of aggregation built into the eight categories on a priori grounds, so that they will exhibit "a certain, publicly recognized, status ordering" (Hope, 1981a: 132). Given this consideration, one might well imagine that several partitions of the initial categories induce global structures of internal homogeneity, so long as the underlying a priori ordering of these eight categories is preserved, and this is in fact the case.[2]

Additional Homogeneity Criteria

Goodman (1981) has recently developed additional homogeneity criteria, and he has employed the British data in a discussion (1981: 641-650) of the relationship of these criteria to the criterion of internal homogeneity. I will further elaborate this relationship with reference to the three-class hypothesis of the preceding section.

The homogeneity model considered in Goodman's article (model 41 in Goodman, 1981: 649) is model 1 in Breiger (1981b: 587), which previously was formulated by Béland (1978; Béland and Fortier, 1981; see also Goodman, 1972). The models differ in that the internal homogeneity model of the preceding section (model 2 in Breiger, 1981b, p. 589) is a generalization of model 1. Stated equivalently, model 1 tests the criterion of internal homogeneity as well as additional homogeneity criteria. I will now characterize these criteria in a manner that departs from Goodman's (1981) treatment.

When applied to the British data (Table 1.1), model 1 yields a chi-square value of 361.06, leaving 45 degrees of freedom (see line 3 of Table 1.3).[3] If the eight entries on the main diagonal of Table 1.1 are deleted and model 1 is applied solely to the off-diagonal entries, the resulting chi-square statistic is 106.26, leaving 37 degrees of freedom (line 1 of Table 1.3). Thus, the three-class hypothesis of this chapter fails to satisfy the homogeneity criteria considered by Goodman (1981).

To understand these findings further, consider a table whose rows represent class origins and whose columns represent occupational destinations. For the three-class hypothesis of this chapter, this table is provided as panel A of Table 1.4. The first row of the data in panel A (corresponding to Class I) is therefore the sum of the first three rows of the data of Table 1.1, and so forth.

Now consider a particular substantive proposition about social mobility, namely: that *occupation* of destination is independent of *class* of origin, for all occupational categories *within* the same class.

To illustrate the import of this proposition, take as examples "professionals" (a shorthand designation for category 1), "managers" (a short-

TABLE 1.3 Components of Homogeneity (internal homogeneity and additional criteria) for the Three-Class Hypothesis of This Chapter (Model 41 in Goodman, 1981; Model 1 in Breiger, 1981b)

Component	*df*	*Likelihood Ratio Chi Square*
1. Internal homogeneity and additional homogeneity criteria, diagonal omitted	37	106.26
2. Occupational inheritance	8	254.80
3. Internal homogeneity and additional homogeneity criteria, all cells estimated directly	45	361.06

hand designation for category 2), Class II, and Class III. Category 1 and category 2 are hypothesized to belong to the *same* class. The proposition of the preceding paragraph mandates that the odds of origins in Class II, rather than in Class III, should be *identical* for respondents who are "professionals" (column 1 of panel A) and for respondents who are "managers" (column 2 of panel A). Similar absence of association should hold for any two classes, with respect to any two categories hypothesized to belong to the same class.

Since this proposition pertains to the relation *between* occupational categories and hypothesized classes, I will refer to it as a proposition concerning *external* homogeneity.

The burden of the remaining discussion is to show that the test of this substantive proposition and the test of one other that is directly analogous to it provide exactly the set of supplementary criteria that Goodman's model (equivalently, model 1 in Breiger, 1981b) *adds* to the criterion of internal homogeneity.

The usual model of independence (defined, for example, by equation 36 in Goodman, 1981: 647) may be applied to each of the three subtables of panel A that results from partitioning its eight *columns* into the three classes hypothesized in this chapter. Each of these three applications tests the criterion of homogeneity for occupational destination with respect to class origin, for all destinations hypothesized to belong to the *same* class. These three applications are reported in Table 1.5 (lines 1-3).

TABLE 1.4 Data on Social Class Mobility, Derived from Table 1.1

A. Class Origins, Occupational Destinations

Father's Class	Son's Occupation 1	2	3	4	5	6	7	8
I	78	94	125	92	53	119	37	26
II	13	28	70	133	65	229	92	44
III	12	37	135	234	126	838	464	354

B. Occupational Origins, Class Destinations

Father's Occupation	Son's Class I	II	III
1	95	15	19
2	90	29	31
3	112	101	132
4	89	150	279
5	22	48	86
6	142	252	961
7	25	61	372
8	17	47	323

C. Class Origins, Class Destinations

Father's Class	Son's Class I	II	III
I	297	145	182
II	111	198	365
III	184	360	1656

A similar proposition states that *class* destination is independent of *occupational* origin, for all occupations hypothesized to belong to the same class. This is an additional proposition of external homogeneity. This proposition is evaluated with reference to the data of panel B of Table 1.4. The usual model of independence is applied to each of the three subtables of panel B that results from partitioning its eight *rows* into the three classes hypothesized in this chapter (see lines 4, 5, and 6 of Table 1.5).

Panel C of Table 1.4 reports mobility within and between the hypothesized social classes. These data also were derived from Table 1.1. The

TABLE 1.5 Components of Homogeneity for Table 1.4

Component	*df*	*Likelihood Ratio Chi Square*
1. Table 1.4a, columns 1, 2, 3	4	57.53
2. Table 1.4a, columns 4, 5	2	0.54
3. Table 1.4a, columns 6, 7, 8	4	34.60
4. Table 1.4b, rows 1, 2, 3	4	78.46
5. Table 1.4b, rows 4, 5	2	0.88
6. Table 1.4b, rows 6, 7, 8	4	41.09
7. Subtotal	20	213.10
8. Table 1.4c	4	593.43

TABLE 1.6 Decomposition of Association for Table 1.1

Component	*Source*	*df*	*Likelihood Ratio Chi Square*
1. Internal homogeneity	Table 1.2, line 4	25	147.96
2. External homogeneity	Table 1.5, line 7	20	213.10
3. Subtotal	Table 1.3, line 3	45	361.06
4. Homogeneity within and between social classes	Table 1.5, line 8	4	593.43
5. Total: Independence applied to Table 1.1	Text	49	954.49

usual model of independence, when applied to the data of panel C, yields results reported in line 8 of Table 1.5.

The relation between the model considered in Goodman's (1981) article and the internal homogeneity model may now be clearly understood within the perspective of this chapter. As previously reported in the text, the usual model of independence, applied to the British data (Table 1.1), yields a chi-square value of 954.49 leaving 49. degrees of freedom. Table 1.6 reports a decomposition of this "total association" for the British data.

Total association in the mobility table is the simple sum of (a) the criterion of internal homogeneity (line 1 of Table 1.6); (b) the criteria of external homogeneity stating that, among all categories hypothesized to belong to the same class, occupational destination is independent of class origin and that class destination is independent of occupational origin (line 2 of Table 1.6); and (c) the association of class of destination and class of origin (line 4 of Table 1.6).

The model considered in Goodman's (1981) article (model 1 in Breiger, 1981b) tests criteria a *and* b; see line 3 of Table 1.6 (equivalently, line 3 of Table 1.3). The model of internal homogeneity tests criterion a alone. The three-class hypothesis of this chapter induces internal homogeneity for all off-diagonal entries of the British data (line 1 of Table 1.2). The criteria of external homogeneity are satisfied for Class II (lines 2 and 5 of Table 1.5) but are not satisfied globally (line 7 of Table 1.5) for the regions of the data that result from the partition of categories considered here.

Conclusion

A mobility table portrays the occupational structure conceived "as consisting of the relations among its constituent subgroups" (Blau and Duncan, 1967: 23). An important early motivation for the development of log-linear models for the mobility table–a motivation that has occasionally been slighted in subsequent developments and expositions–is the desirability of "methods that focus attention in turn on various subsets of the entire table" (Goodman, 1968: 1093).

The question of which "subsets of the entire table" are relevant for depicting "relations among . . . constituent subgroups" is a question of structural sociology. In my opinion, the unwillingness or inability of quantitative analysts to explicate structural formulations as the *basis* for their statistical models is what accounts for the rising criticism that "ransacking mobility tables, however coruscating a methodological exercise, may produce findings that are extraordinarily difficult to interpret" (Huber, 1980: 7).

An alternative is clearly evident in recent research of Pappi (1981: 111):

> Classes form out of coalitions and collective conflicts, in the exchange of economic resources. Status groups are formed via affectually positive relations among the basic units, so that . . . [one must study] consolidation of interaction zones on the one hand and a hierarchic order due to nonmutual choices on the other hand.

Specifically, Pappi (1981) formulates ideal-typical images of an "antagonistic class structure" and a "status group structure" as blockmodel images (White et al., 1976; Breiger, 1981c), which he then examines with reference to German data on four mobility relationships among seventeen occupational categories: inter- and intragenerational mobility of men, marriage mobility of women, and shared memberships in trade unions and occupational organizations (1981: 113). One claim is that "it is difficult to understand" the "popular practice among empirical social researchers of working with clearly hierarchic classifications of strata. . . . A middling position on indicators of social status . . . does not tell us enough; it tells us neither about the structure of relations between the strata, nor about the many aspects of social behaviour" (Pappi, 1981: 118; on the relevance of the approach of this chapter for models of network structure, see Breiger, 1981a, and Holland and Leinhardt, 1981).

Analysts of mobility tables have bracketed the questions of social classes and underlying theoretical images of social structure in order to make progress in the statistical analysis of mobility patterns and trends. The statistical frameworks themselves, however, rest on prior commitments about structural images and boundaries. Recognition of the priority of social structure in the formulation of statistical models has led to the developments presented in this chapter.

NOTES

1. Thus, consider conceptualization and empirical analyses of the generation of mobility from the creation of vacant positions in dual person-position systems (White, 1970; Stewman, 1975; Sørensen, 1977), typical career trajectories as definitive of organizational and labor market structure (Spilerman, 1977; Rosenbaum, 1979), the effects of contact networks on occupational mobility (Katz, 1958; Granovetter, 1974; Boorman, 1975; Lin, Ensel, and Vaughn, 1981), the mobility table as a multidimensional structure of positions (Laumann, 1966; Blau and Duncan, 1967: 67-75; Haller and Hodge, 1981), and–of greatest direct relevance to this chapter–the formulation and empirical analysis of social class hypotheses as partitions of occupational categories of the mobility table (Vanneman, 1977; Pappi, 1981; see also Hartigan, 1980).

2. Employing the model of line 1 of Table 1.2 (model 2 in Breiger, 1981b), this statement applies, for example, to none of the two-class partitions but to five of the three-class partitions that preserve the initial eight-category ordering. These findings reinforce Hope's (1981a: 163) point that "it is possible that familiarity has blinded us (a) to the distinction between the denomination of the categories and their interpretation as status groups and (b) to the relation between the hypothesized status ordering and the empirical investigation to which it was subjected."

3. This model was fitted according to procedures described in Breiger (1981b: Appendix A). Equivalently, the model can be tested according to procedures similar to those presented by Goodman (1981: 614-623). First, apply the model of quasi-independence to Table 1.1 with all entries deleted except those in categories 4 or 5,

thus obtaining a chi-square value of 18.65 and leaving 13 degrees of freedom. Second, combine categories 4 and 5 and apply the quasi-independence model to the resulting 7 × 7 table after deleting all entries except those in the last three rows or last three columns. This test of quasi-independence yields a chi-square value of 150.03 and leaves 20 degrees of freedom. Third, combine the last three categories of the 7 × 7 table, and apply the quasi-independence model to the resulting 5 × 5 table after deleting all entries except those in the first three rows or the first three columns. This application yields a chi-square value of 192.38 and leaves 12 degrees of freedom. Observe that the sum of these three applications (a chi-square value of 361.06 = 18.65 + 150.03 + 192.38, leaving 45 = 13 + 20 + 12 degrees of freedom) is identical to the test reported on line 3 of Table 1.3.

On a Structural Analysis of Occupational Mobility

LEO A. GOODMAN

Some readers of Breiger's foregoing article may be misled by comments about results in Goodman (1981) and by Breiger's presentation of his structural analysis of the British mobility data. In addition, further clarification is needed about the relationship between Breiger's two articles (1981b and in this volume) and results in Goodman (1981). The present note will rectify these matters.

(1) Breiger (this volume) states that "[Goodman] (1981: 615) is unduly pessimistic about . . . [the] applicability [of Breiger's framework] to the 'classic' British mobility data of Glass (1954)." I shall now explain why this statement may mislead readers about results in Goodman's article.

Goodman's exposition on the cited page (p. 615) provides a *proof* of the following result:

> Breiger's definition and application of the term 'internal homogeneity' *cannot* be helpful (i.e., it *cannot* provide any useful information)

AUTHOR'S NOTE: Financial support under grant SOC76-80389 from the National Science Foundation is gratefully acknowledged.

> when applied by the researcher to determine whether two given occupational categories in an occupational mobility table can be combined to form a given 'class.'

This result holds true for *any* occupational mobility table. The classic British mobility data served only as an example of an occupational mobility table. (The example was used in Goodman's article for expository and illustrative purposes.) Thus, from Goodman's article (1981: 615), we see that for any occupational mobility table Breiger's definition and application of the term "internal homogeneity" *cannot* provide useful information when applied in the context in which the researcher wishes to determine whether two given occupational categories can be combined to form a given "class."

The *proof* of the above result is straightforward. This result is *not* "unduly pessimistic"—a *correct* result *cannot* be "unduly pessimistic."

As I have already noted, the result stated above is correct in the context in which the researcher wishes to determine whether two given occupational categories can be combined to form a given "class." This context describes an elementary situation, and a criterion of "homogeneity" should be helpful in this situation. Since Breiger's definition and application of "internal homogeneity" are not helpful in this situation, other homogeneity criteria are needed, and they are introduced in Goodman (1981).

While the result stated above from page 615 in Goodman's article is correct in the context described, it should also be noted that in other contexts different results are obtained; see, for example, pages 641-644 in Goodman's article. For the study of the "homogeneity" of the occupational categories within each "class," Breiger's "internal homogeneity" criterion is vacuous in the context described above, and it is insufficient in other contexts as well (for example, when the researcher wishes to consider the combination of three or more occupational categories, or when all occupational categories are partitioned into two or more "classes"). Both in the context described above, and in other contexts as well, additional homogeneity criteria are needed (see Goodman, 1981).

(2) Breiger (this volume) states that (a) he will demonstrate the applicability of his framework to the British data, (b) he will provide "a test [using the 'internal homogeneity' model] of the claim that [the] eight categories [in the 8 X 8 British mobility table] may be aggregated into three classes," and (c) his "application of the internal homogeneity model to the British data" is "successful." I shall now explain why readers may

be misled by these statements in Breiger's presentation of his structural analysis of the British data.

Goodman (1981) showed that, with respect to any proposed class structure, if the study of the "homogeneity" of the occupational categories within each "class" is limited to the application of the "internal homogeneity" model, then misleading results can be obtained. (The applications in Breiger, 1981b, were limited in this way, and the results in Table 1.2 of Breiger's article in this volume are also so limited.) If the analysis of the 8 X 8 British mobility table is limited to the application of the "internal homogeneity" model, then the reader will conclude that the eight categories in the mobility table "may be aggregated into three classes." On the other hand, by applying the full set of homogeneity components introduced in Goodman's article, rather than the "internal homogeneity" model introduced in Breiger (1981b), we would conclude that the eight categories in the mobility table can *not* be aggregated into the three classes. From the results in Table 1.5 of Breiger (this volume), we see that the occupational categories in the first class are not homogeneous with respect to the distribution of class origins for the occupational destinations, nor are they homogeneous with respect to the distribution of class destinations for the occupational origins; and a similar result holds true for the occupational categories in the third class.

(3) Breiger's presentation in this volume may leave the reader with an incorrect impression about the relationship between Breiger's two articles (1981b, this volume) and results in Goodman (1981). For the sake of further clarification, I shall now describe briefly some of the results in Goodman's article that are related to topics considered in Breiger (1981b, this volume).

On page 641 of Goodman (1981), I showed that, with respect to the total chi-square value obtained in testing homogeneity in the context in which the researcher wishes to determine whether two given occupational categories can be combined to form a given "class," none of the components of this total chi-square value pertains to Breiger's definition of "internal homogeneity" if the entries on the main diagonal of the occupational mobility table are deleted; and one of the components pertains to this term if the entries on the main diagonal are not deleted. In addition, from the results on pages 641-644 of Goodman's article, we see that the total chi-square value obtained in testing "homogeneity" will depend on the particular context under consideration (that is, on the researcher's proposed partitioning of the occupational categories into a particular set of "classes"); and the number of "internal homogeneity" components (of this total chi-square value) will also depend on this context (and on whether or not the entries on the main diagonal are deleted). To illustrate these general points, Goodman (1981) considered several examples:

(a) The 8 × 8 occupational mobility table in the context in which the researcher wishes to determine whether two given occupational categories can be combined to form a given "class," and the entries on the main diagonal are deleted (p. 615).
(b) The 8 × 8 occupational mobility table in the context described above in (a), but the entries on the main diagonal are not deleted (p. 641).
(c) The 4 × 4 occupational mobility table in the context in which the researcher's proposed partitioning of the four occupational categories consists of a set of three "classes," and the entries on the main diagonal are not deleted (p. 642).
(d) The 4 × 4 occupational mobility table in the context described above in (c), but the entries on the main diagonal are deleted (p. 643).
(e) The 4 × 4 occupational mobility table in the context in which the researcher's proposed partitioning of the four occupational categories consists of a set of two "classes" (combining, say, occupational categories 1 and 2 to form the first "class," and occupational categories 3 and 4 to form the second "class"), both in the situation where the entries on the main diagonal are deleted and where they are not (p. 644).

These examples in Goodman's article served to illustrate the general points noted above concerning the dependence of the total chi-square value obtained in testing "homogeneity" on the particular context under consideration, and the dependence of the number of "internal homogeneity" components (of this total chi-square value) on this context. The analysis in Breiger (this volume) of the 8 X 8 British mobility table serves as still another example to illustrate these general points in the context in which the researcher's proposed partitioning of the eight occupational categories forms the given set of three "classes."

From the results on pages 646-648 of Goodman's article, we see that, with respect to the researcher's proposed "class structure," the likelihood-ratio chi-square statistic for testing the hypothesis of null association in the full occupational mobility table can be partitioned into a component to test the hypothesis of null association in the mobility table pertaining to the proposed classes, and a component to test the homogeneity model. The latter component is equal to the total chi-square value obtained in testing "homogeneity" in the context of the researcher's proposed class structure, as described in Goodman's article and earlier herein. As noted earlier here and in Goodman's article, this total chi-square value can be partitioned further into components that pertain to "internal homogeneity" (when the researcher's proposed class structure is such that there are components pertaining to this) and components that do not pertain to "internal homogeneity."

The result stated above, for the partitioning of the chi-square statistic in the full occupational mobility table into two components (namely, a component obtained from the mobility table pertaining to the proposed classes and a component to test the homogeneity model), can be applied in the situation in which none of the entries in the full occupational mobility table is deleted. (When some of the entries are deleted, complications arise that can *not* be ignored.) For related results in the situation in which some of the entries in the full occupational mobility table are deleted, the reader is referred to Goodman's article.

A Reply to Professor Goodman

RONALD L. BREIGER

The thoughtful comments of Professor Goodman provide a welcome opportunity for continued discussion of the contributions of structural sociology to the reorientation of mobility studies.

Professor Goodman writes of "misleading" statements, but he has never claimed, either here or elsewhere (Goodman, 1981), that published results pertaining to the log-linear model of internal homogeneity (Breiger, 1981b, and in this volume) are incorrect. I surmise from the fifth paragraph of Professor Goodman's comment that a *correct* result *cannot* be misleading—except when interpreted from one set of paradigmatic commitments, as opposed to another set. As the reader of our articles may independently verify, the disagreement between Professor Goodman and

AUTHOR'S NOTE: Financial support under grant SES80-08658 from the National Science Foundation is gratefully acknowledged.

myself does not concern issues of fact, but rather assertions of "relevance" (on one side) and the dissemination of "misleading" statements (on the other). The advances resulting from the new models and their enlightening applications to data (Breiger, 1981a, 1981b; Goodman, 1981, this volume) stand independent of these charges, which result from the confrontation of a statistical paradigm by a structural paradigm.

(1) The correctness of Professor Goodman's factual statements is not in dispute. The criterion of internal homogeneity applies vacuously to the special case in which the analyst desires to consider the partition of R categories into exactly R-1 classes (Goodman, 1981: 615). Regarding all other cases, including all cases treated in my publications, the applicability of the internal homogeneity criterion has not been questioned. Indeed, the homogeneity model of Goodman (1981) is a special case of the model of internal homogeneity (Breiger, this volume); stated equivalently, Professor Goodman's model tests the criterion of internal homogeneity as well as additional homogeneity criteria (Goodman, 1981, this volume; Breiger, this volume; see also note 15 in Breiger, 1981b: 599-600). The reader of our articles can arrive independently at a judgment as to whether Professor Goodman's correct statements on the applicability of the internal homogeneity model to the "classic" British mobility data are "unduly pessimistic." The question of whether the partition of R categories into R-1 classes is an "elementary situation," as Professor Goodman asserts, in contrast to the partition of R categories into *two* classes, evokes paradigmatic commitments, which I have addressed elsewhere (Breiger, 1981a: 51).

(2) As mentioned above and discussed elsewhere (Goodman, 1981; Breiger, this volume), Professor Goodman's homogeneity model (model 1 in Breiger, 1981b) provides a more stringent test than does the internal homogeneity model. His development and formulation of additional criteria constitutes one among a number of important contributions that Professor Goodman (1981) has made to the modeling framework that I presented (Breiger, 1981b), and I have sought to acknowledge and incorporate this contribution (Breiger, this volume). In particular, I believe that separate tests of the criteria of internal homogeneity and external homogeneity (see Table 1.6 in this volume) will prove quite useful in understanding the social structure of homogeneity.

(3) I fully agree with Professor Goodman that "the analysis in Breiger (this volume) of the 8 × 8 British mobility table serves as still another example to illustrate these general points (of Goodman, 1981) in the context in which the researcher's proposed partitioning of the eight occupational categories forms the given set of three 'classes.' " Indeed, one of my purposes (Breiger, this volume) was to incorporate certain contribu-

tions of Professor Goodman *within* the general framework for the analysis of mobility and class structure that I presented earlier.

It is especially gratifying to me that Professor Goodman (1981) has contributed substantially to the development of log-linear models for the assessment of partitions that the research worker hypothesizes will induce homogeneous structure, since my concern with this research problem was motivated in large part by blockmodel analysis (Breiger, 1981a), a development within structural sociology. Recent contributions of Professor Goodman (1981 and in this volume) further the advances in log-linear analysis that have been made, and that will continue to be made, in confrontation with a paradigmatic commitment of structural sociology, namely, that "the aggregation of rows and columns . . . [is] the fundamental theoretical issue in mobility table analysis, rather than an exogenous 'given' to be decided upon prior to the construction of explicit models" (Breiger, 1981b: 604).

2

Class and Prestige Origins in the American Elite

GWEN MOORE and RICHARD D. ALBA

The relation of economic privilege to political power is a prominent issue in American social science, and one approach to its study has led to the examination of elite recruitment and activity. All studies of this topic have found considerable overrepresentation of men from upper- and upper-middle-class families in top positions in powerful public- and private-sector institutions (for example, Matthews, 1960; Keller, 1963; Mintz, 1975; Dye, 1979). Prewitt and Stone (1973: 136) summarize the evidence with the statement:

> The tiny group, consisting primarily of men, that directs the political economy of the United States is overwhelmingly recruited from the wealthier families of society. Few persons reach elite positions in political and economic life unless they are born to wealth, acquire it fairly early in life, or at least have access to it.

Moreover, privileged social origins characterize large proportions of leaders in all groups examined not only in the United States but also in dozens of other countries (see Putnam, 1976, for a review of the literature).

Most research, measuring social origins by father's occupation, has found that those with professional or managerial fathers are disproportionately represented in elite positions (see Keller, 1963). Others attempt to identify a far smaller group (less than 1 percent of the population), the upper class, and study its occupancy of top positions (Domhoff, 1967, 1971; Dye, 1979). Domhoff (1967, 1971), using such facts as attendance at an elite prep school or membership in an exclusive social club as indicators of upper-class membership, concludes that the upper class is found in top institutional positions far in excess of its proportions in the population as a whole. He argues further that its overrepresentation is due to its cohesion and group consciousness. In his view, upper-class cohesion rests on an exclusive nationwide network of informal connections, including attendance at select private schools, membership in exclusive private clubs, vacations at specific resorts, and intermarriage (1967, 1971; Baltzell, 1964; Blumberg and Paul, 1975). Members of the upper class, sharing both similar origins and experiences and linked indirectly and directly, tend to trust one another more than outsiders. As a result, nonmembers are handicapped in the achievement of an elite position because they are excluded from the social institutions in which important informal relations are forged.

Despite the overwhelming consistency of the evidence on social origins and elite recruitment, very important questions remain. Thus, while the social homogeneity of American elites in the past is well documented, the current extent of homogeneity is open to question, as some have found heterogeneity to be increasing. For example, reviewing the social class origins of elite members in several institutional sectors through the early 1960s, Keller (1963: 205-207) found some evidence that the representation of those from working-class origins was growing. Nevertheless, she declared that social class factors continue to play a significant role in elite recruitment. Also without a definitive answer is whether the relative importance of social origins for elite entry varies by institutional sector. Putnam, for one, after reviewing numerous studies of elite recruitment, concludes that business elites tend to come from the most privileged origins, followed by top-level federal officials and then by federal legislators (Putnam, 1976: 22-26).

Little is known about the role of social origins once an elite position has been attained. If Domhoff's argument on the importance of interaction in upper-class social institutions is correct, one would expect upper-class origins to be advantageous even within elite groups. This would result in differentiation *within* elite groups according to social origins, with key positions and network centrality being disproportionately held by those from the upper class. But this expectation is contradicted by the implications of the pluralist view. In general, pluralists contend that the link between class background and policymaking behavior is weak (see Polsby, 1980). Implied is that, although privileged social origins may be an asset in the achievement of an elite position, they are of little consequence to activities or positions within the elite.

A final related issue concerns the kind of origins that matter for the achievement of an elite position. As some recent research has emphasized (for example, Wright and Perrone, 1977; Wright, 1979; Robinson and Kelley, 1979), the bulk of American stratification research over the last few decades has concerned dimensions of *status*; that is, it is based on a conception of stratification as a continuum of fine distinctions, without sharp breaks or boundaries, and has focused on what might be taken as indicators of generalized prestige, such as occupation and education. In contrast to this tradition, recent research in a neo-Marxist spirit has revived the categorical notion of *class,* which derives from the organization of production. A measure of class position in the social relations of production has been found to be at least as useful as the traditional status variables in predicting income (Wright and Perrone, 1977; Wright, 1979).

With some notable exceptions, such as the work of Domhoff, most research on elite origins derives from the status conception of stratification. But both status and class deserve consideration in an examination of the impact of social origins on elite position. On behalf of a consideration of class, the view of Marxist class analysis can be noted–namely, that ownership of a business and control over the labor of others confer distinct advantages to members of the bourgeoisie, petty bourgeoisie, and, in contemporary capitalism, managers. These groups are seen as uniquely able to accumulate wealth and political power (Wright, 1979: 224). In addition, growing up in a property-owning rather than a laboring family might offer related cultural and social skills, such as experience in giving rather than taking orders, and a belief in one's leadership ability.

In this chapter we examine the relationship of class and status origins to elite positions, using a unique sample of interviews with top position holders in powerful public- and private-sector organizations in 1971-1972. We address the following major questions: (1) What is the representation of individuals from different class and status groups in the American elite? (2) To what extent are there differences along these lines within the elite in such matters as routes of entry into it or current standing in it? (3) Are there marked tendencies for interaction within the elite to take place along class or status lines?

Data

The data we use are taken from the American Leadership Study, conducted by the Bureau of Applied Social Research, Columbia University, in 1971-1972. These data are well suited to examining the above questions, since they include extensive social background, current activity, and sociometric information for a sample of 545 elite position holders in a variety of institutional sectors that have a broad impact on policymaking and political processes in the United States. Ten sectors were selected for study on the basis that their leaders appear to exert significant influence on electoral politics, governmental actions, the definition of national issues, or public opinion. These are Fortune 500 industrial corporations, Fortune 300 nonindustrial corporations, holders of large fortunes (these first three we combine into a single "business" sector), labor unions, political parties, voluntary organizations, mass media, Congress, political appointees in the federal government, and federal civil servants.[1] We refer to the top position holders in these institutions as the elite, although we recognize that others might define the national elite in somewhat different terms.

Within each sector, a random sample of approximately 50 persons were interviewed. The 484 resulting interviews constituted the positional sample. It was supplemented by a snowball sample of 61 other persons named as influential by several of the original respondents. However, the analysis reported here uses data only from the positional interviews. We exclude the snowball interviews because a comparison of the social origins of snowball and positional sample members revealed that the former group had a greater proportion of fathers with high-status occupations and college degrees. The completion rate for the positional sample was 73 percent.

The design in terms of sectors, although a necessity in a broad elite study, causes problems for any analysis. The definition of the sampling universe varies by sector so that, in this sense, the study is composed of ten distinct samples. Moreover, the sectors probably do not have equal influence on national policy, although it is not possible to assign a meaningful weight to the influence of each. To deal with these problems, wherever possible we report results by sector or, at least, control for sector in our analysis. Nonetheless, for convenience in summarizing, we at times use figures for the overall sample.

The data include detailed social origins, such as the occupation and education of the respondent and his or her parents, as well as extensive information on his or her attitudes on national issues, current activities, and organizational memberships. These last two items are of special relevance for an elite study. For example, from the very detailed information about organizational memberships, we are able to identify whether the respondent belongs to any upper-class social clubs (listed by Domhoff, 1971: Chapter 1) and whether he or she is a member of the major policy-planning organizations (Moore, 1979: 685). Each respondent was also asked to report memberships on boards of trustees, boards of directors, and federal government advisory committees; testimony before congressional committees; and recent press or television interviews, speeches given, and other indicators of communications output. We use this information to create measures of elite-related activities (for details, see Moore, 1979: 684-689). Finally, the interviews focused in part on the respondent's policy-related activities on a national issue in which he or she recently had been deeply involved. A series of sociometric questions asked for the names of persons with whom he or she discussed the issue as well as those the respondent believed to be nationally influential on it. We use these to construct various sociometric measures.

Classifying Elite Members' Social Origins

In classifying elite social origins, we use both a neo-Marxist definition of class and the more usual parental occupation and education variables. Because the class variable is less familiar and its categories are subject to dispute (see Robinson and Kelley, 1979; Attewell and Fitzgerald, 1980; Aldrich and Weiss, 1981), we explain in detail our definition and operationalization of it.

According to Wright and Perrone (1977: 33), the traditional Marxist concept of class results in the identification of three major classes in capitalist society: (1) capitalists: those who own the means of production and employ others, (2) the petty bourgeoisie: those who own the means of production but do not employ others, and (3) workers: those who do not own the means of production and work for others. Wright and Perrone argue that in contemporary capitalist society, it is reasonable to distinguish a fourth important group, managers: those who do not own the means of production but who supervise the work of others (Wright and Perrone, 1977: 34).

One difficulty with this scheme is the absence of a clear boundary between the capitalist class and the petty bourgeoisie (Wright and Perrone, 1977; Aldrich and Weiss, 1981: 280-282). It is not clear whether one employee is sufficient to make one a capitalist or whether a distinction should be made between large and small employers. Aldrich and Weiss (1981), in particular, argue that workforce size is a crucial variable that must be considered in analysis of the capitalist class. In order to incorporate a distinction based on workforce size, we have chosen to classify business owners with ten or more employees as capitalists and those with zero to nine employees as petty bourgeoisie. Although somewhat arbitrary, this cutting point has the virtue of allowing a comparison to the class composition of the United States as determined by Wright and Perrone.

Hence, we classify individuals on the basis of father's social class according to the following categories:

(1) capitalist: owner of business with at least ten employees
(2) petty bourgeois: owner of business with zero to nine employees
(3) manager: supervises work of others but not self-employed
(4) worker: not self-employed and does not supervise the work of others.[2]

Our classification of elite individuals according to father's occupation and parental education follows more conventional lines. In classifying by father's occupation, we distinguish professional, proprietary, and managerial occupations from other white-collar occupations; additionally, we retain a broad category for blue-collar occupations and one for farm owners. In terms of parental education, we distinguish college-educated parents from others.[3]

Social Origins in the American Elite

The first question to be addressed is: What are the class and status origins of the American elite? Related to this is the question of how the social origins of the elite compare to those of the general population. Are those with high-status parents overrepresented in the elite, as past studies have found? Do disproportionate numbers of the offspring of the capitalist class occupy elite positions? We answer these questions in this section. In the next, we consider the relationship of social origins to position and activities within the elite.

Table 2.1 presents the basic data on social origins, including father's class, occupation, and education, and mother's education. It shows these by institutional sector as well as for the entire elite sample. In order to assess over- or underrepresentation, the table also provides comparable parental class, occupation, and education data for the American population.

The general population data for father's occupation and parents' educations are calculated from the combined NORC General Social Surveys for 1972-1980. Since nearly all members of the elite sample are male (95 percent) and were over 40 at the time they were interviewed (94 percent), these two characteristics have been used to define the relevant American population for comparison.[4] There is great difficulty in obtaining population data for father's social class as we have defined it. Ideally, the data

TABLE 2.1 Class and Status Origins in the Elite Sample (percentages)

Sector	Father's Class					Father's Occupation							Father's Education		Mother's Education	
	Capi-talist	Petty Bourgeois	Manager	Worker	(N)	Professional	Proprietor	Manager	Other White-Collar	Blue-Collar	Farm Owner	(N)	College Graduate	(N)	College Graduate	(N)
Overall elite	21.3	27.3	35.4	16.0	(381)	21.9	21.0	15.9	6.7	25.6	9.0	(434)	32.0	(409)	20.1	(402)
Business	27.0	23.0	36.0	14.0	(100)	19.7	24.8	26.5	6.0	15.4	7.7	(117)	34.5	(113)	28.2	(110)
Labor	7.1	14.3	38.1	40.5	(42)	9.5	7.1	2.4	0.0	76.2	4.8	(42)	14.7	(34)	3.1	(32)
Party	21.1	44.7	23.7	10.5	(38)	27.3	25.0	13.6	6.8	22.7	4.5	(44)	31.8	(44)	26.2	(42)
Voluntary org.	21.6	35.1	29.7	13.5	(37)	13.3	24.4	15.6	6.7	24.4	15.6	(45)	33.3	(39)	28.6	(42)
Media	18.2	25.0	45.5	11.4	(44)	40.8	24.5	12.2	10.2	10.2	2.0	(49)	44.9	(49)	16.3	(49)
Congress	32.3	35.5	22.6	9.7	(31)	19.0	23.8	4.8	7.1	23.8	21.4	(42)	17.6	(34)	8.8	(34)
Political appt.	21.4	28.6	40.5	9.5	(42)	17.8	17.8	20.0	8.9	22.2	13.3	(45)	37.8	(45)	15.9	(44)
Civil Service	17.0	23.4	40.4	19.1	(47)	28.0	14.0	14.0	8.0	30.0	6.0	(50)	29.4	(51)	16.3	(49)
U.S. population	1.6	10.1	37.4	49.2	(1502)	4.7	12.2		5.3	47.8	30.0	(2295)	5.1	(1756)	2.8	(1919)

* Population figures for social class are calculated from Wright and Perrone (1977: 36-37, Table 3 and note 7); for occupation and education, these figures are calculated from the combined NORC Social Surveys, 1972-1980, for men born before 1932.

would characterize the older male population from which the elite is drawn, referring, in historical terms, to the class composition of the population during the 1920s and 1930s, when most of our respondents were growing up. But we could not find this information. We use instead the only data we could locate on class composition of the U.S. population as defined here, taken from the 1969 Survey of Working Conditions, as reported by Wright and Perrone (1977). In comparison to the 1920s and 1930s, these data probably overstate the proportion of managers while understating those of workers and members of the petty bourgeoisie. Nonetheless, we think that the general pattern of class origins in the elite is clear enough to withstand any ambiguity caused by the absence of an exact standard of comparison.[5]

The most striking result in the table is the strong overrepresentation of those from capitalist families in the elite. More than one in five members of the elite sample come from such origins, but only one in sixty members of the comparable population group is in this category. Also overrepresented in the sample are persons from petty bourgeois origins, with over a fourth of the sample but only 10 percent of the population in this group. Combining the two categories of ownership shows that nearly one in two sample members had a father who owned his own business. On the other hand, workers' sons and daughters are greatly underrepresented in the sample—about 16 percent versus nearly half of the population. The children of managerial fathers are found in the elite sample in roughly the same proportion as in the population.

Moreover, the children of business owners are not concentrated in just a few sectors but are overrepresented in all the sectors in the survey. The labor sector has the sparsest representation of this group and by far the highest representation of the sons and daughters of workers. With the additional exceptions of the civil service and the media, at least half of every sector is composed of the children of owners. This proportion rises to two-thirds among party leaders and those in Congress. Indeed, nearly a third of Congress is composed of the children of capitalist fathers; this group also comprises over a quarter of business leaders.

The elite sample is also unrepresentative of the general population in terms of father's occupation. Nearly three out of five fathers of elite sample members were in high-status white-collar positions (professional, proprietor,[6] manager), compared to about one in six in the comparison group.

Most sectors roughly approximate the occupational distribution of the sample as a whole, with about 50 to 60 percent having high-status white-collar fathers. As was true of father's social class, the major sectoral exception from the general pattern is found among labor leaders: Three-fourths are the children of blue-collar or service workers, a far higher proportion than in the sample as a whole (or the population, for that matter), and only 19 percent have high-status white-collar fathers. An exception in the other direction is the media, where three-quarters have high-status fathers, including 40 percent who are the children of professionals. Business leaders also have a high percentage (71 percent) of high-status fathers. Congress is unusual for its higher proportion of farm-owner fathers, probably reflecting the rural origins of many members of that sector.

The overrepresentation of the children of high-status fathers in most elite sectors suggests that elites' parents had more education than most others of their generations. This is indeed the case, as the last two columns of Table 2.1 show. One-third of fathers and one-fifth of mothers of elite sample members graduated from college, at times when tiny proportions of the population had as much education. In specific sectors, namely Congress and labor, fewer mothers and fathers of elite members had college educations, but only for the mothers of labor leaders does the proportion in an elite sector come close to that of the population. Again, the media are an exception in the other direction; a very high proportion of their fathers, but not of their mothers, had a college education. In other sectors, the percentage of parents who are college graduates is close to that in the overall sample.

The combination of class and status dimensions sheds interesting light on Putnam's (1976: 22-26) well-known generalization that business leaders are from more privileged origins than political administrators, who in turn have higher origins than legislative elites. The differences in status origins among sectors generally are in accord with Putnam's statement. Thus, in comparison to political appointees and members of Congress, a very high percentage of the fathers of business leaders fall into the three high-status occupational categories; and of the three sectors, Congress has the lowest percentage of fathers in the top occupational categories and also the lowest percentage of parents with college educations. But in terms of the class dimension, the members of Congress move from the bottom to the top. They have the highest percentage of fathers who were owners and also the highest percentage of capitalist fathers. The discrepancy is a result of the high percentage of fathers of members of Congress who were farm owners, a group that falls into the owner class but is placed low in terms of occupational prestige. Accordingly, the class dimension imparts a different perception of elite social origins than do the status dimensions.

Overall, the class and status origins of the elite sample are far different from those of the comparison groups in the U.S. population. Elites are far more likely to come from occupationally and educationally privileged families than are nonelite persons. This is not, of course, a surprising finding, but what is striking among the differences in social origins of elite and nonelite persons is the large percentage of elites from capitalist families. Origins in the capitalist class appear to be a significant advantage in achieving a top-level position in a powerful public or private institution.

Differentiation by Socioeconomic Origins Within the Elite

Two broad questions concerning differences by class and status origins within the elite remain. First, are elite members from different class and status backgrounds similar with respect to other background factors, such as types of education? It may be, for example, that whatever their origins, elite members tend to have attended the most prestigious colleges and that these schools serve as entry portals, even for those from the least favored backgrounds. Second, do social origins coincide with differences in elite position, as indicated by current activities or influence? Much of the literature suggests that common origins and common culture form the cement for powerful informal networks within the elite. If so, then those entering the elite from less favored backgrounds may remain on the periphery of influence, while those from the most favored backgrounds may be at its center.

Both of these questions are addressed by the results reported in Table 2.2. The table shows the results of regression analyses of five social background characteristics, seven current activity measures, and three sociometric variables.[7] Because we are interested in whether these variables are related to class and status background, they are the dependent variables in the regressions. The class and status background variables, which are represented by sets of dummy variables,[8] are independent variables in regressions run separately for each of them. For each, the first column reports the increment to R^2 produced when the variable is added to an equation already containing sector.[9] The remaining columns for the variable report the coefficients of its dummy variables. These coefficients have been calculated in such a way that they represent differences, in standard deviation units of the dependent variable, and with sector controlled, between each category represented by a dummy variable and the so-called omitted category. The significance tests for the coefficients are, then, tests of those differences; the overall effect of each class or status variable is tested by its increment to R^2.

An example may help to clarify this approach. The R^2 increment of father's social class to the equation for the COLLEGE variable shows that class background is significantly related to the quality of the college attended by an elite sample member, even with sector controlled. The coefficient of petty bourgeois origins shows that those from such origins were less likely, by .50 standard deviation units, to attend high-prestige colleges than were those from capitalist origins, who form the omitted category. This difference is with sector controlled.

To begin with, class and status background is related, and sometimes strongly so, to the other aspects of social background that we have analyzed here. The relation of father's class to the background variables generally demonstrates the advantages of those with capitalist origins (the omitted category). These are visible in the overall pattern of differences in the education variables and especially in the differences in attendance at an elite private high school (PREPSCHL). Contrary to what might be expected, however, the children of small entrepreneurs are not the next most advantaged group. Indeed, in educational terms, they seem the least advantaged of the four groups. There is little difference between the children of managers and those of workers, although it deserves note that the former come from the oldest American families (GENRES).

Regarding father's occupation, advantages in background adhere to those with professional fathers (the omitted category) or managerial ones, with the children of proprietors and other white-collar workers generally not far behind. Specifically, the children of professional and managerial fathers are the most likely to have attended elite private schools and high-quality colleges. Falling at the bottom in both respects are the children of blue-collar and farm origins. These two groups are clearly the least advantaged in general background, as they also have less education (OWNED) than those in the four white-collar categories. In addition, the children of blue-collar fathers come from the most recently arrived families.

Finally, in terms of parental education, the children of college-educated parents are generally the most advantaged in overall social background. Although the differences made by mother's education are not large, as indicated by the relatively small R^2 figures, the differences associated with father's education are defined fairly sharply. The children of fathers who earned at least a baccalaureate have attended more prestigious educational institutions, and the children of fathers with the very highest educational credentials, a postbaccalaureate degree (the omitted category), have them-

TABLE 2.2 Regression of Social Background, Current Activities, and Sociometric Measures[a] on Class and Status Background, Net of Sector

	Father's Social Class[d]				Father's Occupation[e]					
		Semistandardized Coefficients[c]				Semistandardized Coefficients[c]				
	R^2 Net of Sector[b]	Petty Bourgeois	Manager	Worker	R^2 Net of Sector[b]	Proprie-tor	Manager	Other White-Collar	Blue-Collar	Farm Owner
Social background										
GENRES	.026*	.04	.29*	-.16	.076**	-.55**	-.05	-.33	-.67**	-.05
AGE	.014	.15	-.11	.16	.024*	-.08	-.19	-.26	-.24	.31
PREPSCHL	.061**	-.71**	-.44**	-.52**	.061**	-.37*	-.18	-.59**	-.66**	-.64**
COLLEGE	.031*	-.50**	-.21	-.16	.028*	-.22	-.05	-.22	-.44**	-.46*
OWNED	.011	-.29*	-.10	-.13	.019*	-.04	-.04	-.07	-.34**	-.35*
Sociometric measures										
CENTRAL C	.004	-.05	.09	-.02	.017	-.24	.00	-.03	-.31*	-.22
INTVOTES	.001	-.05	.01	-.01	.002	-.01	.10	-.06	.08	.08
REPVOTES	.001	.03	.08	-.00	.004	-.16	-.12	-.18	-.15	-.07
Current activities										
ELITEORG	.005	-.18	-.04	-.13	.033**	-.39**	-.23	-.55**	-.37*	-.57**
FEDADV	.009	-.19	.05	-.08	.012	-.23	-.26	-.33	-.24	-.06
TESTCONG	.001	-.04	.00	-.09	.009	.06	-.01	-.02	-.20	-.19
COMMOUT	.012	-.20	-.13	-.36*	.023	.23	-.17	.12	-.05	-.25
NONPROF	.019*	-.38**	-.23	-.34*	.022*	-.06	.04	-.14	-.33*	-.38*
CORPDIR	.004	-.14	-.04	-.18	.014	-.25*	-.02	-.21	-.20	.09
ELCLUBS	.021*	-.40**	-.22	-.35*	.015	-.15	-.05	-.18	-.34*	-.30

	Father's Education[f]					Mother's Education[g]			
		Semistandardized Coefficients[c]					Semistandardized Coefficients[c]		
	R^2 Net of Sector[b]	College Graduate	Some College	High School Graduate	Not a High School Graduate	R^2 Net of Sector[b]	Some College	High School Graduate	Not a High School Graduate
Social background									
GENRES	.066**	.25	.14	-.15	-.42*	.051**	-.06	-.30*	-.63**
AGE	.011	.21	.29	.25	.36*	.003	.00	.03	.14
PREPSCHL	.083**	.03	-.56*	-.54**	-.66**	.029*	-.27	.03	-.37*
COLLEGE	.037**	.03	-.05	-.48*	-.26	.005	.00	-.05	-.19
OWNED	.039**	-.33*	-.50**	-.21	-.61**	.003	-.09	-.05	-.17
Sociometric measures									
CENTRAL C	.022	.17	-.08	-.05	-.24	.014	.25	.02	-.15
INTVOTES	.008	.20	-.08	.07	-.01	.003	.11	.01	.12
REPVOTES	.023*	.31	.07	-.01	-.10	.001	-.11	-.09	-.09
Current activities									
ELITEORG	.025*	.36	.08	.00	-.07	.008	-.21	-.14	-.28
FEDADV	.013	.06	.32	.14	-.05	.011	-.35*	-.21	-.23
TESTCONG	.002	.05	.02	.13	.05	.006	.02	-.16	-.04
COMMOUT	.012	.05	.25	.01	-.12	.001	-.05	-.04	-.10
NONPROF	.025**	.02	-.17	-.21	-.39*	.004	-.07	-.04	-.18
CORPDIR	.012	.12	-.22	.03	-.12	.003	.16	.09	.03
ELCLUBS	.026*	-.02	-.19	-.13	-.41*	.005	-.06	.03	-.15

a Descriptions of the variables in this table are in note 7.
b These columns report the increment to the R^2 produced by adding a particular class or status variable, expressed as a set of dummy variables, to an equation already containing sector.
c The semistandardized coefficients report the differences, in standard deviation units of the dependent variable, between the categories heading the columns and the omitted category.
d The omitted category contains those with capitalist fathers.
e The omitted category contains those with professional fathers.
f The omitted category contains those whose fathers had postgraduate educations.
g The omitted category contains those whose mothers earned at least the baccalaureate degree.

selves the highest educational attainment. Father's education is also associated with generations of residence in the United States.

By and large, the differences we have just described form a set of related differences in background that, broadly speaking, constitute what most would expect to find. It is worth noting, nonetheless, that the parallels do not hold in every detail. There are not, for example, neatly graduated differences for each step in father's social class; recall the above-mentioned extreme differences within the sample between the children of capitalists and those of the petty bourgeoisie.

We are now at the point of asking what these differences in class and status origins imply about current position within the elite. The answer, first of all, is: less than one might think. For most of the indicators of current position and influence in the elite, class and status origins make little or no difference when their effects are assessed by a difference-of-R^2 test. Among the sociometric indicators, for instance, there is only one significant relation by this test. Among the indicators of current activities and visibility, there are no significant differences for the number of federal advisory boards (FEDADV) or corporate boards (CORPDIR) on which an individual sits, the number of times he or she has testified before Congress (TESTCONG), or the level of that person's communications output (COMMOUT). Although there are occasionally significant regression coefficients for some of these variables (such as for the children of workers on level of communications output), their presence does not change the general pattern of little or no relation.

On the whole, those indicators of current activities for which class and status origins make the most difference are the ones often thought to reflect the influence of an "upper class," expressed in large part through informal connections. These indicators include membership in exclusive social clubs (ELCLUBS), on the boards of trustees of nonprofit organizations (NONPROF), and in influential policy-planning organizations (ELITEORG). By and large, the differences on these indicators correspond with the differences in general social background we have identified previously.

Judging again by a difference-of-R^2 test, membership in exclusive social clubs is associated with father's class and education. In terms of class origins, the children of capitalists are the most likely to belong to such clubs, followed by the children of managers. In terms of father's education, the children of college graduates or those with postgraduate educations are the most likely to belong, while the children of fathers who did not graduate from high school are the least likely. Membership on the boards of trustees of nonprofit organizations is associated with father's class, occupation, and education. The differences according to father's class and education parallel those for club membership. In terms of father's occupation, those of blue-collar and farm origins are less likely to be nonprofit board members than are the children of white-collar fathers.

The biggest differences by background are for membership in elite policy-planning organizations, such as the Business Council and the Council on Foreign Relations, that are thought to be key channels for upper-class influence on national policy (see Domhoff, 1979; Dye, 1979). But father's class is not related to this sort of membership; rather, father's occupation and education are. The differences associated with father's education are somewhat unanticipated, as the children of fathers with postbaccalaureate degrees are among the least likely to be members. The differences associated with father's occupation are more expected and also large in magnitude. The children of professionals, followed by the children of managers, are most likely to belong; the children of lower white-collar workers and of farm owners are least likely.

These differences in elite activities are worthy of attention because of the significance that is often attributed to them. But it must be noted that the differences associated with background are, on the whole, not large, as is indicated by the size of the R^2 increases reported in the table and the magnitudes of the regression coefficients. Only in one instance does a background variable add more than 3 percent to the variance explained by sector membership; and only a few of the differences among categories of a background variable are larger than .4 standard deviation units. That these are indeed signs of relations of only modest strength is brought out by a comparison to the regression results for the other social background variables, such as attendance at a select prep school.

In terms of a larger picture, the results of this section are quite fundamental. We have already noted that class and status background has an important bearing on entry into the elite. This is especially true, of course, for father's social class. Further, according to the results presented early in this section, class and status origins correspond with other background differences that might be expected to affect position and influence within the elite. They affect not only the amount of education received but the prestige and quality of the educational institutions an elite person has attended. In addition, they correspond with differences in generations of family residence in the United States. But class and status origins are surprisingly weak in predicting indicators of *current* elite position and influence. These origins are consistently related to only a few indicators, such as membership in exclusive social clubs. These few indicators do have an important theoretical status, but they are only weakly associated with class and status background.

Homophily in Elite Interaction

The proposition that informal relations tend to occur on the basis of common origins and culture is often viewed as central to the presumed hegemony of elite individuals of upper-class origins. This proposition is an instance of the homophily principle, which holds that persons tend to interact with others like themselves (Lazarsfeld and Merton, 1954). We have already tested it indirectly through the relation of class and status origins to sociometric indicators such as the number of interaction nominations an individual receives from others in the elite sample. These tests are indirect because the indicators were constructed by aggregation; hence, the equality of individuals of different socioeconomic origins could mask a tendency for interaction at the individual level to run along lines determined by origins.

To test the homphily principle directly, we use part of the data that provided the basis for the sociometric measures of the last section—specifically, the nominations respondents provided when asked to name those with whom they were in personal contact concerning their issue of activity.[10] In this section, we report briefly an analysis of who named whom, focusing specifically on the extent to which respondents named others with the same class and status origins as themselves. Our analysis is based on who-to-whom tables, in which characteristics of respondents are tabulated by the same characteristics of the persons they named.

In constructing such a table, we can only use nominations to other sample members, since only for these do we know the socioeconomic backgrounds of both the respondents and the persons they named. A total of 645 nominations were to sample members; they were made by 279 sample members. However, because of missing data, not all of these nominations can be tabulated in each who-to-whom table. As a result, the tables are based on relatively small portions of the data, and it is impossible to control for sector, as we have done elsewhere in the study. Obviously, our conclusions must be tentative.

We have constructed a who-to-whom table for each class and status variable, and we have run each table in two different ways, one with the nomination as the unit that is counted (hence, respondents contribute unequally to the table) and one with the respondent as that unit (weighting his or her nominations in inverse proportion to their number). Space

TABLE 2.3 Who-to-Whom Tables for Father's Social Class

a. Nominations Counted

Nominator's Class Background	*Nominee's Class Background*				
	Capitalist	*Petty Bourgeois*	*Managerial*	*Worker*	*(N)*
Capitalist	30.9%	23.5	35.3	10.3	(68)
Petty Bourgeois	30.3	31.6	31.6	6.6	(76)
Managerial	23.4	29.7	34.2	12.6	(111)
Worker	30.6	30.6	30.6	8.2	(49)

$X^2 = 4.36$ with 9 df ($p > .8$)

b. Respondents Counted

Nominator's Class Background	*Nominee's Class Background*				
	Capitalist	*Petty Bourgeois*	*Managerial*	*Worker*	*(N)*
Capitalist	33.3%	17.1	38.5	11.0	(37)
Petty Bourgeois	32.4	27.4	33.9	6.3	(45)
Managerial	20.4	28.7	36.6	14.3	(60)
Worker	27.8	37.7	30.7	3.8	(27)

$X^2 = 7.63$ with 9 df ($p > .5$)

constraints prevent a full presentation of these tables, but some representative results, for father's social class, are presented as Table 2.3. The results are quite consistent for all the tables: There is no trace of a systematic pattern. None of the X^2 values is significant; none, in fact, even borders on significance. Inspection of the percentages reveals variations that are too weak and inconsistent to support even a qualified conclusion on behalf of homophily, as Table 2.3 illustrates.

In sum, there is no evidence here of homophily along lines determined by social origins. The fact that this conclusion is based on tables constructed from only parts of the data is partly redeemed by the consistency of the results. Although they are far from definitive, our results suggest that elite interaction patterns may be constrained by instrumental interests. Many writings about elites that presume a cohesion within ethnic- or class-derived groups assume that elite interactions are based to some degree on "elective affinity." But our results imply to us that instrumental interests may counteract the "taste" for others like oneself, and consequently cohesion based on social origins may be only of minor magnitude *within the elite.*

Conclusion

The relation of political power to the other axes of stratification is one of the classic issues in sociology and political science, dating back at least as far as the famous dictum in *The Communist Manifesto* that "political power, properly so-called, is merely the organized power of one class for oppressing another." The perspective inherent in this remark has influenced many descriptions of the American elite. It is visible in such well-known works as C. Wright Mills's (1956) *The Power Elite* and those of G. William Domhoff, and in many related pieces of empirical research (for example, Domhoff, 1975). The point of view these works represent is a familiar one, but not the only one. We start with it because it offers a useful background to the empirical findings we have presented here.

To begin with, this point of view is generally taken to imply a link between social origins and elite recruitment. Its adherents tend to identify the elite as extremely selective in terms of the social origins of its personnel, with social class of origin an especially important criterion of entry. Dye's work emphasizes this fundamental point as he finds that at least 25 percent of elites in major sectors come from upper-class origins (1979: 169-170). This perspective also identifies a mechanism through which such narrow recruitment occurs: Selection is accomplished through special socialization agencies, such as select private schools, which provide individuals with the social and cultural wherewithal to qualify as *potential* elite members. These institutions are, by and large, open chiefly to those of privileged origins.

Our research on the class and status origins of the American elite has produced results that in part agree with, but also in part differ from, this familiar portrayal. Agreement seems strongest on the selectivity of the elite. As others have noted, the children of professionals, proprietors, and managers are overrepresented in the elite, as are individuals with highly educated parents. But none of these concentrations of individuals with favored status origins seems sharp enough to impart a dominant character to the elite.

Such a character does appear in our findings on father's social class, and here too we are in broad agreement with the familiar portrayal. Truly striking is the proportion of individuals whose fathers were owners of businesses. Such persons make up about half the elite sample, and although we are unable to determine precise U.S. population figures to compare against the sample, it is obvious that the children of owners are highly overrepresented. This seems especially true for the sons and daughters of those we have labeled "capitalists," employers of ten or more persons. This concentration along lines determined by class of origin becomes even more sharply defined when we include the children of managers in our reckoning. Thus, the children of men who controlled either property or the work of others make up an astounding 85 percent of the elite sample.

But we differ from the familiar portrait on the precise nature of class advantages. Domhoff and others describe elite selectivity in terms of a very small group of extremely privileged families, the upper class, whose members are highly overrepresented in the elite, although they are not a majority of it. We have found a broader stream of recruitment, from the families of business owners. This produces a considerable overrepresentation of individuals who do not have upper-class origins—for example, the children of farm owners or of the petty bourgeoisie. It also leads to a stronger representation of a class group within the elite than is true of the upper class, as the children of business owners form a majority or a near majority of nearly all elite sectors.

Our findings are also at variance with the familiar portrait on the impact of social origins on current position and influence *within* the elite. We are unable to find much impact, despite the abundant evidence that class and status origins affect elite recruitment. We have examined the relation of social origins to activities and organizational memberships that might either reflect or magnify an elite individual's influence. Examples of the indicators we have considered are the number of times a person has testified before Congress and memberships in exclusive social clubs. But the background variables are only occasionally related to these indicators and even these few relations are modest in magnitude. The same basic pattern is found in our analysis of interaction within the elite, both in the analysis of aggregated sociometric indicators and in our homophily analysis. In short, we find little or no evidence that the influence of those with privileged origins is consolidated further by informal patterns of elite interaction or the solidarity cultivated in exclusive institutions.

Finally, although this is not clear from the empirical findings we have presented, we differ from the familiar portrait on the mechanisms giving rise to elite selectivity. This is an important difference because the selective character of the elite with respect to class origins is a phenomenon that demands some explanation. As we noted before, Domhoff and others explain the class selectivity of the elite in large part by pointing to the role of specific institutions in channeling individuals into the elite. These institutions, it is argued, provide individuals with a cultural patina shared by elite members and with a set of connections, ultimately including some to potential sponsors within the elite, that assist in elite entry. Chief among these institutions are schools, and this explanation takes on added plausibility since very specific educational credentials seem prerequisites for elite positions in some other societies like France and England (Bottomore, 1964). But the evidence on behalf of this explanation is not very compelling as far as the United States is concerned. Only a small proportion (10 percent) of our sample has attended an exclusive private school, and even the proportion who attended a high-quality college (37 percent) is not large. As we indicated earlier, class and status origins are related to the prestige and quality of the educational institutions an elite individual has attended. We suspect that having attended a prestigious school is a definite advantage for entry into the elite. Nonetheless, the representation of individuals with this sort of education does not seem large enough to account for class advantage.

Two other categories of explanation, involving culture and wealth, seem plausible to us, although we can only advocate them in a speculative way. The influence of cultural values on social position is an important theme in sociology and has been discussed often in relation to ethnic differences in mobility (see Steinberg, 1974). In that context, a critical distinction has been made between groups with entrepreneurial experiences in their countries of origin, Eastern European Jews being perhaps the preeminent example, and those without those experiences, such as Southern Italians (Schooler, 1976). A classic argument traces the broad mobility differences between these groups to the cultural values engendered by these different backgrounds. We see the possibility of a similar argument in relation to entry into the elite, although we are not certain as to the exact details. In its essence, such an argument would depend on an outlook specific to the controllers of property (and perhaps also controllers of persons). Involved would be such factors as attraction to risk, commitment to the notion of a "career" that is independent of a specific organizational context, and a high value placed on control over the lives of others and over one's own work.

Wealth, of course, is useful in many concrete ways, such as the attainment of an elite education. Further, wealth and other material resources may interact with or even make possible the outlook that predisposes some toward an elite career. We have no direct data on inherited wealth in our sample, and in all probability the bulk of the sample members with owner fathers did not inherit great wealth (a majority of these fathers were in the petty bourgeois category). But it is likely that most of the children of owners inherited some wealth. In our view, wealth is significant in that it enables individuals to weather the vicissitudes of an elite career, especially in its early stages, when the improbability of success may drive men and women of lower social origins into a more stable career path.

To sum up, we believe that the major value of our research on the class and status origins of the American elite is in documenting the significant advantages enjoyed by the children of business owners, rather than merely the scions of the upper class, in attaining a national elite position in the United States. However, additional research is required to delineate the precise mechanisms through which such origins facilitate an elite career. It is also essential to examine further the consequences of this class selection for policy-influencing and policymaking behavior.

NOTES

1. Detailed descriptions of the universe for all sectors are given by Barton (1974); capsule descriptions are presented by Moore (1979: Table 1). The descriptions of a few sectors here may help to give the flavor of the study design. The universe for the political appointees sector, for example, included secretaries, under- and assistant secretaries, and general counsels of cabinet departments, as well as heads and deputy heads of independent agencies. The civil servants sector included individuals in the two highest civil service grades (GS 17 and 18) from all cabinet departments and independent agencies. In industrial corporations, the chief executive officers of the 500 largest corporations constituted the universe.

2. In classifying respondents, we use information they provided on a vita form pertaining to the work of their fathers when the respondents were 16 years old. Specifically, they were asked about their fathers: Was he self-employed? Did he employ others? Number he employed? Did he supervise others? The information gathered by these questions was sufficient to classify the class origins of nearly 80 percent of the positional sample members.

3. The parental education and occupation variables are constructed from the considerable information about family background that respondents provided on the vita form. The information about parental education is straightforward, but some of the information about father's occupation (when the respondent was 16 years old) is coded according to somewhat unconventional categories. We report these unconventional categories below, followed immediately in each case by the occupational categories in which we have placed them: "subprofessional (nurse, surveyor, personnel)" professional; "armed services, policemen, firemen, other protective services," blue-collar; "unemployed, disabled," blue-collar; "politics," professional; "business

man, no further information," managerial. It should be noted that the number of respondents classified in these unconventional categories is very small (N = 20).

For each of the background variables, the percentage of missing data is as follows: father's occupation, 10.3 percent; father's education, 15.5 percent; mother's education, 16.9 percent.

4. In terms of age, the American population selected for comparison is that part over 40 at the time of the elite interviews. These are men born before 1932.

Some of the occupational categories in the elite sample and the NORC surveys are not precisely comparable. The farm-owner category in the elite sample includes only owners of farms, while in the NORC surveys this category includes farm tenants as well. Also, the NORC survey does not have a separate category for proprietors, but combines these with managers.

5. The standard is less than fully exact for two reasons not mentioned in the text. The study used by Wright and Perrone includes women and excludes persons out of the labor force. The inclusion of women undoubtedly depresses the class distribution by comparison with that which holds for men only, while the exclusion of those out of the labor force probably works in the other direction, as individuals primarily in the lowest-class category are dropped from the sample. We are uncertain as to the overall effect of these two features of the study.

6. Some readers may find it puzzling that the two occupational categories of ownership (proprietors and farm owners) contain a smaller percentage of the sample than do the categories of ownership for the class variable. The discrepancy is explained by the fact that many respondents whose fathers were self-employed described the kind of work their fathers did (for example, lawyer, butcher) in answering the occupational question. In short, the discrepancy results from a meaningful distinction between the class and status dimensions. The same point holds for differences between the managerial categories.

7. The variables are: GENRES, generations of residence in the U.S. (range 1-4 with 1 = foreign born, 4 = 4 or more generations); PREPSCHL (1 = attended elite prep school, 0 = did not attend one); COLLEGE, quality of college attended (1 = attended high prestige college, 0 = did not attend one), OWNED, years of education; AGE (in years); ELITEORG, number of memberships in seventeen elite policy-planning organizations; FEDADV, number of memberships on federal advisory committees; TESTCONG, number of congressional testimonies given (range 1-3, 1 = 0, 2 = 1, 3 = 2+); COMMOUT, level of communications output (range 1-7 with 1 = low); CORPDIR, number of corporate directorships held; NONPROF, number of nonprofit directorships held; ELCLUBS, elite club membership (0 = no, 1 = yes); INTVOTES, number of interaction nominations received from other sample members (range 0-5 with 0 = 0, 1 = 1 . . . 5 = 5+); REPVOTES, number of reputation nominations received from other sample members (range 0-5 as in INTVOTES); CENTRAL C, central circle membership (0 = no, 1 = yes). The central circle, a key feature of the elite network, is described in detail by Moore (1979). The lists of elite prep schools and clubs are taken from Domhoff (1971: Chapter 1).

8. In our regression results for mother's and father's education, we have provided finer breakdowns of these variables than we report in Table 2.1.

9. Because the elite sample is actually composed of separate sector samples, sector is controlled throughout the analyses reported in this section.

10. Respondents were not constrained in making these nominations. They were, for example, allowed to make as many nominations as they liked and were not provided with predefined lists of names from which to choose.

3

Studying Personal Communities

BARRY WELLMAN

Old and New Campaigns

Generals often want to refight their last war; academics often want to redo their last study. The reasons are the same. The passage of time has made them aware of mistakes in strategy, preparations, and analysis. New concepts and tools have come along to make the job easier. Others looking at the same events now claim to know better. If only we could do the job again!

With such thoughts in mind, I want to look at where network analyses of communities have come from and where they are likely to go. However, I propose to spend less time in refighting the past (in part, because the battles have been successful) than in proposing strategic objectives for the present and future. In this chapter, I take stock of the current state of knowledge in three ways.

First, I relate community network studies to fundamental concerns of both social network analysis and urban sociology. I argue that while community network studies have evolved easily out of the postwar realization that communities have continued to thrive since the Industrial Revolution, they have made unique contributions to the study of community through their focus on structured social relationships and their deemphasis of local solidarities.

Second, I assess the current limitations of community network studies by discussing the one whose problems I know best: my own (see Wellman

AUTHOR'S NOTE: Brenda Billingsley, Christina Black, Jennifer Gullen, Sharon Kirsh, and Edward Lee contributed greatly to the development of the research reported here. Bonnie Erickson commented incisively on an earlier draft. Portions of et al., 1973; Wellman, 1979). Community network analysts have created a strong base for further research by establishing the importance of networks of community ties for providing sociability and informal aid to network members. They have used network analysis as a metaphor and method to demonstrate the persistence of community in contemporary societies. It is now time to move beyond these initial achievements and use network analysis as a more comprehensive structural approach to studying how communities fit in large-scale divisions of labor.

Third, I report on my enactment of the generals' and scholars' dream. My research group has mounted a new study of community, using some of our original "East Yorker" respondents. We are investigating what kinds of community networks are likely to be prevalent under various structural conditions, analyzing how different kinds of community networks affect the quality of urban life, and discovering how variations in the personal situations of individuals (such as their stages in the life course) affect the kinds of communities in which they are involved. I present this study's analytic concerns and research design, as well as preliminary findings about the composition and content of East Yorkers' community ties.

Where We Are Coming From

The Rediscovery of Community

Network analysts have made both incremental and revolutionary contributions to the study of communities. In the 1950s, many community scholars looked around and realized–contra Toennies (1887/1963), Simmel (1950a) and Wirth (1938)–that the large-scale social transformations of the past 150 years had not destroyed small-scale ,communities. Hanging around on street corners, sipping tea through interviews, and ringing doorbells in surveys, they found an abundance of useful community ties with kin, friends, neighbors, and workmates (see the reviews in Craven and Wellman, 1973; Fischer, 1976; Warren, 1978).

Against all odds and arguments, urbanites had "saved" communities from the storm of the Industrial Revolution's large-scale changes. As urban

---

this chapter were discussed at the annual meetings of the American Sociological Association, Toronto, August, 1981. Our research has been supported by grants from the Center for Studies of Metropolitan Problems (NIMH), the Joint Program in Transportation of York University and the University of Toronto, the Social Sciences and Humanities Research Council of Canada, and the Structural Analysis Programme and the Gerontology Programme of the University of Toronto. Throughout the decade-long course of the East York research, the Centre for Urban and Community Studies, University of Toronto, has been a sociable and supportive base.

scholars came to realize this in the 1960s, they made the persistence of urban communities their new orthodoxy. Policymakers shifted emphasis from slum-clearing, urban renewal, and bureaucratic support services to Jacobsean (1961) urban preservation and informal support networks. Social network research fit easily into this movement, documenting the persistence and usefulness of community ties. In the common enterprise, network analysts evolved distinctive points of view, emphasizing the study of structures of communities rather than of solidary local communities.

Personal Communities: The Network Approach

Boundedness. Network analysts argued that sociologists should study community in terms of types of social relations and not look only at the local clustering of these relations. They suggested conceiving of a community as a *personal community*—a network of ties—and not as a *neighborhood*—a local area containing sets of potential relations (see Tilly, 1974; Wellman and Leighton, 1979).

This switch in perspective encouraged sociologists to look for community ties and support systems extending beyond neighborhoods. It helped dethrone local or group solidarity as the criterion for viable communities and opened up discussion of the alternative consequences of different network configurations. It encouraged analysts to evaluate different types of ties—kin or friends, strong or weak, local or long-distance, egalitarian or patron-client—in terms of the kinds of access to resources that they provide. On the debit side, it deemphasized analyses of neighborhoods as real ecological entities in which all inhabitants must rub shoulders. Moreover, the analysts' concentration on small-scale interpersonal networks often led them to neglect considering the larger institutional contexts in which such networks were embedded.

Ties or Norms? When they first started doing community research, many network analysts had treated structural patterns as just another set of intervening variables. They hoped, for example, that network density might increase explained variance a bit. In time, network analysts began to explain social behavior more in terms of the structural pattern of community ties and less in terms of internalized norms and values. They increasingly treated all of social structure as a network phenomenon. They argued that the pattern of ties in a network ordered people's access to scarce resources—that is, that these patterns greatly determined the opportunities and constraints for their social behavior (see Alba, 1981; Berkowitz, 1982; Wellman, 1982a). They showed how network patterns could affect the activities of network members. Densely knit networks, for example, could mobilize resources more rapidly than networks in which resources would flow to some members through longer chains (see Bott, 1971).

This focus on structural patterns is quite different from normatively driven analyses, which study how people first become socialized and then behave in accord with their internalized norms. Such normative explanations, based on internalized motives for action, are ultimately individualistic. Moreover, as they tend to assume that community members share attitudes, they often assume that viable communities are solidary bodies.

The difference in the two approaches is clear in Third World studies of urban social networks. Normatively driven analyses are plausible for studying differences among persons whose lives are totally contained within such concrete, bounded groups as solidary villages. Yet migrants from rural areas to cities are no longer members of village solidarities. Conventional modernization theory, as heavily indebted to Durkheimian anomie as the old "loss of community" argument, suggests that when rural villagers migrate to cities, they are ripped asunder from their local solidarities to become rootless, normless members of urban "mass society" (see Kornhauser, 1968). Their only hope, according to normative analyses, is to receive a healthy inoculation of achievement norms upon leaving home so that they can become modern operators on the urban scene (see McClelland and Winter, 1969).

Normative, "uprooting" analyses received a jolt when researchers discovered that migrants rarely come to the city alone and disconnected. Rather, they use links with kin and village mates who have migrated earlier to find friends, housing, and jobs. Nor are their old ties disconnected: The migrants use links in both the cities and their ancestral villages to gain access to diverse resources. Thus, normative analyses just do not have the necessary payoff: Many migrants' norms do not change in the city, and the migrants' heterogeneous, cross-cutting social networks contradict explanations of their behavior in terms of local solidary group norms (see Howard, 1974; Mayer with Mayer, 1974; Roberts, 1973).

From Personal Attributes to Social Relations. Network analysts also started interpreting behavior more in terms of social relationships and less in terms of personal attributes (see Burt, 1980c; Berkowitz, 1982; Wellman, 1982a). They were concerned that studies based on personal attributes (such as "gender" or "socioeconomic status") inherently treated social system members as astructural, independent units of analysis. Because such studies analyze the aggregated attributes of discrete individuals, their inherent "methodological individualism" leads them "to the neglect of social structure and of the relations among individuals" (Coleman, 1958: 28). At best, such analyses use personal attributes as proxy measures of how social structure constrains behavior.

The shift from personal attributes to relational analysis is quite evident in the study of "community support systems." Early social studies of health usually related the aggregated personal attributes of individuals to their symptoms and well-being (see Srole et al., 1975). However, support system researchers have recently begun to link network phenomena to mental and physical health. They have shown that supportive ties and densely knit networks foster good health directly, provide useful resources for dealing with stress, and give network members helpful feedback about their behavior. There is some evidence that network characteristics explain more about social support than do the personal attributes of network members (see Gottlieb, 1981; Hammer, 1981; Wellman et al., 1973). Thus, network analysts have become more inclined to study social structural patterns directly and to avoid using personal attributes as proxy measures of structured social relationships.

The First East York Study

Background

In the late 1960s, the first East York study entered directly into the then-heated "loss of community" debate. We wondered if English-Canadians continued to maintain communities in a modern metropolis and if their close community ties were giving them social support to deal with stressful situations (Wellman, 1968; Coates et al., 1970). Rather than studying "community," we studied "community ties." That is, we did not study a local area comprehensively, but asked a large number of urbanites about their informal relationships with persons outside of their households. This enabled us to find out how both local and more distant ties fit into "personal communities," that is, networks of community ties providing sociable companionship and supportive resources to participants.

We concentrated on studying the residents of East York, a densely settled, inner residential "borough" of metropolitan Toronto (1971 population = 104,785). East York then had a broad housing mix of lowrise and highrise dwellings. Its population was homogeneously British-Canadian in ethnicity and a mixture of working-class and middle-class in socioeconomic status. The respondents' relatively homogeneous social backgrounds enabled us to focus on the effects of ties and networks on the provision of support without having to allow for potentially confounding differences in ethnicity and social class (see Gillies and Wellman, 1968).

Many East Yorkers saw their borough as a tranquil, integrated community, insulated from the metropolitan hurly-burly. Certainly, it had had a long tradition of active social service agencies and communal aid (see East York, 1976). Yet East York had also participated integrally in the postwar transformation of Toronto: It had always been a part of the metropolitan—and North American—economic system; its basic municipal political decisions had been taken over in 1954 by a metropolitan government; it had long been integrated into regional transportation and communications systems. Although the British-Canadian residents remained staunchly in their small homes, their children and kin were dispersed throughout North America. Thus the borough and its residents were quite thoroughly knit into larger social structures, despite their insular self-images.

The Survey

We based the original study on a two-hour survey of 845 randomly sampled adult East Yorkers. The survey gathered information about each respondent's socially close community ties: their relationship to the respondent, where they lived, how often they were in contact (both in person and by telephone), the strength of their closeness (or intimacy), and whether they helped each other in everyday or emergency situations.

The survey had a number of strengths: It used a large, well-designed, and well-collected sample; it obtained separate, systematic information about each of the six socially close "intimates"; it did not assume, a priori, that these intimate community members were kin or neighbors; it enabled some structural analysis by obtaining reports from respondents on the ties between their intimates; it differentiated crudely both between everyday and emergency assistance and between the help that respondents and intimates each gave to the other.

The study's basic conceptual strength was that it treated community as a network of ties and not as a local area containing sets of potential relationships (for some similar treatments, done at about the same time, see Shulman, 1972, 1976; Laumann, 1973; Fischer et al., 1977; Verbrugge, 1977; Walker, 1977; Caulkins, 1980). This switch in perspective enabled us to look for community ties that extended well beyond neighborhoods. It helped dethrone local or group solidarity as the criterion for viable communities. It encouraged us to evaluate different types of ties–kin or friends, strong or weak, local or long-distance–in terms of the access they provided to resources.

By defining community as a network phenomenon, we found that most ties were not local; indeed, three-quarters of them stretched beyond East York's boundaries. Neighboring in East York remained an important, but less intense, relationship (see Gates et al., 1973). Furthermore, the availability of assistance from intimates in both everyday and emergency situations depended more on whether they lived within the metropolitan Toronto area than on whether they lived in the same neighborhood.

We found that most East Yorkers had a differentiated set of intimate community ties. While kin–especially parents and adult children–played very important roles in most East Yorkers' lives, half of the intimate ties were with unrelated friends, neighbors, and workmates. Intimate networks were not solidary wholes: Only one out of every three potential ties between an East Yorker's intimates actually existed (that is, network density equaled .33). Furthermore, East Yorkers did not count on most of their intimates to provide them with assistance in dealing with either everyday or emergency situations, although most East Yorkers had at least one intimate they could count on for such help (see Wellman, 1979, for more details).

Limitations

Despite such useful findings—preventing community from being "lost" even if it had moved out of the neighborhood—we were troubled that our research had some serious limitations:

(1) *By emphasizing networks, these studies had deemphasized the role of neighborhoods (and other spatial areas) as real ecological entities in which all inhabitants must rub shoulders.* What was the effect on personal communities of differences in the opportunities and constraints available in various neighborhoods? Did being isolated in suburbia or packed in the downtown core make a difference? To what extent did the pool of available choices—of people and resources—affect the kinds of ties formed and resources used?

(2) *We had limited our inquiries to only six close ties.* However, many persons had far more than six ties in their personal communities and their ties did not form homogeneous sets. How did the composition, structure, and use of these less intimate ties affect the ways in which personal communities were connected to the larger world?

(3) *We had thin, albeit extensive, data.* We had collected closed-ended information for computerized analysis. We had only minimal information about the nature of the resources network members transmitted to each other. We knew nothing about the opportunities and contingencies these individuals confronted in their lives.

(4) *We had treated network variables as just a few among many, rather than as a basic conceptual approach.* Since the time of our original study, the network approach had developed into a thoroughgoing structural formulation of sociology (Wellman, 1982a)—a sensibility that could profitably inform our entire study design.

(5) For a study that had billed itself as "network analysis," *we did not know much about the structure of the respondents' networks.* We had only the respondents' reports of the structure of these small, six-person, "intimate" fragments of their larger "personal communities." We had treated all ties as symmetric and voluntaristic. Our only measures of network structure were density and centrality.

(6) *We were not well-equipped to relate what happened in these small-scale personal communities to the structured opportunities and constraints created by large-scale divisions of labor.* Our concentration on

small-scale interpersonal networks often had led us away from considering the macrostructural contexts in which these networks were embedded (but see Laumann, 1973). In order to address the Community Question more adequately, we needed to know more about how capitalism, bureaucratization, industrialization, technological change, and urbanization affected the structure and content of personal communities.

The New East York Study

Strategy

It is interesting that Claude Fischer's and our research group have taken two different, but complementary, routes to dealing with the limitations of the early community network surveys. Fischer (1982) analyzes the effects of urbanization comparatively, using a series of surveys administered in California localities ranging in size from rural villages to San Francisco. We, in contrast, have sought to understand a small number of personal communities in depth, using lengthy reinterviews with a subsample of the original East York survey respondents.

Our basic strategy has been to juxtapose the original survey's statistical precision and diverse population with the new interviews' richer and more extensive information about the composition and dynamics of a small number of personal communities. We explicitly designed our interviews to fill the gaps left by the original survey. The interviews provide information about many more ties than the six intimates studied in the original survey and more information about each tie. We are especially concerned with the kinds of resources that flow between community members and the ways location in the larger social network affects interaction between network members. The interviews' information about a much greater number of ties helps to place in perspective our survey-based knowledge of intimate ties and to give more information about the structural complexities of these networks. At the same time, the original large, random-sample survey provides information about subgroups that is difficult to obtain in a small set of focused interviews.

Picturing Community

Our new study has five linked aims: Our first aim is based on the realization that much of the debate about the Community Question has been about *sheer description:* Just what do contemporary communities look like? Hundreds of survey analysts and ethnographers have gone forth to find out if they can now best describe community as a Lost mass of disconnected souls, a Saved solidarity joyously communing, or Liberated networkers maneuvering among their differentiated ties (Wellman and

Leighton, 1979). While most urban scholars now agree on the continuing abundance of community ties—the initial concern of the Community Question—we still wonder about their composition, structure, and content.

Studying Network Structure

Our second aim comes from the developing network analytic paradigm that deemphasizes explanations of behavior based on internalized norms or personal attributes, looking instead to explanations of behavior in terms of the structural patterns of networks. We want to study network structures in a variety of ways, since the traditional structural measure, network density, has both conceptual and methodological limitations.

When community theorists think principally in terms of network density, they get a chronic case of "pastoral syndrome": They nostalgically compare contemporary community networks with the well-integrated solidary networks supposedly prevalent in preindustrial communities (see Bender, 1978). This high-density norm leads analysts to treat complex, ramified networks as tattered residues of defunct solidarities. By removing the normative criterion of density, analysts can inquire into the effects different structural forms have on the availability of resources to network members. We are especially interested in the extent to which respondents have the structural ability to maneuver and "shop around" for appropriate help among their multiple social circles.

Density also is an ambiguous variable because networks with the same density value may have markedly different structural forms (Friedkin, 1981). Hence, while a density statistic reveals the amount of connectivity within the overall network, at intermediate values it gives poor information about network structure. Networks with the same density values vary markedly in their number of subgroups, number of triads, the size of their largest clump, and their degree of centrality—even when they contain the same numbers of persons and ties. Among these networks, those with well-connected cores seem to occur much more frequently, while those with ringlike or starlike forms rarely occur.[1]

Large-Scale: Small-Scale

Our third aim is to consider some of the ways in which large-scale structural phenomena—such as bureaucratization, capitalism, industrialization, technological change, and urbanization—affect the composition, structure, and dynamics of personal communities. Since Toennies (1887/1963), sociologists have argued over the extent to which such large-scale phenomena are the principal causes of our contemporary community condition. Indeed, even those who agree on a cause cannot agree on its effects: They debate, for example, whether capitalism has destroyed, saved, or liberated community (see Shorter, 1973; Scott and Tilly, 1975).

Our study cannot address such ultimate questions comprehensively, as it is not comparative and tracks only the 1968-1978 decade. However, we can tease out some implications of these large-scale factors by looking at how East Yorkers' structural location in systems of production and reproduction affects both their access to resources and the opportunities and pressures that come their way. We are doing this by treating such "personal attributes" as occupation, stage in the life course, and sex as structural locations in contemporary divisions of labor. For example, we are analyzing community members' occupations according to the types of control they have over capital, information, their own labor power, and the labor power of others.[2]

Preliminary analyses have already shown some of the ways in which East Yorkers' structural locations affect the composition, structure, and content of their personal communities (see Table 3.1). For example, the networks of "singles," living alone, resemble Community Lost depictions of urban life–transitory, sparsely knit, with few links to friends and kin–while the networks of "houseworkers," raising children and husbands, resemble Community Saved depictions–neighborhood and kinship-based support groups exchanging much emotional aid, small services, and household items.[3] We hope that our study will discover something about the "political economy of community": the place of personal communities in large-scale systems of reproduction and production. We are finding, for example, that adult women with families often serve as a "reproduction reserve army," providing low-cost, flexible support services to kin and neighbors at times of overloading stress.

From Support System to Social Network

Our fourth aim is to specify the conditions under which personal communities provide supportive resources to members. We want to go beyond documenting and celebrating the supportiveness of contemporary communities to understanding the circumstances under which resources do–and do not–flow through them. For example, "support system" research into community mental health often has assumed unwisely that communities are solidary groups composed only of supportive ties. This goes against empirical reality and creates the dubious expectation that solidary systems are invariably more desirable. Furthermore, by ignoring conflicts of interest between community members, the "support system" approach has inherently invoked the false premise of a common good (see the reviews in Gottlieb, 1981; Hammer, 1981).

Clearly, a support system is an analytically constricted social network that takes into account only supportive ties and that assumes these ties can

TABLE 3.1 Summary Table of Differences in the Composition, Structure, and Content of Personal Communities

Structural Type	*"Producers"*	*"Reproducers"*	*"Double Loaders" (prod. & reprod.)*	*"Singles" (prod. & reprod.)*
Employment status	Employed	Houseworkers, retired	Employed	Employed, students
Marital status	Married	Married, single mothers	Married, single mothers	Single, live alone
Sex	Men	HW: women Ret.: women, men	Women	Women, men
Network composition	Predominantly kin; some workmates	Neighbor intimates; kin nonintimates; no nonlocal friends	Kin; some workmates; no neighbors	Predominantly friends; no neighbors
Structure	Solidary kin; women central	Solidary neighbors; women central	Solidary kin; women central	Sparsely knit
Content	Sociable; exchange of small services and items; no emotional aid	Sociable; exchange of much emotional aid; exchange of many small services and items	Exchange of much emotional aid; sociable	Emotional aid; small services and items; sociable

only form a single, integrated structure. We can escape these limitations by defining personal communities more broadly—without regard to social support—and only later inquiring about the flows of supportive resources through each of the ties constituting the networks. This approach opens up the consideration of supportive ties to anywhere in an East Yorker's personal community and does not assume that aid is available only from solidary groups or specified social categories (such as kin). Moreover, it enables us to take into account the many community ties that are not supportive, to study which kinds of supportive resources flow through which ties, and to analyze the circumstances under which supportive aid is, or is not, symmetrically reciprocated (see also a more extended discussion in Wellman, 1981).

Longitudinal Studies

Our fifth aim is to take advantage of our study's longitudinal design. For one thing, we want to analyze how changes in personal situations affect changes in personal communities. To date, most such studies have looked only at one type of tie (for example, kin or neighbors) or one type of situational change (such as aging or residential mobility). We look forward to studying possible changes in a wide range of community ties as experienced by East Yorkers undergoing three different types of situational change: movement through the life course, residential mobility, and occupational mobility. This should enable us to evaluate differences and similarities in the impact of such situational changes on personal community composition, structure, and content.

We cannot assume, though, that the characteristics of personal communities are always passive consequences of changes in personal situations. There also is reverse causality: How do different sorts of personal communities facilitate changes in personal situations by structuring opportunities for East Yorkers? Many East Yorkers use their communities actively, to change their situations, rather than passively, to respond to stressful situations. They use community ties to change jobs, find mates, find housing, and extend their personal communities. Moreover, the composition and structure of personal communities affect the kinds of resources that flow to East Yorkers, whether or not they are aware of it.

We also intend to study longitudinal changes in the composition and structure of the personal communities themselves. Ties and networks also have careers, yet there has been little systematic analysis of how such open systems change. Do they have natural histories? Can they be manipulated? We shall look at the ways in which individuals "network"—forge links that can aid them in maintaining and developing their lives. For example, we wonder about the extent to which East Yorkers deliberately forge heterogeneous weak ties in order to get better access to diverse resources (see Granovetter, 1973, 1974; Welch, 1980; Lin, Ensel, and Vaughn, 1981).

Tactics

We reinterviewed (1977-1978) thirty-four of the original respondents for the new study, selecting them equally from four residential mobility categories:

- nonmovers since the 1968 survey;
- currently residing elsewhere in East York or near its borders;
- currently residing elsewhere in the Municipality of Metropolitan Toronto; and
- currently residing elsewhere in southern Ontario.

We chose respondents randomly within each residential mobility category from the subsample of those whom Shulman had resurveyed in 1969, thereby leaving open the possibility of studying the same persons' communities at three points in time (Shulman, 1972, 1976). Twenty-five percent of the potential respondents we originally selected were not available for reinterviewing, and we randomly replaced them.[4]

The interview design attempts to remedy the limitations of the original survey. Instead of closed-ended forms, interviewers went out with open-ended guides (Leighton and Wellman, 1978). The tape-recorded interviews usually lasted ten to twelve hours, over several sessions.

The interviews elicited more information about more community ties than had earlier community network studies. Instead of asking only about six (or fewer) "close" intimates, we asked about all those persons with whom respondents were significantly "in touch" informally.[5] We recorded detailed information about the personal situations of these "community ties" (CTs): sex, age, family status, residential location, type of housing, income, education, employment status, social class, religious affiliation, ethnic background, and transportation access. We also gathered much information about respondents' accounts of the nature of the relationships between themselves and their ties: formal role (such as kin, friend, neighbor, and workmate), level of intimacy, frequency of contact (face-to-face, telephone, or "other," such as by letter or CB radio), how relationships began, duration, problems and changes encountered, social and physical contexts of interaction, and component sociable and supportive strands.[6] In addition, we replicated key questions of the 1968 survey to facilitate longitudinal analysis.

We gave a good deal of attention to studying the reported flows of supportive resources between East Yorkers and their CTs. Instead of asking about generalized support, we asked about specific flows in each direction of fifteen different types of resource, such as nursing care, emotional aid, or help with the mortgage.[7] We also asked about how respondents had obtained help for dealing with specific problems (or, if the problems had not arisen, how they believed they would obtain such help). This is helping us to study the principles under which a respondent mobilizes available ties, the extent to which assistance flows regardless of mobilization activities, the degree of situational specialization of these ties, and the articulation of various relationships within the respondents' overall networks.

In order to study the structure of these personal communities, we asked the respondents to tell us about the links of personal community members with each other. We confined our question here merely to knowing whether two CTs were "in touch" (the same criterion used to select CTs originally), as we doubted that respondents could give consistently accurate information about their CTs' ties with each other. However, our data collection approach also enables the study of role relationships, as we know which CTs are kin, neighbors, workmates, or friends of each other.

We recorded these data in three complementary ways:

(1) Complete interview transcripts, 150-200 pages in length, that report nuances of interactions and the meanings respondents ascribe to them.

(2) Large qualitative matrices for each network, with each CT recorded on a separate line. These summarize information about the CTs' personal situations and the dynamics of their relationships with respondents and each other. Scanning a matrix provides a broad overview of the composition, structure, and dynamics of a personal community (see Wellman, 1982b, for a diagram of such a matrix).

(3) Three linked data files for computerized analysis of (a) the respondents and the summary characteristics of their personal communities, (b) their CTs and, (c) CT-CT links in the personal communities.

What Do Communities Look Like?

Multiple Definitions of Community

We have started our analyses by describing East Yorkers' community ties and networks. Instead of assuming that East Yorkers participate only in a single community, we have allowed for the possibility that they encounter different *sets* of community ties for different reasons: The persons with whom they are in touch for routine sociability may be significantly different from those who aid them in major emotional crises.

Hence we have sorted East Yorkers' ties according to three relational criteria: frequency of contact, the content of ties, and the respondents' feeling of closeness (or intimacy) to the other (see Table 3.2). Because our purpose here is accurate description, a community tie can appear in more than one network set. In the extreme case, an intimate contacted five times a week, who gives both sociable companionship and some sort of support, will appear in every set.[8]

Sorting the ties according to relational criteria reveals marked differences in the composition of personal communities even though our procedure allows the same tie to appear in more than one set. East Yorkers only actively maintain about three-quarters of their total ties; the rest are latent. On the average, they feel intimate with 40 percent of their active ties and are in routine contact with 25 percent. Immediate kin–especially siblings–comprise nearly half of all intimate ties, while neighbors and workmates form a larger majority of routinely seen (three times per week) ties. Twenty-nine percent of the active ties give no support of any kind to East Yorkers. We certainly cannot identify these diversified personal communities as local, solidary "support systems."

Resource Access

While not all ties are supportive, most are, and all East Yorkers receive a broad range of support through their networks. Yet it is clear from Table 3.3 that community ties vary markedly in the kinds of resources flowing through them; for example, many more network members lend ladders than mortgage money. Moreover, the kinds of resources provided differ widely according to the type of network. While intimates are most apt to provide emotional assistance and such major help as long-term nursing or child care, persons seen frequently are more apt to provide information about new jobs or housing.

Despite the prevalence of support–and supportive ties–in East Yorkers' personal communities, there are many reasons why it is misleading to describe these communities as solidary clusters of mutual supporters. For one thing, much of the business of these ties is not direct aid but help in getting resources from corporate bureaucracies. With the McDonaldization of life, such corporate entities now operate much of the social reproduction business–food, clothing, housing, education, and emotions. Consequently, people need "connections" as well as "supporters." Instead of directly feeding or nursing their friends, East Yorkers now often help them get government checks and medical connections.

Second, many community ties are not supportive. For example, 24 percent of East Yorkers' total ties reportedly provide no supportive aid in either direction. These ties are purely sociable–or even destructive.

TABLE 3.2 Composition of Community Ties by Relational Criteria

Net Type	*Total*	*Active*	*Intimate*	*Sociable*	*Routine*	*Support*
N =	526	404	163	274	99	306
Net Composition						
% of total net	--	77	31	52	19	69
% of active net	--	--	40	68	25	88
Mean net size	16	12	5	8	3	11
Role Type						
% Immediate Kin	19	21	29	26	14	22
% Extended Kin	24	22	18	19	12	18
% Friend	11	11	26	18	5	12
% Neighbor	15	18	9	13	29	18
% Workmate	10	13	4	6	36	8
% Former neighbor	8	4	7	7	1	8
% Former workmate	5	3	4	4	0	5
% Organizational	4	5	1	3	0	4
Residential Distance						
Median mileage (quartiles)	10 (2-75)	9 (1.5-49)	10 (3-39)	10 (3-58)	2.5 (0.5-9)	10 (1.5-39)
% Same building or block	15	18	11	12	33	18
% Same neighborhood (0.2-1 mile)	6	6	8	6	9	6
% Metro Toronto (1.1-30 miles)	45	47	51	49	51	47
% Southern Ontario (31-100 miles)	15	12	15	16	7	16
% Further away	20	16	15	17	0	13

NET TYPE DEFINITIONS:

Total: All ties that R actively maintains or are latent but could still be activated.

Active: All ties that R actively maintains. Typically, this is contact (in person, phone, letter) at least 1x/year, but may include less frequently contacted ties, temporarily absent. Does not include frequently contacted – but trivial – ties (e.g., casual office acquaintances).

Intimate: All ties whom R defines as "close."

Sociable: All ties whose company R enjoys and whose absence R would miss.

Routine: All ties in contact with R (in person, phone, letter, etc.) at least 3x/week (156x/year).s,

Support: All ties who give R at least 1 of 15 (surveyed) types of supportive aid. (Information available only for 28 networks.)

TABLE 3.3 Type and Direction of Supportive Resources by Relational Criteria

Net Type	*Total*	*Active*	*Intimate*	*Sociable*	*Routine*	*Support*
N =	526	404	163	274	99	13
			Personal Services			
Minor Household Help						
%R→CT	11	11	20	13	13	13
%CT→R	7	8	10	8	9	9
%Both Ways	25	27	33	31	27	35
Minor Services						
%R→CT	13	14	19	13	18	17
%CT→R	6	7	9	8	3	9
%Both Ways	29	32	36	37	31	42
Major Household Help						
%R→CT	5	6	10	7	7	8
%CT→R	4	3	4	3	3	5
%Both Ways	7	9	12	10	10	10
Major Services						
%R→CT	3	4	7	4	7	5
%CT→R	3	3	5	4	2	5
%Both Ways	3	4	6	5	4	5
Organizational Help						
%R→CT	7	7	7	6	7	9
%CT→R	3	4	4	4	6	5
%Both Ways	5	6	7	6	8	7
			Material Aid			
Household Items						
%R→CT	6	6	10	5	9	7
%CT→R	5	6	8	6	6	7
%Both Ways	27	29	39	36	39	38
Small Amounts of Money						
%R→CT	6	7	13	7	9	8
%CT→R	5	6	6	6	6	8
%Both Ways	7	8	9	8	9	10
Mortgage Money						
%R→CT	1	1	2	1	2	1
%CT→R	3	3	4	4	3	4
%Both Ways	0.2	0.3	0	0.4	0	0.3
Large Amounts of Money						
%R→CT	2	2	4	1	1	2
%CT→R	3	4	5	4	8	5
%Both Ways	0.2	0.3	1	0.4	1	0.3

TABLE 3.3 Type and Direction of Supportive Resources by Relational Criteria (Continued)

Net Type	*Total*	*Active*	*Intimate*	*Sociable*	*Routine*	*Support*
N =	526	404	163	274	99	306
			Emotional Aid			
Family Advice						
%R→CT	10	9	13	11	12	12
%CT→R	9	10	9	10	8	12
%Both Ways	25	29	38	32	28	36
Minor Emotional Aid						
%R→CT	9	8	13	7	10	8
%CT→R	7	8	7	8	7	10
%Both Ways	36	38	53	45	38	51
Major Emotional Aid						
%R→CT	9	8	11	11	10	12
%CT→R	7	8	8	9	2	10
%Both Ways	21	24	37	28	30	30
			Information			
Job Leads						
%R→CT	5	6	6	5	4	8
%CT→R	5	6	7	6	11	8
%Both Ways	1	1	1	1	4	2
Job Contacts						
%R→CT	3	3	3	3	4	4
%CT→R	4	5	5	5	10	6
%Both Ways	0.5	1	1	0	2	1
Housing Leads						
%R→CT	5	5	8	4	6	7
%CT→R	3	3	4	3	2	4
%Both Ways	1	1	2	2	3	2

Indeed, when East Yorkers fear that seeking aid through a tie may disrupt that tie, they often deliberately limit their claims upon it.

Third, East Yorkers often do not exchange equal amounts of a specific resource, such as financial aid, with other network members. Table 3.3 shows that most major sorts of resources–such as mortgage aid, long-term care, and major emotional aid–are transmitted asymmetrically, although minor amounts of resources–such as small amounts of money, quick services, and quick sympathy–are more symmetrically exchanged. Furthermore, there is often an imbalance between two persons in overall exchanges of support, when all kinds of assistance are taken into account.

East Yorkers make careful distinctions between the support they give to others and the support they get from them.

The prevalence of such asymmetric ties means that community ties are not bound up in solidary clusters, permeated with symmetric support. Many ties are asymmetric, varying in content and intensity, and fitting into unevenly knit, loosely bounded networks. While the networks often contain substantial internal differences in power and resources, their structural form also gives members ramifying, indirect connections to other social circles.

Fourth, despite the usefulness of decomposing overall ties into narrower strands, overall ties link persons and not specific strands. Thus, the link between Jack and Jill encompasses more than help in carrying a pail of water; we must interpret what came between them on the hill in the context of their overall relationship. When we focus narrowly on types of support, we obscure the ways in which the strands of a tie can change to fit new situations. For example, many East Yorkers count on intimates to bring help in a wide range of situations, without necessarily being able to predict just what these situations will be and what help they will require.

Fifth, we have dealt only with the tie as the unit of analysis, not the network. But for East Yorkers, the crucial question is whether they will get mortgage money from anyone in their network, not how many will provide it. They do not expect—nor necessarily want—broad support from everyone. For with support comes often-intrusive invasion of privacy and claims for reciprocity.

Structures or Choices?

The limited supportiveness of so many ties—even intimate ties—calls into question the "voluntaristic" assumption, which many support system analyses make, that network members maintain all of their ties because they actually enjoy them or perceive direct benefits to be gained through the dyad. Our data show that about one-quarter of East Yorkers' ties are with persons whom they do not like and with whom they would not voluntarily form a twosome. Such "structurally embedded" ties become involuntary parts of network membership packages. Most are ties to persons with whom the participants have to deal seriously in their neighborhoods, in a solidary kinship group, or at work. While such ties often are neither egalitarian nor reciprocal, they can be important in terms of the time spent on them, the resources that flow through them, the way they constrain other network members' activities, and the indirect access they give to other relationships. Communities are not necessarily nice things.

NOTES

1. This assertion is based first on the statistical evaluation of all observed networks comprising six persons and five ties, as compared with their expected distribution (calculated by Ove Frank), and second, on more cursory analysis of the entire data set by myself and Edward Lee.

2. Our analytic scheme was developed by Barry Wellman and Edward Lee, partially based on Erik Olin Wright's advice and work (1979, 1980). See Wellman (1982b) for our Social Class Coding scheme.

3. Sharon Kirsh has collaborated on this part of the study; see also Kirsh (1981).

4. We chose this sampling design because one research group member had proposed to do doctoral research comparing changes in personal communities under different conditions of residential mobility (see Crump, 1977). Most failures to interview resulted from death, severe illness, or long-distance moves (although we did follow one respondent who moved to Alberta in mid-interview). While the final sample is not strictly representative of any population, its characteristics broadly resemble those of the original East Yorker survey sample. Note that as the minimum age for the survey sample was 18 in 1968, all our respondents were at least 28.

5. For example, the interview item for kin was: "Please list the relatives you are in touch with who do not live in your household." Similar questions were asked about neighbors, former neighbors, workmates, former workmates, organizational ties, and friends. Compare this with the 1968 survey item: "I'd like to ask you a few questions about the people outside your home that you feel closest to; these could be friends, neighbors, or relatives."

6. Bernard, Killworth, and Sailer (1981) have argued vigorously against trusting the accuracy of respondents' accounts of network composition and dynamics. Certainly, analysts must constantly bear in mind that our data sets (and others like them) are respondents' reports of interaction and not observed interactions. In analyzing our interviews, we have some problems of recall and sanitization (for example, only one extramarital affair is reported). Nevertheless, while the reports may be inaccurate in detail, we are persuaded of their broad validity by the consistency of responses to different questions given in multiple interview sessions.

7. Some of this information was elicited in a focused follow-up questionnaire in 1981.

8. Strictly speaking, these data are about *sets* of ties (or "stars" in Barnes's [1972] terminology) and not networks. We have aggregated ties from all thirty-three networks, and we do not take into account here any information about the structure of these ties in the networks.

4

Structural Constraints on Intergroup Contact

Size, Proportion, and Intermarriage

STEVE RYTINA

Simmel introduced the sociological topic of number through his analyses of the effects of sizes. As Kanter (1977b) pointed out, the effect of proportions has been more neglected. Her analyses of the effects of skewed sex ratios on face-to-face interaction helped fill this gap, but, like those of Simmel, her mechanisms were often of a social psychological nature. Yet such effects are no less present in large collectivities, even if the mechanisms are less amenable to introspective understanding.

Proportions constrain interaction. In particular, they constrain choices of interaction partners. The effect is most apparent if the interaction is dyadic and mutually exclusive. The tension of the erotic triangle, where conventional notions of balance fail realization, is a striking example. A somewhat subtler but no less compelling set of constraints is found in the proportional composition of large collectivities.

The purpose of this chapter is to examine empirically how proportional composition affects marital choices. Marriage is the most intimate (and best recorded) of social ties, and its extent delimits the boundaries of social groups. Intermarriage between members of different groups indicates the weakening of their boundaries, while the rate of intermarriage is an inverse index of the strength of such boundaries. An intermarriage typically entails the overlapping of primary ties across a boundary, and thus the extent of intermarriage tells us the degree to which a collectivity is divided into discrete social worlds. To the extent that such discrete worlds are the loci of conflicting values and standards for conduct, the degree of intermarriage is an index of the integration of a social structure.

The combination of an interest in integration and proportion is the core of Blau's (1977a, 1977b) primitive theory of social structure. Blau has suggested that size distributions have a direct impact on intergroup association and therefore on the integration of large social structures. Accordingly, one of the purposes of the following analysis is to provide an empirical test for parts of Blau's theory.

That is not so straightforward as it might seem. Blau's theory can be analyzed in more formal terms than most, because its operative terms are quantitatively precise. An operational test of the theory must be sensitive to the original formulation. But a formal analysis of its terms (reported more extensively in Rytina, 1980a, 1980b) reveals that the theory is a mixture of tautology and contingency. A test of it must separate these components. That is another goal of the following analysis.

It should not be assumed that the tautological part is somehow bad and the contingent part good. The tautologies at the core of Blau's theory are numerical and not merely verbal (see Schelling, 1978, on the analytic utility of numerical tautology). They capture logically necessary relations among numerical elements of a structural description. These can be written as algebraic equations that describe theoretical constraints on possible observations. For example, there is a logically necessary relation that holds among heterogeneity, intergroup contact, and salience as these are defined by Blau.

This leads to an interesting problem in statistical analysis that can be labeled the contrast of rule and residual. To describe the impact of Blau's concerns, a three-step process will be carried out repeatedly. First, an unconstrained specification will be estimated to determine the amount of covariation among the various size variables. As a second step, the unconstrained result will be factored in light of criteria of theoretical content and/or parsimony. As a third step, the rulelike part will be factored out and the process will begin again with the residual covariation as an object of analysis.

Through this process, Blau's broadest claim that size matters will be unpacked and the impact of the particular pattern of size relationships called for in his theory will be examined. What is derived from Blau is not just a theory, but a strategy for analyses of size effects. At the outset, it will be seen that size makes a great difference. At an intermediate stage, it will be shown that heterogeneity does indeed lead to an increase in intermarriage. After many steps, the issue of whether differentiation leads to a decline in barriers to intergroup association will be examined. So, in addition to untangling the formal or statistical relations among these questions, the analysis will show that numerical minorities do experience a very noticeable decline in barriers to intermarriage.

The starting point of this exercise rests on a particular view of Blau's theory that motivated the choice of data and the functional forms analyzed. That view is more extensively presented in Rytina (1980a, 1980b) and Rytina and Morgan (1982). The key abstraction is a summary of network contacts among members of different social categories in a representation called a tie accounts table. For marriages the unit of analysis for each table is the individual. For the concrete instance of race, a tie accounts table would contain four entries: (1) the number of nonwhites married to nonwhites, (2) the number of nonwhites married to whites, (3) the number of whites married to nonwhites, and (4) the number of whites married to whites. Such a table is square, symmetric in the off-diagonal and symmetric in the margins. This form arises at the basis of Blau's theory, where a population is assigned into mutually exclusive groups and contact or interaction is numerically symmetric—that is, where the result of assessing amount of contact is independent of the choice of members of the interacting dyads.

Although Blau contrasted discrete and continuous dimensions (which he called parameters) of social positions, much of his reasoning about continuous dimensions rested on the device of dichotomizing (see Blau, 1977a: Chapter 3). Furthermore, Blau abstracted from the cultural contents that might be attributed to different sorts of dimensions, and simply treated them as sources of sizes. The same strategy will be followed here for the three chosen variables of race, mother tongue, and education.

The unit of analysis of the theory is not the individual but the social structure. For empirical purposes, the units are 118 standard metropolitan statistical areas (SMSAs). For each of these and for each social attribute (race, education, and mother tongue), a tie accounts table was constructed. Its entries are the variables that characterized each SMSA.

The data were provided by Professor Blau. He started with the 1/100 Public Use Sample of the 1970 Census. From this he selected every marital pair that involved a female who was under 25 and had lived in the same county five years previously; 17,341 marital pairs were included. This selection rule ensures that the structural conditions of the SMSA of residence were constraints on the observed marital pairs.

The classifying variables used to form inmarriage and intermarriage totals were (1) mother tongue, a dichotomous classification of language spoken in the family of origin into English and non-English; (2) race, originally white and nonwhite but later classified as black and white, since nonwhite nonblacks (mostly people from various Asian countries) account for the bulk of the "racial" intermarriages; and (3) education, dichotomously divided into fewer than twelve years and high school or more.

The original goal was to examine the joint effects of a continuous (and achieved) characteristic and a discrete (and ascribed) characteristic. Thus, the original plan was to examine the effects of race and education. Education was treated as a dichotomy for a first approximation, a feature retained in the present analysis. Race had to be dropped as a central topic of analysis once the marginals were examined. Only 187 interracial marriages occur in the 17,341 marriages observed (about 1 percent), and only 59 of these involved whites and blacks. With the SMSA as unit of analysis, racial intermarriage is almost invariantly zero and therefore will not be mentioned until a later section, where higher levels of aggregation than the SMSA are invoked.

Mother tongue was then selected as an alternative ascribed characteristic. To be non-English is reasonably common (18 percent of sampled persons are), and the proportion non-English varies from zero to 77 percent. Unfortunately, mother tongue is largely unrelated to education, and therefore the effects of consolidation are slight and not of much interest. But what remains to be examined are the effects of category size and proportion on intermarriage.

The final data set analyzed consisted of measures for 27,316 persons in 13,658 marital pairs for which no variables had missing values. These measures were aggregated into within- and between-group totals for each of the 118 SMSAs that had both English and non-English speakers in the sample. All measures are based on the sample. It is this feature that induces the tautologies that govern each case.

The strategy of analysis is one of guided exploration. The initial functional specifications are rather undemanding and give rise to fairly obvious results. But at each stage, more demanding and more theoretically meaningful forms are imposed. This requires a combination of algebraic and statistical manipulation. Three concerns guide this presentation. First, it is desirable to present as much information as possible about the observed patterns so that others with alternative theoretical agendas might make some use of these results. Second, it is desirable to assess the amount of empirical impact that may be accorded to Blau's theoretical concerns. Third, a pattern of some importance emerges, which is that proportional size determines the strength of group boundaries. In the conclusion, some of the theoretical implications of this will be considered.

In what follows, standard tools of statistical inference will be employed, although they are not strictly appropriate. The random sampling scheme that generated these data was on persons, while the variables are sample totals for different SMSAs. While a weighting scheme could have reflected this error structure, it would have complicated things enormously for the sake of a dubious gain in precision. Most of the observations are estimates from moderate to large samples and are fairly accurate numbers. More important, the functional forms employed in estimation were selected for their algebraic properties and not their statistical properties. But it still is useful to characterize the size of coefficients in terms of the residual variability and the intercorrelation of the various estimates, as standard errors do. These provide some guide, in a very familiar metric, to the sensitivity of the results to jiggles in the dependent variable. That provides a heuristic justification for this exploratory analysis.

The first functional specification to be examined resembles an economic production function. It is plausible that intermarriage arises as the coming together of the different groups. The number of possible points of contact is the product of the two groups' sizes. To estimate the dependence of intermarriage on the product of sizes, the following logarithmic equations were estimated for mother tongue and education:

$$\log(FE) = a + b_1 \log(F) + b_2 \log(E) + u \quad [1]$$

$$\log(HL) = a + b_1 \log(H) + b_2 \log(L) + u \quad [2]$$

FE and HL are the number of English-foreign and high education-low education marriages, while E is the number of English speakers, F is the number of non-English speakers, L is the number of persons with less than high school education, H is the number of persons who completed high school, and u is a disturbance term with the usual properties. The results are shown in lines 1 and 2 of Table 4.1.

This specification fits the observations rather closely, as the multiple Rs of .922 and .959 indicate. Of somewhat more interest is the observation that regression coefficients in both equations are close to one-half. To investigate this possibility, constrained specifications were estimated:

$$\log(FE) = a + b_1(\log(F) + \log(E)) + u \quad [3]$$

$$\log(HL) = a + b_1(\log(H) + \log(L)) + u \quad [4]$$

The results appear in lines 3 and 4 of Table 4.1. The increment in explained variation associated with one more coefficient can be used to form an F ratio to assess the constraint. For mother tongue, the F ratio is

(Text continued on p. 90)

TABLE 4.1 Regression Equations Relating Components of Size for Education and Mother Tongue

log(FE)	= −1.971 +	.491 log(F) +	.607(log(E))		Multiple R =	.922
		(.507)	(.034)		Exp. SS =	133.514
1.		.348	.708		Resd. SS =	23.395
		78.4	304.2		Overall F =	244.8
log(HL)	= − .908 +	.487 log(H) +	.525 log(L)		Multiple R =	.959
		(.061)	(.057)		Exp. SS =	76.804
2.		.458	.529		Resd. SS =	6.757
		63.6	84.9		Overall F =	653.6
log(FE)	= −2.236 +	.568(log(F) + log(E))			Multiple R =	.921
		(.022)			Exp. SS =	133.084
3.		.921			Resd. SS =	23.826
		647.9			Overall F =	647.9
log(HL)	= −1.302 +	.508(log(H) + (log(L))			Multiple R =	.959
		(.014)			Exp. SS =	76.798
4.		.959			Resd. SS =	6.762
		1317.4			Overall F =	1317.4
log(FE)	= −1.150 +	.775 log(F) +	1.400 log(E) −	1.129 log(N)	Multiple R =	.930
		(.058)	(.263)	(.319)	Exp. SS =	135.829
5.		.904	.992	−.765	Resd. SS =	21.080
		179.1	28.4	12.5	Overall F =	244.8
log(HL)	= − .908 +	.875 log(H) +	.697 log(L) −	.562 log(N)	Multiple R =	.959
		(.650)	(.294)	(.943)	Exp. SS =	76.825
6.		.819	.702	−.522	Resd. SS =	6.736
		1.8	5.6	.3	Overall F =	433.4
log(FE/N)	= − .457 +	.775 log(F) +	1.400 log(E) −	2.129 log(N)	Multiple R =	.821
		(.058)	(.263)	(.319)	Exp. SS =	43.601

7.		1.408	1.545	−2.246	Resd. SS =	21.080
		179.1	28.4	44.5	Overall F =	78.6
log(HL/N) =	− .215	+ .875 log(H)	+ .697 log(L)	− 1.562 log(N)	Multiple R =	.365
		(.650)	(.294)	(.943)	Exp. SS =	1.037
8.		2.687	2.303	−4.753	Resd. SS =	6.736
		1.8	5.6	2.7	Overall F =	5.8
log(FE/N) =	− .202	+ .782 log(F/N)	+ 1.429 log(E/N)		Multiple R =	.820
		(.057)	(.260)		Exp. SS =	43.463
9.		1.090	.437		Resd. SS =	21.228
		187.1	30.1		Overall F =	117.7
log(HL/N) =	−1.208	+ .919 log(H/N)	+ .719 log(L/N)		Multiple R =	.364
		(.636)	(.287)		Exp. SS =	1.030
10.		.442	.765		Resd. SS =	6.743
		2.1	6.3		Overall F =	8.8
log(FE/N) =	−1.053	+ .680 log(H_{mt})			Multiple R =	.805
		(.046)			Exp. SS =	41.889
11.		.805			Resd. SS =	22.809
		213.1			Overall F =	213.1
log(HL/N) =	− .816	+ .583 log(H_{ed})			Multiple R =	.361
		(.140)			Exp. SS =	1.013
12.		.361			Resd. SS =	6.760
		17.4			Overall F =	17.4
log(FE/N) =	−1.193	+ 1.429 log(H_{mt})	− .646 log(F/N)		Multiple R =	.820
		(.260)	(.221)		Exp. SS =	43.463
13.		1.69	.900		Resd. SS =	21.228
		30.1	8.5		Overall F =	117.7
log(HL/N) =	− .758	+ .919 log(H_{ed})	− .200 log(L/N)		Multiple R =	.364
		(.636)	(.370)		Exp. SS =	1.030

(Continued)

TABLE 4.1 Regression Equations Relating Components of Size for Education and Mother Tongue. (Continued)

14.			.569	−.213	Resd. SS =	6.743
			2.1	.3	Overall F =	8.8
log(FE/N)		0	+ 1.0 log(H_{mt})	+ 1.0 log(K_{mt})	Multiple R =	1.0
			(.000)	(.000)		
15.			1.184	.704		
			x.x	x.x		
log(HL/N)		0	+ 1.0 log(H_{ed})	+ 1.0 log(K_{ed})	Multiple R =	1.0
			(.000)	(.000)		
16.			.619	.968		
			x.x	x.x		
log(K_{mt})	=	−1.193	+ .429 log(H_{mt})	− .646 log(F/N)	Multiple R =	.582
			(.260)	(.221)	Exp. SS =	10.870
17.			.721	−1.278	Resd. SS =	21.228
			2.7	8.5	Overall F =	29.4
log(K_{ed})	=	− .758	− .081 log(H_{ed})	− .200 log(L/N)	Multiple R =	.271
			(.636)	(.370)	Exp. SS =	.535
18.			−.052	−.22	Resd. SS =	6.742
			.0	.3	Overall F =	4.6
log(K_{mt})	=	−1.138	− .287 log(F/N)		Multiple R =	.568
			(.038)		Exp. SS =	10.369
19.			−.568		Resd. SS =	21.729
			55.3		Overall F =	55.3
log(K_{ed})	=	− .741	− .246 log(L/N)		Multiple R =	.271
			(.081)		Exp. SS =	.534

						Statistic		Value
20.			−.271			Resd. SS	=	6.744
			9.2			Overall F	=	9.2
$\log(K_{mt})$	=	−1.150	− .225 log(F)	+ .400 log(E)	− .129 log(N)	Multiple R	=	.586
			(.058)	(.263)	(.319)	Exp. SS	=	11.017
21.			−.581	.627	−.194	Resd. SS	=	21.080
			15.1	2.3	.2	Overall F	=	19.8
$\log(K_{ed})$	=	− .908	− .125 log(H)	− .302 log(L)	+ .438 log(N)	Multiple R	=	.273
			(.650)	(.294)	(.943)	Exp. SS	=	.542
22.			−.396	−1.032	1.376	Resd. SS	=	6.736
			.0	1.0	.2	Overall F	=	3.0
$\log(K_{mt})$	=	− .896	− .217 log(F/N)	+ .429 log(E/N)		Multiple R	=	.582
			(.057)	(.260)		Exp. SS	=	10.870
23.			−.430	.186		Resd. SS	=	21.228
			14.5	2.7		Overall F	=	29.4
$\log(K_{ed})$	=	− .814	− .080 log(H/N)	− .281 log(L/N)		Multiple R	=	.271
			(.636)	(.287)		Exp. SS	=	.535
24.			−.040	−.309		Resd. SS	=	6.743
			.0	1.0		Overall F	=	4.6
$\log(K_{mt})$	=	−1.004	− .250 log(F/E)			Multiple R	=	.580
			(.033)			Exp. SS	=	10.781
25.			−.580			Resd. SS	=	21.317
			58.7			Overall F	=	58.7
$\log(K_{ed})$	=	− .584	− .170 log(L/H)			Multiple R	=	.269
			(.056)			Exp. SS	=	.526
26.			−.269			Resd. SS	=	6.752
			9.0			Overall F	=	9.0

KEY: The first line presents the regression coefficients; standard errors are in parentheses; standardized coefficients are below; and F ratios for the coefficients are given last.

2.1, while for education it is 1.02, so that in both instances the equality of coefficients is not rejectable. But the constrained equation for mother tongue does indicate, in contrast with education, that an exact value of one-half is not consistent with the observations.

This is both good and bad. A value of one-half would denote a process strikingly independent of scale. If population size and subgroup sizes were increased in equal proportion, intermarriage would follow in exact measure. That would be tidy and symmetric but rather boring. As shall soon be seen, that result is more nearly characteristic of education and it is mother tongue that will yield the more interesting pattern.

As a first attempt to assess the effects of scale more directly, the following specifications were estimated:

$$\log(FE) = a+b_1\log(F)+b_2\log(E)+b_3\log(N) + u \qquad [5]$$

$$\log(HL) = a+b_1\log(H)+b_2\log(L)+b_3\log(N) + u \qquad [6]$$

The results are shown in lines 5 and 6 of Table 4.1. The contrast between mother tongue and education is more sharply revealed. Inspection of the correlation matrix in Table 4.2 and the pattern of standard errors indicates what is happening. For mother tongue, log(N) is relatively independent of log(F), although closely related to log(E). Therefore, total size makes an independently significant contribution. In contrast, log(N) is quite closely related to both log(H) and log(L) and the rather large regression coefficient for log(N) is nonsignificant as a result of multicollinearity. What this means, as shall be shown more directly, is that for mother tongue it is necessary to take account of proportional size, the joint effects of F, E, and N, while for education, effects of proportional and absolute size are not distinguishable with these data.

Another way to factor out scale effects is to examine proportion outmarried rather than absolute number. This leads to the specifications

$$\log(FE/N) = a+b_1\log(F)+b_2\log(E)+b_3\log(N) + u \qquad [7]$$

$$\log(HL/N) = a+b_1\log(H)+b_2\log(L)+b_3\log(N) + u \qquad [8]$$

with estimates reported in lines 7 and 8 of Table 4.1. These results are closely related to the last results. All that has happened is that log(N) has been subtracted from both sides of the equations. The only change in coefficients is that the coefficient for log(N) is less by unity and is no longer statistically negligible. The residual sum of squares is unaffected. But the total sum of squares and the explained sum of squares are reduced in proportion to the covariation of absolute outmarriage and sheer scale.

TABLE 4.2 Correlation Matrices

a. Mother Tongue

	logFE	*logF*	*logE*	*logF+logE*	*logN*	*logFE/N*	*logF/N*	*logE/N*	$logH_{mt}$	$logK_{mt}$
log FE										
logF	.869									
logE	.676	.463								
logF+logE	.921	.922	.770							
logN	.772	.646	.961	.885						
logFE/N	.743	.673	.039	.501	.148					
logF/N	.550	.816	-.124	.533	.086	.765				
logE/N	-.226	-.558	.294	-.273	.018	-.372	-.742			
$logH_{mt}$	.558	.816	-.069	.557	.105	.805	.985	-.615		
$logK_{mt}$	.066	-.416	.172	-.224	.033	.067	-.568	.505	-.538	
logF/E	.511	.801	-.161	.506	.076	.723	.992	-.820	.955	-.580

b. Education

	logHL	*logH*	*logL*	*logH+logL*	*logN*	*logHL/N*	*logH/N*	*logL/N*	$logH_{ed}$	$logK_{ed}$
logHL										
logH	.927									
logL	.935	.887								
logH+logL	.959	.969	.973							
logN	.953	.988	.947	.995						
logHL/N	.380	.035	.185	.116	.081					
logH/N	-.109	.135	-.329	-.108	-.021	-.292				
logL/N	.178	-.072	.395	.175	.079	.342	-.959			
$logH_{ed}$	.221	-.018	.425	.217	.119	.361	-.872	.975		
$logK_{ed}$	.252	.047	-.080	-.019	.007	.802	.256	-.271	-.267	
logL/H	.158	-.092	.378	.156	.061	.329	-.98	.996	.952	-.269

The relatively uninteresting pattern of education is now sharply revealed. A great deal of the variation is simply scale and, compared to mother tongue, the effects of subgroup size (and proportion) are small. However, a substantial amount of variation in proportion outcontact is still explained by subgroup sizes.

The last results can be further manipulated to eliminate the remaining effects of absolute scale by the specifications:

$$\log(FE/N) = a+b_1 \log(F/N)+b_2 \log(E/N) + u \qquad [9]$$

$$\log(HL/N) = a+b_1 \log(H/N)+b_2 \log(L/N) + u \qquad [10]$$

The estimates are reported in lines 9 and 10 of Table 4.1. A comparison with the previous results indicates that, within an acceptable degree of approximation, all effects may be represented as proportional effects with no independent scale effect.

It is now possible to factor out the effect theoretically suggested by Blau. One of his central results was that intergroup contact increased with heterogeneity. The index of heterogeneity he proposed was $H=1-\Sigma P_i^2$, where P_i is the proportion of the population in group i. In the present case, it happens that $\log(H)=\log(1/2)+\log(F/N)+\log(E/N)$ and similarly for education. The effects of heterogeneity can be seen by estimating the equations

$$\log(FE/N) = a+b_1 \log(H_{mt}) + u \qquad [11]$$

$$\log(HL/N) = a+b_1 \log(H_{ed}) + u \qquad [12]$$

where H_{mt} and H_{ed} are heterogeneity measures for mother tongue and education, respectively. The results in lines 11 and 12 of Table 4.1 indicate that heterogeneity has a significant effect in both cases and a substantial effect for mother tongue. Of course, these are just constrained forms of equations 9 and 10 and comparisons indicate that nearly all the action in educational intermarriage that can be accounted for is due to heterogeneity while for mother tongue a substantial amount remains for proportional size. This is shown by the estimates in Table 4.1 for

$$\log(FE/N) = a+b_1 \log(H_{mt})+b_2 \log(F/N) + u \qquad [13]$$

$$\log(HL/N) = a+b_1 \log(H_{ed})+b_2 \log(L/N) + u \qquad [14]$$

which are really just factorings of equations 9 and 10. Only one of the subgroup proportions can be employed if perfect collinearity is to be avoided. The choice of the smaller proportion, non-English and low education, is not entirely arbitrary. In what follows, there is reason to examine these results in terms of the smaller group and not the larger group with which it is in contact. One of the tenets of Blau's theory is that it is the smaller of the two groups that is most affected by changes in boundaries. And it is statistically true that the logged proportion of the smaller group has the greater range of variation and thus is the most suitable carrier for clarifying patterns of variation.

The last result can be rendered tautological in an interesting way. In Blau's scheme, intergroup relations are a joint result of heterogeneity and salience. Salience is a measure of boundary strength defined as the extent to which intergroup contact falls below that expected by chance. Since H is the amount expected by chance, then the ratio of the outcontact rate to H, which I have elsewhere (Rytina, 1980a) named K, is an index of salience. It is definitionally true that outcontact is equal to the product of K and H or of salience and heterogeneity.

That observation leads to the tautological specifications

$$\log(FE/N) = \log(K_{mt}) + \log(H_{mt}) \quad [15]$$

$$\log(HL/N) = \log(K_{ed}) + \log(H_{ed}) \quad [16]$$

where K_{mt} and K_{ed} are the saliences of mother tongue and education, respectively. Results appear in lines 15 and 16 of Table 4.1. Here, the regression coefficients are of little interest, while the standardized coefficients reveal the relative impact of the two terms. Several observations are indicated. The relative impact of heterogeneity is greater for mother tongue than education. Furthermore, in both equations, the effect of heterogeneity is suppressed by the negative relation of heterogeneity and salience. This effect is greater for mother tongue than for education.

Blau's theoretical scheme is tautological for any single dichotomized population. But the foregoing indicates that such a tautological conceptualization admits of something very like falsification. The relative weights of heterogeneity or number and salience (which might be identified with culture but is not independent of number, as shall be shown) depend on relative amounts of variation. Blau's sensitizing notions could have been revealed as misleading if his factor, heterogeneity, varied much less than its competitor. Moreover, his scheme could have been falsified if the correlation of salience and heterogeneity were sufficiently negative as to lead to substantial suppression in the zero-order relationship. But as was seen above, examination of the zero-order relationship without consideration of the tautological relation governing each observation produced significant regressions of intermarriage on heterogeneity that must be counted as substantial confirmation of the theory.

Another falsifiable assumption is Blau's axiom of in-choosing, that persons sharing memberships interact (and intermarry) more than is expected by chance. To examine this, it is useful to consider a different index, which I have elsewhere called I, that is an index of salience defined as 1-K. I takes on values from zero, when the category boundary has no effect on contact, to unity, where no intergroup contact occurs. It can also take on negative values, when intergroup contact exceeds the rate expected by chance.

I is, among other things, analogous to a mover-stayer parameter. It describes the proportion of contacts or marriages that stay within group boundaries as contrasted with those randomly distributed across groups. For polytomous tables, it can be shown that a single value of I characterizes a population where out-group choice is random among out-groups and the total number of contacts is constant. For the present dichotomous case, a single value of I necessarily characterizes both groups, since there is but one degree of freedom for intermarriage. I for the present case has extraordinarily nice statistical properties. It is equal to the difference in proportions in the two rows of the table so that the usual test of a difference in binomial means is applicable. Simple algebra reveals that the statistic sqrt(N)*I is distributed normally with zero mean and unit variance under the assumption that marital choices are random with respect to group boundaries.[1]

The result of calculating z statistics for salience is reported in Table 4.3. For mother tongue, the results are not overwhelmingly supportive of the theory. Of the 115 SMSAs, 39 (34 percent) have z's less than 2, and 28 (24 percent) actually have negative z's. For education, only 2 z's are negative and only 15 percent are less than 2. Overall, the amount of in-choice far exceeds chance, though many exceptions are visible. Many of the exceptions should not be taken seriously, however. The approximation that underlies the test requires a reasonable marginal distribution. Using as a cutoff the conventional rule of thumb that no expected cell value should fall below 5, the results in panel 3(c) indicate that only 18 percent of SMSAs where the test is applicable have mother tongue intermarriage patterns that are plausibly due to chance. The great bulk of the negative z's are eliminated.

To provide still another comparison, panel d in Table 4.3 reports the results for black-white intermarriage for SMSAs with blacks in the sample. It should come as no surprise that the low rate of black-white intermarriage is nowhere attributable to chance.

TABLE 4.3 Z Scores to Test the Axiom of In-Choosing for SMSAs

a. Z Scores for Mother Tongue

	N	*%*
$-2<z<0$	28	23.7
$0<z<1$	3	2.5
$1<z<2$	8	6.8
$2<z<3$	14	11.9
$3<z<4$	7	5.9
$4<z<6$	24	20.3
$6<z<15$	29	24.6
$15<z<100$	5	4.2
	118	99.9

b. Z Scores for Education

	N	*%*
$-2<z<0$	2	1.7
$0<z<1$	7	5.9
$1<z<2$	8	6.8
$2<z<3$	14	11.9
$3<z<4$	23	19.5
$4<z<6$	37	31.4
$6<z<15$	25	21.2
$15<z<60$	2	1.7
	118	100.1

c. Z Scores for Mother Tongue with Small Expected Values Removed

	N	*%*
$-2<z<0$	8	8.6
$0<z<1$	3	3.2
$1<z<2$	8	8.6
$2<z<3$	13	14.0
$3<z<4$	7	7.5
$4<z<6$	22	23.7
$6<z<15$	27	29.0
$15<z<60$	5	5.4
	93	100.0

d. Z Scores for Race (black-white) with All-White Samples Excluded

	N	*%*
$4<z<6$	6	5.5
$6<z<15$	88	80.7
$15<z<60$	15	13.8
	109	100.0

That intermarriage rates in some SMSAs reflect almost no boundary effect suggests the importance of examining the pattern of variation in the impact of boundaries. To take a first glance at this, a further residualization of the previous equations is carried out so that variation in log(K) or salience can be examined. The specification is

$$\log(FE/NH_{mt}) = \log(K_{mt}) = a+b_1(H_{mt})+b_2\log(F/N) + u \qquad [17]$$

$$\log(HL/NH_{ed}) = \log(K_{ed}) = a+b_1(H_{ed})+b_2\log(L/N) + u \qquad [18]$$

and the estimates are in lines 17 and 18 of Table 4.1. In both cases, the effect, which parallels the last residualization, is to take out the variation due to heterogeneity and to reduce the heterogeneity regression coefficient by unity, which reduces its statistical impact to nil. In the case of education, neither independent variable has a significant independent effect, although it is clear that heterogeneity is the lesser of the two.

Eliminating heterogeneity as an independent variable in the specifications

$$\log(K_{mt}) = a+b_1\log(F/N) + u \quad [19]$$

$$\log(K_{ed}) = a+b_1\log(L/N) + u \quad [20]$$

produces the rather similar regression coefficients of around .25 found in lines 19 and 20 of Table 4.1. Sorting through the effects of logs and the transformation of K to I, what this shows is that the impact of group boundaries declines as a function of proportional size. The effect for mother tongue is slightly greater and the range of variation is much greater, so that the amount of variance accounted for is more impressive.

This specification is not the only one consistent with these data. To establish a baseline, the unconstrained specifications

$$\log(K_{mt}) = a+b_1\log(F)+b_2\log(E)+b_3\log(N) + u \quad [21]$$

$$\log(K_{ed}) = a+b_1\log(H)+b_2\log(L)+b_3\log(N) + u \quad [22]$$

were estimated; results are reported in lines 21 and 22 of Table 4.1. If one degree of freedom is allowed for the difference between these specifications and the proportional form, which is rather generous, one cannot reject the hypothesis that the difference is not due to chance. It is, however, nearly so for the mother tongue equations, since the relevant F ratio is 3.5.

In spection of the correlation matrix in Table 4.2 indicates that no absolute size, F, E, H, L, or N, acting alone will fit the data. Estimation of the twin proportional specifications

$$\log(K_{mt}) = a+b_1\log(F/N)+b_2\log(E/N) + u \quad [23]$$

$$\log(K_{ed}) = a+b_1\log(H/N)+b_2\log(L/N) + u \quad [24]$$

indicates that it is the proportion of the smaller group that accounts for the variance. In a way, this is artifactual, since the log of the smaller proportion has the greater variance, but it shall be seen that the greatest effect is for very small groups. Finally, alternative specifications that do fit well are

$$\log(K_{mt}) = a+b_1\log(F/E) + u \quad [25]$$

$$\log(K_{ed}) = a+b_1\log(L/H) + u \quad [26]$$

as shown by the results in lines 25 and 26 in Table 4.1. The regression coefficients are more different than for lines 19 and 20. Equations 25 and 26 produce slightly better fits than 19 and 20, but there is no statistical ground for discriminating among the alternative specifications. The reason is not difficult to find. Log(E) and log(H) are very highly correlated with log(N) so that the two different specifications are nearly identical in practice. The first specification, that salience depends on the proportion of the smaller group, is favored on grounds of similarity of coefficients, but either specification is consistent with the observed pattern of variation. The one conclusion that is forced is that relative and not absolute size is the determining condition.

To allow a closer look at the relationship without the inconvenience of logarithms, a smoothed representation is presented in Table 4.4. The SMSAs were divided into strata by proportion in the smaller group and the saliences for the entire strata were calculated. This provides an especially useful look at the SMSAs with very few non-English, since the observations for particular SMSAs are subject to rather large potential sampling errors. The sixth column presents the predicted values from the linear regression of aggregated salience on average proportion. The seventh column presents the residuals around the linear fit. The regular pattern of pluses and minuses indicates the curvilinearity of the relationship. There is an especially steep decline in the lower range of proportional size. The further panels in Table 4.4 indicate a similar curvilinear pattern for education and for race (white-black). It is the latter result that is especially striking. Black-white intermarriage is nearly taboo, and still proportional size works its magic. Although the effect is not great, it is overcoming an extremely powerful cultural force.

This result offers further support for Blau's theory, although the argument is nearly paradoxical. It has been shown that the total rate of intergroup marriages increases with heterogeneity. Heterogeneity increases as the groups are of more equal size. But as groups are of less equal size, as the proportion of the smaller group falls, the potency of the group boundary as a barrier to social association declines. Thus, even as the total rate of intermarriage falls, the rate of intermarriage for the small group is subject to a doubly determined rise. If salience were maintained at a constant level, the rate of intermarriage would rise with declining size, since it is equal to $K(1-P_i)$. But since salience declines as P_i falls (that is, since K increases), the amount of increase is greater than the fall in proportional size.

If this result is true for polytomous social attributes, and its generality across the three different attributes examined suggests that it may well be,

TABLE 4.4 Estimates of In-Choosing for SMSAs Group by Proportion in the (usually) Smaller Group

a. Mother Tongue

		Proportion Non-English		*I*	*Î*	
Persons	*SMSAs(N)*	*Range*	*Average*	*Salience*	*(From Linear Regression)*	*Residual*
2524	16	0–.03	.018	.027	.107	–.080
2164	13	.03–.05	.036	.096	.134	–.038
3506	22	.05–.10	.070	.257	.183	.073
3684	15	.10–.15	.121	.361	.257	.104
4092	15	.15–.20	.170	.381	.328	.052
4718	14	.20–.25	.229	.415	.414	.000
2782	17	.25–.30	.268	.484	.471	–.006
1348	10	.30–.40	.349	.543	.588	–.046
2498	6	.40+	.450	.656	.735	–.079
27316	118					

$\hat{I}$ = .080 + 1.41 (proportion non-English)
r = .9504

b. Education

		Proportion Less Than High School		*I*	*Î*	
Persons	*SMSAs(N)*	*Range*	*Average*	*Salience*	*(From Linear Regression)*	*Residual*
896	8	.10–.20	.171	.235	.250	–.015
3204	16	.20–.25	.225	.297	.287	.010
5574	21	.25–.30	.276	.352	.323	.029
2180	14	.30–.325	.311	.341	.347	–.006
8626	23	.325–.35	.335	.378	.363	.014
4142	20	.35–.40	.377	.377	.393	–.016
2994	16	.40+	.450	.426	.443	–.017
27316	118					

$\hat{I}$ = .13 + .69 (proportion low education)
r = .960

c. Race (black-white) for non-Southern* SMSAs with Blacks in the Sample

		Proportion Black		*I*	*Î*	
Persons	*SMSAs(N)*	*Range*	*Average*	*Salience*	*(From Linear Regression)*	*Residual*
2136	20	0–.03	.023	.875	.919	–.044
1175	15	.03–.05	.039	.955	.923	.032
2392	20	.05–.10	.067	.954	.931	.023
2478	11	.10–.15	.109	.925	.943	–.018
4821	10	.15–.20	.175	.979	.962	.017
1146	10	.20+	.296	.988	.997	–.009
14148	86					

$\hat{I}$ = .9121 + .2869 (proportion black)
r = .7165

* There was only one black-white marriage in the samples from the South.

then the more general picture is highly favorable to Blau's scheme. In the dichotomous special case, increases in heterogeneity can only be due to an equalization of group sizes. In the more general case, increases in the number of groups as well as equalization of sizes will increase heterogeneity. This second pattern of increase is equivalent to a decline in proportional size for the average group. Thus, all groups could be simultaneously subject to the twin effects of an increase due to increasing out-group proportion and the declining strength of group boundaries. The total result is an increase in intergroup contact that far exceeds that tautologically required by the increase in heterogeneity alone.

The pattern is broadly supportive of Blau's theory as well as supportive of his prediction that social pressures against practices such as outmarriage will decline with increases in the frequency of such practices. Also, it is parallel to Coleman's (1964) argument that proportionately smaller groups have to maintain more extreme out-group discrimination to sustain a given rate of in-group association. The results indicate clearly that smaller minorities do not succeed in doing so.

The pattern implicitly sustains Blau's argument about penetrating differentiation. A group that is small will exist in smaller average proportion if it is evenly dispersed among SMSAs. But if group membership is consolidated with spatial distribution, that is, if a group's members are concentrated in a few SMSAs, then sufficient proportional size to sustain a sizable rate of endogamy may be maintained. Groups that are not consolidated will rapidly cease to exist as endogamous social formations. Culture is not without its impact, as the example of race shows. But the effects of size, pure and simple, are large enough to merit further attention. The degree to which a social category denotes a closed social formation or group is very much dependent on the effects of number.

I hope this helps to demonstrate both the subtlety and the utility of Blau's approach. Size is a ubiquitous variable and one that is easily and accurately measurable. But it is not merely an incidental nuisance that should be controlled and thereby given short shrift. The successive residualizations of the previous analysis amount to imposing controls for size. But at two different levels these revealed effects of size. Heterogeneity, which is a measure of proportional diversity of differentiation, has a substantial impact on the amount of intermarriage. While this is in some degree tautological, it still means that differentiated social structures promote intergroup contact. Second, small groups are subject to a diminution of barriers to intermarriage. For race, this is a theoretically interesting effect imposed on a background of very substantial segregation. But for education and especially for mother tongue, the barriers nearly disappear.

To the degree that the maintenance of group identity rests upon endogamy, the groups identified by these attributes do not last beyond a single generation when they are in small proportion. In that sense, Blau's central argument that diversity promotes integration is quite strikingly confirmed.

NOTE

1. I is equivalent to Freeman's (1978) index of network segregation. Its inferential properties for this special case are considerably simpler than those derived by Freeman.

II.

Social Networks and Individual Outcomes

The analyses of social structure reported in the chapters in Part I are stimulating, and they have bearing on important theoretical and substantive issues in social science. Nonetheless, as Laumann (1979: 394) puts it, "the hallmark of a network analysis . . . is to explain, at least in part, the behavior of network elements (i.e., the nodes [or actors]) and of the system as a whole by appeal to specific features of the interconnections among the elements." The four chapters in Part II offer theoretical discussions and empirical illustrations of the way in which a structural analysis can inform studies concerned with individual outcomes such as attainments, attitudes, and behaviors.

In Chapter 5, Granovetter reviews studies that were stimulated by his influential paper, "The Strength of Weak Ties" (Granovetter, 1973). In that paper, he tentatively defined the strength of a tie as "a (probably linear) combination of the amount of time, the emotional intensity, the intimacy (mutual confiding) and the reciprocal services which characterize the tie" (Granovetter, 1973: 1361). He argued that weak ties, because they frequently "bridge" between nonoverlapping sets of actors, are a key to social integration and are often sources of novel information for the actors linked by them. He thus called for increased attention to weak ties (such as acquaintances) as distinct from strong ones (such as relatives and friends). Much research since 1973 has heeded this call. Here, Granovetter reviews work on the impact of weak ties on the job search and income attainment processes of individuals, on the diffusion of cultural and scientific innovations, and on the social organization of peer groups, communities, organizations, and conflict groups. He also provides a useful discussion of strong ties and their value.

Significant contributions to the line of research reviewed in Granovetter's chapter have been made by the research program directed by Lin. Lin's chapter outlines a theory of instrumental action that argues not only for the importance of weak ties in Granovetter's sense, but also for the importance of the social resources accessed by such ties. Thus, it is not simply the use of a weak tie that enhances the success of an instrumental action like seeking a job; it is the use of a weak tie to a person in an advantageous position in a social structure that is crucial. After stating the three propositions that form the core of his theory, Lin reviews three research efforts to test the theory: a "small world" study tracing chains of personal connections between pairs of unknown persons, and two studies of the role of social ties in occupational attainments.

Kadushin takes up a theme that appears in many classical social theories, that of the relation of social density to individual responses. Like the classic formulations, Kadushin suggests that a dense and cohesive social environment should be capable of rendering support to the individual it surrounds and should therefore serve as a bulwark against mental disturbances. The classic views, however, posited that industrialization and urbanization would destroy such sources of social support (but see Wellman's chapter in Part I), resulting in increased rates of both social and individual disorder. Kadushin argues that the density of the "interpersonal environment" surrounding an individual is what matters, not the spatial density of the person's residential community or the modernity of the society in which he or she lives. Analyzing data on a sample of young men, many of whom were exposed to the traumatic stressor of heavy combat in Vietnam, he shows that high social density in the interpersonal environment is, in fact, associated with low stress reactions.

The last chapter in this part of the book, by Erickson, is concerned with the role of social structure in the development of ideologies (attitudes shared by the incumbents of a social position) and belief systems (sets of common dimensions underlying the varying attitudes of an interrelated set of individuals). She argues that dense relations among those in a social position are likely to generate an ideology. Further, she maintains that the network structure most likely to lead to the development of a belief system is one in which there is a clear mapping of persons into distinct social positions, but in which there is also connectedness between such positions. Erickson's argument is distinctive in its emphasis on the social structural foundations of attitude organization; much previous work has stressed cognitive development or other individual characteristics as sources of variation in attitude structure.

Taken together, the chapters in Part II make a case for the plausibility of measuring and including social structural variables based on network analyses in explanatory models for social behaviors and attitudes. It is to be hoped that social research in the 1980s will make further use of such a strategy of explanation, extending applications to include some of the refined structural concepts and measurements that have been developed recently.

5

The Strength of Weak Ties

A Network Theory Revisited

MARK GRANOVETTER

In this chapter I shall review empirical studies directly testing the hypotheses of my 1973 paper, "The Strength of Weak Ties" (hereafter SWT), and work that elaborates those hypotheses theoretically or uses them to suggest new empirical research not discussed in my original formulation. Along the way, I reconsider various aspects of the theoretical argument, attempting to plug some holes and broaden its base. First, it will be useful to restate briefly the original assertions.

The Argument Recapitulated

The argument asserts that our acquaintances ("weak ties") are less likely to be socially involved with one another than are our close friends ("strong ties"). Thus, the set of people made up of any individual and his or her acquaintances will constitute a low-density network (one in which many of the possible relational lines are absent), whereas the set consisting of the same individual and his or her *close* friends will be densely knit (many of the possible lines present).

The overall social structural picture suggested by this argument can be seen by considering the situation of some arbitrarily selected individual—

AUTHOR'S NOTE: I am indebted to Everett Rogers, who first suggested this study, inviting it for a special session of the International Communications Association meetings on the weak-ties hypothesis. The first version was delivered at this session in call him or her "Ego." Ego will have a collection of close friends, most of whom are in touch with one another—a densely knit "clump" of social structure. In addition, Ego will have a collection of acquaintances, few of whom know one another. Each of these acquaintances, however, is likely to have close friends in his or her own right and therefore to be enmeshed in a closely knit clump of social structure, but one different from Ego's. The weak tie between Ego and his or her acquaintance, therefore, becomes not merely a trivial acquaintance tie, but rather a crucial bridge between the two densely knit clumps of close friends. To the extent that the assertion of the previous paragraph is correct, these clumps would not, in fact, be connected to one another at all were it not for the existence of weak ties (SWT: 1363). It follows that individuals with few weak ties will be deprived of information from distant parts of the social system and will be confined to the provincial news and views of their close friends. This not only will insulate them from the latest ideas and fashions, but also may put them in a disadvantaged position in the labor market, where advancement can depend, as I have documented more fully in my 1974 book, on knowing about appropriate job openings at just the right time. Furthermore, such individuals may be difficult to organize or integrate into politically based movements of any kind, since membership in movements or goal-oriented organizations typically results from being recruited by friends. While members of one or two cliques may be efficiently recruited, the problem is that, without weak ties, any momentum generated in this way does not spread *beyond* the clique, with the result that most of the population will be untouched.

The macroscopic side of this communications argument is that social systems lacking in weak ties will be fragmented and incoherent. New ideas will spread slowly, scientific endeavors will be handicapped, and subgroups that are separated by race, ethnicity, geography, or other characteristics will have difficulty reaching a *modus vivendi.* These themes are all taken up in greater detail, with supporting evidence, in SWT.

My review of the past eight years' literature on "weak ties" will follow this outline. First, I will review work focusing on the impact of weak ties on individuals; then that relating to the flow of ideas and the sociology of

---

Acapulco on May 21, 1980. A version closer to the present one was delivered at the Albany Conference on Contributions of Networks Analysis to Structural Sociology, April 4, 1981. I am indebted to participants in these two conferences for their generous comments—especially Fernando Morett, Scott Feld, Nan Lin, and Ronald Rice. The chapter has also leaned heavily on the comments and literature review of Ellen Granovetter.

science; finally, work evaluating the role of weak ties in affecting cohesion in complex social systems.

The Impact of Weak Ties on Individuals

An early draft of SWT was entitled, "Alienation Reconsidered: The Strength of Weak Ties." In this draft I argued that weak ties, far from being productive of alienation, as one might conclude from the Chicago school of urban sociology–especially from Louis Wirth–are actually vital for an individual's integration into modern society. Upon further reflection it is clear that this argument is closely related to certain classical themes in sociology. In the evolution of social systems, perhaps the most important generator of weak ties is the division of labor, since increasing specialization and interdependence result in a wide variety of specialized role relationships, in which one knows only a small segment of the other's personality (see the perceptive comments of Simmel, 1950b: 317-329). As against the emphasis of Wirth, and also Toennies, that such role segmentation results in alienation, is the Durkheimian view that the exposure to a wide variety of different viewpoints and activities is the essential prerequisite for the social construction of individualism.

In a provocative article, Rose Coser (1975) takes up some of these themes. She describes the "complexity of role set"–to use Robert Merton's expression for the plurality of others with whom one has role relations–as a "seedbed of individual autonomy." In Simmel's view, she recalls, "the fact that an individual can live up to expectations of several others in different places and at different times makes it possible to preserve an inner core, to withhold inner attitudes while conforming to various expectations" (1975: 241). Furthermore, persons "deeply enmeshed in a *Gemeinschaft* may never become aware of the fact that their lives do not actually depend on what happens within the group but on forces far beyond their perception and hence beyond their control. The *Gemeinschaft* may prevent individuals from articulating their roles in relation to the complexities of the outside world. Indeed, there may be a distinct *weakness in strong ties.*" (1975: 242).

Coser (1975: 254) then elaborates the cognitive ramifications of this conundrum: "In a *Gemeinschaft* everyone knows fairly well why people behave in a certain way. Little effort has to be made to gauge the intention of the other person. . . . If this reasoning is correct . . . the manner of communication will tend to be different in a *Gesellschaft.* Hence, the type of speech people use should differ in these two types of structures." She relates this difference to Basil Bernstein's distinction between "restricted" and "elaborated" codes of communication. The former is simpler–more meanings are implicit and taken for granted, as the speakers are so similar to and familiar with one another. The latter is more complex and universalistic. More reflection is needed in organizing one's communication, "when there is more difference between those to whom the speech is addressed" (Coser, 1975: 256). While, of course, some weak ties may connect individuals who are quite similar, there is, as I pointed out in SWT (1362), "empirical evidence that the stronger the tie connecting two individuals, the more similar they are, in various ways." Thus, Coser's argument applies directly to the distribution of weak and strong ties. She concludes that in "elaborated speech there is a relatively high level of individualism, for it results from the ability to put oneself in imagination in the position of each role partner in relation to all others, including oneself" (1975: 257). She goes on to argue that the social structure faced by children of lower socioeconomic backgrounds does not encourage the complex role set that would, in turn, facilitate the development of "intellectual flexibility and self-direction" (1975: 258).

This discussion casts an interestingly different light on some of the arguments of SWT. There, I argued that while West Enders, for example, did have some weak ties, they were of the type that were embedded within each individual's already existing set of strong ties, rather than bridging to other groups. I interpreted this as inhibiting organization because it led to overall fragmentation and distrust of leaders. Coser's argument suggests further that *bridging* weak ties, since they do link different groups, are far more likely than other weak ties to connect individuals who are significantly different from one another. Thus, in addition to the overall macrostructural effect of bridging weak ties, I could also have argued that they are exactly the sort of ties that lead to complex role sets and the need for individuals to develop intellectual and cognitive flexibility. The absence of such flexibility may have been still another factor that inhibited organization against urban renewal, since the ability to construct and function in complex voluntary organizations may depend on a habit of mind that permits one simultaneously to assess the needs, motives, and actions of a great variety of different people.

There is no special reason why such an argument should apply only or even best to lower socioeconomic groups; it should be equally persuasive for any set of people whose outlook is unusually provincial as the result of homogeneous contacts. In American society there is thus some reason for suggesting that upper-class individuals as well as lower-class ones may suffer a similar lack of "cognitive flexibility." Baltzell (1958) and others have described in nice detail the cloistered features of upper-class interaction; Halberstam (1972) has suggested that such a social structure generates inflexibility in the form of arrogance and a sense of infallibility, and that American involvement in the Vietnam War was in part the result of these.

At a more mundane level, I argued (SWT: 1369-1373; 1974: 51-62) that weak ties have a special role in individuals' mobility opportunities—that there is a "structural tendency for those to whom one is only *weakly* tied to have better access to job information one does not already have. Acquaintances, as compared to close friends, are more prone to move in circles different from one's own. Those to whom one is closest are likely to have the greatest overlap in contact with those one already knows, so that the information to which they are privy is likely to be much the same as that which one already has" (1974: 52-53). In my empirical study of recent job changers (1974), I found, in fact, that if "weak ties" are defined by infrequent contact around the time when information about a new job was obtained, professional, technical, and managerial workers were more likely to hear about new jobs through weak ties (27.8 percent) than through strong ones (16.7 percent), with a majority in between (55.6 percent).

Three pieces of empirical research offer partial confirmation of this argument. Langlois (1977) studied a large sample of men and women in a branch of the Quebec provincial government. Langlois (1977: 217) notes that even though this branch had "attempted to formalize the recruitment of its members as much as possible," 42.7 percent of the 2553 individuals in the sample found their jobs through personal contacts. Also using frequency of recent contact as the definition of tie strength (but with slightly different cutting points from mine), he found that weak ties were indeed often the ones that resulted in a new job, but that the pattern varied strongly by occupation. Specifically, administrative or managerial employees had a pattern very much like the one I reported, with 35.5 percent using weak ties, 15.8 percent strong ones, and 48.7 percent intermediate. Professionals and office workers also were heavy users of weak ties (30.8 percent and 25.8 percent, respectively), but, unlike managers, used strong ties even more frequently (51.0 percent and 44.4 percent). Semiprofessionals found only 13.1 percent of jobs through weak ties, and blue-collar workers 19.1 percent; the former found 44.9 percent of jobs through strong ties, the latter only 19.1 percent.

Ericksen and Yancey (1980: 14-15) studied a probability sample of 1780 adults aged 65 and under living in the Philadelphia area in 1975. Respondents "who had significant help from another person" in finding their current jobs were classified as "having used ties." If the person "providing the help was identified as a relative or friend of the respondent, the tie was classified as 'strong.' If the person was classified as an acquaintance, the tie was classified as 'weak.' " Ericksen and Yancey note that most acquaintances were work-related, and about two-thirds of the strong ties were relatives. A majority of respondents used "some form of personal connection to land the job." Of the non-self-employed, 41.1 percent used strong ties, 15.6 percent weak ties, and 43.3 percent formal means or direct application. It is difficult to compare this classification of ties to my trichotomy, because the operational definitions are different, there are two categories instead of three, and the population at risk here is of broader socioeconomic background.

One set of results is of special interest, however. Ericksen and Yancey (1980: 24) found that "less well educated respondents were those most likely to use strong ties for jobs. The rate drops among respondents who attended college, and is balanced by a correspondingly large increase in the likelihood of using weak ties and a slight increase in the use of bureaucratic procedures." In fact, 31 percent of managers used weak ties in finding jobs, a figure close to that found by Langlois, though 30 percent used strong ties, a larger figure than in the Canadian sample. Regression analysis was then employed to determine whether the strength of ties used had any impact on income, net of other variables. Results indicated that the use of strong ties had no consistent impact; for weak ties, the overall effect on income was substantial and *negative,* opposite to the predictions of the weak-ties hypothesis. But there was a significant interaction between weak ties and education, so that

> weak ties actually leads to a reduction in income among the poorly educated, but . . . this reduction grows smaller with increasing levels of education such that there is a small increase among high school graduates . . . and this increase grows larger with further increases in education. Thus, for that group of well educated respondents where weak ties are most likely to be used we see that the effects of using the weak ties are most positive [Ericksen and Yancey, 1980: 24-25].

Lin, Ensel, and Vaughn (1981) use similar definitions of weak and strong ties to probe the relation between tie strength and occupational status attainment for a representative sample of men aged 20-64 in an urban area of upstate New York. Those ties identified by respondents as acquaintances or friends of friends were classified as "weak," whereas friends, relatives, or neighbors were considered "strong" ties. Lin et al.'s

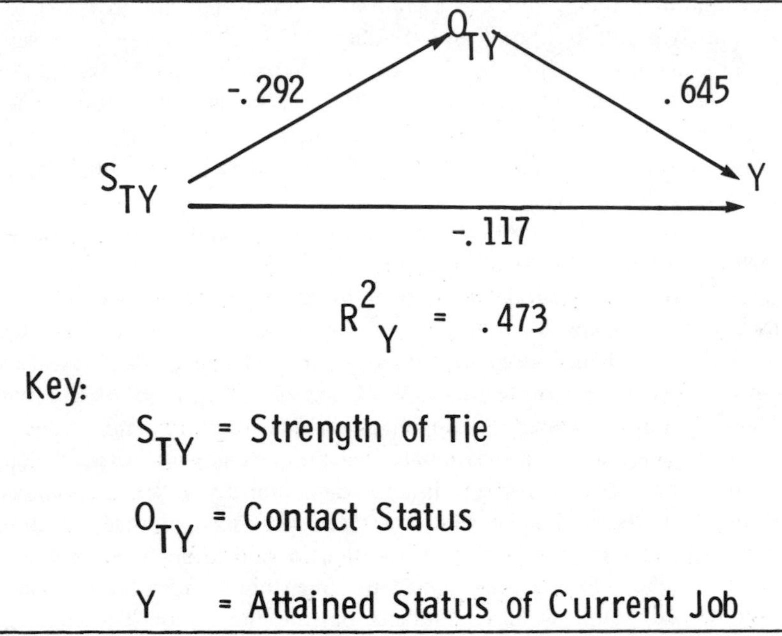

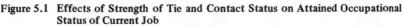

Figure 5.1 Effects of Strength of Tie and Contact Status on Attained Occupational Status of Current Job

SOURCE: Lin, Ensel, and Vaughan, 1981: Figure 2. Reprinted by permission of the authors and the American Sociological Association.

method was similar to that used by researchers such as Blau, Duncan, and Featherman: the construction of structural equation models, or "path analyses," to measure the relative contribution of different independent variables to some dependent variable–in this case, occupational status (as measured by the Duncan Socioeconomic Index). Their central finding is as follows: The use of weak ties in finding jobs has a strong association with higher occupational achievement only insofar as the weak ties connect the respondent with an individual who is well placed in the occupational structure. This is illustrated in their path diagram, reprinted here as Figure 5.1. For first job, the direct contribution of tie strength is negligible; for the current one it is larger but still less than the indirect effect. In numerical terms, this results from the fact that the great majority of weak ties used in finding jobs connected respondents to relatively high-status individuals: 76.2 percent of weak ties (as compared to 28.9 percent of strong ones) for the first job and 70.7 percent (as compared to 42.9 percent of strong ones) for the current job were to informants of high occupational status (defined as a score of 61-96 on the Duncan scale). The most likely interpretation of these findings is that, in general, weak ties are more efficient at reaching higher-status individuals, so that if such ties are available, they are preferred. But since only 34 percent of jobs in this sample were *found* through weak ties (among those whose jobs were found through social ties), it appears that many individuals had no choice but to fall back on strong ones.

These studies help clarify the circumstances under which weak ties will provide unusual advantage. The argument of SWT implies that only *bridging* weak ties are of special value to individuals; the significance of weak ties is that they are far more likely to be bridges than are strong ties. It should follow, then, that occupational groups that make the heaviest use of weak ties will be those whose weak ties *do* connect to social circles different from one's own. In Langlois's Canadian study, the most frequent users are managers and professionals, just the persons who, to use Robert Merton's terms, are most likely in an organization to be "cosmopolitans" rather than "locals"–most likely to deal with acquaintances in other organizations or other branches of the same organization. More generally, Homans (1950: 185-186) has argued that high-status individuals are more likely in all groups to have contacts outside the group. Ericksen and Yancey also find managers to be the group with the highest frequency of jobs found through weak ties. How should we interpret the interaction effect, in their data, between weak ties and education in determination of income? I suggest that in lower socioeconomic groups, weak ties are often not bridges, but rather represent friends' or relatives' acquaintances; the information they provide would then not constitute a real broadening of opportunity, reflected in the fact that the net effect on income of using such ties is actually negative. In higher groups, by contrast, weak ties do bridge social distance, so that if there are no lucrative job openings known to one's own social circle at a given moment, one may still take advantage of those known in other circles. Here, the net effect of weak ties on income is strongly positive.

Consistent with this interpretation is Lin et al.'s finding that weak ties have positive effects on occupational status only when they connect one to high-status individuals. For those of lower status, weak ties to those of similar low status were not especially useful, whereas those to higher-status contacts were. In the latter case, the status difference alone strongly suggests that the ties bridged substantial social distance. When high-status respondents use weak ties of similar status, there is no status difference on which to seize for evidence that such ties bridge; here we must speculate that the hypothesized tendency of high-status individuals to have more bridges among their weak ties is in effect.

Though consistent with these data, the above interpretations could be better supported by more detailed field reports of the exact circumstances under which respondents used weak ties. Some findings (such as Langlois's) of heavy strong-tie use by professionals and sparse weak-tie use by semiprofessionals are simply not explained by the arguments of SWT and await further theoretical speculation.

Excursus on the Strength of Strong Ties

Lest readers of SWT and this chapter ditch all their close friends and set out to construct large networks of acquaintances, I had better say that strong ties can also have some value. I did not discuss this point in SWT, since I was trying to establish a counterintuitive argument; but proper balance requires us to think clearly about the circumstances under which different types of ties are of instrumental use to individuals. Weak ties provide people with access to information and resources beyond those available in their own social circles; but strong ties have greater motivation to be of assistance and are typically more easily available. I believe that these two facts point the way to understanding when strong ties play their unique role.

A general formulation is suggested by Pool (1980), who argues that whether one uses weak or strong ties for various purposes depends both on the number of ties one has at various levels of tie strength and on the utility of ties of different strength. Thus, someone for whom weak ties are much more useful than strong may still be constrained to use the latter if weak ties make up an extremely small portion of his or her contacts; conversely, one for whom strong ties are more useful may be socially isolated and forced to fall back on weak ties. Thus, the analytic task is to identify factors that affect these variations. Pool argues, for example, that the number of weak ties is increased by the development of the communications system, bureaucratization, population density, and the spread of market mechanisms. Furthermore, he suggests that average family size affects this, since where "primary families are large, more of the total contacts of an individual are likely to be absorbed in them" (1980: 5).

Peter Blau has suggested that since the class structure of modern societies is pyramidal and since we may expect individuals at all levels to be inclined toward homophily (the tendency to choose as friends those similar to oneself), it follows that the lower one's class stratum, the greater the relative frequency of strong ties. This results because homophilous ties are more likely to be strong, and lower-status individuals are so numerous that it is relatively easier for them to pick and choose as friends others very similar to themselves.[1] An overly literal interpretation of this comment would lead us to expect upper-status individuals to have large numbers of weak ties, since there are so few others of high status; it would further follow that many of these weak ties would then be to others of lower status, since the latter would be so numerous. This does not jibe with ethnographic accounts of upper-class life which stress the importance of strong ties to other members of the upper class. But it does suggest why the upper class must invest so many resources in institutions such as private clubs, special schools, and social registers: The effort to maintain a network of homophilous strong ties is more difficult here than for lower strata (see, for example, Baltzell, 1958).

Interesting as these speculations are, and important as it may be to know what an individual's total network looks like before we can assess the meaning of that person's use of a strong or weak tie, there exist few data that allow us to take this factor into account. It may be that recent work on the sampling of large social networks will allow us to make progress in this area (see, for example, Granovetter, 1976; Frank, 1981).

More can be said about the value to individuals of ties of different strengths. Here, Pool (1980: 5) observes that "the utility of weak links is a function of the security of the individual, and therefore of his wealth. A highly insecure individual, for example, a peasant who might starve if his crop fails, is under strong pressure to become dependent upon one or a few strongly protective individuals. A person with resources on which he can fall back can resist becoming dependent on any given other individual, and can explore more freely alternative options."

This hypothesis can be strongly supported empirically. In my study of job-finding, for example, I found that those whose jobs were found through strong ties were far more likely to have had a period of unemployment between jobs than those using weak ties (1974: 54), and I suggested that those in urgent need of a job turned to strong ties since they were more easily called on and willing to help, however limited the information they could provide. Murray et al. (1981) studied social and physical scientists at one Canadian and one U.S. university: Most found jobs through strong rather than weak ties. They interpret this as being "contrary to Granovetter's hypothesis that salient job information derives from 'weak ties.' " (1981: 119). But more than 80 percent of their data concern first academic jobs–situations of considerable insecurity for new Ph.D.s, who have few usable contacts in their discipline as yet and typically rely on mentors and/or dissertation advisers who know both them and their work well (the definition of "strong tie" used by Murray et al.). They do find that the proportion using strong ties for jobs subsequent to the first is still high–47 percent versus 58 percent for first jobs–but the data for the 47 percent figure consist of about fifty individuals in one university, where the response rate barely exceeded 50 percent. Even if the figure were representative, it would need to be disaggregated by career stage; thus, the present hypothesis suggests that as professors move further away from their first academic jobs, their reliance on strong ties should decline. The question of whether or not respondents face unemployment also would be relevant here; when individuals are denied tenure, for example, one would expect a greater reliance on strong ties, other things equal, than if it were not strictly necessary to find a new job.

A purely theoretical model from economics bears directly on this question: Boorman (1975) used economic theory and network ideas to suggest when rational economic actors might choose to allocate their time and energy to weak as compared to strong ties. He assumes: (1) that strong ties require more time to maintain than weak ones, and (2) that if one hears of a job, one offers the information to strong ties if any are unemployed, and otherwise to weak ties. These simple assumptions lead to a complex mathematical model. The results, however, can be summed up simply: If the probability of unemployment in the system is low, rational individuals will invest *all their time* in weak ties, and such a situation will be a Pareto-optimal equilibrium; for a *high* probability of unemployment, on the other hand, the only stable equilibrium is one in which only strong ties are maintained, though such an equilibrium is not Pareto-optimal (that is, some actors could have their situations improved without any other suffering). This model, based on assumptions and ideas entirely different from those reported in my theoretical and empirical work, ends up with remarkably similar conclusions. This suggests that in such studies, more attention ought to be paid to the level of employment security enjoyed by different participants in the labor market. (The Boorman model is elaborated and extended in important ways by Delany, 1980.)

Employment difficulty is not the only occasion that prompts the use of strong ties. All sorts of everyday problems have this result. Summing up studies of helping networks in a Toronto suburb, Wellman (1979: 1222-1223) indicates that the "closer [stronger] the intimate relationship [as measured by the respondents' ordinal ranking of the intimates], the more the perceived availability of help becomes a salient defining component of that tie. Closeness is apparently the single most important defining characteristic of helpful intimate relationships; . . . 56% of the first closest ranked intimates are relied on in emergencies . . . while only 16% of the sixth closest intimates are."

A number of studies also indicate that poorer people rely more on strong ties than do others. Ericksen and Yancey (1977: 23, 28) in a study of Philadelphia, conclude that the "structure of modern society is such that some people typically find it advantageous to maintain strong networks and we have shown that these people are more likely to be young, less well educated and black" and that "strong networks seem to be linked both to economic insecurity and a lack of social services. As long as the unemployment rate is high the threat of living in poverty is real, and as long as large segments of the population find access to medical services, day care, and social welfare services problematic, we can expect to find reliance on strong networks to continue among them."

Two ethnographic studies demonstrate the same point: Stack (1974) studied a black, urban American, midwestern ghetto; Lomnitz (1977), a shantytown on the fringes of Mexico City. Without apparent knowledge of one another's work, and despite the enormous cultural differences between these two populations, the investigators came to nearly identical conclusions. Stack (1974: 32, 33, 40): "Black families living in the Flats need a steady source of cooperative support to survive. They share with one another because of the urgency of their needs. . . . They trade food stamps, rent money, a TV, hats, dice, a car, a nickel here, a cigarette there, food, milk, grits and children. . . . Kin and close friends who fall into similar economic crises know that they may share the food, dwelling, and even the few scarce luxuries of those individuals in their kin network. . . . Non-kin who live up to one another's expectations express elaborate vows of friendship and conduct their social relations within the idiom of kinship." Lomnitz (1977: 209): "Since marginals are barred from full membership in the urban industrial economy they have had to build their own economic system. The basic social economic structure of the shantytown is the reciprocity network. . . . It is a social field defined by an intense flow of reciprocal exchange between neighbors. The main purpose . . . is to provide a minimum level of economic security to its members." The similarity extends also to the use of fictive kinship as both effect and cause of further reciprocity.

This pervasive use of strong ties by the poor and insecure is a response to economic pressures; they believe themselves to be without alternatives, and the adaptive nature of these reciprocity networks is the main theme of the analysts. At the same time, I would suggest that the heavy concentration of social energy in strong ties has the impact of fragmenting communities of the poor into encapsulated networks with poor connections between these units; individuals so encapsulated may then lose some of the advantages associated with the outreach of weak ties. This may be one more factor that makes poverty self-perpetuating. Certainly, programs intended to provide social services to the poor have frequently had considerable difficulty in their outreach efforts. Such difficulty would be expected from the network arguments advanced here.

Weak Ties in the Spread of Ideas

In SWT (pp. 1365-1369) I suggested application of the argument on weak ties to the study of innovation diffusion. This suggestion has been taken up by Everett Rogers in his analysis of family-planning adoption outcomes over a ten-year period in rural Korean villages; in combination with other network variables, this argument helps explain the level of adoption in these villages (Rogers, 1979: 155-157; Rogers and Kincaid, 1981: 247-249).

In addition to the diffusion of innovations, such an argument logically applies to the diffusion of any set of ideas or information. It has been taken up especially with regard to the spread of cultural and scientific ideas. Fine and Kleinman, for example, in an article entitled, "Rethinking Subculture: An Interactionist Analysis" (1979), assert that the idea of "subculture," as used in sociology, is deficient because it is stripped of its interactional origins and conceived of mainly as a set of disembodied ideas and symbols. Fine and Kleinman confront, in particular, the paradox that large numbers of individuals, most of whom have never been in contact with one another, nevertheless manage to sustain common understandings and meanings—as in the example of "youth culture." They reject the view that such a common culture can be mostly explained by the pervasive influence of mass media: "While media diffusion can result in widespread knowledge, one must not equate the extent of information spread with method of transmission. Much that is communicated by the mass media is not transmitted or used by audiences." Furthermore, many cultural items never transmitted by the media are known throughout an extensive network. "Youth cultures offer excellent examples of subcultures which provide a set of communication channels external to the media. Much material which is common knowledge among young people—dirty jokes, sexual lore, aggressive humor . . .—is not communicated by the adult-controlled media" (1979: 9). They go on to suggest that the

> speed at which children's lore is spread across great distances . . . suggests the role of weak ties. In addition to the school peer group, children who have been geographically mobile may maintain friendships over many miles. The childhood pastime of having pen pals is an example of this phenomenon. Likewise, the distant . . . cousins who populate American extended families provide children with others with whom to compare their life situations and cultures. Since children's culture has both regional and local variations, these kin ties can provide a mechanism by which cultural traditions breach geographical chasms. . . . The spread of culture from an individual in

> one local social network to an acquaintance in another local social network seems to be a critical element for the communication of cultural elements within a subculture [1979: 10-11].

One suggestive empirical study that is consistent with this argument was carried out by Lin, Dayton and Greenwald (1978). Volunteers in a tricity area of the eastern United States agreed to attempt forwarding a booklet to designated but previously unknown target persons, through a chain of personal acquaintances (compare Milgram, 1967). Lin et al. investigated this question more systematically, defining strength of tie in two different ways: by recency of contact and by the type of relationship named by respondents in sending the booklet along to the next person. Data based on both measures showed that successfully completed chains made much more use of weak ties. The authors sum up by saying that "participants in the successful chains tended to utilize fewer strong ties in their forwarding effort. The successful terminals [that is, those who reached the target] dramatically showed that they had weak ties with the targets" (1978: 163). While this experiment is artificial in the sense that no information or ideas were actually being transmitted with these booklets, the efficacy of weak ties in reaching socially distant and unknown targets suggests that the process cited by Fine and Kleinman to explain the diffusion of cultural ideas and symbols across wide segments of a society—via weak ties—may indeed operate as hypothesized.

What makes cultural diffusion possible, then, is that small cohesive groups that are liable to share a culture are not *so* cohesive that they are entirely closed; rather, ideas may penetrate from other such groups via the connecting medium of weak ties. It is a seeming paradox that the effect of weak ties, in this case, is homogenization, since my emphasis has been on the ability of weak ties to reach out to groups with ideas and information different from one's own. The paradox dissolves, however, when the process is seen as one that occurs over a period of time. The ideas that *initially* flow from another setting probably are new, given regional and other variations. Homogeneous subcultures do not happen instantly, but rather are the *end point* of diffusion processes. What cannot be entirely explained from arguments about diffusion is why groups in California and New York, with initially different orientations, *adopt* enough of one anothers' cultures to end up looking very similar. Weak ties may provide the possibility for this homogenization, but the adoption of ideas cannot be explained purely by structural considerations. Content and the motives for adopting one rather than another idea or symbol must enter as a crucial part of the analysis. The active role of individuals in a culture cannot be neglected, lest the explanation become too mechanistic. Fine and Kleinman (1979: 12-13) note that "culture usage consists of chosen behaviors. . . . Culture can be employed strategically and should not be conceptualized as a conditioned response. Usage of culture requires motivation and, in particular, identification with those who use the cultural items. Thus, values, norms, behaviors and artifacts constitute a subculture only insofar as individuals see themselves as part of a collectivity whose members attribute particular meanings to these 'objects.' "

This point can be clarified by contrasting the diffusion of subcultural items to that of scientific information. The scientific case is different in that the adoption of innovations is supposed not to be arbitrary, as in subcultures, but to be governed by agreed-upon tests and standards. That the supposed difference is only one of degree is suggested by Chubin's (1976) model of scientific specialization, which is similar to the Fine-Kleinman analysis of cultural groups. He points out that despite considerable division of labor in science, few problem areas are likely to be sociometrically closed–that any scientific field has a center and a periphery, and the periphery may be defined by its members' weak ties with the center and to *other* scientific groups.

The importance of this is that if "the innovativeness of central units is shackled by vested intellectual interests (or perspectives) then new ideas must emanate from the margins of the network" (Chubin, 1976: 460). Furthermore, as I suggested in SWT (1367) for the case of high-risk innovations, Chubin (1976: 464) asserts that marginals, in science, can better afford to innovate; the innovations, if useful, are seized on by the center. This sequence of events is relatively invisible because the "adoption is sure to affect the innovator's position in the specialty as well. Weak ties are transformed; the former marginal may become the nucleus of a cluster." A similar position is taken by Collins (1974), who reports an empirical investigation of eleven laboratories in Britain, the United States, and Canada, involved in the development and production of a particular type of laser. Based in part on his data and in part on theoretical considerations, Collins argues that the idea of an "invisible college" is misleading, because it suggests too coherent an internal structure. For Collins (1974: 169), the likely importance of weak ties in scientific innovations throws "further serious doubt on the validity of the questionnaire response as a direct indicator of the flow of real scientific innovatory influence."

The most comprehensive attempt, in a scientific setting, to test empirically the validity of my arguments on weak ties is that of Friedkin (1980). He sent questionnaires to all faculty members in seven biological science departments of a large American university (anatomy, biochemistry, biology, biophysics, microbiology, physiology, and pathology), receiving

97 responses, 71.3 percent of the relevant population. Two alternate definitions of "weak tie" were used, with similar outcomes. The results reported rest on the following definition: Two scientists were said to have a weak tie if one reported talking with the other about his or her current work, but the other made no such report. Where both made this statement about one another the tie was defined as "strong" (see SWT, p. 1364n, for discussion of the definition of mutual choices as strong ties).

Friedkin tests systematically a number of my propositions. One concerns what I called "local bridges"–ties between two persons that are the shortest, and often the only, plausible routes by which information might travel from those connected with one to those connected with the other (SWT: 1364-1365). I argued that while not all weak ties should be (local) bridges, all such bridges should be weak ties–an argument central to the assertion that weak ties serve crucial functions in linking otherwise unconnected segments of a network. Friedkin (1980: 414) found that there were eleven local bridges in the network; *all were weak ties.* Moreover, this result is much stronger than might have been expected by chance: 69 percent of ties among respondents were weak and 31 percent were strong. By a binomial test of significance, therefore, the chance of such a result, if ties were randomly chosen to be local bridges, would be only .017.

Other findings predicted in SWT materialize strongly in these data. I argued, for example, that the stronger the tie between two people, the greater the extent of overlap in their friendship circles, and that people with strong ties to third parties are more likely to be acquainted than are those with weak ties to those parties, who in turn are more likely to be acquainted than if they had no mutual friends. All these are verified in substantial detail (Friedkin, 1980: 415-417). Friedkin (1980: 417) concludes that this "evidence suggests that local bridges tend to be weak ties because strong ties encourage triadic closure, which eliminates local bridges. Other things being equal, weak local bridges will tend to be maintained over time, while strong local bridges will tend to be eliminated." Finally, the hypothesis that intergroup ties (as compared to intragroup ones) consist disproportionately of weak ties is assessed: 77 percent of interdepartmental ties, as compared to 65 percent of intradepartmental ones, are weak ties ($p = .002$).

The assertions about bridging can also be cast in terms of transitivity: the tendency of one's friends' friends to be one's friends as well. In SWT I asserted that transitivity could be expected of strong ties but not especially of weak ones, since the rationale for transitivity–that if A chooses B and B chooses C, it is cognitively inconsistent for A not to choose C–is irrelevant for weak ties: A may not even know C, and if he or she does, will not find it inconsistent not to be interacting with his acquaintance's acquaintance (SWT: 1377). In a study of an Israeli kibbutz with 280 members, Weimann (1980: 10) measured the strength of ties by "tenure, importance and frequency." Using a program written by Samuel Leinhardt (SOCPAC II), which compares the frequency of transitive triads to that expected by chance, Weimann (1980: 16-17) found that "networks of strong ties are significantly tending to transitivity, while networks of weak ties lack this tendency, and in some cases even tend to intransitivity. . . . Weak ties, relatively free from the tendency to transitivity, are less structured, thus enabling them the role of bridging separate cliques or subgroups, carrying information to all the network's segments."

Weimann finds also, however, that strong ties are not irrelevant in information flow—that speed of such flow, credibility, and especially influence are all greater through strong ties, and that, in fact, "most of the influence is carried through strong ties" (1980: 12). He suggests a division of labor between weak and strong ties: weak ties provide "the 'bridges' over which innovations cross the boundaries of social groups . . . whereas the influence on the decision making is done mainly by the strong ties network within each group" (1980: 21).

Weimann (1980: 19-20) also points out that weak ties play an important cohesive role in the kibbutz—a social unit formerly thought of as tightly organized: "Encouraged by growing heterogeneity, the process of segmentation . . . limited the power of traditional social forces and threatened some of the basic principles of the kibbutz, namely direct democracy, equality and participation. . . . Conversation networks in a kibbutz play . . . the role of social control mechanism: gossip becomes one of the social forces suppressing deviants and keeping the obedience to the common norm. . . . By the transmission of gossip items (mainly in weak ties, as shown in this research), the kibbutz social system can keep solidarity, sanctions and obedience in an heterogeneous, segmented social group."

Friedkin (1980: 421-422) points to the need for more precision about the regularity and type of information transmitted through different kinds of ties:

> Granovetter's theory, to the extent that it is a powerful theory, rests on the assumption that local bridges and weak ties not only represent opportunities for the occurrence of cohesive phenomena . . . but that they actually do promote the occurrence of these phenomena. A major empirical effort in the field of social network analysis will be required to support this aspect of Granovetter's theoretical approach. . . . It is one thing to argue that when information travels by means of these ties it is usually novel, and, perhaps,

important information to the groups concerned. It is another thing to argue that local bridges and weak ties promote the regular flow of novel and important information in differentiated structures. One may agree with the former and disagree with the latter. If we accept the proposition that regular flows of information depend on the presence of multiple short paths between persons, then a local bridge does not represent a likely path of information flow, though it represents a possible path of such flow. . . . One might argue that such information as does flow by means of local bridges is crucial to the social integration of differentiated populations, i.e., that regular flows of information between differentiated groups are not crucial to their systemic integration. If so, one is asserting that there are different bases of macro and micro integration; for example, that macro integration can be based on weak ties which permit episodic transmissions of information among groups, while micro integration is based on a cohesive set of strong ties which permit regular transmissions within groups.

Weak Ties and Social Organization

Friedkin's emphasis on weak ties as the basis of macro rather than micro-level integration is similar to Peter Blau's (1974: 623) argument that since "intimate relations tend to be confined to small and closed social circles . . . they fragment society into small groups. The integration of these groups in the society depends on people's weak ties, not their strong ones, because weak social ties extend beyond intimate circles (Granovetter, 1973) and establish the inter-group connections on which macrosocial integration rests."

In this section of the chapter, therefore, I will consider a number of studies that address the role of weak ties in organizing groups larger than the primary groups of microsociology. Two such studies consider the problem of integration of diverse groups within formal organizations. Karweit, Hansell, and Ricks (1979: 1) do not present new data but rather a stimulating review of the literature on "how features of peer groups within schools affect the educational orientations, aspirations and achievements of their individual members." "Close friends in school," they note, "have long been considered as important sources of influence, and numerous investigations have sought to document the socializing power of the peer group" (1979: 11). "The dyadic view implies that peer socialization to different values occurs only through close friendship ties. However, other peer relationships—such as admiration for someone quite different from oneself—may be more important socialization sources than close friendships" (1979: 19). (Recall the evidence cited in SWT: 1362, that ties to those very different from oneself are much more likely to be weak than strong). Further, they question whether it is a proper policy goal to attempt to create a situation where the values of one group in school (such as high achievers) can be most efficiently assimilated by others. An "alternative, perhaps more desirable peer structure would be one in which diverse cultures can exchange information and support without necessarily becoming more similar" (1979: 19).

In particular, Karweit et al. (1979: 20), consider how my argument about weak ties may be applied to biracial school settings in the United States, suggesting that "racial integration in the classroom can be achieved by arranging classroom structures to produce enough weak contacts to connect black and white cliques, rather than by encouraging strong biracial friendships [the usual strategy]. This result would be immediately applicable in schools because weak ties are easier to stimulate through realistic organizational innovations. If the idea that racial integration has to occur in strong contacts at the dyadic level can be relaxed, many possibilities for planned intervention in schools to foster racial accommodation become feasible." Finally, Karweit et al. (1979: 26) suggest that a "good deal of students' alienation from school may be associated with their lack of indirect contacts with student leaders and their consequent inability to contribute to student decision-making processes." This point is reminiscent of my argument in SWT that West Enders in Boston may have been loathe to join an organization to fight urban renewal because a lack of bridging weak ties left most of them without even indirect access to leaders of such an organization. If the same argument applies to school settings, it may be that the strategy of encouraging bridging weak ties, suggested by Karweit et al., could have not only the effect of linking culturally different groups, but also the broader macro effect of reducing overall feelings of student alienation and increasing general social solidarity.

Judith Blau (1980) presents a case study of successful integration in a children's psychiatric hospital in New York City and argues that this integration can only be understood by considering the role of an extensive network of weak ties. This public hospital has a staff of 200 and serves children whose level of impairment is quite high. Treatment is difficult and outcomes uncertain. Comparable institutions elsewhere "are marked by high levels of staff turnover and low morale. This is decidedly not the case at the Childrens' Center" (1980: 2). Blau argues that the reason for this is the surprising predominance of weak ties among staff members—so many that "all 200 staff members are on a first name basis" (1980: 6). Interaction is so evenly distributed that "there is an absence of cliques" (1980: 8). Nevertheless, "a dissection of the content of interaction reveals a highly differentiated system of specialized staff relations" (1980: 8), forming stable subnetworks.

These subnetworks have many different foci of organization, reflecting the complex arrangement of the hospital into departments (such as psychology and nursing), committees, programs (such as art and recreation), residential units, and clinical teams focused on particular sets of patients. If the ties in these stable subnetworks were strong, by my argument, this would tend to close them off from one another, so that they would develop into cliques; the overwhelming predominance of weak ties, even if structured, produces and maintains, instead, a situation in which each subnetwork overlaps extensively with many others and a large number of the weak ties serve bridging functions. Blau (1980: 20-21) found, for example, that neither "homogeneous work groups nor strong friendship relations could be identified. . . . The institution's intolerance of close dyadic ties is expressed by the ritualized avoidance patterns among those who have a sexual or family alliance outside of the institution. . . . This suggests . . . that in a complex structure . . . extensive weak networks can remain viable only when close ties are prohibited. . . . For when dimensions of structure intersect and staff are integrated in subnets of multiple crosscutting role relations, close bonds with some will threaten working relations with others." Further, "an individual's access to opportunities and resources can only be fully exploited if he or she is linked with others in diverse positions furnishing different information, but strong ties tend to involve closed circles that limit [such] access. . . . Since information is so widely diffused throughout the hospital structure, it is imperative for staff to sustain bridging intergroup connections, further weakening bonds of ingroup solidarity" (1980: 21).

Relating her findings to organization theory, Blau notes that the problem of integrating large numbers of diverse specialists in a formal setting is not simple; in the present case, there are psychiatrists, social workers, doctors, dentists, teachers, art and music therapists, and learning disability specialists, as well as the usual lower-level categories of aides. The standard solution to this problem is strong mechanisms of control built into a formal hierarchy. An alternative to this formal solution has been an attempt of some clinics to generate "family-like and egalitarian relations." Blau (1980: 19) points out, however, that both of these solutions "exhibit forms of strong ties." In the bureaucratic solution, the ties are hierarchical; in the "democratic" clinics, many of which have reacted against the more formal model, "ubiquitous and tenacious ties provide a matrix of close primary group relations unifying the entire structure. These strong ties strikingly resemble patterns observed in small communities, summer camps and Jesuit monastic orders" (1980: 20). Thus, the weak-tie "solution" of the Bronx psychiatric hospital seems importantly different from either of these patterns. Blau implies that it is better by associating the hierarchical pattern with ineffectual coordination of health care delivery; one might assume, moreover, that the "democratic" solution, which depends on a network of strong ties to bind an institution together, would be highly limited as to the size of the system that could be so bound. Attempts to extend the size of such institutions would confront the constraint that individuals could not sustain the requisite number of strong ties, leading to a fragmentation of the institution into cliques and a corresponding loss of morale and integration.

If, in fact, the weak-tie mode of organizational integration *is* efficient and generates high morale and good services for the general theoretical reasons Blau suggests, an important question would then be to what extent the model can be exported to other such settings. This requires more understanding of how such a pattern came about originally. Blau suggests that there was some conscious attempt to develop a new kind of structure, but it is unclear whether the founders understood the structural implications of their early decisions.

In a larger setting, that of entire communities, Breiger and Pattison (1978) use the methods of blockmodeling (see White et al., 1976) to argue that weak ties play the bridging roles I have suggested in integrating communities, and that, moreover, it would be possible to infer the weak versus strong quality of given types of ties entirely from algebraic manipulation and reduction of the raw sociometric data, without having any other information. In particular, they analyze sociometric data collected by Laumann and numerous associates (Laumann and Pappi, 1976; Laumann et al., 1977) in a German city, "Altneustadt," and an American one, "Towertown" (both pseudonyms). Though the patterns are different in the two cities, Breiger and Pattison show that they share certain structural features that suggest the importance of weak ties. In technical terms, the "joint homomorphic reduction" of the two blockmodel semigroup multiplication tables generates a common structure in which certain algebraic relations are satisfied—relations that would be predicted by the arguments of SWT. The analysis is made for the three types of ties analyzed in the two communities: social, community-affairs-related, and business-professional. It is found that social ties function as strong ties, business-professional ones as weak, and that community-affairs ties are strong in relation to business ones but weak in relation to social ones (1978: 222-224). This characterization is consistent with the ethnographic accounts of the communities, even though it can be developed without those accounts actually being used. While it is not possible in this chapter to give an adequate treatment of the mathematical complexities of the Breiger-Pattison analysis, it should be stressed that the algebraic role structure that they predict on the basis of the weak-ties argument is not one that can be "found" empirically by any variety of curve-fitting; the hypothesis is entirely falsifiable, but it is, in the present case, confirmed for the two communities.

In SWT I suggested that individuals with few weak ties were unlikely to be able to mobilize effectively for collective action within their communities, arguing that the West Enders described by Gans were for this reason ineffective in fighting against urban renewal (see Gans, 1962, and my exchange with Gans on this question in the *American Journal of Sociology*, September 1974). Steinberg (1980) puts this suggestion into a more general context, noting that there are "two dominant schools of thought on the relationship between community attachment and participation in organized protest." One is the mass society argument, asserting that protest results from the "sudden activation of previously 'unattached' individuals or uprooted collectivities"; the second, largely in response to the first, argues that "attached individuals or organized collectivities are most likely to engage in sustained protest" (1980: 2). To argue the importance of weak ties in organization is a position halfway between these two; "attachment" theorists have had little to say about the nature of preexisting social ties, and Steinberg (1980: 3) notes the surprising "paucity of empirical research which systematically examines the social ties of the members of protest groups. . . . We need systematic micro-level inquiries that examine the social ties of initiators and initial recruits before and after the formation of conflict groups in different contexts as well as the effects of these ties."

Steinberg's own work is a "longitudinal study which analyzed the politically relevant social ties of the initiators and initial recruits in five conflict groups mobilized around [different] educational issues in a suburban community" (1980: 3). In all five cases, local school authorities resisted the dissidents' goals; as a result, they "were forced to initiate new groups" (1980: 4). For all groups, Steinberg asked about preexisting ties between initiators and initial recruits, those among the recruits, and those between group members and nongroup members relevant to educational affairs. She found that of the seven individuals responsible for initiating the five groups, none was heavily integrated into the community; all were women who "occupied a marginal position in relation to the network of groups and individuals active in community affairs" (1980: 17). Furthermore, "of 20 initial core members recruited directly by initiators, 19 stemmed from preexisting ties and 15 of these were weak," with the other four being concentrated in one group ("strong" ties were those described by respondents as representing "good friends"). The group recruited on the basis of strong ties "was linked to the fewest organizations and individual memberships were concentrated in the same organizations which formed a dense network. Later recruits tended to join the same groups as the founders. Groups formed on the basis of weak ties, on the other hand, were linked to more organizations that were loosely knit and individual memberships tended to be scattered throughout these organizations" (1980: 19). The strong-tie group was ultimately unsuccessful, whereas three of the other four groups were able to implement many of their aims. Steinberg (1980: 25) concludes that although the initiators of successful groups were marginal individuals in the community, they "were able to recruit some individuals who had occupied leadership positions and who were linked to a dense network of school activists. . . . The evidence suggests, tentatively, that where innovations are controversial, a mobilization strategy based on the activation of weak ties is more likely to facilitate adoption of the goal and integration into the school decision-making structure."

Here we see the intricate interplay between weak and strong ties in structuring outcomes and mediating the competing claims of various community groups. The final study to be reported also points to such an interplay and contains elements of conflict and cohesion. The study itself reports only the cohesion achieved by the business community; left implicit is the extent to which this cohesion may implement the goals of that community in conflict with those of competing groups such as labor or consumers. Bearden et al. (1975) studied interlocking directorates among American corporations, defining a "tie" between two corporations to exist when at least one individual sits on the boards of directors of both. It has long been noted that such interlocks are possible vehicles for interfirm control or collusion.

Since the investigation of interlocking directorates began early in the twentieth century, one of the persistent issues has been whether the corporate network consists of "cliques" (or "interest groups") that might be seen as competing with one another, or of one large, densely connected web, reflecting the overarching influence of unity among capitalist leaders. A number of studies (reviewed in Bearden et al., 1975: 1-16) have generated inconclusive results on this question.

The study to be reviewed here, by Bearden et al. (1975), is described in a widely circulated (though unpublished) paper; it is the largest study of interlocking directorates ever carried out in the United States, covering the 1131 largest American corporations during the period 1962-1973. From various sources, Bearden et al. collected data on all 13,574 directors of these companies in 1962. In resolving the issue of interest groups versus one large, connected network, Bearden et al. (1975: 27) comment that if "all interlocks are treated as having equal strength, the whole network is so highly connected that the identification of cliques is very difficult." They point out, however, that when an officer of firm A sits on the boards of firms B and C, two types of interlocks are created. The A-B and A-C interlocks are "functional" or "strong" interlock ties, in that there is a direct connection between an officer of one corporation and the board of the other. This is the kind of interlock that might occur, for example, "when one company places someone on the board of another company because of stock ownership, a buyer-seller relationship or another functional relationship" (Bearden et al., 1975: 27). On the other hand, the individual from firm A also creates an interlock between the boards of firms B and C, which may have no direct business ties with one another. This interlock can be seen then as incidental, or weak. Another type of interlock that can be seen as a weak tie is that created between two companies when an individual from outside the corporate world entirely—from a university or law firm, for example—sits on both boards.

Bearden et al. argue that in order to uncover "cliques" or interest groups, it is necessary to compare the corporate network as a whole to that formed only by "strong" interlock ties. They find that when the *entire* network is analyzed, there is "no sign of interest groups . . . [but] lack of clustering reflects the prevalence of weak ties in the interlock network" (1975: 60). When only strong ties are analyzed, definite cliques appear, "with banks playing the central roles in all the clusters" (1975: 68).

> Recent interlock literature has produced contradictory indications about the survival of the "interest" groups uncovered by pre-World War II research. . . . It is our contention that both sides of the dispute are correct: the integration of New York, Boston, Chicago, Philadelphia and California centers of business into a national and even international network of corporations has occurred simultaneously with the maintenance and further development of interest groups. . . . The intensive clusters are created by strong ties . . . : interfirm stockholding, . . . indebtedness, enduring economic interdependence. . . . Like the small groups studied by Granovetter, these intense ties tend to produce cliques which are in some ways competitive and exclusive of each other. The extensive national network is formed from weak ties. . . . They do not imply specific interfirm economic connections; instead they reflect an overall common orientation and interest, the need for common action across cliques and a growing sense of national and international interdependence among large corporations. Thus . . . the network . . . contains both the coordinative leverage of weak ties and the cliquishness of strong ties; national cooperation among most firms as well as competitive antagonism between clusters; unity and conflict simultaneously [1975: 51-52].

The argument of Bearden et al. is oriented, then, to the force of weak intercorporate ties in generating cooperation and coordination in the national network of firms. It seems likely also that such ties play a role analogous to that highlighted by Fine and Kleinman, in helping to maintain a common *cultural* consciousness among the managers of large corporations—in transmitting information and influences on stylistic matters, political judgments, and broad social trends. It could be argued that such cultural homogeneity is a necessary condition for any large-scale corporate coordination.

Conclusions

In this account of empirical research inspired by or bearing on the argument of SWT, I have shown that that argument has, in fact, been useful in clarifying and explaining a variety of phenomena, ranging from effects of social relations on individuals to the diffusion of ideas and innovations to the organization of large-scale social systems. It is certainly gratifying to have been able to document this.

But one may still usefully ask: Do these studies show that the argument is empirically verified? Here we are on shakier ground. Many of the studies cited did not actually set out systematically to test the argument of SWT. In some cases, that argument came in handy to explain empirical findings that otherwise would have been anomalous. This is the case for Rogers, Judith Blau, and Bearden et al. While these studies certainly lend credence to the argument, the procedure for finding them—either personal contact between the authors and myself, or the authors' citation of SWT—is not an unbiased procedure for *testing* the argument. There is no way to know, for example, about empirical studies in which the SWT argument was considered, rejected, and not mentioned because it did not fit the facts; authors can hardly be expected to cite every argument that did not help to explain their anomalies.

Furthermore, a number of the studies cited are mainly theoretical, proposing that, in their subject area, weak ties can be seen as serving important functions, but not actually bringing any substantial body of empirical data to bear on this assertion. The work of Coser, Boorman, Fine and Kleinman, Chubin, and Karweit et al. fits this category. This work provides stimulating leads for future research; it is that research which will, however, help to verify or falsify the argument.

Other studies cited *have* set out, as part of their work, to put the argument to systematic test. Langlois, Lin et al. (1978 and 1981), Ericksen and Yancey, Murray et al., Rogers, Breiger and Pattison, Weimann, Steinberg, and Friedkin have done so. The results of these studies are very encouraging but not conclusive. As Friedkin points out, one needs to show not only that ties bridging network segments are disproportionately weak, but also that (1) something flows through these bridges–they actually serve as conduits bringing information and influence to groups they would otherwise not get, and (2) whatever it is that flows actually plays some important role in the social life of individuals, groups, and societies. While some of these studies help make such a showing, the case remains incomplete.

This review should also have served to highlight a crucial feature of the original argument that has important bearing on its falsification or verification: I have not argued that all or even most weak ties serve the functions described in SWT–only those that act as bridges between network segments. The importance of weak ties is asserted to be that they are disproportionately likely to be bridges, as compared to strong ties, which should be underrepresented in that role. This does not preclude the possibility that most weak ties have no such function. It follows that an important part of further specifying the argument would be more systematic investigation of the origin and development of those ties that bridge, as compared to those that do not. In SWT (p. 1375) I suggested that "for a community to have many weak ties which bridge, there must be several distinct ways or contexts in which people may form them." I went on to point out that Charlestown (in Boston), which successfully fought urban renewal, as compared to the West End, which did not, had a rich organizational life, and its male residents worked within the community. The implication was that weak ties formed in these contexts were more likely to bridge than weak ties that result from "meeting friends of friends . . . in which case the new tie is *automatically* not a bridge" (SWT: 1375; emphasis added). None of the work reviewed here has taken up this point; a recent paper by Feld (1981), however, develops a new theoretical perspective based on the issue of what social "foci" organize the formation of social ties. Work proceeding from this perspective may shed new light on the issues raised here. In general, the most pressing need I see for further development of network ideas is a move away from static analyses that observe a system at one point in time toward more systematic accounts of how such systems develop and change. Only by more careful attention to this dynamic problem can social network analysis fulfill its promise as a powerful tool in the analysis of social life.

NOTE

1. Discussant's comments on this paper at the Albany Conference on Contributions of Networks Analysis to Structural Sociology, April 4, 1981.

6

Social Resources and Instrumental Action

NAN LIN

I would like to sketch a theory explaining why certain goal-oriented actions are more successful than others. This theory covers only certain types of actions. First, it deals only with those actions that are taken to achieve a goal for the benefit of the individual who takes the action. This is the class of actions that are defined as instrumental in nature. For example, looking for a good job and searching for a stranger in a community are such actions. Secondly, it only concerns those instrumental actions that require the use of a personal contact. Under certain conditions, an instrumental action may be accomplished without going through a personal contact or any contact. For example, in a perfect market system, where all job vacancies and their required skills were known to all who seek jobs and where the recruitment of an applicant to fill the job depended entirely on the matching of the required skills and the skills possessed by each candidate, there would be little need to use a contact; direct application should accomplish it. Similarly, if the searcher knew everyone else in the social system, there would be no need for him or her to go through a contact to locate someone. A contact becomes a requirement only when the searcher does not know the target person directly. Thus, the theory applies in an imperfect market where the diffusion of the information about the goal is less than perfect. I am assuming this condition covers most real market situations.

There are situations in which other than personal contacts are used as means in the instrumental action. For example, in seeking jobs, people do use employment agencies or read newspaper ads. The present theory does not deal with these actions. I hope to treat this topic elsewhere.

The benefit of an individual in an instrumental action discussed here focuses on the resources valued by the members in the social system. *Resources* are defined as valued goods in a society, however consensually determined, the possession of which maintains and promotes an individual's self-interest for survival and preservation. The resources may include both ascribed elements, such as sex and race, and acquired elements, such as prestige and authority. The values are normative judgments rendered on these goods. For most societies, they correspond to wealth, status, and power. The theory focuses on those instrumental actions that are taken for the purpose of gaining valued resources.

A Theory of Instrumental Action

The theory begins with an image of the social structure consisting of a network of persons whose positions are rank-ordered according to certain normatively valued resources such as wealth, status, and power. It further assumes that the structure has a pyramidal shape in terms of accessibility and control of such resources. The higher the position, the fewer the occupants; and the higher the position, the better the view it has of the structure (especially down below). Both in terms of number of occupants and accessibility to positions, the pyramidal structure suggests advantages of positions nearer to the top.

A position nearer to the top of the structure has greater access to and control of the valued resources not only because more valued resources are intrinsically attached to the position, but also because of the position's greater accessibility to positions at other (primarily lower) rankings. I define *social resources* as resources embedded in one's social network. They are not possessed goods of the individual. Rather, they are resources accessible through one's direct and indirect ties (Lin, Vaughn, and Ensel, 1981). Then, an individual occupying a higher position, because of its accessibility to more positions, also has a greater command of social resources.

What is implied in such an image of the social structure, and of social resources, is that there is a direct relationship between the level of a position in the hierarchical structure and the amount of influence it may exert on other (lower) positions for instrumental purposes (obtaining additional resources), as well as the amount of information it possesses about the locations of resources in the structure. The influence factor derives from the ability of higher positions to cumulate resources at a higher rate than lower positions. Thus, any "favor" the lower position may provide can be expected to have a greater future "payoff," since the higher position has more to offer the lower position than vice versa. The information factor is associated with asymmetric network relations across levels of the positions. A higher position tends to have more information or a better view of the structure than a lower position; thus, it is more capable of locating the specific resources embedded in the structure.

Given that the embedment of the resources in the hierarchical positions is as postulated in such a pyramidal structure, it is possible to formulate propositions concerning the use of personal contacts in instrumental actions. A simple strategy in instrumental action is to reach a contact that provides the necessary influence and information. Thus, the first and most obvious proposition is: *The success of instrumental action is associated positively with the social resources provided by the contact.* As one reaches up to a contact with better resources, the chances increase that the contact's resources and command of social resources will help in achieving the goal of the ego's instrumental action. I will call this *the social resources proposition.* It is the primary derivation from the conceptualization of the social structure described above. It is also the most primitive derivation, because even if the proposition is valid, the factors determining the likelihood of reaching such social resources remain to be resolved. I propose below that the primary factors involve the strength of positions and the strength of ties.

The principle of homophily has been used to describe normative and expressive interactive patterns. This principle suggests that persons, for expressive reasons, tend to interact with others who are like themselves. Thus, it is also known as the like-me principle (Laumann, 1966). In general, empirical data have shown that frequency of interaction and intensity of relationship are more likely to occur among individuals who share similar characteristics. There is also evidence that in terms of preferred interaction partners, persons tend to name others of higher prestige and status. The prestige principle also characterizes some normative interactions. In any event, the homophily and prestige principles both suggest interactions with others at similar or higher positions in the social structure.

When these principles are applied to the issue of who tends to reach better social resources, it should be obvious that those whose initial positions are relatively high in the social structure should have the advantage over others. The initial position may be inherited from parents or achieved by the individual. Once such an initial position is located, the normative interactive patterns for the particular occupant of the position link it with others at similar or higher positions. The higher the initial position, the more likely the occupant will have access to better-valued resources. Thus, we may hypothesize that *the level of the initial position is positively related to social resources reached through a contact.* I will call this *the strength-of-positions proposition.*

The upshot of this proposition is that the structural opportunity for reaching better social resources is much better for those whose initial positions are relatively high. It is not as good for those whose initial positions are relatively low. The next question is whether there is a mechanism by which persons at relatively low initial positions can reach better social resources. The concept of the strength of ties provides clues as to how the action of those at relatively lower initial positions may be instrumentally successful.

The strength-of-ties perspective builds on the principle of homophily. If the principle of homophily characterizes the normative interaction patterns, then it must also tend to be true that frequency of interaction and intensity of relationships decrease for those who have dissimilar characteristics. In other words, strong ties characterize the intimate social circle of individuals with similar characteristics and weak ties characterize the infrequent interactions and peripheral relationships among dissimilar individuals. Granovetter (1973, 1974) has pointed out that there are indeed advantages to using weak ties, because these ties provide possible linkages with individuals who have dissimilar characteristics. By breaking out of one's own intimate, close social circle through weak ties, one can access information or influence not otherwise available.

The strength-of-ties perspective, therefore, leads to another proposition linking individuals with better social resources: *Weak ties rather than strong ties tend to lead to better social resources.* If reaching up in the hierarchical structure corresponds to obtaining better social resources, then breaking out of one's intimate circle increases the likelihood of reaching a contact at a higher social position. I will call this *the strength-of-ties proposition.* The strength-of-positions proposition, regarding the relationship between the initial position and access to social resources, specifies the expected advantage of being at a higher initial position. The strength-of-ties proposition, on the other hand, specifies the communication strategy optimal for instrumental action, even if one's initial position is relatively low.

However, this latter relationship should be less than overwhelming, because weak ties may link one to individuals at lower social positions. In fact, the strength-of-ties probably makes an insignificant impact on reaching better social resources for those initially in high social positions. As one's initial position gets nearer to the top of the structure, there should be greater advantage of using strong ties to reach positions with similar (and better) social resources. In the limiting case, at the very top level of the structure, one should find strong ties rather than weak ties to be instrumentally important, as weak ties there would simply increase the likelihood of reaching lower positions in the structure. In general, I expect an interaction effect of initial position and strength of ties on social resources reached. The greatest effect of the strength of ties on social resources reached should occur when one's initial position is very low.

To recapitulate, a theory of instrumental action, focusing on the use of social contacts, has been proposed. Based on an assumption about the distribution of resources among the hierarchical positions in the social structure, it is postulated that higher positions possess greater resources as well as social resources. Therefore, it is expected that the success of instrumental actions depends largely on the social resources of the contact used. The likelihood of reaching good social resources is dictated by (1) the initial position of the person taking the instrumental action (the strength-of-positions proposition), and (2) the use of weak ties rather than strong ties (the strength-of-ties proposition) in reaching a contact. Further, there is an interaction between the initial position and the strength of the ties: the effect of using weak ties rather than strong ties increases as the initial position is lower. These propositions are depicted in Figure 6.1.

A program of research has been designed and carried out to test various aspects of this theory. So far, three studies have been conducted: (1) a Small World study, (2) the Albany study, and (3) the New York study. I will now describe each of these studies and briefly discuss findings relevant to this theory.

The Small World Study

The Small World technique maps chains of communication by tracing the forwarding processes involved in the delivery of a packet to a described target person. In this technique, a target is selected and described (name, address, age, sex, occupation, and so on) in a packet that is then sent to a starter. The starter is asked to send the packet either directly to the target (if the target is an acquaintance of the starter) or to a person who may know the target or a friend of the target. By keeping track of the persons (links) who send and receive the packets until the packet either successfully reaches the target or terminates, it becomes possible to gather data on the communication flow and the characteristics of the participants. The

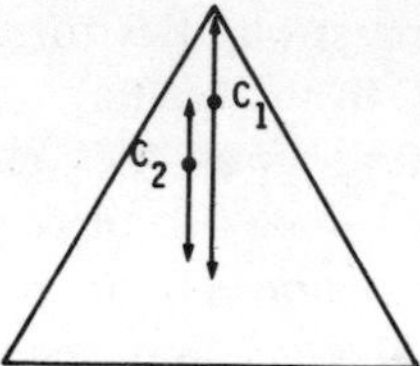

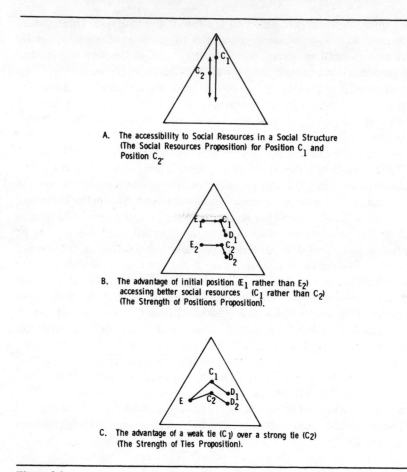

A. The accessibility to Social Resources in a Social Structure (The Social Resources Proposition) for Position C_1 and Position C_2.

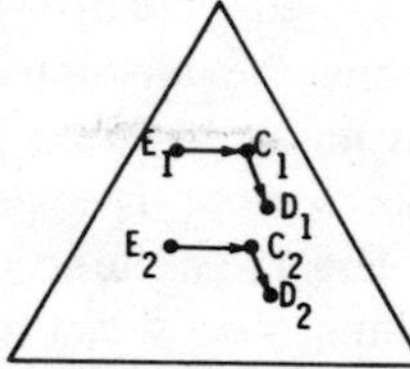

B. The advantage of initial position (E_1 rather than E_2) accessing better social resources (C_1 rather than C_2) (The Strength of Positions Proposition).

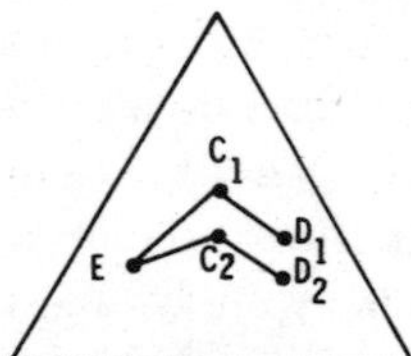

C. The advantage of a weak tie (C_1) over a strong tie (C_2) (The Strength of Ties Proposition).

Figure 6.1

Small World technique was useful to examine the instrumental task of searching for a stranger through contacts (intermediaries). For this reason, we selected a study site within one urbanized area, rather than cross-country, as is the usual case in such studies. We assumed that restricting both starters and targets to the same urbanized community would mean that most of the forwarding activities would take place within the same area and that the mapping would therefore approximate the networks within and across certain socioeconomic strata in a community. The study site selected was the tricity area of Albany-Schenectady-Troy in the state of New York. It is classified as a single urbanized area by the U.S. Census Bureau.

Four targets were used: (1) a white male, (2) a white female, (3) a black male, and (4) a black female. They were selected and matched in terms of their length of residence in the community, age, marital status, and social involvement (participation in religious and civic activities). They all resided in Schenectady.

A random sample of the households in the largest city of the area, Albany, was drawn from the city directory. A letter soliciting participation in the study was sent to each household, with an attached business reply postcard to indicate whether the head of the household, the spouse, or both would be willing to participate as starters in the study. The final list of starter households included the first 300 volunteer households whose returned postcards reached us. Analysis showed that the volunteer participants are of slightly higher social status than the adult population in the area, with ethnic minorities underrepresented.

Each starter received two packets describing two different targets. There was concern as to whether each starter would send both packets to the same receiver. Analysis showed that 92 percent of the started packets were sent to different persons by the starters. None of the starters knew about the targets; therefore, in all cases, contacts (intermediaries) were used.

By identifying chains in which packets were successfully forwarded to the targets (about 30 percent) as well as those in which they were not, we were able to assess the relationship between various social resources and a chain's likelihood of success. The specific resource characteristics examined were race, sex, and the occupational prestige of the intermediaries in each chain. Details of the data and analyses are available elsewhere (Lin et al., 1977, 1978). I will briefly discuss pertinent results here.

The data showed the packets had difficulty crossing the racial boundary. White participants had difficulty sending packets to black intermediaries in order to reach the black targets. While there were too few black participants to allow assessment of the flow of packets from the blacks to the whites, it was evident that communication flows mainly within ethnic groups.

Within the racially defined network, communication flow is more effective downward in the hierarchy—from males to females rather than from females to males, and from persons with higher occupational status toward targets of relatively low occupational status, rather than from persons with moderate or low occupational status to those of higher occupational status.

These data supported the proposition that the success of instrumental action is associated positively with the social resources provided by the contact. The prevailing valued resources in American society (sex and occupational status) clearly influenced the likelihood of a packet reaching its target. The better the resources (males rather than females, and higher rather than lower occupational status), the greater the likelihood of success. The race variable also shed light on the segmentation of American society in terms of communication flow. The phenomenon is so prevalent that it defines the structural boundary for two segments of the population (the white and the black). Communication flows follow the predicted pattern within each segment.

Further analyses showed that participants in the successful and unsuccessful chains are distinguished quite clearly, in that the former tended to forward the packets to others higher in occupational prestige than themselves and much higher than the targets. Participants in the unsuccessful chains, on the other hand, tended to forward the packets to persons with prestige levels similar to their own. We then examined the possibility that the starters in the successful chains were themselves of higher occupational prestige than those in the unsuccessful chains, so that they were originally capable of reaching persons of even higher prestige. This was not true; the starters in the successful chains did not have higher prestige than those in the unsuccessful chains.

Thus, there was evidence that as the packet was forwarded upward on the hierarchical pyramid, the likelihood of eventually locating the target at a relatively low position increased. We also noted that the last intermediaries (or terminals) in the successful chains (those who eventually sent the packets to the targets) tended to have lower prestige than those immediately preceding them in the chains. This "dipping" relationship suggests that the up-the-status-slope effort paid off when the packet reached a participant of sufficiently high prestige to be able to identify someone below and to be certain that this someone could deliver the packet to the target. Only then did the forwarding take a dip in the pyramidal structure.

We then investigated the recency of the last contact between each participant and the person next in the chain ("How many days ago did you last see this person?"). Here, the strength of ties is indexed by the recency of contact. The data showed that participants in successful chains tended to forward the packets to persons of less recent contact, as compared to those in the unsuccessful chains. The successful strategy was to reach persons who did not have strong ties to the senders. Thus, the participants in the successful chains tended to turn to weak ties. These ties finally were able to forward the packets to the last intermediaries (the terminals), who uniformly had a large reservoir of social ties (in terms of the mean number of friends).

Further to verify the fact that weak ties rather than strong ties were more useful, we examined the relations between each pair of senders and receivers in the chains. Each sender was asked to indicate the relationship between himself or herself and the person to whom the packet was forwarded. We computed the percentage of mentions of strong ties (relatives, friends, and neighbors). The results confirmed the strength of weak ties. The participants in the successful chains tended to utilize fewer strong ties in their forwarding efforts. The successful terminals dramatically showed that they had weak ties with the targets.

The Small World study provided support for the general proposition linking social resources to the success of instrumental action and indirect support for the proposition concerning the use of weak ties and social resources reached. It is a crucial test, since the instrumental action involved actual behavior (forwarding a packet) rather than a paper-and-pencil test. It does have limitations, however. For one, the instrumental action (searching for a stranger) was not a socially significant act. For another, the data base, consisting of chain positions in successful and unsuccessful chains, was insufficient for meaningful multivariate analysis. For these reasons, we conducted the next study on the job-seeking activities of a representative sample of male adults in Albany.

The Albany Study

The data were collected in Spring 1975 with a modified random sample of males, aged 20 to 64 years, residing in the Albany-Schenectady-Troy, New York, area. All respondents were then or previously had been members of the United States civilian labor force. Of a total sample of 440 persons, 399 cooperated, resulting in a 91 percent completion rate. In the interview, we asked questions regarding how they found their first and last jobs. If they used personal contacts in finding the jobs, we then asked a series of questions about the characteristics of the personal contacts. For this discussion, I will focus only on those respondents who used personal contacts. Social resources were indicated by the occupational status (as measured by the Duncan socioeconomic status scale or the SEI scale) of the contact. In all, 57 percent of the respondents used personal contacts to find their first jobs, and 59 percent of them did so in finding their last jobs. Again, details of the findings have been presented elsewhere (Lin, Vaughn, and Ensel, 1981; Lin, Ensel, and Vaughn, 1981).

In the usual analysis of such status attainment data, the occupational statuses of the first job and last job are used as the dependent variables to be explained, and the father's educational and occupational status as well as the respondents' own education are used as the independent, explaining variables. Regression analysis is usually employed. The finding is that education has a strong direct effect on the son's occupational status attainment, while father's education and occupation have substantial effects on the son's educational achievement. The interpretation is, therefore, that the achievement factor (education) rather than the ascription factor (family background) is more important in the status attainment process in the United States (Blau and Duncan, 1967). This model and finding have been generally validated in industrial nations.

Our Albany data showed that there is a strong relationship between social resources, as indexed by contact status, and attained job statuses. The zero-order correlation between contact status and the attained status of the first job was .65, and between contact status and the last job status the correlation was .68. When we incorporated contact status into the basic status attainment regression model (also known as the Blau-Duncan model), we found the explained variance for the statuses of attained jobs increased substantially (from .41 to .53 for the status of the first job and from .55 to .65 for the status of the last job). Further, contact status became the dominant explaining variable for the first job status, replacing education; and it was as important as education in predicting the status attained in the last job.

Thus, there is convincing evidence that social resources affect the success of instrumental action when we consider contact status as indicating social resources and the status of attained jobs as indicating the success of an instrumental act. This relationship remains strong and valid, even when other significant factors are also taken into account in a multivariate analysis.

The data also provided an opportunity to assess the strength-of-positions proposition (the extent to which social resources are affected by one's initial position). We took father's education and occupation as indicators of the initial socioeconomic position of each respondent, and it then was possible to determine whether such initial positions, compared to educational achievement, were more important in determining the likelihood of reaching a contact with high status. The regression analysis showed that for the first job nearly 85 percent of the explained variance in contact status can be attributed to family background, directly or through its effect on education. Family background also accounted for, directly or indirectly, 71 percent of the explained variance of the status of the contact in seeking the last job. Thus, it is evident that the initial position to a large extent influences social resources obtained, a confirmation of the strength-of-positions proposition.

We then examined the relationship between the strength of ties between the respondent and the contact and social resources obtained. Strong ties were represented by relatives, friends, and neighbors, and weak ties by acquaintances. The strength of ties did not have any significant direct effect on the status of the first or last job obtained. Rather, it was significantly related to contact status (zero-order correlations of -.40 for the first job and -.292 for the last job). Thus, the strength of ties makes a difference in the status of the contact. It has only an indirect effect on the eventual status of jobs obtained by the respondent. These results support the strength-of-ties proposition. See Figure 6.2 for these results.

Finally, we examined the interaction between the initial position and the strength of ties on social resources. As mentioned earlier, the theory predicted that the effect of strength of ties on social resources obtained would increase as the initial position becomes lower in the structure. The result of this examination is shown in Figure 6.3. Here, we can see that the benefit of using a weak tie rather than a strong tie was most significant when the status of the origin (father's occupational status) was the lowest. The benefit gradually diminishes as one's original status improves. When the original position is at or beyond the upper-middle status range, the benefit of weak ties over strong ties is insignificant.

In conclusion, the Albany study confirmed the social resources proposition, the homophily proposition, and the strength-of-ties proposition, within the context of the status attainment process.

The New York Study

Our confidence in the Albany data is strong, because the data verified the Blau-Duncan model and showed patterns among variables comparable to national studies. The fact remains that the data came from a particular metropolitan area and were restricted to males. We took advantage of a New York State survey to replicate some portions of the findings. The survey was conducted in November–December of 1978 with a sample of male and female adults residing in various New York State utility areas. A total of 1623 respondents were interviewed. Of these, 764 were 20-64 years of age and currently employed in the civilian labor force in the state. Analyses were conducted for that portion of the sample. For males, father's education and occupation indexed family background, while for females, mother's education and occupation were used. This decision

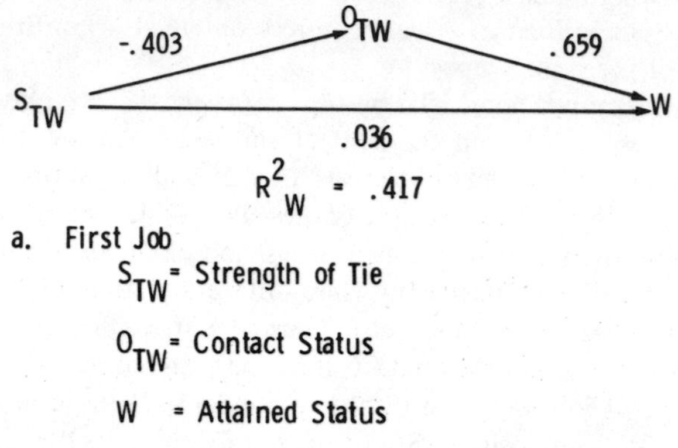

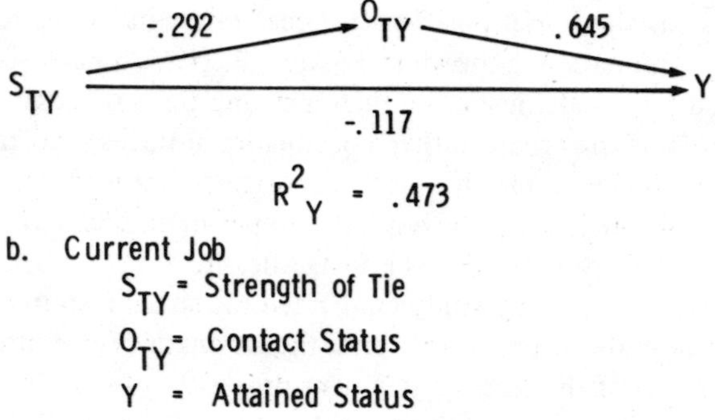

Figure 6.2 Effects of Strength of Tie and Contact Status on Attained Occupational Status

resulted in the further reduction of the number of female respondents, because about three-fifths of the mothers did not work and therefore had no occupational status. But this decision was theoretically sound (the like-sexed inheritance), empirically validated (fathers show influence on both sons and daughters, mothers show greater influence on daughters than on sons, and the father-son effect is comparable to the mother-daughter effect), and reliable (there were no significant differences in status characteristics between the females with working mothers and those without). Details of the findings are reported by Ensel (1979).

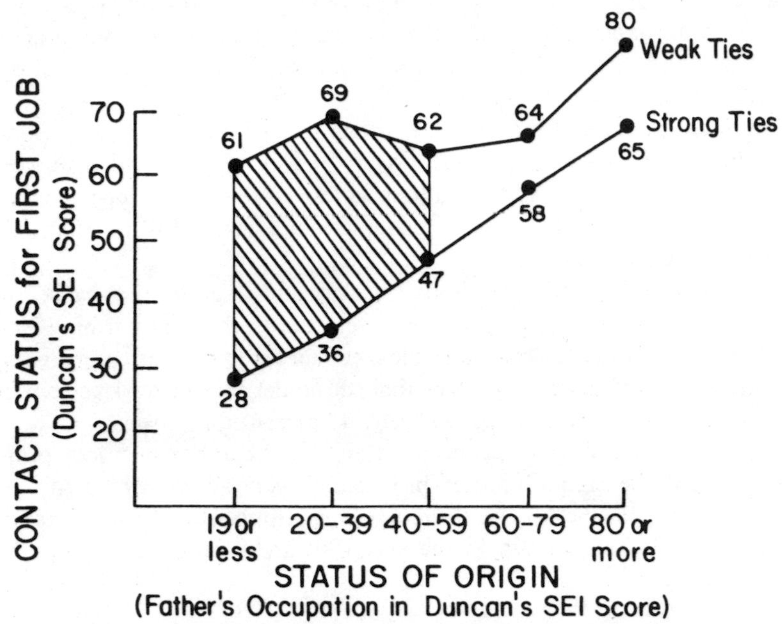

Figure 6.3 Relations Between the Status of the Origin and the Contact Status Through Weak and Strong Ties (shaded area indicates significant statistical differences)

One significant difference in the contacts the male and female respondents used in finding jobs was in the sex of these contacts. For most males, the contacts used were males (about 90 percent for both the first and current jobs). For females, 57 percent used female contacts for the first job and 45 percent used female contacts for the current job. Thus, we included the sex of the contact as an additional variable in the analysis.

The data on the male respondents generally confirmed the findings from the Albany study. Contact status was the most important factor in explaining the status of the first job obtained. It was as significant as the status of the first job in explaining the current job. Contact status, in the case of seeking the first job, was best explained by father's occupational status and then by the strength of ties. For the current job, contact status was explained by education, father's occupational status, and the status of the first job. Thus, these data confirmed the social resources proposition as well as the strength-of-positions and strength-of-ties propositions.

For females, the attained status was more affected by family background than it was for males. For the status of both first and current jobs, mother's occupational status and education played an important role, along with contact status. In other words, ascribed status continues to have a direct effect on the females' job status long after such a direct effect has waned among the males.

Further, in finding the first job, females relied on family background (mother's occupation and education) to seek weak ties and male ties. These male and weak ties tended then to lead to contacts of higher status. In other words, access to social resources, for females, has an additional barrier to overcome: sex.

The persistent effect of family background and the sex barrier in seeking and obtaining high-status contacts makes the explanation of job advancement more problematic and less certain for females as compared to males. This is reflected in the fact that the model explained 61 percent of the current job status for males and only 47 percent for females.

Again, the social resources proposition, the strength-of-positions proposition, and the strength-of-ties proposition were all confirmed for the female sample. In fact, such effects are even stronger for females than for males, because reaching up in the social hierarchy requires crossing the sexual boundary.

Concluding Remarks

The research program is continuing. Currently, I am examining the social ties individuals have in the occupational structure. In the Albany study, we presented a list of twenty occupations, ranging from "lawyer" to "laborer," and asked each respondent to indicate whether any of his relatives, friends, or acquaintances had such an occupation. If the respondent answered affirmatively, we also asked him to indicate how frequently he interacted with that tie and the physical distance between them. Preliminary analyses (Lin and Dumin, 1982) show that respondents at higher initial positions have greater access (social ties) to various occupational groups; such extensity of access is primarily due to ties to occupations of higher rankings. Friends and acquaintances rather than relatives account for such extensive access. Thus, these data further confirm the strength-of-positions and the strength-of-ties propositions. There is also evidence that weak ties (acquaintances) are more useful (in terms of their possible effect on the status of attained jobs) if they are nearby, whereas strong ties (relatives) remain useful even if they are far away (outside the area). There is a clear interaction of social and physical distance affecting the success of instrumental action. These data are important because they cover all respondents, rather than only those who used social contacts in obtaining jobs.

It is now possible, I believe, to comment on the implications this theory of instrumental action has for understanding the interactions between individuals and the social structure. The fact that success in society may be related to "who you know" modifies both the functional explanation of social mobility and structural determinism of individual behavior. This theory and the data show that while structural characteristics impose the range of behaviors possible, individuals hold certain degrees of freedom in the manipulation of the social structure for their own benefits. Such freedom results from a combination of structural characteristics as well as strategic choices. Individuals are actors.

At a still broader scope, this theory reminds us that both instrumental and expressive behaviors have social significance. Expressive behaviors, which have received much research attention, point to the type of social interactions that promote horizontal linkages among individuals of similar characteristics. Such behaviors reinforce the solidarity and stability of social groups. However, instrumental behaviors dictate equally significant social interactions providing vertical linkages. Such behaviors allow greater social mobility and greater sharing of resources in society.

There is intrinsic complementarity as well as tension between the two types of behaviors. Excessive instrumental actions risk the loss of group identity and solidarity, as one attempts to move up from one position to another. On the other hand, excessive expressive behaviors promote the stagnation of social segmentation and nurture the development of class consciousness and class conflict. The relative frequency and intensity of instrumental and expressive interactions in a society, I believe, hold the key in determining the dynamics of stability and change. I postulate that the persistence of a given social structure depends on the relative amount of expressive and instrumental interactions actually taking place among its members. Further, the optimal points of such interactions for both persistence and change should be focal points of theoretical and empirical investigations.

7

Social Density and Mental Health

CHARLES KADUSHIN

The concept of social density has had an honored place in theories of the social etiology of mental disorders. If social density is defined as the ratio of the number of social relations that actually exist in a system to the number of possible such relations,[1] then social density is said to be positively related to mental health, and vice versa. To be sure, classical social theory does not necessarily speak in such formal language, although this is the drift of much of the theorizing about social forces in mental disorder. Despite the prevalence of such theorizing, however, there has been little hard evidence consistent with the theories.

This chapter presents, to my knowledge, the first substantial empirical demonstration that there is indeed a negative relation between social density and mental disorder; or, conversely, high social density is associated with mental health.

The data come from a probability sample of 380 men interviewed in the spring of 1977 in Brooklyn and Westchester County, New York State, and in Bridgeport, Connecticut. An additional 1001 interviews were conducted by our research group in other parts of the country. These data, collected under congressional mandate, are not yet publicly available. Men between the ages of 24 and 37 who were eligible to serve in the Vietnam War were the target.[2] This age range, while restricted in terms of examining some general correlates of mental health, is ideal for investigating the

AUTHOR'S NOTE: This chapter represents a substantial revision of two drafts. The first was by Kadushin, C. R. Ziviano, and L. M. Roth and was presented at the 1979 Annual Meetings of the American Sociological Association. The second was a longer impact of relations with friends upon mental health. Recent national survey data (Antonucci and Bornstein, n.d.) show that persons in this age group, as compared with others, are more likely to visit with their friends and more likely to utilize informal social support when they are worried or unhappy.

In this chapter I shall first review the theoretical basis for expecting a relationship between social density and mental health and will discuss some causes of density. Then I shall present a simple model linking the causes of density, density itself, stressors, and reactions to stress. Given the character of the sample, the stressor is defined as a traumatic stressor—the experience of heavy combat in Vietnam. Finally, I shall speculate on the difference between those social contexts in which social density has direct effects on mental health, by producing a more benign environment, and those in which density leads to social support once persons have been exposed to a severe stressor.

The Theory of Social Density and Mental Health

There is a deep-rooted connection in the minds of classical social theorists between industrialization and social and mental disorder. As Inkeles and Smith (1974: 261) have put it:

> In our experience, no belief is more widespread among critics of industrialization than that it disrupts basic social ties, breaks down social controls, and therefore produces a train of personal disorientation, confusion and uncertainty, which ultimately leads to misery and even mental breakdown among those who are uprooted from the farm and herded into great industrial cities.

There is scarcely an important social scientist of the nineteenth and early twentieth centuries who has not contributed to the development of this argument. Included are Marx (1844/1972), Morgan (1877/1964), Toennies (1887/1963), Durkheim (1897/1951), Weber (1922/1978), Freud (1930/1962), and many others. There is also a specific strand of theorizing that has tied the changing nature of relations between personal behavior

---

working draft by the above authors and G. Boulanger and J. Martin. The author of this chapter acknowledges with gratitude the help of these colleagues. Naturally, the present author bears full responsibility for this version. The research was supported by grants from the National Institute of Mental Health and the Veteran's Administration.

and social structure to the nature of the city and urbanization.

Contemporary network theorists (Kadushin, 1966; Fischer, 1975b; Fischer et al., 1977; Wellman, 1979) have shown that the implication of theorizing by Durkheim (1902/1960), Simmel (1950a), Park (1916/1969), and Wirth (1938) has been to associate urbanization with the weakening of primary relations and the lessening of social ties and thus with lower social density. This situation is said to result in anomie, alienation, and deviant behavior. The evidence is, in fact, mixed. There is indeed an "association between urban residence and unconventionality" (Fischer, 1975a) when the unconventional is defined to include such socially approved behaviors as invention, artistic behavior, and political dissent as well as such obviously disapproved behaviors as crimes against property, alcoholism, and other matters that contravene standard morality. But there is little evidence that city dwellers, with their allegedly low social density, are more likely than rural dwellers to exhibit high rates of alienation or anomie (Fischer, 1975a). On mental health itself, the record is mixed. It remains unclear as to whether there are substantial differences between urban and rural dwellers in their overall rates of mental disorder. Some of the data suggest that rural residents are more likely to suffer from psychoses and urban dwellers are more prone to character disorders and neuroses (Dohrenwend and Dohrenwend, 1974). Other studies suggest that there are no systematic rural-urban differences (Srole, 1980). If social density has increased in modern times, there is no evidence that there has been a parallel increase in rates of psychosis (Goldhammer and Marshall, 1955). Finally, Inkeles and Smith (1974: 264) summarize their findings by saying, "Quite the contrary to popular expectation . . . one is forced to conclude that, if anything holds in this realm, it is that the more modern the individual, the better his psychic adjustment as measured by the Psychosomatic Symptoms Test."

One reason the relation between modernity, urbanization, and personal disorder has been so difficult to demonstrate in any consistent fashion is that the mediating factors have been poorly specified. As a first step, I shall speculate on the way the interpersonal environment (Rossi, 1966; Wallace, 1966) mediates stress reaction and discuss some factors that may, in turn, offset this environment.[3]

By interpersonal environment I mean the set of all persons with whom the focal person directly interacts in some meaningful way. In some terminologies (Mitchell, 1969; Barnes, 1969; Boissevain, 1974), the persons who form a ring about the focal person are called the first-order zone. To be sure, those whom the focal person can reach only through at least one intermediary–the second-order zone–also affect his or her life, but I am trying to simplify. Even so, the individual's entire first-order zone or interpersonal environment may include as many as one or two thousand individuals (Pool and Kochen, 1978). For practical research purposes, therefore, the size of the interpersonal environment must be sharply restricted by focusing only on a few types of relationships. In some studies the research concerns those who contacted the focal respondent or were contacted by the respondent with respect to some particular issue, say birth control (Verbrugge, 1978). In other situations, data are collected on those others who have helped the respondent in a particular situation (McAllister and Fischer, 1978). Typical "sociometric" questions of this kind ask for the respondent's best friend or friends. One might ask for those with whom the respondent plays chess or with whom he or she has any other kind of direct relationship. In this case, I am interested in the respondent's friends at various points in the life course and those to whom he or she turns for help with serious personal problems.

Let us for the moment invoke the classic notion of a traditional or *Gemeinschaft* society, in which everyone knows everyone else and in which, therefore, the interpersonal environment is very dense. Let us contrast this situation with modern *Gesellschaft* society, in which social relations are generally more sparse and in which, therefore, we can expect the immediate interpersonal environment to be less dense. It is possible, however, for a person to live in a modern society and yet also experience a very dense interpersonal environment (Gans, 1962). At the same time, some persons in modern society indeed do have sparse social relations accompanied by an interpersonal environment in which few of their friends know one another. Note that I am talking not about the sheer *number* of friends, but about a structural property of the relationship *between* these friends. Given this lack of a one-to-one correlation between the density of the interpersonal environment and the characteristics of modern life, it is no wonder that it has been next to impossible to produce a clear-cut correlation between modernity and mental health. It is the interpersonal environment within which a person "swims," however, that counts most in establishing levels of mental health.

A Model Linking Stressors, Density, and Stress Reaction

What is it about density that makes it likely to be related to mental health in the first place? The classic literature suggests that if everyone knows everyone else, then norms are more likely to be clear-cut and consistently enforced, and that this clarity is highly beneficial. Thus, density has a direct effect on mental well-being by producing a more benign social environment. But there are also indirect effects. Suppose that for one reason or another, persons do become subject to stressors. Then, in a dense interpersonal environment, there is a greater likelihood that one's friends both are available to give social support and actually do come forth with it. There is considerable evidence that among persons who are stressed, social support with respect to the particular stressful problem results in lowered levels of mental distress, whereas such support is obviously less relevant to those not subjected to stressors (LaRocca et al., 1980).

There has been some controversy in the literature as to whether social support has a direct effect on mental health (Lin et al., 1979; Dean and Lin, 1977; Warren, 1976; Gore, 1980), shows its effects only among those stressed and thus operates as a "coping strategy" (LaRocca et al., 1980), or, indeed, has no effects at all (Pearlin and Schooler, 1978; Gore et al., 1979). Obviously an umbrella term, "social support" has been used to cover a wide variety of perceived or actual social interactions as well as to imply situations in which these interactions are merely possible or in which they are actually facilitated. No wonder findings have been mixed. My present concern is focused. I wish to show that a particular *structural* aspect of the interpersonal environment, social density,[4] is directly related to lowered levels of stress reaction.[5] Whether social density also has indirect effects by creating a situation in which specific helpful interactions are more likely once the respondent has been stressed is another matter, which I shall consider in further work.[6] The stressor used in this study is heavy combat in Vietnam.[7] This stressor is clearly located in time *prior* to any current measurement of stress reaction. Unfortunately, many of the daily life stressors reported in the mental health literature may include ongoing events such as moving to a new home or beginning school. In such cases, specifying a causal sequence that leads from stressor to stress reaction is, to say the least, highly problematic (Boulanger, 1981).

Social density itself can be viewed as a dependent variable as well as one that impacts on the relationship between stressors and reaction to stress. Classical views of social density regard it as dependent on the global characteristics of an entire society. This position does not allow for much variation in social density at the level of individuals. The concept of interpersonal environment, however, does allow for such variation. Most important for the present topic of social density and mental health, it is possible that severe stressors may alter an individual's ability to manage and maintain an integrated interpersonal environment. Low density might therefore be an outcome of the kinds of stressors that also result in lowered levels of mental health. Further, one might expect that persons with more extensive interpersonal environments will have lower social densities in their environments than will persons with more limited interpersonal environments. There are two reasons for this: first, the sheer numbers involved. The larger the environment, the more practical difficulties there are in ensuring that everyone gets to meet everyone else. The generally observed lower densities for large sociomatrices are not only numerical artifacts, but also a social reality. Second, extensive interpersonal environments are likely to encompass many different social worlds or social circles within which relations are likely to be dense but between which there may be few connections (Simmel, 1922/1955b). The "circle phenomenon," therefore, tends to produce interpersonal environments whose *overall* density is low. These facts suggest that persons of higher social class will have lower social densities in their interpersonal environments. First, the higher the class, the more likely that the interpersonal environments will be larger (Boissevain, 1974; Pool and Kochen, 1978). Further, given the nature of modern life, it is the occupational component of class that is most likely to lead to a widespread network. A capitalist might live within the confines of a narrow circle, but a physician must necessarily involve a great many diverse persons in his or her network.

One last and rather obvious candidate for predicting density is the stability of one's friendships.[8] Other things being equal, persons who have had the same friends for many years are also likely to have friends who know one another. Friendship stability may in turn be affected by geographic mobility. On the other hand, friendship stability may be the result of a "corner boy" (Whyte, 1955) style of life rather than merely the outcome of geographic mobility.

Some of the predictors of density may also be predictors of mental health. I have already noted that a severe stress reaction may affect both density and mental health. High occupation is anomalous, since it is predicted to be negatively related to density but most studies have shown it to be positively related to mental health.[9] Stability may promote both density and mental health. The standardized path regression depicted in Figure 7.1 shows the model and the findings for this sample (Table 7.1 presents means, standard deviations, and correlations for the variables in the model).

The main finding of the chapter is contained in the predicted negative association between density of the interpersonal environment and stress reaction. This finding holds true regardless of the occupational standing of the respondent, his exposure to the stress of combat, or the stability of his friendships. The latter two factors also contribute directly to stress reaction, and indirectly, through their influence on interpersonal environment density. In this sample, occupational prestige affects stress reaction only by affecting the density of the interpersonal environment. Some comments on the variables and the model are indicated.

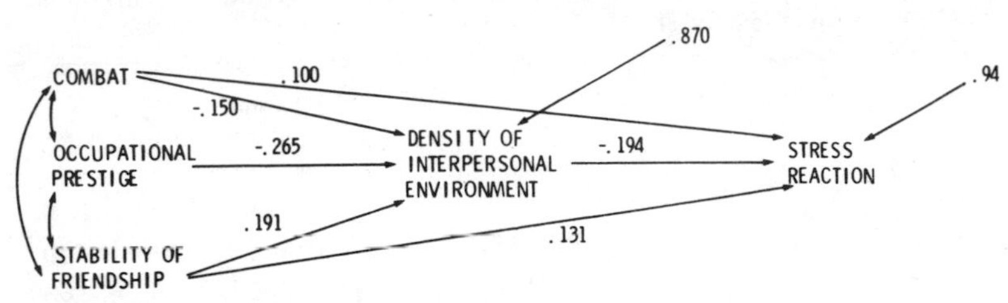

Figure 7.1 Standardized Path Regression Model for Predicting Density and Stress Reaction

It should be noted that the model is more successful in accounting for the variance in density than in stress reaction. This is not surprising, since the variables that predict density are mainly structural and belong to the same system reference as density, whereas stress reaction is an individual psychological variable. Unlike many studies in which coping behavior or indicators of support are themselves psychological variables based on the perceptions of respondents, in the present study the predictors of density have no direct face validity connection with the items that compose the stress reaction scale. I might also note that density is uncorrelated with a measure of social desirability contained in the PERI scales (Dohrenwend and the Social Psychiatry Research Unit, 1977). By and large, the findings are as predicted and are self-evident.

The measure of occupational prestige used is the Duncan occupational prestige scale (Reiss et al., 1961). It performs better than the Edwards (1943) scale, though not by much. Income and education drop out when occupation is introduced into the equation, suggesting that the theory that specifies occupation per se rather than class in general is correct. Occupation does not in this sample relate to stress reaction, though it does so in most studies. Nor does weighting the sample change the picture. There seems no obvious explanation of why occupation is unrelated to stress reaction in the present sample, though the narrow age range may partly account for the lack of a relationship.

Stability of friendship does exhibit the surprising characteristic of being positively related to high stress reaction. I interpret this finding as an indication that in the Northeast, stability, in part, indicates a "stick-in-the-mud" mentality and thus indicates the possession of few resources. Almost half of the sample has at least one friend left over from boyhood days, a surprisingly high proportion. It should be remembered that Brooklyn is in many respects a middle-sized city with strong ethnic and neighborhood traditions. The film *Saturday Night Fever* gives a good sense of

TABLE 7.1 Means, Standard Deviations, and Correlations of Variables in the Model

	Mean	*Standard Deviation*	*N*
Combat	.592	.325	360
Occupational prestige	47.033	24.608	360
Stability of friendship	.472	.500	360
Density	.592	.325	360
Stress reaction	10.012	1.002	360

Correlation Matrix

Correlation (Significance)

	Combat	*Occupational Prestige*	*Stability of Friendship*	*Density*	*Stress Reaction*
Combat		–.078 (.071)	.011 (.416)	–.129 (.007)	.126 (.008)
Occupational prestige			.024 (.323)	–.251 (<.001)	.015 (.391)
Stability of friendship				.192 (<.001)	.095 (.036)
Density					–.181 (<.001)

what many of the men in the sample were like. Lower Westchester County and Bridgeport are similar to Brooklyn, being "middle-sized." Thus, I do not expect the relation between stability and stress reaction necessarily to hold in the rest of the country, though its presence in this sample reveals much about the nature of the locale and the young men within it. Though it is not included in Figure 7.1, geographic mobility does slightly affect stability ($r = .124$, significant at the .01 level), but its effect on density washes out when stability of friendship is introduced; and geographic mobility also has no direct effect on stress reaction.

A number of logical candidates for inclusion in these equations failed. Included in the set of poor predictors for this sample are race (no relation to density and poor relation to stress reaction, once other variables are introduced), the number of friends, and age.

Discussion

The relation between high social density of the interpersonal environment and lowered stress reaction has been demonstrated, at least for young men in some moderately sized urban areas, some of whom were exposed to traumatic stress. Further, it has been shown that density is itself a consequence of a stressor, when the stressor has clearly taken place prior to current social density. Consistent with theory, a position in society that allows for extended social relations also leads to lower levels of social density, but not necessarily to higher levels of stress reaction. This suggests that future work in exploring density and mental health should take into account the Simmel hypothesis that metropolitan residents may belong to several circles, each of which may have minimal overlap with the others. This phenomenon is more likely, I suspect, for persons of high occupational levels. Once the overlap or lack of overlap of circles is taken into account, density may not be associated with occupational level.

The fact that I have demonstrated direct effects for stress on social density and on mental health does not rule out interaction effects between the stressor and density. The larger social context may well affect the relationship between density and mental health. Whether high density implies a high level of social support, a high level of normative consistency, or both may very much depend on the context. It is possible, for example, that in large metropolitan areas (without taking the multiple circle phenomenon into account), normative consistency on neighborhood issues but not on more general political or emotional issues does not necessarily lead to social support with respect to mental health problems. Some urban circles may be knowledgeable and supportive with respect to mental health issues but others may not be (Kadushin, 1968). Thus we might find interaction effects for social density and a stressor; such effects might be indicative of the fact that the density of the general interpersonal environment leads to emotional support as well as to general normative consistency in smaller cities and perhaps in rural areas, but not in large, undifferentiated metropolitan areas.

NOTES

1. Social density means meaningful relations, not physical crowding or proximity. Hence, propositions and literature on the relation (or lack of relation) between crowding and mental health is basically beside the point in the present discussion. See Gove and Hughes (1980a, 1980b) and Booth et al. (1980a, 1980b) for a discussion of some current issues in crowding and mental health.

2. To maximize the efficiency of a small sample, the design called for an even split between Vietnam-era veterans and nonveterans, between men under 29 and

those over 29 years in age, and between blacks and whites. Veterans were split between those who served in Vietnam and those who did not. Nonveterans were split between college- and noncollege-educated men. Telephone screening from recent reverse directories was used to obtain a probability sample of men who met the desired characteristics. The overall refusal rate for men with these characteristics was 30 percent. Interviews lasted approximately four hours and respondents were paid $20. While the sample can be weighted to reflect the "true" nature of the population (as revealed by the screening interviews), this analysis is presented unweighted in order to "control" for some of the key variables known to affect the behavior of the Vietnam generation. The additional 1001 men were sampled in 1979 in Chicago, South Bend, rural Indiana, Atlanta, Columbus (Georgia), rural Georgia, and Los Angeles. For further details of the sample in the Northeast, see Vietnam Era Research Project (1979) and Fine et al. (1979).

3. Rossi is noted as having publicly used the term "interpersonal environment" in 1966. In fact, he coined the term in unpublished memoranda of the Bureau of Applied Social Research in the 1950s. The concept grew from the Bureau's interests in "personal influence" and in the use of survey research to measure the impact of significant others on various decision-making processes in studies of voting and other situations.

4. The method used to collect density of the interpersonal environment follows the techniques reported in Shulman (1976) and McAllister and Fischer (1978). Claude Fischer first brought these methods to my attention and he and Norman Shulman each graciously made available to me the research instruments they were developing. In the present application, up to fifteen names of friends were solicited: the three best friends when the respondent was 18, the three buddies in the military or an equivalent time period for civilians; the person who found the respondent his present job, the person with whom the respondent lives (usually the spouse), four current friends, and three Vietnam veteran friends. The current personal environment obviously excludes the first two *relationships,* though the same *person* could conceivably fall into all six types of relations. The maximum number in the current interpersonal environment is therefore 9 and has in this sample a mean of 5.3. In addition to a number of questions about the characteristics of these friends, respondents were shown a matrix of their friends' names and asked to indicate with an "X" who knows who. Density is the number of connections indicated divided by the number possible given the size of the current interpersonal environment of the respondent. Because of the limits of human interaction, the more persons one knows, the lower the density. Controlling for size of the interpersonal environment does not, however, affect my results. Hence, to equalize the size of the environment for married or single persons, the spouse or partner was excluded from the density calculations. Otherwise I would also enter into a discussion of the support system of marriage, a topic for another paper.

5. The present stress reaction scale represents an attempt to subset from the PERI scales (Dohrenwend and the Social Psychiatry Research Unit, 1977; Dohrenwend, 1979) those items which DSM III (American Psychiatric Association, 1980) notes as indicative of Post Traumatic Stress Disorder, the mental measure of major concern to a study of Vietnam-era men. The items are listed in the appendix. The scale has a reliability (alpha) of .88. The items were selected from the PERI items by G. Boulanger and A. Egendorf. L. M. Roth scaled the items. We are grateful to Bruce and Barbara Dohrenwend for making the PERI scales available to use while they were being developed. G. Boulanger (1981) has developed a different scale, administered in the 1001 further interviews, that more directly measures the symptoms noted by DSM III. While the analysis presented here is similar when the more general mental

health measures developed by the Dohrenwends from the PERI scales are used, the "Stress" measure is, as one would expect, more sensitive to the impact of combat.

6. Demonstrating interaction effects requires a larger sample and a wider variety of social contexts than are now available to me with the sample of 380 men from the Northeast of the United States. The present data do not show clear interaction effects. Only 40 of the 380 respondents were subjected to heavy combat. I expect that the additional 1000 cases collected from other parts of the country may prove helpful in teasing out interaction effects, if any, between social density, the stressor, and stress reaction.

7. Since combat in Vietnam had no "front line" as it is commonly understood, an index has to be created. It is defined as the sum of the following experiences, weighted by the number of times they were experienced: receiving incoming fire; receiving sniper fire; encountering mines, boobytraps, or ambush; being wounded or seeing people killed; and various ways of engaging the enemy. The index is for present purposes dichotomized as a "dummy variable" defined for all men, including nonveterans.

8. Stability is measured as the percentage of one's current friends who were also one's friends at age 18. Since only a few values are possible here, given a maximum of four current friends, the measure is dichotomized into (0) no current friends were also given as friends at age 18, and (1) at least some current friends were also friends when the respondent was 18.

9. Though entering the military during this time period is class-related, being in heavy combat is not highly related to class, since some officers volunteered for combat to advance their careers. Thus, among men who were in Vietnam, high class is slightly associated with high combat. Overall, the relation between combat and class for men in the Northeast (weighted or unweighted) is negligible. The same is true for occupation, current or parental. Thus, the relation between density and occupation in this study is not spurious.

APPENDIX:
STRESS SCALE (alpha = .88)

- How often in the last 12 months have you felt angry?
- How often in the last 12 months have you felt like a powder keg ready to explode?
- How often in the last 12 months have you gotten easily irritated?
- Now, if you go back more than 12 months, was there ever a time when you felt extremely angry?
- In the last 12 months, how often have you had personal worries that get you down physically, that is, made you physically ill?
- How often in the last 12 months have you feared something terrible would happen to you?
- How often in the last 12 months have you felt anxious or tense?
- How often in the last 12 months have you been bothered by feelings of restlessness?
- How often in the last 12 months have you feared being left all alone or abandoned?

- How often in the last 12 months have you felt you deserved to be punished?
- How often in the last 12 months have you felt guilty about things you do or don't do?
- How often in the last 12 months have you blamed yourself for everything that went wrong?
- How often in the last 12 months have you felt like crying?
- How often in the last 12 months have you been in very low or low spirits?
- How often in the last 12 months have you felt completely helpless?
- How often in the last 12 months have you felt completely hopeless about everything?
- Did you *ever* think about taking your own life?
- How often in the last 12 months have you been bothered by cold sweats?
- How often in the last 12 months did your hands ever tremble enough to bother you?
- In the last 12 months, how often have you had trouble with your heart beating hard when you were *not* exerting yourself?
- In the last 12 months, how often have you had chest pains?
- During the last 12 months, how often have you had shortness of breath when you were *not* exerting yourself?
- How often in the last 12 months have you felt that people were trying to cheat you?
- How often in the last 12 months have you felt that people avoid you?
- How often in the last 12 months have you felt that people dislike you?
- How often in the last 12 months have you felt that people were trying to pick quarrels or start arguments with you?
- In the last 12 months, how often have you had the following difficulties in sex: Having no interest in sex? Getting no pleasure from sex? Trouble getting or keeping an erection? Trouble in reaching climax?
- How many times have you been in a physical fight in the last five years?
- Did you ever hurt a person you were fighting with pretty badly?
- Have you ever had anything in your hands, like a knife or a stick or a gun, during a fight?

8

Networks, Ideologies, and Belief Systems

BONNIE H. ERICKSON

This chapter discusses two important and frequently confused aspects of the effects of network structure on attitudes. On the one hand, structure is related to attitude agreement, as in the familiar finding of agreement within cliques. On the other hand, networks with a particular range of structures can give rise to belief systems. Belief systems will receive special attention because they are a more complex and less well understood topic, but their analysis presupposes arguments and concepts from the analysis of attitude agreement.

A belief system is an organized diversity of attitudes, or a number of opinions on multiple issues that can be summed up by a few underlying dimensions. Converse (1964) argues that the members of the U.S. political elite shared a belief system with just one major dimension, the liberal-conservative axis. For each issue, alternative positions are judged more or less liberal and people choose the position closest to their own liberal-conservative identifications. Since liberal people tend to take the liberal positions, moderates adopt the moderate views, and conservatives choose conservative options, issue positions are highly correlated over people. Thus, a single dimension captures most of the variance in opinions. Belief systems may have more than one dimension so long as a small number of dimensions sums up most of the variation in views. For example, the U.S. political elite data used by Converse proved to have three dimensions when later factor analyzed (Kritzer, 1978). Clearly, organization is a matter of degree. At its lowest degree, attitudes are random and no *system* of beliefs exists.

Belief systems are an important aspect of culture wherever they exist. The importance of U.S. political belief systems, in particular, is clear from the extent of the related literature and from the theoretically central themes addressed. For example, Converse (1964) argues that an individual's knowledge of the liberal-conservative dimension is crucial for effective political choices, while Sartori (1969) argues that belief systems primarily benefit the elites who create and control them. At the individual or the structural level, belief systems play a central part in discussions of how politics works. Since interest in this particular kind of belief system is great and the empirical and conceptual materials are relatively extensive, I will use it as the primary example throughout this chapter. However, the same kind of analysis can be used for subcultures generally (Mueller and Judd, 1981).

The vast literature stemming from Converse's work has one curious and important thin area. Very little has been said about the possible structural bases of belief systems or the kinds of social network structure that would permit development of a belief system. Since scholars in other areas (such as Mueller and Judd, 1981) are beginning to adopt the procedures and concepts developed in this literature, they, too, may neglect structural aspects of this problem. In this chapter I argue that belief systems do have characteristic structural foundations, and the available evidence is consistent with this view, though not appropriately designed to test it. I will begin with a brief review of the essential points from existing literature and then turn to a more structural approach and its contributions.

Political Belief Systems in the United States

Converse (1964) defines a belief system as a set of ideas and attitudes somehow constrained to vary together. Such constraint is not usually a matter of logic, since many combinations of ideas are logically possible and can be linked by a plausible argument with sufficient ingenuity. Constraint usually has social sources: Some ideas or attitudes go together because they are in the interests of people in shared structural locations and/or because they have been plausibly linked by ideological innovators and then have diffused as a package. Constrained belief systems tend to be stable over time, since a change in just a few elements would create perceived inconsistencies for the individual, while change to another constrained combination would require a major reorientation. Stability is especially strong for the more central items that provide the unifying themes in the system. For the more well educated and politically well informed, the central items in political belief systems are useful abstractions, most notably the liberal-conservative dimension. For those less able to use abstractions, the central items may be attitudes toward concrete groups like classes, political parties, or races. For those still less sophisticated, the central ideas are still less general—for example, party evaluations may be discussed in terms of one or two narrow issues. Finally, some people have no policy orientations at all. The more analytically a person's political ideas are organized, the more efficiently he or she can evaluate and remember political information and the more easily he or she can make political decisions consistently and appropriately. Thus, the more analytic the organization, the more constrained the political attitudes (one can readily predict one issue position from another), the more consistent the person's party choice with issue position, and the more consistent party choice with class.

Now the greater the education and political involvement, the greater is political information, including information about analytic dimensions currently organizing issue positions. Further, the higher the education, the more directly a person has access to the elite circles in which idea packages and their rationales are generated. Thus, more educated people have more specific items of political information, more understanding of what issue positions go together and why, more constraint in their own views, a more analytic basis for this constraint, and more appropriate political choices. In particular, political elites have levels of analytic constraint dramatically different from those of mass publics. Elite members may not realize just how dramatic the differences are, since they interact largely with other elite or higher-status people who also use the same abstract organization of political ideas. In fact, the bulk of the mass public consists of people with very little, if any, abstract grasp of politics and very little, if any, constraint of issue positions.

Converse marshaled survey data to support a number of points in this argument. Respondents were coded in terms of use of more or less abstract ideas in open-ended comments on politics; few of them used the most abstract (the liberal-conservative dimension). This measure was related to years of formal education and political activity, as well as the strength of relationship between class and vote. The survey respondents were also contrasted as an aggregate, the mass public, with an elite sample of congressional candidates. The elite sample showed much stronger constraint, that is, correlations among issue positions and between issue positions and party identifications. To counter the possible objection that mass publics may include a variety of idea organizations concealed by aggregation, Converse argues that any form of organization should lead to stability; but a panel study shows that mass attitudes are not very stable over three waves of interviews two years apart. He had no corresponding data for elites, but a later study of an Italian political elite group (Putnam et al., 1979) did show considerable stability of opinions over time.

Converse's work has stimulated a blizzard of methodological, historical, and analytic debate. As methodological examples, Smith (1980) shows that measures of levels of abstraction have poor test-retest reliability; many (especially Bennett, 1975) note that Converse examined constraint for a small and perhaps biased set of issues; others note that correlational measures of constraint can produce artifacts (Barton and Parsons, 1977; Weissberg, 1976). Historically, Nie et al. (1976) argue that Converse happened to have data on a period when mass belief systems were weak because the salience of political events was low. More recently, constraint in mass samples has increased because political events have been more dramatic and related issues have been more coherently packaged by major political actors and the media. Nie et al. have their own critics. For example, there is some doubt whether any change has actually occurred since key questionnaire items are not fully comparable over time (see Sullivan et al., 1979; Bishop et al., 1979). Bennett (1975) sums up some of the major analytic criticisms. Converse evaluates mass ideas in terms of their similarity to the belief systems of elites; of course, such similarity is related to social proximity to elites (indicated by education) and self-exposure to elite ideas (indicated by political involvement). But mass publics may include subsets of people with belief systems different from those of the elite, yet in no way inferior. Converse rules out this possibility only by showing that mass attitudes fluctuate over time, but (1) this aggregate result may conceal substantial stability within subgroups with nonelite views, and (2) stability is a poor measure of belief system structure. Nonelite individuals may have views organized by psychological constraints, while nonelite groups and communication networks may have views organized by social constraints. Alternative possible organizations have not been sought in a suitable manner, which Bennett tries to develop for individuals.

Some Gaps in the Current Literature

All participants in this debate have studied not the mass public so much as a nonelite that has been "massified" methodologically. Nonelite respondents are survey respondents, studied without information about the potentially salient social networks in which they are embedded. By contrast, the elite respondents are always taken from a clearly salient network rooted in parties (consider Converse's congressional candidates) or informal ties (Moore, 1979). Social organization is an obvious possible source of attitude organization, yet discussions of mass-elite differences persistently neglect network structure in favor of individual characteristics, such as education or amounts of political information. Here I will start to fill this gap with a heuristic discussion of structural bases of belief systems.

Past discussions have also confounded two quite distinct aspects of attitude organization. The first is similarity of attitude positions, or the extent to which people hold the same views. The second is similarity of attitude structure, or the extent to which people organize their views in terms of a shared set of underlying dimensions. It is possible for people to be similar in either respect while dissimilar in the other. For example, the members of Converse's elite sample shared a liberal-conservative dimension but occupied quite various positions on it, so that they shared attitude structure but not specific opinions. On the other hand, people may agree on a set of specific positions yet think of these as points in different attitude spaces. Similarity of position has been confounded with similarity of structure because both fit one original (Converse, 1964) definition of constraint: Both permit the analyst to predict all of a person's attitudes, given knowledge of some. But the two forms of attitude organization are conceptually distinct and also have distinct structural sources. I shall review the structural sources of attitude agreement, developing some ideas necessary in the ensuing discussion of structural sources of a shared attitude space.

Structural Sources of Similarity of Attitude Positions

Elsewhere (Erickson, forthcoming) I have argued that attitude agreement is related to structural position because structure channels and modifies interpersonal processes, especially the social comparison processes, which play a major role in attitude formulation and change. Different models of structure emphasize different aspects of social networks, and therefore lead to somewhat different predictions for attitude agreement.

Social comparison (Festinger, 1954; Suls and Miller, 1977) occurs when people are not certain of the correctness of their attitudes. Lacking an objective standard of judgment, people perforce evaluate their existing attitudes or alternative possible attitudes by comparison with those of suitable other people. Broadly speaking, "suitable" others are those similar in respects salient to the attitudinal topic, or those to whom one is strongly attracted. The person comparing is motivated to agree with the comparison others, for only then can he or she reduce initial uncertainty and the resulting discomfort. Thus, one can predict attitude agreement by predicting patterns of social comparison, which in turn derive from patterns of social relationships.

Existing social comparison theory has little to say about network structure, but is instead confined to laboratory investigations of the responses of strangers or to a modest number of field studies of dyads and cliques. However, the theory can be extended by combining it with currently available models of overall network structure. One kind of model emphasizes detection of cliques, or sets of people who are relatively densely tied to each other. The greater the density in a clique (that is, the more of the possible ties that actually exist), the more likely it is that clique members will use each other as suitable comparison others. They will do so because they are available (social comparison rarely occurs in any consequential way between strangers), because they are attracted to each other (density tends to increase the strength of dyadic ties and of the overall attractivensss of the group itself), and because they have opportunities to compare salient attitudes (clique density tends to increase communication volume). Further, the multiple redundant paths of communication in a dense clique increase the accuracy with which attitudes of others are perceived and hence increase the agreement of one person's attitude with another's, as opposed to the agreement of one with the perhaps incorrectly perceived views of the other. See Cartwright (1968) on clique properties and Festinger et al. (1950) for an empirical example of the correlation of density and agreement.

Another kind of model emphasizes similarity of structural position. People in structurally equivalent positions may not have any direct ties to each other (quite unlike a clique), but they do have very similar patterns of ties to third parties. For example, the peripheral members of a core-periphery system may share asymmetric ties to the core and an absence of ties with each other. (For a more extensive contrast of clique and structural equivalence models, see White et al., 1976; Burt, 1980c). Since equivalent people have ties to similar others, they are likely to compare with similar others, and therefore to be similar in their attitudes. The similarity is greater if people are densely tied as well as equivalent. If their density is very low, then they cannot coordinate their individual selections of comparison others and may well select differently, in line with differences in salient attributes. Density also increases agreement by facilitating direct social comparison within a set of equivalent people, much as for cliques.

Social networks may also be modeled as social spaces, with people closer in the space if they are more strongly tied in the social network. Since attraction is a basis of social comparison choices, those closer in space should agree more in their attitudes. For a more extended discussion of these models and their implications, including the complications raised in considering asymmetry and multiplexity, see Erickson (forthcoming).

Attitude Agreement in Politics

The literature on political belief systems has many examples of constraint, in the sense of similar attitude positions, which appear to be products of structural effects like those outlined above. For example, Weissberg (1976) reports that blacks have more agreement on civil rights issues than whites, consistent with the relatively homogeneous structural positions of blacks and their more extensive density of ties based in civil rights activist networks. McClosky et al. (1960) report data showing that the leaders of a party agree with each other more than the followers do, consistent with the greater density of ties to be expected among leaders.

Occupants of a social location, whether a clique or block, often have a characteristic profile of opinions. I suggest that we call any such profile an "ideology." At first glance, this definition may seem to remove all the romance from ideology. But the proposal has the substantial advantages of objectivity and sociological focus, while many traditional definitions are evaluative and individualistic. Converse, for example, argues that an ideologue uses an abstract dimension in a fully conscious manner and is stable in opinions. Some components of this view are arguable and, indeed, much-criticized evaluations. Is stability a sign of clear thinking, or merely rigidity? Is a left-right dimension more abstract than a group-interest organization, or merely more conventional? Some components of this view raise intractable measurement problems. Given the relationship between formal education and ability to articulate views in a standard interview, it is as hard to measure the consciousness of ideology fairly as it is to develop a culture-free intelligence test. Thus, biases of measurement are added to subjectivity of evaluative criteria. More generally, there is no objective way to assess the ideological status of an individual's opinions. But for a set of people we can objectively measure interpersonal agreement.

Some traditional sociological analyses have used sets of people as units but have defined these sets more categorically than structurally, thus missing the concrete structural units within which agreement is generated. By contrast, Brym (1978) describes the highly varied political beliefs within a rather narrowly defined category, Russian Jewish intellectuals. He shows that these beliefs were related to the social networks in which the intellectuals were embedded. Here I argue that the presence and consistency of an ideology should be examined within structural units specified by the above theory of structural sources of agreement.

The Structural Basis of the U.S. Elite Belief System

Let us now turn to attitude constraint in the second sense, that is, the sharing of a common attitude structure rather than similar specific positions. While similarity of attitude positions would be measured by a lack of variation in opinions, similarity of attitude structure would be measured by the amount of variation accounted for by a small number of underlying dimensions. Converse's (1964) analysis of persons in the U.S. political elite indicates that much of the variation in their views is explained by a liberal-conservative dimension. He argues that social sources of such orderliness include structurally vested interests, with ideas covarying because they serve the interests of the same people. This alone is not sufficient, however, because perceived interests can vary and also the overall pattern of self-interested views may be far from simple. Most important, Converse argues that the core abstractions in a belief system can only be made by unusually creative individuals, from whom they diffuse to others, with diffusion most rapid and complete for the most educated and interested. Thus, he finally emphasizes individual variables, with their stratification hierarchies being the only macrosociological element seriously considered. Even given this view, however, structural analysis is essential because of its importance for perceptions (even of ideological innovators) and diffusion.

I contend that belief systems are most likely to emerge in social networks with a particular range of structures. A shared attitude space requires both disagreement (else there is no variation to speak of and hence no dimensions) and agreement on the basic issues underlying the different views (else there is too much variation for a few dimensions to summarize). These requirements are most likely to be met in social structures that simultaneously provide secure social bases for differing opinions *and* extensive connectedness of these bases. A network including distinct cliques or blocks can support differing attitudes, as argued above.

If representatives of these different opinion pools interact frequently, they will gradually develop generalizations summing up the patterns of disagreement they observe, and these generalizations are the basis for the dimensions in a shared attitude space.

The U.S. elite appears to have just this kind of structure as well as this kind of attitude space. National leaders in the early 1970s (Moore, 1979) had both small, specialized cliques and extensive connectedness, including one large, central circle with representatives from all major segments of the country. Barton (1974) reports considerable attitudinal differences between segment representatives in this elite. These differences are maintained both by the smaller cliques within the elite and by external support from their publics. These differences are also communicated and discussed as elite members meet, so that elites come to agree on the nature of their most basic disagreements. Much the same structure probably held for the earlier (and entirely political) elite studied by Converse (1964), for members of this elite are compelled to represent and form alliances and yet also interact with other members with different issue stances.

The Emergence of a Belief System

Consider any network in which subunits are distinctly bounded, yet connected. As people involved in interunit links interact with each other, they have opportunities to observe the covariation of those attitudes that differ from one subunit to another and that are salient in the network context so that they are likely to be discussed or revealed sooner or later. Whether or not people are consciously aware of these patterns, they come to take them for granted as the natural state of affairs. They have frequently seen that people who believe X also believe Y; thus, they assume X and Y belong together. Exceptions to the overall correlations of attitudes may be numerous to start with, but once the correlations are taken for granted the exceptions seem dissonant or imbalanced. Exceptions thus become less common, the correlations seem even more natural because they become stronger, and the patterns of relationships among attitudes thus simplify so that much of their variation can be summed up in a space of a modest number of dimensions.[1]

This is why experiments in balance or dissonance are often successful, even though there is no general way to define balance or dissonance. The experimenters, as members of the same social settings as their subjects, know what "naturally" goes together. This is also why attitude scales are so easy and popular to construct; again, the investigator defines sets of related attitudes in ways similar to those of the other members of his or her social world. Such scales will usually be stable over moderately long time periods in the same social setting, but they can vary greatly over major cleavages in network boundaries, if the argument above is correct; indeed, attitude scales tend to be useful over time in the population for which they were constructed, but they often transfer poorly from one population to another.

A more subtle aspect of the emergence of an attitude space is suggested by an experiment by Tesser (1971). He asked subjects to give their attitudes on a variety of topics and to arrange them in related sets. Later these subjects were given attitude profiles apparently belonging to other people but in fact manipulated to be more or less similar to a subject's own answers in one of two senses: similar in specific attitudes, or similar in attitude structure. A profile similar in attitude structure had internal consistency on attitudes the respondent thought were related, though the consistency could take the form of uniform agreement or of disagreement with the respondent's own positions. People similar in attitudes or in attitude structure were rated more attractive than those dissimilar in either respect. People similar in attitude structure were also rated consistent, predictable, and intelligent. Now people who disagree but share an attitude space have similarity of attitude structure in Tesser's sense. Therefore, they are likely to find each other attractive interaction partners, and interaction between disagreeing people is an essential component in maintaining an attitude space. Further, the attractiveness of attitude-structure similarity suggests that interactants would approve of and hence reinforce this structure in each other, even while disagreeing on attitudes.

In political networks, anecdotal materials include numerous examples of political opponents who think well of each other and enjoy discussing political matters with each other. Opponents sometimes "speak a common language" and thus find each other attractive and rewarding interaction partners, at times even more rewarding than others with whom they agree on more positions but with whom they do not share a framework for discussion.

Effects of Different Network Structures

If a network includes fully connected but distinct subunits, then, as argued above, an attitude space will emerge. In large networks, some members of subunits may not have ties to other units and hence may not be directly involved in the processes described. They must then acquire the emerging attitude space (or its foundation, information about correlations

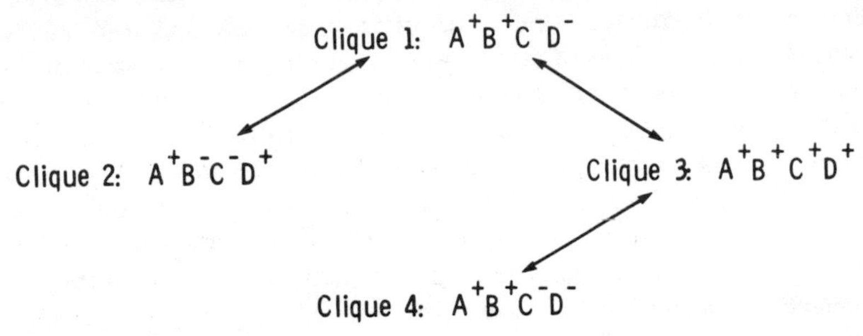

Figure 8.1

among attitudes) from others in more integrative positions. It is at this point that Converse's argument enters the picture. The U.S. political elite links representatives of various interests and publics and generates dimensions summarizing the major attitudinal disagreements of the day; then, as Converse argues, these dimensions diffuse to varying degrees to others. The present argument differs in emphasizing the relational aspects of this diffusion, which are not likely to be dependent merely on the individual traits that Converse emphasizes. Even those traits that are relevant may have some network sources; for example, Coser (1975) argues that analytic sophistication is a product of the complexity of role sets. The present argument also differs in predicting that nonelite networks will often have belief systems of their own, provided only that the networks have the appropriate structure and the analyst does the fieldwork necessary to identify issues salient in that network. In one instructive study, Luttbeg (1968) factor analyzed positions on ten local issues for an elite and a nonelite sample from two Oregon communities. The amount of variance explained by extracted factors differed little between elites and nonelites, or between more and less politically involved nonelites. This study comes closer than Converse's to a comparison of elite and nonelite networks, because the nonelite populations were relatively small.

Next, consider networks with distinct subunits, only some of which are connected to each other. People in different subunits may then observe different attitude correlations and hence abstract different dimensions. Consider a hypothetical example showing the average positions for four cliques on four attitudes, A through D (see Figure 8.1). Members of clique 3 will perceive that "everyone," or all their potential social comparitors or reference groups, is for A and for B, which then play no part in their attitude space because of insufficient variation. Clique 3 members will also perceive that it is natural and appropriate to be for C and D, or against both. Members of clique 4 will share the resulting attitude space of one dimension, C^-D^- to C^+D^+. Members of clique 2, on the other hand, will see A^+ and C^- as common ground, while B^+D^- to B^-D^+ form a different one-dimensional space. Finally, members of clique 1 can take only A^+ as given and observe no uniform correlations among B, C, and D so that their attitude space may have three dimensions. Thus, both the nature and the number of dimensions could vary and the network as a whole may not generate a single, uniform attitude space.

The sparser the links between subunits, the less likely it is that an attitude space will emerge. In the extreme, a network with some unconnected regions, the lack of interunit links implies the absence of any interpersonal mechanisms for the development of a shared belief system. One example is the mutual incomprehensibility of fieldworker and members of another culture, who at first find each other bizarre and unpredictable because neither side knows how the other's culture packages ideas.

An attitude space may also fail to emerge if links between subunits are *too* numerous, so that subunit boundaries are indistinct and the network is in effect one large clique. By the processes outlined in the first half of this chapter, such a network may develop such uniformity of attitudes that there is not enough variation to form a space. Some possible political examples are discussed in Barton and Parsons (1977), Mueller and Judd (1981), and Weissberg (1976).

Effects of Types of Ties and Roles

Attitude agreement results from processes that vary with the types of relationship involved. Most notably, social comparison takes place more often the more strong and positive a relationship is. A shared attitude space, however, results from processes of observation and generalization that can occur in a wider variety of relationships. Conflict between subunits of a network may well prevent attitudinal agreement between them or even increase their disagreements through negative comparison with outgroups, but it need not prevent the emergence of a shared belief system. It may do so in extreme cases, when conflict escalates to the point that communication effectively ceases (Coleman, 1957). But, as Simmel (1955a) points out, conflict is usually a mutually socializing experience.

Contending parties must attend to each other's positions and must engage in some forms of interaction.

Interaction and mutual attention are facilitated by several factors when present. The conflicting parties may exist within a shared institutional framework, as the U.S. political elite works within a political structure and set of rules of the game supported by all. The contenders may share superordinate goals (for their role, see Sherif et al., 1961), as the U.S. political elite agrees on the importance of peace or full employment, though not on just how to achieve these. Parties to a conflict may yet share some vested interests, as persons in the U.S. political elite share a stake in their high positions. Finally, opponents may be partially united through cross-cutting ties, as the U.S. political elite includes people who are opponents on some issues but allies on others and people who belong to some networks in common.

Converse implies the importance of a special role, that of ideological innovator, credited with the creation of belief systems. People performing this role observe major dimensions of disagreement, abstract them, articulate them, and provide a rationale. Converse does not discuss the structural position such people might have. From the current point of view, such people might be occupants of a position (White et al., 1976) with extensive links to a variety of network subunits. Such a position would permit easy observation of existing nascent dimensions, as well as fostering analytic orientations (Coser, 1975). People in positions with more limited external linkages may still be creative but may well create generalizations based only on their special perspective (see the preceding section), which therefore will have little appeal to other network members. Ideological innovation leading to a shared belief system is thus perhaps most likely for people both talented and well located. If so, then the production of belief systems by elites is a function not simply of their individual training and ability, but also of their pivotal social location. Structurally similar people in nonelite networks may also produce belief systems that are less well known to us, simply because these networks have less access to the media and other avenues of ideological dissemination.

Conclusions and Discussion

I have argued for some major conceptual and theoretical revisions to Converse's (1964) analysis of belief systems. First, one should distinguish the two topics confounded by the original usage of the term "constraint," that is, the predictability of one attitude from another. One may be able to predict attitudes because people in a social location have very similar attitudes, or what I have called an ideology. Alternatively, one may be able to predict attitudes because people in a network share an attitude space, which I have called a belief system. Second, in either case one should trace the ideology or belief system to its structural roots. I have argued that ideologies are most likely for cliques or structurally equivalent sets of people, especially if these cliques or sets have high density. Belief systems, on the other hand, are most likely for complex networks containing distinct but interconnected subgroups of people with differing attitudes.

Wherever belief systems do emerge, they are important because they are consequential social facts. They are external to individuals, being founded in and shared in a network. They are constraining upon individuals, who experience imbalance or dissonance in the face of attitude combinations not part of their belief systems. Individuals also use attitude spaces to organize their perceptions. The importance of this use is suggested by the distress and disorientation experienced when an established framework breaks down (see Kadushin, 1974: 78-80).

What is constraint for individuals is also facilitation for many important social processes. To continue in Durkheimian language, a shared belief system is a kind of precontractual element, an often unacknowledged but essential precondition for such processes as routinized conflict, negotiation, exchange, and the definition and resolution of issues. The reader will find models of many of these processes in the next part of this volume (see Cook, Knoke and Laumann, and Marsden). All of these processes require complex communication and mutual predictability, both facilitated by a shared attitude space. For example, such a space defines the issues that belong together and hence should be negotiated together, and it permits people to predict that an opponent (or ally) holding some views will also hold other, related ones. Thus it would be useful to have structural research on both the sources and effects of belief systems, in addition to the heretofore more popular research on attitude agreement.

NOTE

1. Abelson (1979) offers an alternative, more formal model deriving belief systems from networks. He assumes that people who communicate more effectively become more similar, separately for each kind of opinion. Since opinion on each topic becomes more and more similar within clusters of people, opinions become correlated over clusters. Eventually, the links between clusters lead to a complete homogenization in which everyone agrees. His model differs in that (1) it is suggested for any connected network of any structure, (2) it includes no role for actor perceptions of opinion correlations and resulting balance processes, and (3) it offers no mechanism for stable belief systems enduring for some substantial period of time.

III.

Purposive Action in Social Networks

Numerous important theoretical works in sociology (for example, Parsons, 1951; Collins, 1975) have dealt with the tension between the purposefulness, intentionality, and creativity of individual actors in attempting to realize goals or interests and the constraints imposed on such action by preexisting structures of social relations. The chapters in this part are all concerned with the interplay of social structure and purposive action; they deal with issues concerning the creation of social networks and the use of networks as social resources in exchange and collective action.

Cook's chapter suggests that exchange theory constitutes a framework within which many of the questions of interest to network analysts can be formulated. She argues that microlevel processes of social exchange can serve as a basis for understanding social networks as structures of resource dependency. Her paper reviews the basic concepts used in her work with Emerson on exchange theory and the relation of these to network concepts. She then discusses results of the experimental work done by her research team on power and network position, power and network centrality, commitment, and power redistribution mechanisms. Cook closes with a consideration of forms of exchange other than those examined in her

EDITORS' NOTE: These introductory remarks are in part patterned after the comments made by James S. Coleman, at the Albany Conference on Contributions of Networks Analysis to Structural Sociology, on presentations of the authors of the chapters in Part III. Of course, the editors take full responsibility for the descriptions and comments made here.

experiments to date: agent-mediated exchanges, in which some actors act on behalf of others, and systems of generalized and productive exchange.

The relationship between power and network centrality with which Cook deals is also a theme of Marsden's chapter. He suggests that when exchanges among a set of actors must be conducted using only a restricted set of the possible linkages among them, at least two types of purposive action by strategically positioned actors are possible: exploitative and brokerage behavior. Here, he focuses on brokerage behavior, in which actors on indirect channels between others lacking direct access to one another arrange transactions for those other actors, in return for resource commissions. This process is formulated as an extension of Coleman's (1973a) mathematical model of purposive action. Marsden's simulation results indicate that power gains through brokerage accrue to those actors central in the senses of betweenness and closeness (see Freeman, 1979) in the network of access restrictions defining the possible brokered transactions.

The concept of interdependence among actors plays a central role in the work of both Cook and Marsden, and a network approach does seem a natural vehicle for capturing this concept. Burt's contribution here is concerned, in part, with the manner in which the dependence of one actor on a second, or the constraint posed by the second actor for the first, should be conceptualized. He argues that constraint is more than the intensity of resource or exchange relations linking the occupants of a pair of social positions; it also must consider the overall structure of resource relations and, specifically, the degree to which occupants of a social position are capable of collective action on their own behalf. Burt operationalizes his concept of constraint using data on interindustry sales and purchase transactions and industry concentration levels in the 1967 American economy. He proceeds to show that constraint thus conceived is helpful for understanding the structure of a much-studied interorganizational network: the network of interlocking directorate ties among industrial corporations. Burt's results show that directorate ties are patterned as if they were purposively established with the object of coopting crucial sources of market constraint.

Galaskiewicz is also concerned with the creation of relations among organizations, but he approaches this question from a more microanalytic perspective than the one used by Burt. Galaskiewicz examines donative transfers from business corporations to nonprofit charitable organizations, focusing on the transactional difficulties posed by the level of uncertainty surrounding such relations (see Williamson's [1975] discussion of similar transactional problems for business firms). Galaskiewicz discusses the advantages and disadvantages of strategies of marketing, the use of brokerages, and the use of peer groups or reference groups as information sources; these are alternative devices for coping with the uncertainties of donative transfers. In the final portion of his chapter, he speculates on conditions under which each of his three modes of resource allocation should succeed or fail. He argues that some coping strategies will be more feasible than others, given the nature of the relationships among the various parties to the transactions studied.

In the last chapter in Part III, Knoke and Laumann develop a model of the agenda-setting process in policy domains of the national society. Policy domains are defined as sets of elite actors having interests in and resources with which to influence the development of national policy in specific issue arenas, such as health or energy. Knoke and Laumann center their attention on the agenda-setting process, arguing that the nature of the social organization of a domain will affect this process, and set limits on the ability of individual actors to place proposals in which they have interests on the agenda for governmental action. Knoke and Laumann present several hypotheses linking structural dimensions of domains—such as centralization, polarization, constitutional bases, and resource distributions—to features of the agenda-setting process—such as the number of policy options generated per unit time, the speed with which options reach the governmental decision agenda, and the development of coalitions or collective actors.

These five chapters, all in different ways, consider the intentionality of actors in the presence of structured social relations. They do not, of course, solve the extraordinarily involved theoretical problems in this area, but they do show that the adoption of a network orientation does not require that one embrace a blind structural determinism. Networks are created in part by the self-interested efforts of actors to pursue interests, and, once in place, networks channel and constrain choices made by actors rather than determine such choices. They also provide opportunities for action not available in the absence of network structure.

9

Network Structures from an Exchange Perspective

KAREN S. COOK

Within exchange theory, Blau's (1964) original work, along with more recent theoretical advances–by Emerson (1972a, 1972b) on exchange networks, Coleman (1972) on systems of social exchange, and Ekeh (1974) on generalized exchange–have moved exchange analysis from a focus on relatively isolated dyadic exchange relations at the micro-level to a more macro-level consideration of exchange systems where dyadic relations are viewed as components of larger social structures. While there remains much to be understood about isolated dyadic exchange relations (see Molm and Wiggins, 1979), it is this shift in theoretical emphasis to larger systems of exchange or networks of connected exchange relations that holds promise for providing theoretical grounding for processes of interest to network theorists–including structural determinants of power, modifications in network structure as a result of power-balancing mechanisms, the emergence of corporate actors, the normative regulation of exchange in networks, and exchange systems in which ongoing negotiations are managed or controlled by agents, brokers, or intermediaries of some sort.

AUTHOR'S NOTE: This article reports on the collaborative research efforts of the author with Richard M. Emerson, Mary R. Gillmore, and Toshio Yamagishi, funded by the National Science Foundation (SOC7825788). I would like to thank my collaborators for stimulating theoretical discussions on which this report is based and Bertie Conrad for help in the preparation of the manuscript.

Various network theorists, predominantly anthropologists, have commented on the natural affinity between exchange theory and the analysis of social networks. Mitchell (1974) cites both Kapferer's (1972, 1973, 1976) research and the work of Whitten and Wolfe (1973) as exchange-based network analyses. Whitten and Wolfe (1973: 52) argue: "It is with exchange and action theory that we find the theoretical basis for network analysis." They conclude by saying, "without exchange theory the notion of network would appear quite abstract, divorced from the realities of human life, in specific social and cultural settings." Sociologists Marsden and Laumann (1977), Burt (1975, 1977b), and others, ground their analyses of network phenomena explicitly in exchange notions based primarily on Coleman's (1973a, 1974) work. In addition, Anderson and Carlos (1976) in an article, "What Is Social Network Theory?" explicitly acknowledge exchange theory[1] as an important source of input into a developing "theory" of social networks.[2] Thus, current developments both in exchange theory and in network research bring these traditions into closer theoretical contact. In this chapter I discuss ways in which the experimental research on exchange networks may contribute to this emerging synthesis.[3]

Basic Concepts

Many interesting forms of social structure can be represented as networks (often multiplex and overlapping) composed of sets of connected exchange relations.[4] These networks may include as "nodes" or actors both "natural persons" (Coleman, 1974) and corporate groups, which operate through agents. Thus, exchange relations between two or more actors form the basic building blocks for larger structures of theoretical interest.

Exchange Relations

An exchange relation between any two actors A and B each possessing one or more resources ($x_{1 \ldots n}$, $y_{1 \ldots m}$) valued by the other party is conceived longitudinally. That is, the relation is defined as a "temporal series containing opportunities for exchange which evoke initiations which in turn produce or result in transactions" between the *same parties over time* (Emerson, 1972a: 59). The exchange relation, not a single transaction between a pair of actors, is the primary unit of analysis.[5] Various factors govern behavior in exchange relations. These factors include the value of the resources to the actors involved, comparison levels for alternatives, numbers of alternative sources, and the degree of primacy of each relation to the actors involved in the network.

An *actor* is conceived as a point (or node in a network) where many exchange relations connect (Emerson, 1972a: 57). Some of these relations lie in the same exchange domain,[6] while others lie in different domains. Exchange *categories* are sets of actors that occupy the same domain;[7] that is, they are "substitutable" because they have the same resource(s) to offer in exchange. The significance of this concept is that actors can be identified as alternative sources of the same resources, and access to alternative sources is an important determinant of power in an exchange network. Exchange relations in the same category or domain, therefore, are alternative relations, whereas relations in different domains are not. We use the term *intracategory exchange* to refer to exchanges within the same domain (such as the exchange of friendship or affection)[8] and the term *intercategory exchange* to refer to exchange in different domains (such as advice for esteem or status).

Exchange domains within social network theory are often referred to as different relational "contents." For example, sentiment relations, information-exchange relations, and advice-giving and influence relations represent separate domains of social interaction or activity (that is, different types of ties) and thus *separate networks* (see White et al., 1976; Boorman and White, 1976; White and Breiger, 1975; Breiger, 1979). The exchanges represented in such networks are defined, within our framework, as intracategory exchanges because they are exchanges within the same domain.[9] Other network theorists, most notably the anthropologists (such as Mitchell, 1969; Barnes, 1972; Boissevain, 1974) *merge* different relational contents or types of ties, representing them as "multiplex" or multistranded network bonds.

Since any given exchange relation may include transactions in more than one domain, the relation can "mediate" more than one type of valued outcome or resource (Emerson, 1972a: 57). This means one can speak of the "primacy" of an exchange relation as an index of the extent to which the relation mediates a variety of valued outcomes and has few if any alternatives. The example of a low-primacy relation given by Emerson (1972a: 57) is a customer-sales clerk relation (with many alternative relations and a highly restricted set of mediated outcomes). In contrast, a parent-child relation might be classified as a high-primacy relation, since it mediates a wide range of valued outcomes and has few alternatives. Thus, relational primacy is a joint function of (1) the range (or variety) of valued outcomes mediated by a given exchange relation, and (2) the number of alternative sources of those valued outcomes. Multistranded ties or multiplex bonds represent links between actors that are connected by a number of exchange relations in a variety of different exchange domains; thus, multiplexity is directly related to primacy. Primacy can also be linked to what some network theorists refer to as the "intensity" of a relation, since a high-primacy relation is likely to be more intense, involving more frequent interaction, than a low-primacy relation.

Exchange Networks

Introduction of the notion of exchange networks by Emerson (1972a, 1972b) has facilitated the analysis of more complex social structures from an exchange perspective. An *exchange network* is a set of two or more connected exchange relations. Exchange relations are defined as *connected* if exchange in one relation is contingent on exchange or nonexchange in the other relation (that is, the magnitude or frequency of transactions in one relation is affected by the magnitude or frequency of transactions in another relation). The connection is defined as *positive* to the extent that exchange in one relation increases the likelihood of exchange in the other relation; the connection is *negative* to the extent that exchange in one relation decreases the likelihood of exchange in the other relation (Emerson, 1972b). Examples of positively connected networks range from the Kula Ring (Malinowski, 1922) to vertically integrated markets and channels of distribution (El-Ansary and Stern, 1972). Examples of negatively connected networks given by Cook and Emerson (1978: 725) include competitive economic market structures, dating networks, and some friendship networks. In addition to the sign of the contingency linking exchange relations, network connections can vary in strength. As a result, networks have empirically definite boundaries where the exchange contingencies approach zero.

Introduction of the notion of exchange connections is significant for two reasons: (1) It allows for the direct empirical assessment of the degree of linkage within a network by explicit criteria, and (2) the distinction between types of connections resolves the theoretical controversy that has existed in exchange theory concerning the relationship between competition and exchange. Chadwick-Jones (1976: 329) cites Blau (1964) on the relationship between exchange and competition: "Where there is competition there cannot be exchange since the parties each aim to maximize . . . what they obtain of scarce resources, while exchange, *in contrast* [emphasis added], involves sharing and interdependence." This theoretical position has led to a corresponding overemphasis on the cooperative, voluntaristic side of exchange processes.[10]

The distinction between negative and positive connections removes the necessity of separating in theory competitive processes from exchange processes. In our framework, negatively connected exchange relations represent *competition* over valued resources *within* an exchange network. Furthermore, competitive arrangements, or negatively connected networks, can evolve into cooperative, or positively connected, network arrangements through "product differentiation," specialization, or other forms of division of labor or "market" segmentation, especially under the condition of scarcity.[11] Members of the same exchange category or domain can be viewed as potential competitors who, under certain conditions, choose not to remain competitors, perhaps by adopting alternative "roles" within the network. Similarly, through various mechanisms, cooperative relations can evolve into competitive relations (for example, two firms engaged in a joint venture might eventually become competitors). Modifications in network structures that result from changes over time in the nature of the exchange connections among actors in the network merit closer examination in network research.

This general conception of a network connection or link provides an explicit mechanism for determining whether or not it makes empirical sense to "connect" two or more separate exchange relations *into a network* of some particular size and shape.[12] For example, a three-actor system in which all three parties are engaged in mutual exchange relations does not represent an exchange network unless contingencies empirically exist at some nonzero level (either positive or negative as defined above) linking the sets of exchange relations. Other network models tend not to provide a clear, theoretically meaningful conception of what constitutes a network tie or link.

In exchange theory, network linkage is determined by the strength of the contingencies affecting the *actual* flow of resources within the network. One difficulty with this conceptualization of relational contingencies is that it requires data not easily obtained from sociometric-type measures. Three actors, A, B, and C, might "choose" each other as friends on a sociometric questionnaire of some sort, and thus in some network models would be defined as a "social exchange network"[13] (see Burt, 1977a); however, these three dyadic friendship relations do not necessarily form a *network of connected exchange relations.*

Depending in part on the social circumstances surrounding the A:B, A:C and B:C exchange relations, these friendship relations might be simply noncontingent social relations.[14] For example, A and B might be old college roommates exchanging cards and gifts on significant social occasions, B and C might be neighbors exchanging coffee and conversation weekly, and A and C might share rides to work in a carpool. While all three actors are mutual friends or acquaintances, the flow of resources in any single dyadic exchange relation is noncontingent upon the flow of resources in either of the other two dyadic relations. On the other hand, in a different situation in which A, B, and C are mutual friends, the time A spends with B might mean that C must do without A's company. In this case the A:B and A:C exchange relations form a negatively connected network in which B and C end up competing for "time spent with" A. Resource flow in the A:B relation is contingent on the flow of resources in the A:C relation to a nontrivial degree. This suggests that the study of resource flows and exchange connections is an important topic for empirical research in its own right. Most current network research, our own included, makes certain simplifying assumptions about such connections without checking these assumptions empirically.[15] Research on this topic will become even more critical as we move to the analysis of larger, more complex network structures.

Power and Position in Exchange Networks

Once exchange relations are viewed empirically as connected either positively or negatively to form an exchange network, power can be examined in relation to position or location in that network structure. Sociologists frequently speak of power as a function of position either in some hierarchy of interrelated roles or statuses or in some other strategic location within a set of relations. For example, Kanter (1977a) defines power in terms of access to important resources provided by position within an organization. Burt (1977b) presents a comprehensive treatment of the various conceptualizations of the link between network position and community power.

In an exchange network, all actors with structurally similar locations within the overall structure occupy the same *position* in the network. This notion allows us to simplify the analysis of complex network structures. In conceptualizing network positions, we have relied on relatively simple graph-theoretic concepts identifying networks as digraphs or flow networks in which points represent positions (occupied by actors) and lines represent exchange relations.[16] We use the notion of residual graph from graph theory to specify what we mean by position in an exchange network. If the network as a whole is treated as a "parent graph," then a "residual graph" can be obtained by removing a specified point from the parent graph (see Emerson, 1981, for a more detailed discussion). *Position* can thus be defined in graph-theoretic terms as a "set of one or more points whose residual graphs are isomorphic" (Emerson, 1981: 40).[17] In

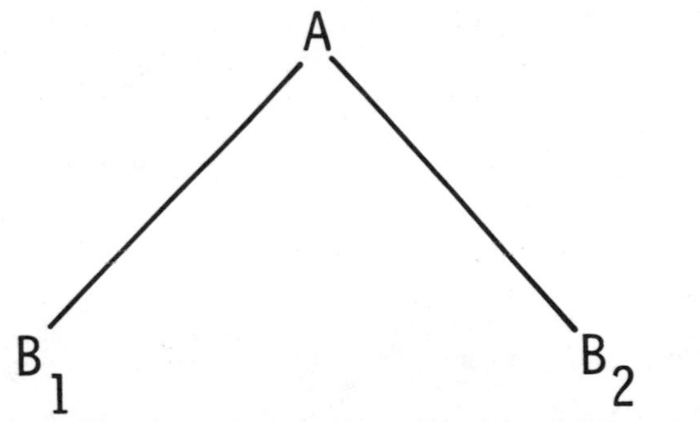

Figure 9.1 Exchange Network Including Three Actors, Two Positions

this way, positions are defined in relation to the overall structure of the exchange network.[18]

Power-dependence principles (Emerson, 1962, 1972a, 1972b; Cook and Emerson, 1978) can be applied to the analysis of network positions in order to ascertain the loci of power within a network. It is clear, for example, that in the simple three-actor, two-position, negatively connected network presented in Figure 9.1, A occupies the more powerful position due to A's monopolistic control over the resource(s) of value to the occupants of position B. In a straightforward application of power-dependence reasoning, $P_{AB_i} > P_{B_iA}$; in other words, the occupants of position B are more dependent upon A than A is upon B_i for valued resources. The main source of this power is the existence of alternative sources (B_1 and B_2) of the resource(s) of value to A and the absence of alternative sources for the occupants of position B in the network.

According to Emerson (1962, 1972a, 1972b), power is a function of dependence, which is determined jointly by two factors: (1) access to alternative sources of valued resources, and (2) the relative values to each actor in the network of the resources to be obtained through exchange. Exchange networks thus represent the structure of resource dependencies across positions in the network. Recently researchers at the macro level have adopted a similar conception of networks (see Pfeffer and Salancik, 1978; Laumann and Pappi, 1976; Marsden and Laumann, 1977). Marsden and Laumann (1977: 245, note 4), for example, claim that their "treatment of a network as a system of power-dependence relations" is basically consistent with variants of Coleman's (1973a) purposive action model. In addition, Marsden and Laumann (1977: 216) argue that "the mechanism

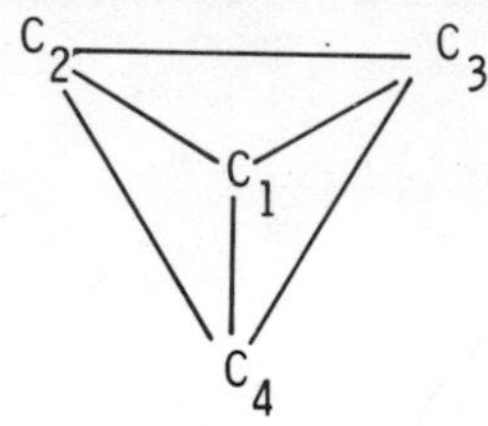

(a) Power-Balanced Exchange Network Including Four Actors, One Position

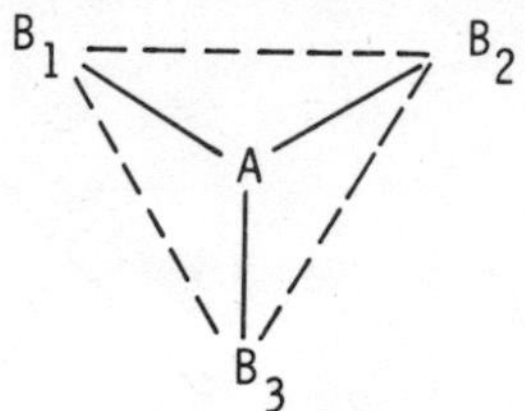

(b) Power-Imbalanced Exchange Network Including Four Actors, Two Positions

Key: Lines represent communication links (exchange opportunities). Solid lines represent high value exchange relations. Broken lines represent low value exchange relations. Letters identify "positions" and numerical subscripts identify actors as "occupants" of positions.

Figure 9.2 Graphic Representation of Exchange Networks Investigated in Cook and Emerson (1978)

generating proximity and distance in the network is resource dependency."

Structural Determinants of Power

Within exchange networks, various factors have been examined empirically in relation to power use. Cook and Emerson (1978) report findings from a laboratory study of four-party exchange networks that demonstrate a direct link between network position and level of power use. The networks included in that study are diagrammed in Figure 9.2. Figures 9.2a and 9.2b represent the two main types of networks investigated in that study. Figure 9.2a presents a four-actor, one-position, power-balanced network, whereas Figure 9.2b presents a four-actor, two-position, power-imbalanced network. The imbalanced network includes one actor in the powerful position (A) and three actors who simultaneously occupy the less powerful position (B) within the network.

In this study (discussed in greater detail in Cook and Emerson, 1978), exchange relations, represented by lines in Figure 9.2, are negatively connected because we established through experimental manipulation that all relations involving the same actor were exchange *alternatives* for that actor. That is, exchange with one party precluded (by experimental control) exchange with any other party during a given time period. We began our program of research with the analysis of negatively connected networks because of ease of operationalization and clear theoretical linkage to power-dependence notions.

In the networks diagrammed in Figure 9.2, actors joined by solid lines have a larger amount of profit to divide through negotiation, whereas actors joined by broken lines have a much smaller amount of profit to divide through negotiation. The manipulation of the value of the alternative exchange relations in this manner enabled us to manipulate the relative dependence and thus the power of the actors in the network.

It was predicted that over time more valued outcomes would accrue to the occupants of the powerful position (A) in the network of Figure 9.2b (see Cook and Emerson, 1978, for an exposition of these theoretical predictions). No differences in outcomes obtained by the various occupants of the less powerful position (B) in this same network were predicted. Furthermore, in the power-balanced network (Figure 9.2a), containing no structurally based power differentials, no differences were predicted to occur in the distribution of the exchange outcomes across the entire network. Any observed differences in outcome would have to be attributed to differential bargaining skill or some other individual difference factor, since the occupants of the sole position (C) in this network were equally powerful (or powerless) in structural terms. The data on exchange outcomes (or profits) in these networks provide general support for these predictions. The data also suggest that when equity concerns enter the bargaining process, they tend to dampen power use, but more so for females than males in our experimental setting. This result is interpreted in Cook and Emerson (1978) as partially due to what appear to be differential tendencies among the male and female occupants of powerful network positions to become "committed" to specific exchange partners over time.[19]

Power and Position Centrality

In addition to positional determinants of power advantages and normative constraints on the exercise of power, in subsequent experiments we have inquired into other determinants of power use in exchange networks. Having successfully operationalized relatively simple exchange networks in our laboratory, we decided to examine the link between *position centrality* and power in various types of exchange networks because of widespread theoretical interest in this relationship. Research in various contexts (mainly nonexperimental) indicates that power is a function of centrality. According to Marsden and Laumann (1977: 217), "those persons at the

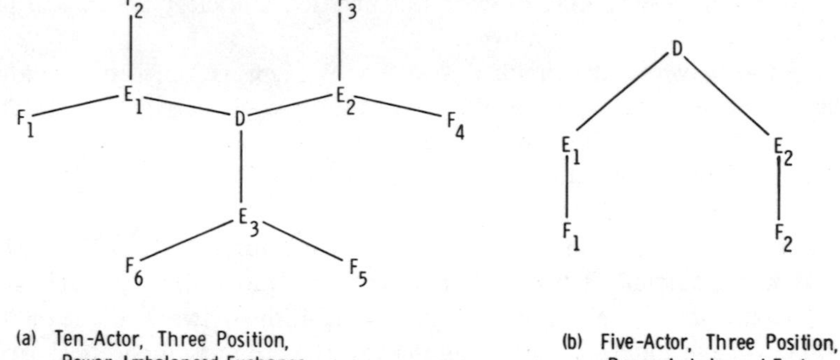

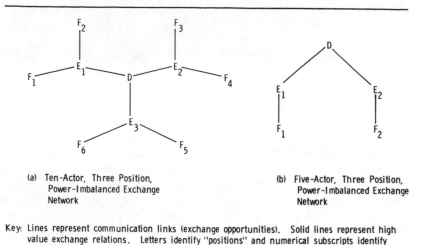

Key: Lines represent communication links (exchange opportunities). Solid lines represent high value exchange relations. Letters identify "positions" and numerical subscripts identify actors as "occupants" of positions.

Figure 9.3 Graphic Representation of Exchange Networks Investigated in Cook, Emerson, Gillmore, and Yamagishi (1980)

center of the network, on whom the more peripheral actors are dependent, are the most powerful actors in the system." In other work (see Laumann and Pappi, 1973, 1976), Laumann refers to this finding as the principle of "integrative centrality."[20] Marsden and Laumann (1977: 224) also note that "power as computed by the Coleman model reflects the relative centrality of an actor in a network of dependency relations." Additional theoretical interest in this topic was sparked by field-historical research conducted by Emerson (1982) on networks similar to the one presented in Figure 9.3a, which suggested that over time power shifted from the center to the occupants of the "intermediate" positions in that network.

Various measures of network centrality have been developed. Early measures of centrality in networks were advanced by Bavelas (1948, 1950), Beauchamp (1965), Sabidussi (1966), and others. The measures they developed were measures of *point* centrality based on the set of shortest distances from a particular point of interest to all other points. Moxley and Moxley (1974) claimed these distance measures were inadequate when applied to unconnected networks; thus, they proposed a solution that Freeman (1977) later described as "arbitrary" and "ad hoc." Freeman (1977) then returned to the original intuitive concept of centrality advanced by Bavelas and, building on others' work (for example, Nieminen, 1973, 1974), formalized new measures based on "betweenness" rather than distance. When applied to the relatively simple graphs in Figure 9.3, however, the differences between these two types of measures of centrality are of little consequence. These particular measures all suggest that D is more central than E in the networks graphed in Figure 9.3. Thus, if power is a function of centrality, as suggested in previous research, then by any measure based on distance or "betweenness" we would predict that $P_{DE_i} > P_{E_iD}$.[21] That is, the occupant of position D should emerge as the most powerful actor in this network.

In contrast to this prediction based on centrality notions, the application of power-dependence reasoning to this negatively connected exchange network leads to the conclusion that $P_{E_iD} > P_{DE_i}$. This prediction follows primarily from the observation that over time the occupants of position E will be drawn into exchanges at the "periphery" (that is, with the occupants of position F) and away from exchange at the center (with D). This will occur because of the extreme dependence of the periphery on the occupants of position E and the inevitable competition between the F_i for access to E (see Cook, Emerson, Gillmore, and Yamagishi, 1980, for a detailed discussion of this argument). Thus, D's power in the network is a function not only of D's dependence on E but also of the dependence of E on F.

An experiment designed to test these competing predictions was conducted on five-person networks as diagrammed in Figure 9.3b.[22] The same basic principles apply to the five- and ten-person networks, so the findings should be generalizable to ten-party networks. (The primary reason for reducing the size of the network was to lower research costs, since the entire network is the basic unit of analysis.) The results of this study are described in Cook, Emerson, Gillmore, and Yamagishi (1980). In short, the main findings support power-dependence reasoning, indicating that within negatively connected exchange networks power is not a simple function of position centrality.[23]

In order to test the generalizability of these findings beyond the five-actor network, we developed a simulation program (described in Yamagishi et al., 1981) that simulates the negotiation of exchanges among actors in n-person networks. The program has the capacity to vary both the size and the "shape" of the network, the number of trials (that is, number of transaction periods), the amount of profit that can be obtained through bargaining in various exchange relations, the number of "offers" and "counteroffers" permitted within a given trial, and the "toughness" of the simulated actors as bargainers.[24]

The results of our simulations of the exchange processes in both of the networks diagrammed in Figure 9.3, the five-actor and ten-actor networks, reproduced the predicted pattern of results based on power-dependence reasoning. This provided additional support for the propositions empirically tested in the actual experiment and allowed us to ascertain the "realism" of our simulation program. The main purpose of the simulation, however, was to "test" the accuracy of our predictions in the larger network. Since we ran the simulation for a longer period of time (increasing by 50 percent the number of trials),[25] we were also able to examine trends in the data over a longer time frame. In these simulated networks, an analysis of the profits obtained over time indicates that E emerges as more powerful than either D or F_i in the network. In addition, it is evident from the profit data that by the final trial block D and F_i have become "equally powerless"; that is, there are no significant differences in their obtained profits. These findings and the results of additional simulation "experiments" are discussed in Cook, Emerson, Gillmore, and Yamagishi (1980) and Yamagishi et al. (1981).

Marsden (forthcoming) presents "artificial data" on hypothetical five- and ten-party action systems partially designed to approximate the conditions in our experimentally examined exchange networks. His model is based explicitly on Coleman's (1973a) model of "purposive action," which he has extended to incorporate the notion of alternative sources (Emerson, 1962, 1972b) and "restricted access." The artificial data he presents in part contradict both our experimental findings and the results of our simulation. Marsden (forthcoming) reports that the actors in position E (of "intermediate centrality") do gain power over actors in positions F ("peripheral") and D ("central"), but that E's power over D is relatively short-lived since it eventually erodes such that E and D have equal power at "equilibrium." This result, Marsden (forthcoming) argues, occurs because dependency relations between these actors are "balanced." Marsden's findings are consistent with a simple *degree*-based measure of centrality[26] (see also note 21) which, for the two networks in Figure 9.3a and 9.3b, predicts equal power for D and E because these actors have an equal number of alternatives (that is, each is linked directly to only two other actors). In fact, Marsden explicitly incorporates a degree-based measure into his model, stating that the exchange ratio between two actors is in part based on the ratio of the numbers of alternatives available to the two actors. As is evident from our empirical results, for negatively connected networks, such a measure is inadequate primarily because it fails to capture the effects of more remote connections on the power of actors in the network. It is for this reason that we have begun the process of extending power-dependence reasoning beyond the dyadic conception originally introduced by Emerson (1962, 1972a).

In a follow-up study, in progress, we are investigating positively connected exchange networks in which theory suggests that power-dependence predictions and notions of centrality may lead to complementary rather than opposing predictions.[27] The nature of the resource dependencies are quite different in positively connected networks, since resource flows across actors in the network are more highly interdependent. The occupants of position E in the positively connected version of the network in Figure 9.3b, for example, function more like intermediaries. Their role is primarily to "pass" on valuable resources. Profit accrues to the occupants of position E as a result of facilitation of *both* the $E{:}F_i$ and E:D exchanges; thus, D's role becomes "central" as the only link between the various $E{:}F_i$ subnetworks. These subnetwork dependencies on D to maintain resource flow to the periphery become a power base for D. We are working toward the development of a conception of centrality based on the concept of network "vulnerability" that might hold up in both negatively and positively connected networks.

Power and Dependence as Determined by Network "Vulnerability"

While power-dependence principles have been well developed theoretically (see Emerson, 1962, 1972a, 1972b) for the analysis of dyadic exchange relations and simple networks, we have only recently begun to extend these notions to apply to more complex networks (Cook and Emerson, 1978; Cook, Emerson, Gillmore, and Yamagishi, 1980; Emerson, 1981). As Emerson (1981: 41) notes in a recent review article, "power-dependence concepts should be raised from the level of exchange relations, where they were first developed, to the more macro level of networks." More specifically, our experimental investigation of centrality and theoretical attempts to apply power-dependence notions to relatively simple networks lead us to conclude that power-dependence reasoning needs to be elevated to the *networkwide* level.

Emerson (1981: 41) poses the question, "Is there a high-level principle regarding power in exchange networks which can subsume the above (contradictory) predictions (concerning centrality)?" In his analysis of these competing predictions he notes, "Position E in the negatively connected network and position D in the positively connected network have one important feature in common: exchange throughout the network *as a whole* is most dependent upon those two positions." *Networkwide dependence* can be evaluated in terms of the functional dependence of resource "flow" within the network on any particular network position.

One way to construct a measure of this system dependence on any given network position is to consider the consequences of *removal* of a particular line or point from the graph representing the network of interest. In previous work (Cook and Emerson, 1978), we have suggested that the "graph theoretic concept of vulnerability (see Harary et al., 1965; Berge, 1962) might prove useful" in this regard, since vulnerability deals with the consequences for the entire graph or specified subgraphs of "removing" specific lines and points.[28] Such a measure, developed by Yamagishi, is reported in Cook, Emerson, Gillmore, and Yamagishi (1980). The basic underlying notion is that the concept "removal" gives an empirical estimate of the extent to which resource flow in a network would be impeded by an actor's refusal to engage in exchange or any other form of "withdrawal" from the network. It is important to note that this type of removal has different implications for resource flow in positively and negatively connected networks. For example, removal of position D in the positively connected network completely stops the flow of value within the network in Figure 9.3a, since in order for the occupants of position E to realize "profit" in their $E{:}F_i$ exchange relations, they must obtain resources of value from D. "Removal" of position D leaves E with nothing of value to exchange with F. By definition, a positive connection implies that the connected exchange relations are interdependent in the sense that what hinders (or facilitates) exchange in one relation also hinders (or facilitates) exchange in the connected relation.

In the negatively connected version of this network, however, removal of D may have no effect on the profit E can accrue through exchange because E can continue to engage in "competitive" exchange relations with the occupants of position F. In the absence of any exchange alternatives, the occupants of position F are totally dependent on E for valued resources. We conclude that in the negatively connected network, system-wide resource flow is only partially impeded by the removal of position D, since value, or "profit," can be independently obtained in the resulting distinct three-actor subnetworks. Additional theoretical and empirical work on this topic is currently in progress.

Power Redistribution Mechanisms in Exchange Networks

Another research topic of major interest from an exchange perspective is structural responses to power imbalance.[29] There are two major aspects of this particular area of inquiry: (1) the nature of the processes by which powerful actors in the network maintain power advantages, and (2) the nature of the processes by which less powerful actors attempt to gain power. Both types of process result in changes in the power structure. To date, our empirical efforts have focused primarily on investigation of "power-balancing" mechanisms that allow the less powerful actors to gain power either by collective action or through specialization or division of labor.[30] These social processes create structural changes in the network that alter the basic underlying power-dependence relation. Specific exchange theoretic formulations of these processes and relevant experimental evidence are reported elsewhere (see Emerson, 1972b; Cook, 1979; Cook, Gillmore, and Little, 1980; Cook, Emerson, Gillmore, and Yamagishi, 1980; a brief summary of some of the findings is presented here).

Two types of power-balancing mechanisms apply at the network level: (1) *network extension,* an increase in the number of exchange alternatives through the creation of new exchange relations or through the addition of new members to the network, and (2) *network consolidation,* a decrease in the number of exchange alternatives by member defection or by the formation of collective actors (a mechanism for gaining power through resource pooling). Our initial research (Cook, Gillmore, and Little, 1980) focused on coalition formation as a type of power-balancing mechanism through network consolidation. This research examines power processes under the condition that individual actors can join together to bargain as a "collective" actor, where one party serves as the agent for the two-party group in subsequent negotiations. Rates of coalition formation in networks varying in degree of power imbalance were examined. The results of this particular study indicate that in three-party negatively connected exchange networks, coalitions of the less powerful actors occur frequently under conditions of power imbalance. Coalition formation enabled the less powerful to gain power and thereby prevent exploitation by the more powerful actor in the network.[31] Coalitions of the powerful actor with one of the less powerful actors in the network occurred early in the exchange process but did not occur later in the process, as the network imbalance became more obvious to all actors in the network.[32] Research is currently being conducted to examine coalition processes in larger networks and to investigate more fully the nature of the conditions that lead to the mobilization of coalitions in exchange networks.

Investigation of the conditions under which coalitions form in exchange networks is significant for two reasons: (1) it extends current coalition theory and research, linking it directly to exchange theory (see also

Komorita and Chertkoff, 1978; Komorita and Tumonis, 1980), and (2) it is linked to the study of "incorporation" or the formation of corporate groups within exchange networks, a topic identified by Emerson (1972b, 1981) as an important area of further theoretical development within exchange theory.

Corporate Actors, Agents, and Principals in Exchange Networks

Recent attention has been devoted to the emergence of what Coleman (1974) refers to as "corporate actors" (that is, corporate groups). This is a consequence of the fact that many events of current interest to individual actors ("natural persons," to use Coleman's term) are now controlled by corporate actors. As suggested by Coleman (1974) and subsequently documented by Burt (1975), ours is a society increasingly dominated by the interests of corporate entities; thus, *power has shifted* in industrialized societies from natural persons to corporate actors. Given this reality, it is important to incorporate into exchange theory an understanding of corporate groups and forms of exchange more complex than elementary exchange (or simple trading relations) in which the actors in the network are "collective" actors.

In the process of "incorporation," individual actors give up some autonomy and control over their own resources by joining or investing in a corporate actor. This occurs apparently in the hope that corporate activity using combined resources will lead to greater benefits than individual activity. According to Coleman (1973b: 3), "When a person decides to yield control of his resources to a corporate body . . . he expects to gain the greater power of combined resources. The decision is between acting independently with more freedom," he argues, "or collectively with more power." Our research on coalition formation indicates one set of conditions under which the gain in power resulting from coalition formation tends to outweigh the costs in loss of freedom of independent action or autonomy.

Other interesting theoretical issues concerning corporate group formation arose in the process of designing our coalition experiments. One such issue of general interest is the nature of agent-principal relations in networks that include corporate groups as actors. Coalition members in our experiments had to grant to one actor the power of "acting for" the group as its agent. That is, the group as principal had to conduct its exchange through a member designated as *agent.* The fact that network exchanges are frequently handled by agents for actors (either natural persons or corporate groups) has important implications that have not been recognized within exchange theory. As Leibenstein (1976: 161) points out:

> Conventional microtheory builds on the notion that in every exchange both parties gain. The logic behind this view is that the parties would not exchange in the first place if each of them did not see the potential for gain. This assumes that the exchange is between principals, or operates as if it were. . . . However, once both agents enter the scene there is no need for both parties to gain in order for transactions to take place. . . . It is possible for the agents to carry out transactions in which both principals lose, and to ignore transactions in which both principals would gain. . . . Thus the situation becomes more complex.

In order to extend exchange theory to apply to more "macro-level" exchange processes, the role of agents in intergroup trade within network structures must be examined. Agents can serve as relatively independent actors, as intermediaries, or as brokers. Given this focus, several interesting research questions arise, especially when agents negotiate "on behalf" of principals in exchange networks. As Leibenstein (1976) indicates, agents typically have split loyalties to their own ends and to their principals' ends—a problem frequently faced by boundary personnel in organizations. Therefore, the nature of the exchanges that take place within the network may be very different when agents are involved. Riker (1962) and Mitnick (1975), for example, suggest that agents may operate more "rationally," in terms of maximizing payoffs on any given exchange episode, than principals, primarily due to the existence of "fiduciary" norms. Furthermore, agents may be less willing to take risks in negotiations than principals and may therefore adopt more "conservative" bargaining strategies. Other research issues include the nature of the negotiations between principals and their agents, the role that sanctions play in the agent-principal relationship, and the corresponding link between the role of sanctions and the bargaining strategies and tactics used by agents in negotiating exchanges for principals.[33] The topic of agency is complex, but research on issues related to agent-mediated exchange will bring important advances for exchange theory and network theory more generally, partly because it will facilitate the analysis of more complex systems of exchange and what Emerson (1981) refers to as "institutionalized" exchange systems.[34]

Systems of Generalized Exchange and Productive Exchange

Within our current experimental format, we have investigated exchange networks in which the exchange relations among the actors in the network involve the joint, relatively concurrent, negotiation of the terms of trade. We refer to this form of exchange as a "transaction." But there are other theoretically interesting forms of exchange that can be investigated in a laboratory setting. Several involve reciprocal "gift-giving" between the same parties or exchanges in which there is no "mutual negotiation" over the terms of trade. Here an exchange is initiated by the giving of something of value to an actor in the network with the expectation of a return, but not from the actor who provided the "gift" initially. This type of exchange is similar to what Ekeh (1974) refers to as chain-generalized exchange (for example, A → B → C → D → E → A).

According to Ekeh (1974: 52), "generalized exchange operates on the principle of what Lévi-Strauss (1969) calls univocal reciprocity. . . . It occupies a unitary system of relationships in that it links all parties to the exchange together in one integrated transaction in which reciprocations are indirect not mutual." Experimental research on generalized exchange will provide evidence concerning the emergence of trust, or the "credit mentality" referred to by Ekeh (1974), which operates to make generalized exchange systems viable as social structures. Issues of the solidarity-generating functions of such exchange systems also may be amenable to experimental research.

In considering more complex forms of exchange, the distinction made by Emerson (1972b) between elementary and productive exchange is an important one.[35] Most networks represent interrelated elementary exchange processes, or what Heath (1976) refers to simply as interconnected "trade" relations. There is no discernible "productive" process involved in these often complex sets of trades. In contrast, some exchanges involve the joint "production" of value—that is, actors must combine their resources in some way in order to obtain any benefit. Many forms of social activity, such as joint problem solving, tennis, and square dancing, as well as forms of economic productive activity, like making toys or vacuum cleaners, are examples of productive exchange typically involving two or more actors.

Productive exchange necessitates "collective action"; thus, this topic links directly to existing theoretical and empirical work on coalition formation and collective action (see Olson, 1965; Oliver, 1980). Central theoretical issues include the nature of the incentives, inducements, or sanctions used to guarantee member contributions as well as distributive justice or equity problems in the distribution of benefit to the contributors to the productive effort and, in some cases, to the noncontributors or "free riders." Research into productive exchange processes will aid theory development along lines that can include corporate entities as "collective" actors in exchange networks, since corporate groups typically form to facilitate productive exchange.

Conclusion

Exchange theory provides a framework within which many of the social processes of interest to network theorists can be formulated. This framework, however, is distinctive in several respects:

(1) It focuses on "purposive action," assuming, for example, that ties or links between actors are established, maintained, or broken primarily in terms of the "value" provided by that exchange relation (or set of relations) directly or indirectly.
(2) Exchange networks fundamentally represent the *flow of resources* within a social structure of "connected" exchange relations, and it is this flow of resources and its social structural consequences that are of basic interest.
(3) Since exchange networks represent the *structure of resource dependencies* among a set of actors, these networks can be viewed as power structures that are dynamic as a result of actors' attempts, through power-gaining and power-balancing mechanisms, to alter the network and thus redistribute power.

Exchange theory provides useful theoretical grounding for networks in which the basic social processes of interest to the researcher can be represented as exchange processes or resource flows. Also, cross-fertilization between exchange theory, and social network "theory" and methods appears promising. It should be clear from this discussion, however, that exchange theory is but *one* possible source of "grounding" for a developing theory of social networks.

NOTES

1. Anderson and Carlos (1976) discuss other theoretical contributions as well. In commenting on the relationship between exchange theory and sociometric research (see Hallinan, 1974; Leinhardt, 1977), they suggest that "sentiment relations

matter most in the earliest phase of the development of network ties. Once a link has become established," they argue, "its fate depends more on the positively or negatively valued outcomes of transactions between group members than on sentiment attachments."

2. There is much debate over whether or not it makes sense to talk about "a theory" of social networks (see Anderson and Carlos, 1976; Wolfe, 1978; Mitchell, 1974; Barnes, 1972; Kapferer, 1973). All of the varying positions on the issue would seem to agree with Burt's (1980c: 134) recent assessment: "In short, the lack of network theory seems to me to be the most serious impediment to the realization of the potential value of network models in empirical research."

3. The primary focus of the research program being conducted by K. S. Cook, R. M. Emerson, M. R. Gillmore, and T. Yamagishi (to be reported in Cook et al., forthcoming) at the University of Washington is the analysis of social structure and structural change within the framework of exchange theory. Our aim is to develop a theory of social exchange that incorporates findings from both laboratory (see Cook and Emerson, 1977) and field-historical investigations of exchange networks.

4. We use Laumann's (1966, 1979: 385) definition of social structure as "a persisting pattern of social relationships among social positions." According to Laumann (1979: 385), a "social relationship is any direct or indirect linkage between incumbents of different social positions that involves mutual but not necessarily symmetric orientations of a positive, neutral, or negative affectual character and/or may involve the exchange of goods, services, commands or information." Our focus is on relations in which exchanges can be said to occur.

5. See Emerson (1972b, 1976) for a discussion of the significance of this focus in distinguishing social and economic theories of exchange. Also, see Cook (1979) for a more general discussion of the distinction between social and economic exchange.

6. Exchange domains are defined in operant terms by Emerson (1972a: 50), employing the concept "satiation" as a basis for "defining boundaries between classes of reinforcers." For our purposes here it is sufficient to note that resources occupy the same domain to the extent that they are "substitutable." We offer no formal definition of substitutability.

7. Resource magnitude is the only variable that may differentiate actors within an exchange domain or category (Emerson, 1972b: 83).

8. Examples of intracategory exchange abound in anthropological field studies. See Trouwborst's (1973) interesting discussion of "food exchanges" and "beer exchanges" in Burundi. Also see Kadushin's (1966) discussion of "social circles" based on intracategory exchange (and Alba and Kadushin, 1976). The important point discussed by Emerson (1972b) is that exchange connections in intracategory exchange networks tend to be negative.

9. Such networks are best viewed as networks of association or affiliation (such as business contacts and social contacts); they do not necessarily represent exchange relations. It is hard to infer the actual existence of exchange relations on the basis of affiliation or association information alone. Even Laumann (1979) makes a distinction between affectual and exchange relations; and while some relations may indeed involve both affect and exchange, if one is interested in the flow of resources it is problematic to assume that affect relations *are* exchange relations.

10. This distinction has led to some theoretical confusion. For example, Schmidt and Kochan (1977) argue that exchange and power dependence represent "competing theoretical approaches."

11. Blau (1964) does acknowledge, however, that competition can evolve into exchange and that exchange can lead to competition.

12. Some social networks can be classified as exchange networks, but not *all* social networks are exchange networks (see Cook, 1979, for a discussion of this distinction). A social network might be conceived as an opportunity structure within which an exchange network might emerge. In this sense, some social networks (as typically discussed by network theorists) represent sets of potential exchange opportunities. Marsden and Laumann (1977: 214) state, "only those persons who are proximately related to an actor are available as partners in potential influence transactions. Exchanges with others who are more distant are unlikely to be made because of a lack of information about resource availability or because of an inadequate basis for establishment of a cooperative relation."

13. Actors are clustered by Burt (1976) into positions in a "social exchange network" based on sociometric responses to the question: "Would you please indicate the three persons from the list with whom you most frequently meet socially?" The "economic exchange network" is derived from responses to a similar question: "Could you now indicate the three persons out of our list with whom you have closest business and professional contact?"

14. If the A:B, A:C, and B:C relations represent communication links or information flows instead, it still remains an empirical issue whether or not information (or some other type of resource) that flows between A and B ever reaches C.

15. Research on social networks and social support (for example, Tolsdorf, 1976; Henderson, 1977; Horowitz, 1978; Pilisuk and Froland, 1978) has attempted to study the nature of network links as support systems.

16. Recently we have begun to examine the relevance of the literature on flow networks (for example, Busacker and Saatz, 1965; Savage and Deutsch, 1960) to the analysis of exchange networks.

17. This definition of positions must be refined for certain classes of networks. For example, in networks in which resource flow along some paths is unidirectional, information about the directionality is lost when positions are defined in terms of point removal (that is, residual graphs). Thus, in a three-person network with unidirectional resource flow (for example, $A \rightarrow B \rightarrow C$), removing either point A or point C produces isomorphic residual graphs; however, in some cases we might want to preserve a distinction between these two positions, since A is a source point and C is the destination point for resource flow in this network. One method of preserving such a distinction based on directionality of resource flow is to define positions using "semiresidual graphs" instead of residual graphs (see Yamagishi, 1981). In semiresidual graphs, the "strength" of all paths related to a point is reduced by half, instead of reducing these paths to zero. In this way, the directionality information is retained while the "effect" or "importance" of a point can still be assessed in the same basic way.

18. This method of identifying network positions probably comes closer to Laumann's spatial technique for position identification than to White et al.'s (1976) blockmodel techniques (see Lorrain and White, 1971; White and Breiger, 1975). Our own theoretical work has not yet proceeded to the point where we deal with "aggregated" exchange networks. At some stage, however, we are hopeful that macro-level attempts to deal with this issue will be informative in this regard. White et al. (1976) comment in a footnote that blockmodels seem a "natural context for a merger" between "restricted exchange and generalized exchange," but precisely how blockmodeling will facilitate this merger is neither indicated nor obvious.

19. In this study, all profits obtained by the actors in each network through exchange were revealed after approximately one and one-half hours of bargaining. The inequalities in these profit distributions raised equity concerns among the

bargainers (see Cook and Emerson, 1978). While the suggested gender difference in concern for equity and level of commitment to exchange partners is interesting, we have not investigated these effects further in this series of experiments because gender differences are not of primary theoretical interest to us at this time. For a general review of results of bargaining studies with respect to gender and other individual characteristics, see Rubin and Brown (1975).

20. Marsden and Laumann (1977: 224) note that "power was also highly associated with centrality in intra-elite networks of business and professional linkages (r = .6)." They argue this is a result of the principle of integrative centrality, according to which "elite networks" are organized (Laumann and Pappi, 1973, 1976). The principle of integrative centrality (Laumann and Pappi, 1973: 219) "holds that persons playing key integrative or coordinating roles in a given structure will tend to be located in the 'central region' of their space."

21. While measures of centrality based on the concepts of "betweenness" and "distance" show D to be the most central position, measures based on the concept "degree" indicate that the positions D and E in the networks in Figure 9.3 are equally central (see Freeman, 1979, for a more complete discussion and critique of these centrality measures). The main point of interest here is that none of these particular measures show E to be *more* central and thus more powerful than D.

22. These theoretical predictions assume that actors *use* their structurally provided power. Actors are assumed to bargain in "rational" or "self-interested" ways, that is, to make offers in order to improve profits over time, to accept offers that provide more gain when given a choice of offers to accept, and to lower offers that go unaccepted. Empirical evidence (from postsession questionnaires as well as behavioral data) provides some support for this general "motivational" assumption.

23. The two factors included in this experiment were subject gender and exchange incentive (high versus low). Subject gender had no significant effect on the results. However, the exchange incentive variable had the anticipated effect: Power differentials emerged more rapidly and had a stronger effect under high exchange incentive (where resource values were higher) than under low exchange incentive (where the motivation to engage in exchange was considerably reduced because there was so little of value to be gained through exchange). We included this factor to give some indication of the nature of the relationship between level of exchange incentives (or importance of the exchanges) and the exercise of power.

24. This factor was introduced to gain information about variation in bargaining styles. In some of our early studies, anecdotal evidence suggested that males might be adopting more "aggressive" bargaining styles than females. Subsequent data have not provided clear-cut evidence on gender differences in bargaining "styles." This factor was also included in order to test the notion that under certain conditions, powerful actors in a network adopt "tougher" bargaining styles or strategies than the more dependent, powerless actors. The simulations reported here do not include any variation on this factor. Relatively "tough" or hard bargaining was assumed for all the simulated actors.

25. Increasing the number of trials further in additional simulations produced no changes in the results.

26. The degree of a point is determined by the number of other points adjacent to it and thus in *direct* contact with it (see Freeman, 1979: 219).

27. This study may link more directly to recent empirical investigations of community power (for example, Laumann and Pappi, 1976), where the typical resource of interest is "influence" over important events (or control over resources that yield influence over such events). Such networks (like communication networks) under certain conditions might best be conceived as positively connected in our terminology.

28. Point and position vulnerability can be treated as conceptually distinct except in the case where there are no positional redundancies in the network (that is, every position is uniquely occupied).

29. In addition, we have investigated what we refer to as normative (rather than structural) resolutions to power imbalance. Under this label we include normative considerations (such as equity/justice concerns), legitimating norms (such as authority), and interpersonal commitment-inducing norms (like the norm of "responsibility" [see Berkowitz and Daniels, 1963] or notions of trust). This work is described elsewhere (see Cook and Emerson, 1978; Cook, 1979; Cook et al., forthcoming). See Cook (1979) for a discussion of normative regulation of exchange processes through enforcement of justice principles, for example.

30. Data from an experiment on resource specialization within exchange networks involving the exchange of multiple resources are not yet fully analyzed.

31. This tradition of research links to Lawler's (1975) work on the mobilization of revolutionary coalitions, since the primary aim is to specify the conditions under which coalitions are likely to be "mobilized" and to identify the effects of such collective action on the social structure (for example, on the distribution of power in the network).

32. Note that it was not advantageous for the powerful actor to coalesce with a less powerful member of the network. Thus, the occurrence of these coalitions can, in part, be interpreted as a strategy adopted by the powerful actor on occasion to thwart coalition formation among the less powerful actors in the network.

33. Another interesting issue is the nature of the role of the "multiple" agent, or the agent representing more than one principal, and the resolution of conflicting interests.

34. See Emerson (1981) for a discussion of field-historical research focusing on "fairly stable, long-term, or institutionalized exchange systems" similar to the Kula Ring described by Malinowski (1922). See also Eisenstadt and Roniger (1980) for a discussion of patron-client relations from an exchange perspective.

35. According to Emerson (1976: 357), "the idea of productive exchange readily accommodates large numbers of actors, thereby freeing exchange theory from its dyadic format. However, productive exchange is uniquely addressed to resource distribution within corporate groups. . . . Networks tie together both groups and individuals as actors. In productive exchange," Emerson notes, "unlike the direct transfer of valued items in simple exchange, here items of value are produced through a value-adding social process. . . . the separate resources of two or more persons . . . are combined through a social process involving a division of labor."

10

Brokerage Behavior in Restricted Exchange Networks

PETER V. MARSDEN

Among the forces motivating the recent surge of interest in network analysis is the idea that social structure, conceived as a routinized pattern of social relations among actors (Laumann, 1973), affects the actions taken by those embedded in it, as well as the outcomes of those actions. There now exists a body of nonexperimental evidence lending support to this general proposition (see Laumann, 1973; Granovetter, 1974; Galaskiewicz, 1979; Wellman, 1979; Burt, 1980a, 1980b; Lin, Ensel, and Vaughan, 1981), and results of some pertinent experimental studies have also been reported (Cook and Emerson, 1978; Freeman et al., 1980; Cook, Emerson, Gillmore, and Yamagishi, 1980).

Of particular concern in establishing a linkage between structure and action is the question of how positions in social structure are transformed into disparities in power among actors. Burt (1977d) discusses three sources of power in a social topology, each of which refers to a distinct way in which actors may obtain power. He suggests that variations in power may be traced to differential levels of control over valuable resources, differential proximity to those having direct control over such resources, and differential levels of influence of actors on one another. Of special interest to network analysts are the latter two types of power (power as proximity to resources and power as influence), because these

AUTHOR'S NOTE: I thank Edward O. Laumann for his helpful comments on this chapter.

sources of power are strictly derived from structures of social relations among actors. Freeman (1979), primarily concerned with communication networks, reviews three conceptions of positional centrality in networks and discusses the associated views on how centrality affects group processes. Concern with degree-based notions of centrality suggests that power disparities can be traced to differences in communication activity;[1] concern with centrality as betweenness implies that the potential to control or interrupt communication is the source of power; while viewing centrality as closeness treats the independence of actors from the control potential of others as the aspect of interest (compare Burt's 1980b, related concept of autonomy).

My object here is to build on earlier work considering mechanisms by which social networks confer power advantages or deficits on the actors within them (Marsden and Laumann, 1977; Marsden, 1981, forthcoming). I am concerned with purposive action in resource exchange networks in circumstances involving at least partial conflict of interest among actors. I argue that one mechanism through which the power of central actors in such networks can be understood is the mechanism of *brokerage,* by which intermediary actors facilitate transactions between other actors lacking access to or trust in one another.

In the next section of this chapter I shall review previous work on networks and purposive action on which the present chapter builds. I then introduce brokerage behavior on a conceptual level. This is followed by a tentative formalization within a mathematical model. Numerical illustration is provided, and the chapter concludes with comments.

Networks and Purposive Action

The basic model of a system of action from which my analysis departs is presented by Coleman (1973a, 1977). The system includes two sets of units of analysis, *actors* and *events,* which are linked to one another by two types of interset relationships, *interest* and *control.* A purposive actor's interest in an event is conceived as the degree to which the actor's well-being is related to the outcome of the event; the model, however, makes no assumptions as to the bases of interest generation, that is, the processes by which actors evaluate the relative contributions of events to their well-being (see Marsden, 1979: Chapter 3, 1981). If the outcome of an event is divisible, an actor's control over it is viewed as the proportion of the event in the actor's possession, while for indivisible events or collective decisions, control is seen as the probability that the actor, on his or her own, can determine the outcome of the event.

Of concern here are configurations of interest and control in which actors do not possess total control over the events of interest to them, for in such configurations, actors are dependent on one another for the realization of their interests. Coleman (1973a) argues that under such circumstances it is rational for actors to exchange their control over events with one another, such that their levels of control over events become consistent with their interests in those events. The postulated process of exchange leads to equilibrium results giving the relative power of actors, the relative value of events, the probable outcomes of events, the expected interest satisfaction or welfare of individual actors and of the collectivity, and the level of internal conflict in the collectivity.

While elegant in its treatment of the interset relationships of control and interest, Coleman's model ignores the intraset relationships—particularly relationships among actors—which are of greatest interest to social network analysts. Social relationships among actors play no part in constraining or facilitating exchanges; an unconstrained, "all-channel" exchange network is assumed.

In previous work, I have attempted to introduce network constraints on action into this model. A study by Marsden and Laumann (1977) provides a foundation for this undertaking by showing, with data on decision making in a community elite, that objective interest dependencies based on interest and control predict one operationalization of dependency relations to only a limited extent. This suggests that there is more to dependency than the intersection of configurations of interest and control, which is the conception of dependency used in Coleman's (1973a) basic model. Marsden and Laumann (1977) also discuss on a conceptual level various imperfections in the exchange market postulated by the basic model; the most prominent of these imperfections is the embeddedness of actors in networks.

Later work builds social networks directly into the purposive action model. In Marsden (1981), influence processes are introduced using a network of influence relations among actors. This modification affects one of the inputs into the purposive action model, the interest configuration, by making the interests of actors interdependent. Simulation results suggest that by comparison with a network-free model, the introduction of influence processes may result in a decline in the level of resource mobilization and an increase in the level of apparent consensus on the outcomes of collective decisions, depending on the configuration of influence relations and the way these are articulated with the interests of actors. Additionally, the presence of the influence network provides actors with indirect control over the use of one another's resources through interest-shaping, and this means that actors with high status—the capacity to influence the use of control by powerful actors—gain in expected interest satisfaction.

Modifications of the basic model introduced in Marsden (forthcoming) have to do with the conduct of the exchange process itself, rather than with one of the inputs into that process. It is argued that for various reasons—including (but not limited to) ideological similarity, limitations of trust, commitment to particular exchange relations, and social homogeneity—an actor will conduct exchanges with only some of the other actors in the system. Taken together across all actors, these operative transaction routes constitute an access network. The assumption that all exchanges taking place are mediated by one of the linkages in this access network introduces new elements into the strategic situation in which actors make decisions about exchanges with one another. Most important, actors will typically differ as to their numbers of accessible exchange partners, which in turn means that they differ as to the number of alternatives they have available in any given exchange relation. Drawing on Emerson's (1962) classic paper on power-dependence relations, discrepancies in alternative exchange relations are combined with objective interest dependencies based on the intersection of configurations of interest and control to yield overall levels of interdependence among actors. It is argued that actors with superior numbers of alternative exchange relations are able to exploit those with fewer alternatives through "price-making" behavior.

Simulations using this modification of the purposive action model lead to an important but problematic result. The effect of including access restrictions and exploitative or price-making behavior within the model is to redistribute power, but *not* in a way consistent with expectations based on network centrality concepts of betweenness or closeness. (Cook, in this volume, points out that these simulation results are consistent with a degree-based conception of centrality.) This conflicts with the positive correlations found in nonexperimental data between betweenness or closeness centrality and power or manifestations of power (for example, Coleman et al., 1966; Laumann and Pappi, 1976; Galaskiewicz, 1979)—correlations that persist when controlled for measures of resource possession. What the inconsistency between the simulation results and the nonexperimental studies suggests is either that exploitative behavior is incorrectly specified in the modified model or that actors take purposive actions other than or in addition to exploitative behavior in the presence of networks restricting the access of potential exchange partners to one another.[2]

The remainder of this chapter will adopt the latter stance. I suggest that actors engage in more than one type of purposive action under conditions of limited access. In addition to exploitative or price-making behavior governed by discrepancies between actors in alternative exchange relationships, brokerage behavior, in which intermediary actors facilitate exchanges between other actors lacking direct access to each other, is a plausible process to be expected under such conditions. Furthermore, the introduction of behavior of this kind may serve to establish the positive correlation involving power and betweenness or closeness centrality that is not present when exploitative behavior only is considered.

Brokerage Behavior

The concepts of centrality used by network analysts are derived in part from the formalism of graph theory (such as Harary et al., 1965) and in part from communication experiments (such as Bavelas, 1950; Freeman et al., 1980). The latter experiments are concerned with the effect of the structure of a communication network on the performance of a cooperative task by a group, and with the distribution of power and satisfaction among actors occupying different positions in that network. During the experiments, subjects pass messages to one another along the network channels made available to them by the experimenters. Freeman et al. (1980) find that power, or reputation for leadership, is attributed to actors in positions with high potential for communication activity and with high potential for control over such activity. Actors high in communication activity are in positions to collect and synthesize information on the group task. Those with high potential for control over communication are located in intermediary positions along "geodesics," or indirect ties linking peripheral actors, and can thus regulate the distribution of information within the system.

An important point pertains to the functions of these indirect ties in communication networks. Implicit in the graph theoretic concern with reachability through indirect ties is the idea that indirect ties serve as functional substitutes for direct communication between actors. Thus, while the conception of centrality as betweenness recognizes that intermediate actors can control the messages passing through indirect channels, it is also recognized that (at least part of the time) the intermediary actors will faithfully pass information from one peripheral actor to another.

This functional equivalence of indirect ties to direct ones is the essence of what is involved in brokerage behavior. It involves more than the happenstance fact that two peripheral actors communicate with a common third party; rather, the broker or intermediary is thought to take into account the needs of the peripheral actors for sending information to and receiving it from one another.

Brokerage behavior, thus described, is to be anticipated in exchange networks as well as in communication networks, if actors have limited access to one another. In the modifications of Coleman's (1973a) basic model of exchange introduced in Marsden (forthcoming), however, brokerage of this kind does not take place. The modified exchange model does permit resources initially controlled by one peripheral actor eventually to reach another peripheral actor through a third party. Such indirect transfers of resources, though, occur on an entirely idiosyncratic basis. They take place only because two dyadic exchanges happen to have one party in common. The indirect exchanges are not based on the relative interests of the peripheral actors in one another, but instead on the relative interests governing their dyadic transactions with the intermediary.

Within an exchange network, brokerage would occur if transactions that could not be conducted by principals themselves, for lack of direct access to one another, were conducted along indirect linkages and mediated by one or more third parties. In such brokered transactions, the indirect tie is to be seen as more than the concatenation of two or more dyadic relationships; it is treated as a functional substitute for direct accessibility, and it is a relationship including at least three actors: the two principals and one or more brokers. Intermediary actors along the indirect ties serve as agents arranging transactions between the (more peripheral) principals to the exchange, and the intermediaries take into account the relative interests of the principals in one another when arranging the terms of exchange. Also, and importantly, the intermediary actors receive resource "commissions," defined here as fractions of the resource flow between principals, for their brokerage services.

I will now outline some of the assumptions I think plausible for initial efforts to modify the exchange model developed in Coleman (1973a) and Marsden (forthcoming) to permit brokerage behavior of the type described. First, actors will use the shortest transaction routes available to them in completing each of their transactions. That is, actors will most prefer a direct connection if one is available, next preferring an indirect connection via a single intermediary, then an indirect connection involving two intermediaries, and so forth. The rationale for this assumption is that by using short transaction routes in preference to lengthy ones, actors will economize on brokerage costs (commissions) involved in the conduct of transactions.

Other necessary assumptions pertain to the commissions involved in brokered transactions. These payments for the arrangement of exchanges are conceived as proportions of the amounts of resources transferred between peripheral actors by brokers. It is assumed that commission fractions vary as functions of the length and uniqueness of the indirect channels available for the conduct of brokered transactions. Thus, commission amounts will be larger if two brokers are required than if only one is necessary; I assume here that total commissions are divided equally among brokers if multiple intermediaries are required, though there are certainly circumstances in which this might not be the case. Further, commission amounts will be largest when there exists only one indirect link through which a given exchange can be brokered.[3] If there are several brokerage routes for a given transaction, then competitive pressures should drive commission fractions down, in the absence of collusion among potential brokers.

Centrally positioned actors in an access network should gain power—by comparison with a model allowing unrestricted exchange—when access limitations are imposed and brokered transactions are permitted. First, central actors will be most likely to be situated on unique chains or linkages joining peripheral actors, and they will therefore be able to extract resources from peripheral actors in the form of commissions. Second, central actors in an access network will be close to most other actors in the system of action. This means both that they will need to have fewer of their own exchanges with others brokered and that they will be able to make use of comparatively short routes for those transactions that must be brokered, thus incurring fewer transaction costs. Overall, therefore, we should expect that the net flow of resources will be toward central actors and away from peripheral ones when exchanges between unconnected principals are mediated by intervening actors.

In the next section, I propose a tentative formalization for brokerage behavior using the assumptions stated above. This effort departs from the mathematical model developed by Coleman (1973a), as modified by Marsden (forthcoming). Readers not interested in specific details of the formalization may skip to the numerical illustration given below, which simulates the redistribution of power in one system of action when brokered transactions of various lengths are permitted.

Formalization

My primary concern in this chapter is with the way brokerage behavior influences the distribution of power in exchange networks. I shall therefore state briefly only the foundations of Coleman's (1973a) model of purposive action that are necessary to achieve this end. Complete mathematical details on the basic model are presented by Coleman (1973a, 1977), while extensions of different kinds are presented by Feld (1977), Marsden and Laumann (1977), and Marsden (1981, forthcoming).

Consider a system of action composed of n actors and m events. Here, these units of analysis are to be regarded at a highly generalized level; thus, actors may be individuals or corporate groups, while events may be collective decisions or private goods and services.

The basic interset relationships of interest and control are conceived in relative terms. Thus, the magnitude of actor j's interest in event i, x_{ji}, is given as a proportion of j's interest in all events. If events are collective decisions, then interests have signs indicating the actor's preferred outcome attached to them, but only the magnitudes x_{ji} are pertinent to the discussion here. Actor j's control over event i is denoted by the symbol c_{ij}. This represents the proportion of all available control over event i that is held by actor j.

From the basic interset relationships of interest and control, it is possible to derive the objective interest dependency of actor j on some other actor j′. This quantity, $z_{jj'}$, gives the extent to which control necessary to realize the interests of actor j is held by actor j′. Objective interest dependency is defined as

$$z_{jj'} = \sum_i x_{ji} c_{ij'}$$

Note that $z_{jj'}$ refers only to the extent to which actor j′ controls events of interest to actor j; it does not consider relative numbers of alternative exchange relations available to each of the actors (see Emerson, 1962; Marsden, forthcoming). Because of the definitions of interest and control as proportions, $z_{jj'}$ is also interpretable as a proportion.

In the basic model, it is assumed that all actors have access to one another for possible exchanges and that the terms of trade in such exchanges will be set according to the relative dependencies of parties to the exchange on one another. Equivalently, exchange rates are set by the relative interests of parties in one another, which in turn derive from the intersection of the profiles of interest and control of the involved actors.

This assumption about exchange leads to the definition of the power of an actor. Conceiving of the power of an actor as that actor's stock of generalized control over events, and making the above assumption about exchange rates, eventually leads to the result

$$p_j = \sum_{j'} p_{j'} z_{j'j}$$

where p_j is the power of actor j at the "equilibrium" point. This point occurs when actors have aligned their control profiles with their interest distributions and hence have no incentive to exchange any further. An actor's power is interpretable as the proportion of the generalized resources in the system under his or her control at the equilibrium point.

A dynamic version of this process is developed in Marsden (forthcoming). Initially, a differential equation model specifying that the rate of change in an actor's power is a function of the discrepancy between the actor's supply of resources and the effective demands of other actors for those resources is postulated. This leads to the result

$$\frac{dp_j}{dt} = \sum_{j'} p_{j'}(t) g_{j'j}$$

where dp_j/dt is the instantaneous rate of change in the power of actor j, $p_{j'}(t)$ is the power of actor j′ at time t, and $g_{j'j}$ is the instantaneous rate at which resources are transferred from actor j′ to actor j in exchanges. The equation states that change in power is a function of the balance of generalized resource transactions taking place during a time period.

The rates of resource transfer $g_{jj'}$ are central to the dynamic version of the exchange process. By altering these rates to take processes thought to operate in the presence of access limitations into account, one can see how the postulated processes affect the equilibrium distribution of power. In Marsden (forthcoming), a functional form for alterations in the rates $g_{jj'}$ that occur as a consequence of exploitative behavior (differences in alternative exchange relations available) is specified, and its consequences are inspected. Here, ignoring (for the present) exploitative behavior, I consider a set of modifications in these rates that are appropriate for brokerage behavior.

Let matrix A refer to a network of access relations. Elements $a_{jj'}$ of A take the value of 1 if actor j has access to actor j′, and the value 0 otherwise. Diagonal elements a_{jj} of this matrix are set to 1, indicating that actors have access to themselves. I assume that A is a symmetric matrix (that is, that $a_{jj'} = a_{j'j}$) and that the access network contains no isolates or isolated subsets of actors exchanging only with one another (that is, that A^{n-1} contains only positive entries). It is assumed that exchanges will take place either along one of the accessible channels for exchange given by A, or along an indirect tie consisting of a chain of such relations.

To discover the two-step indirect ties that may be used to broker transactions between actors j and j′ using a single intervening actor k as a broker, define a three-dimensional matrix B1, with elements

$$b1_{jkj'} = a_{jk} a_{kj'} (1 - a_{jj'})$$

Elements of B1 will equal 1 only if there is an indirect linkage from actor j to actor j′ by way of actor k and there is no direct linkage from j to j′. If there were such a direct linkage, of course, brokerage would be unnecessary.

Next, a commission fraction $f_{jj'}$ must be defined for brokered transactions between actors j and j′. Using some of the assumptions discussed above gives

$$f_{jj'} = d + \frac{e}{b1_{j+j'}}$$

where d is a base commission fraction available in the case of an infinite number of brokers, e is an increment in this fraction that obtains if there is but a single broker available to arrange transactions between actors j and j′, and $b1_{j+j'}$ is the total number of two-step indirect ties that may be used to conduct exchanges between these two actors ($b1_{j+j'} = \sum_k b1_{jkj'}$).

I am now in a position to indicate how the transfer rates $g_{jj'}$ will be altered in the presence of access limitations and brokerage behavior. Assuming that when there are multiple brokers available, it is equiprobable that each will be used for transactions between actors j and j′, the rates $g_{jj'}$ are adjusted to rates $g^*_{jj'}$ as follows, when brokerage via a single intermediary only is permitted:

$$g^*_{jj'} = \begin{cases} g_{jj'} + \sum_{\ell} \left[\frac{d}{b1_{j+\ell}} + \frac{e}{(b1_{j+\ell})^2} \right] b1_{jj'\ell}\, g_{j\ell} & \text{, if } j \neq j' \text{ and } a_{jj'} = 1; \\ (1 - d - \frac{e}{b1_{j+j'}})\, g_{jj'} & \text{, if } j \neq j' \text{ and } b1_{j+j'} > 0; \\ 0 & \text{, if } j \neq j' \text{ and } a_{jj'} = b1_{j+j'} = 0; \\ - \sum_{\substack{\ell \\ (\ell \neq j)}} g^*_{j\ell} & \text{, if } j = j'. \end{cases}$$

The first adjustment occurs when actors j and j′ have direct access to one another. In this case, the dependency-based resource flow $g_{jj'}$ from j to j′ is augmented by the commission amounts expected to flow to j′ for brokering transactions between actor j and third actors ℓ. The second adjustment occurs when actors j and j′ are not directly connected, but are connected by a single intermediary; in this case the dependency-based resource transfer is reduced by the commission fraction. There is no resource flow between the actors if they have neither a direct connection nor a two-step indirect linkage. The final adjustment, given for resource transfer rates from an actor to himself or herself, is made necessary by the mathematical structure of the differential equation model for changes in power. It has no substantive implications apart from those entailed in the first three adjustments.

Given the adjusted rates of resource transfer $g^*_{jj'}$, it is possible to determine the equilibrium power of actors, with brokerage behavior taken into account. Marsden (forthcoming) shows that the equation $\mathbf{P} = \mathbf{P}\exp(\mathbf{G}^*)$ is sufficient for this purpose, where $\mathbf{P}$ is a vector containing the equilibrium power of actors, $\mathbf{G}^*$ is a matrix containing the adjusted rates of resource transfer, and exp indicates exponentiation with Euler's constant as a base.

The above development can be generalized to deal with transactions brokered by more than one intermediary, that is, along indirect ties consisting of three or more links. For three-step brokerage, the development would begin by defining a four-dimensional matrix B2, with elements

$$b2_{jkk'j'} = a_{jk}a_{kk'}a_{k'j'}(1 - a_{jj'})\prod_{\ell}(1 - b1_{j\ell j'})$$

Elements of B2 indicate whether an indirect tie between actors j and j′ via brokers k and k′ is available, given that j and j′ cannot access one another directly or via a single intermediary. To save space, extensions of brokerage behavior to permit multiple brokers will not be discussed further here, but they parallel the above discussion for transactions conducted via a single intermediary.[4]

Numerical Illustration

The proposed modifications incorporating brokerage behavior will be illustrated using one hypothetical system of action including ten actors. Because my concern here is with the effect of network structure on the power distribution, I have specified that all actors have equal control over all events (that is, $c_{ij} = 0.1$ for all i and j). The use of this special control structure means that all actors have equal objective interest dependencies

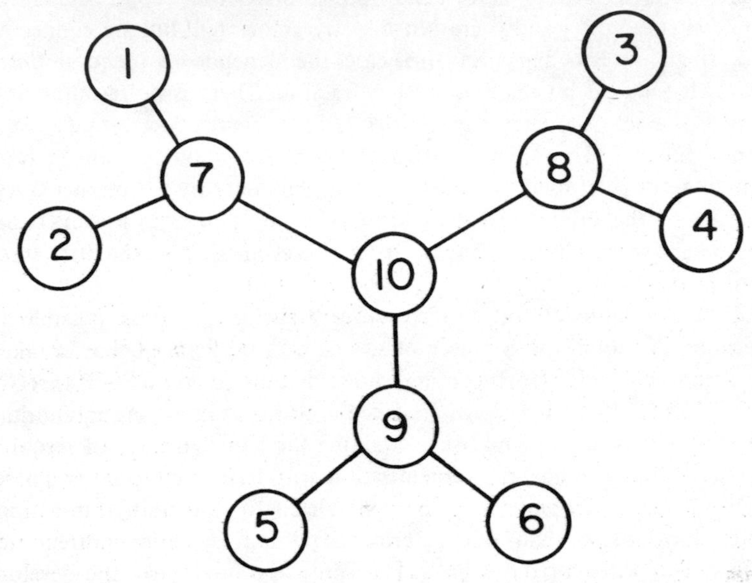

Figure 10.1 A Network of Restricted Access

on one another, regardless of the number of events or the interest distribution across events for actors (that is, $z_{jj'} = 0.1$ for all j and j′). For this reason I do not assume any particular number of events or any particular interest distribution for the simulation. The advantage of assuming the special control structure is that in the absence of restrictions on exchange, it guarantees that all actors will have equal power (that is, $p_j = 0.1$ for all j). So departures from equality in the distribution of power when restrictions are imposed will be attributable to the alterations in resource transfer rates $g_{jj'}$ due to brokerage behavior, not to inequalities in the control over valuable resources or events by actors.

In Figure 10.1, the network of access restrictions A used for the simulation is graphed. This network contains three structural positions: a peripheral one occupied by actors 1-6, a central one (in the sense of betweenness or closeness) occupied by actor 10, and a position of intermediate centrality occupied by actors 7-9. This network is of interest in that neither the experimental results of Cook, Emerson, Gillmore, and Yamagishi (1980; see note 2 of the present chapter) nor the simulation results for exploitative behavior presented in Marsden (forthcoming) show the expected association between centrality conceived as betweenness or closeness and power gains under access restrictions for this network.

Table 10.1 presents results giving the equilibrium distribution of power for the system analyzed, under various conditions of exchange. The first column shows the equal equilibrium distribution of power using Coleman's (1973a) basic model without access limitations, and the second column shows that this distribution is unchanged when restrictions on access are imposed but no purposive action is taken in response to them (see Marsden, forthcoming).

We can begin to see the effect of brokerage behavior on the distribution of power in the third column of Table 10.1. Here, the simulation has assumed that transactions can be brokered by a single intermediary only; no direct or brokered transactions between actors separated by more than two links in the access network are permitted.[5] The position of intermediate centrality occupied by actors 7-9 is the one that gains power under these conditions. The reason for this result is that the intermediate position is the only one to obtain a net gain in resource flow through commissions. Three two-step transactions are brokered by the most central actor, 10, as well as by actors 7-9; this means that actors 7-10 each receive six resource commissions. Actor 10, however, must also pay six resource commissions for transactions with the six peripheral actors, two of these commissions going to each of the actors in the intermediate position. Actors 7-9 pay only two commissions each, both to actor 10 for brokering their transactions with one another. The power of the peripheral actors 1-6 declines, as expected, because each of them must pay three commissions while receiving none. Thus, we see that for the network of access restrictions depicted in Figure 10.1, power gains due to two-step brokerage are not a direct function of betweenness or closeness centrality.

The expected rise in the power of actor 10, in the most central position, does emerge when brokered transactions via two intermediaries are entered into the model (see the fourth column of Table 10.1). The reason for this is that actor 10 is in an intermediate position on *all* three-step paths in Figure 10.1. This means that the central actor receives commissions on all two-broker transactions involving one of the peripheral actors and one of the actors of intermediate centrality. Furthermore, actor 10 need not use any three-step paths in the conduct of his or her own exchanges, and he or she thereby obtains transaction cost economies. These results are accentuated when three-broker transactions via four-step paths are permitted, because actor 10 lies on all of the four-step ties between pairs of peripheral actors (see the last column of Table 10.1).

TABLE 10.1 Power Distributions in Hypothetical Action System, for Brokerage Behavior Along Indirect Ties of Various Lengths

Actor	*No Access Restrictions*	*Restrictions, No Brokerage, No Exploitation*	*Restrictions, Brokerage via 1 Intermediary*	*Restrictions, Brokerage via 1-2 Intermediaries*	*Restrictions, Brokerage via 1-3 Intermediaries*
1	0.100	0.100	0.095	0.094	0.083
2	0.100	0.100	0.095	0.094	0.083
3	0.100	0.100	0.095	0.094	0.083
4	0.100	0.100	0.095	0.094	0.083
5	0.100	0.100	0.095	0.094	0.083
6	0.100	0.100	0.095	0.094	0.083
7	0.100	0.100	0.109	0.105	0.119
8	0.100	0.100	0.109	0.105	0.119
9	0.100	0.100	0.109	0.105	0.119
10	0.100	0.100	0.101	0.124	0.146

Discussion

The problem on which this chapter has focused is that of understanding mechanisms capable of converting an actor's position in a resource exchange network into power advantages. I began with the fact that nonexperimental network studies have generally documented a positive association between centrality conceived as betweenness or closeness and manifestations of power or influence. Other work introducing the mechanism of exploitative behavior by actors in the context of access limitations (Marsden, forthcoming) was unable to reproduce the documented association, and other plausible types of purposive action that would do so were therefore sought.

The mechanism of brokerage behavior is one by which actors lying on indirect channels between other actors lacking access to one another arrange exchanges for the latter, in return for payments in the form of resource commissions. Introducing this mechanism does generate the positive association of centrality and power not successfully modeled in previous work, at least for the case studied here. It should be noted, however, that in the simulation it was necessary to permit transactions to be brokered along rather long chains of direct linkages—involving at least four actors (two principals) and two brokers—before the positive association of centrality and power emerged.

It is important to emphasize that gains in power due to brokerage behavior can be traced to the simultaneous presence of two aspects of centrality identified by Freeman (1979) for communication networks: betweenness and closeness. Gains in power for an actor in the purposive action model are due to net excesses of inflows of resources over outflows. Betweenness is important on the inflow side: An actor positioned along indirect ties between other actors has the potential of receiving commissions for arranging transactions for them; and as the number of appropriate indirect ties grows smaller, commission fractions increase, as does the share of them expected to go to any given broker.

In and of itself, however, central position in the sense of betweenness is not enough to guarantee power gains. Closeness is important in terms of resource transfers on the outflow side. To be close to most actors in the system is to have relatively little need for their brokerage services. An actor central in the sense of closeness is autonomous (Burt, 1980b) in that his or her transactions with others can be conducted largely free of the constraints imposed by requirements that the cooperation of many intervening actors be obtained. Power gains due to brokerage in exchange networks can thus be seen as a joint product of betweenness and closeness–betweenness increasing resource inflows, closeness keeping outflows in the form of transaction costs to a minimum.

The introduction of brokerage behavior as a type of purposive action that may occur under access restrictions in addition to exploitative behavior has successfully modeled the association between network centrality and power gains. To this point, though, the question of the conjoint operation of the two types of behavior has not been addressed; simulations to explore effects of one process have assumed that the other process does not take place. Let us now consider briefly problems that arise when we think of the possibility that both processes may occur simultaneously, using the access network depicted in Figure 10.1 as an example for concreteness.

In Figure 10.1, we see that a peripheral actor (such as actor 1) has no alternative but to exchange with an actor of intermediate centrality (such as actor 7). Because the actor of intermediate centrality has two alternative relations to which he or she may turn rather than exchanging with a peripheral actor (for example, actors 2 and 10), he or she is in a position to exploit the poor strategic position of the peripheral actor, and there is some reason to believe that this will, in fact, happen (Cook, Emerson, Gillmore, and Yamagishi, 1980).

When brokerage via a single intermediary is permitted, the number of effective alternative relations for peripheral actors would appear to increase. For instance, in Figure 10.1, peripheral actor 1 can reach actors 2 and 10 via a single intermediary, in addition to having direct access to actor 7. This would appear to improve the position of the peripheral actor vis-á-vis actor 7; the problem, however, is that the broker for these new alternative transactions is also the actor holding the exploitative advantage based on directly accessible exchange relations. It is not clear that the actor of intermediate centrality will be willing to reduce the leverage he or she holds over the peripheral actor by creating alternative exchange relationships for the latter through brokerage.

I will conclude by mentioning three suggestions of ways for deciding whether brokerage behavior or exploitative behavior will be used by the actor of intermediate centrality in such a situation. One criterion is based on self-interest: If gains available through brokerage exceed those available through exploitation of differences in alternatives, it might be argued that the intermediate actor would choose to broker transactions along indirect ties rather than restricting the peripheral actor's access to alternative sources of supply. The relative gains available through the two strategies would depend on specific values of parameters governing the two types of behavior (for example, parameters d and e dictating the size of commission fractions $f_{jj'}$ for brokers).

Another suggestion as to the conditions under which the two types of behavior might be used is made by Cook (this volume). Cook reviews Emerson's (1972b) distinction between "positively connected" exchange networks, in which the use of one exchange relation makes it more likely or even necessary that other relations also be used, and "negatively connected" networks, in which the use of one exchange relation makes the use of others less likely or even impossible. She cites experimental evidence for the presence of exploitative behavior in negatively connected networks (Cook, Emerson, Gillmore, and Yamagishi, 1980) and suggests (this volume) that in positively connected networks, occupants of a position of moderate centrality, like actor 7 in Figure 10.1, will "function more like intermediaries"—or, in the terms used here, brokers.

A final basis one might use to predict when one type of behavior under limited access of parties to one another will be used is the nature of the distribution of control among actors. Consider again the relationship between actor 7 and actor 1 in Figure 10.1 and the possibility of brokered transactions involving actor 1 and actors 2 and 10. The relevant comparisons here involve the control profile held by actor 7 and those held by actors 2 and 10. If these are complementary profiles, pertaining to different sets of events not substitutable in the view of actor 7, then brokerage behavior might be anticipated. Actor 7 would not drive down the value of his or her own resources by brokering transactions involving actor 1 and actors 2 and 10, and would gain brokerage commissions. If, on the other hand, the profiles of control held by the actor in the exploitative position and those other actors accessible only via his or her agency are competitive with one another, then we might expect the actor in the position of intermediate centrality to capitalize on the isolated position of peripheral actors, maintaining an exploitative stance.

At this point all that can be reliably stated is that the simultaneous operation of exploitative and brokerage processes in exchange networks with limited access is a problem to be dealt with in future work. If such work seeks to elaborate the structure of the mathematical model used here, new directions will be necessary. To take account of some of the suggestions made in this chapter would require the addition of a decision-making apparatus for actors that is sensitive to distributions of control over specific resources or events, not simply a generalized distribution of resources. This would also require the addition of an apparatus for weighing the relative gains available through adopting a competitive (exploitative) stance rather than a cooperative (brokerage) stance in the conduct of transactions.

NOTES

1. A "degree-based" notion of centrality focuses on the number of direct contacts an actor has available in a network (see Freeman, 1979).

2. The experimental results on power in restricted exchange networks obtained by Cook, Emerson, Gillmore, and Yamagishi (1980) are not consistent with the results of Marsden's (forthcoming) modified version of the purposive action model, nor do they conform to expectations based on degree-based, betweenness, or closeness conceptions of centrality. Cook et al. (1980) advance a new conception of centrality, termed "vulnerability," which focuses on reductions in overall resource flow resulting if an actor in a given position is removed from the exchange network together with the exchange relations in which that actor takes part. While this is a provocative proposal, it should be noted that the experimental conditions used in the Cook et al. (1980) study are rather special ones. Actors in the experiment are aware only of the other actors directly accessible for exchanges, and the exchange network is "negatively connected" (see Cook, this volume), which means that actors may engage in one and only one exchange during each experimental trial. It is arguable that these experimental conditions are especially likely to call forth only a special form of exploitative behavior in response to access limitations. For this reason I direct my efforts here toward modifying the basic purposive action model in an effort to produce results consistent with the positive correlation between centrality and power observed in nonexperimental data, rather than attempting to model the results obtained in the Cook et al. (1980) experiment.

3. In Granovetter's (1973) terms, such a unique channel is called a "bridge."

4. An alternative formalization for brokerage behavior was suggested to me in personal communication with James S. Coleman. Coleman suggests that we append n pseudo-events, each of which corresponds to the brokerage services of an actor, to the system. Each actor is assumed to hold total initial control over his or her brokerage services. Other actors would develop interests in brokerage services to the extent that the actor offering them is situated on unique paths linking the other actors to actors with whom they wish to conduct transactions involving large resource transfers—that is, as a function of the betweenness of the actor offering the brokerage services in the access network. For plausible specifications of the way interests in brokerage services are generated, this formalization would lead to results on redistribution of power that are similar to those exhibited below.

5. In conducting the simulation, I have assumed that commission fractions $f_{jj'}$ to brokers amount to one-tenth (0.1) of the dependency-based resource flows $g_{jj'}$. The structure of the access network in Figure 10.1 is such that there is but one indirect linkage available to broker each transaction. For this reason it is not important to specify separate values for the parameters d and e in the formula for $f_{jj'}$ given above; since all brokerage channels are unique, all commission fractions are identical. For transactions conducted by way of two or more brokers, I have assumed that each broker receives a fraction equal to $f_{jj'}$ of the dependency-based resource flow $g_{jj'}$, so that the total commission fraction is a linear function of the number of brokers necessary to complete the transaction.

11

A Note on Cooptation and Definitions of Constraint

RONALD S. BURT

Structural sociologists seem to be in general agreement with the idea that networks of relations have the potential to constrain the perceptions and behaviors of actors in a network. The same scholars begin to diverge sharply when the discussion gets down to the nuts and bolts of how relations pose constraint. My purpose in this chapter is to assess the relative adequacy of two constraint concepts that are applicable in network analysis generally but have been particularly fruitful in the area of organizations and markets. This area is a convenient laboratory for research on alternative constraint concepts: Markets pose constraint and purposive organizations respond with cooptive strategies to circumvent or manage the constraint. The two constraint concepts discussed here do not exhaust the range of possible concepts. They are important alternatives in the area of organizations and markets because both have survived empirical tests and have been useful in understanding cooptive relations between organizations. It is of some moment, therefore, to know not only that the two concepts are adequate, but also which one is better. I shall present data on patterns of buying and selling among sectors of the American economy and patterns of cooptive interorganizational relations through corporate boards of directors. I shall argue that constraint emerges from a

AUTHOR'S NOTE: The work reported here was supported by grants from the National Science Foundation (SOC77-22938, SOC79-25728). The idea for this chapter was taken from an analysis of directorate ties and market constraint in Germany relational pattern rather than an individual relationship. This point will seem obvious to some readers, complex to others. It is neither. I shall build up to the point systematically.

Market Constraint

This discussion is concerned with a refinement of the general resource dependence perspective on organizational behavior. From this perspective, corporate actors are viewed as dependent on resources provided by other actors, or classes of actors, in an organizational environment. This dependence poses a constraint on the freedom corporate actors have to pursue their organization-specific interests. At the same time, however, corporate actors are understood to be purposive in the sense that they can adapt to these constraints and manage their access to needed resources. In a review of the sociology of organizational environments, Aldrich and Pfeffer (1976: 83-84) succinctly summarize the principal theme of the resource dependence perspective:

> Administrators manage their environments as well as their organizations, and the former activity may be as important, or even more important, than the latter. The presumed end result of such strategies is the acquisition of resources and the survival of the organization, as well as the stabilization of relationships with environmental elements. . . . The resource dependence model calls attention to the importance of environmental contingencies and constraints, at the same time leaving room for the operation of strategic choice on the part of organizational members as they maneuver through known and unknown contexts.

The concepts of constraint and cooptive strategies for circumventing or managing constraint are clearly central issues in the resource dependence perspective.

When translated into empirical research on relations among organizations, the resource dependence perspective is typically translated into a concern with the strength of resource and cooptive relations. To the extent that some organization A obtains a large proportion of its resources from some other organization, or class of organizations, B, organization A

---

and Austria that was conducted under Rolf Ziegler's direction at the University of Munich. I am grateful to Professor Ziegler and his colleagues for that original insight. An initial draft of the chapter was improved by incorporating several critical comments from Peter Marsden.

is expected to have cooptive relations to B in order to manage its access to needed resources. The more intense, the stronger, the flow of resources from B to A, in other words, the more likely are cooptive relations between B and A. Empirical research is used to show that interorganizational cooptive relations of various types are predicted by interorganizational resource relations. An illustrative example would be helpful here. There are many studies adopting a resource dependence perspective, but those by Jeffrey Pfeffer with several colleagues are particularly well known and have been conveniently assembled in a book on organizational environments by Pfeffer and Salancik (1978). An extensive review of this and related research up through the mid-1970s can be obtained from chapters in the Nystrom and Starbuck (1981) handbook on adapting organizations to their environments.

A resource dependence measure Pfeffer and his colleagues have found useful is the proportion of all sales and purchases by organizations in some sector j of the American economy that is transacted with organizations in some other sector i. Let z_{ji} represent this proportion. A value of .80 for z_{ji}, for example, would mean that 80 percent of all the sales and purchases by organizations in sector j were transacted with organizations in sector i. To the extent that z_{ji} is high, organizations in sector j obtain a large proportion of their resources from organizations in sector i, which means that organizations in the two sectors should be connected by cooptive relations in order to manage the flow of resources between them. Mergers and joint ventures are explicitly cooptive relations. An organization could coopt another by buying it outright (merger) or agreeing to pool resources with it for a specific project (joint venture). The frequency and strength of these two relations between organizations in separate sectors of the economy increase with the intensity of buying and selling between them, that is, in proportion to z_{ji} for sectors i and j (Pfeffer and Salancik, 1978: 114ff., 157ff.).

Given the increasing popularity of network analysis as a strategy for representing organizational environments, it seems likely that the prediction of cooptive relations from the strength of resource relations will become even more common in future research on organizational behavior. As in past research, there is likely to be a positive association between the strengths of corresponding resource and cooptive relations.

Network analysis brings with it, however, an emphasis on the conceptualization of constraint in the organizational environment. This emphasis goes well beyond a concern with the mere strength of relations. At issue is the structure of relations to actors providing resources and the manner in which those actors themselves are structured. Here again, an example is helpful.

I have elsewhere analyzed constraint as a limitation on structural autonomy, the freedom to act without constraint (Burt, 1980b, 1982: Chapter 7). The structural autonomy model takes the patterns of relations among occupants of each status in a system as input and predicts the relative freedom the status offers its occupants as well as the extent to which that freedom is constrained by role relations with each other status. Shorn of mathematical niceties, the structural autonomy model implies that occupants of status j are constrained by their relations with the occupants of some other status i to the extent that two conditions occur simultaneously: (1) Occupants of status j only have relations with the occupants of status i, and (2) occupants of status i are coordinated so as to act collectively in their own interest. Status group i poses a constraint for some ego occupying status j, in other words, to the extent that ego's relations with occupants of status i are strong *and* the objects of those relations are coordinated so as to be able to impose a constraint. Strong relations to a status occupied by highly disorganized actors would not pose a constraint.

This simple idea has been useful in defining market constraints on corporate profits in the American economy (Burt, 1980b, 1982: Chapter 8, forthcoming: Chapter 2). The "sector" of an input-output table corresponds to a "status" as a jointly occupied network position in a density table. Given data on the dollars of sales and purchases among sectors of the economy and the extent to which organizations within a sector are coordinated in the sense of being dominated by a small number of large firms, the structural autonomy model defines the level of market constraint any one sector faces from its corporate environment. Assuming that organizations within manufacturing sectors of the economy would set prices in their own favor (and accordingly make high profits) to the extent that they were free to do so, the typical profit margin observed in a sector should be a function of the market constraint on the sector. This is precisely what occurred and is reported in the above citations; profit margins increase with decreasing market constraint as defined by the structural autonomy model.

More to the point here, organizations in sector i pose a severe market constraint for organizations in sector j to the extent that two things occur simultaneously: (1) Sector i is the sole supplier/consumer for sector j, and (2) organizations within sector i are coordinated so as to form an oligopoly. The structure of relations is emphasized over the strength of a relation. It is not the mere obtaining of resources from sector i that makes it a source of constraint so much as it is the lack of alternatives. Establishments have alternative actors from which they can obtain needed resources to the extent that they buy and sell with many different sectors, and each sector contains many organizations competing with one another to provide the establishments with their needed resources—needed in the sense of a low price for supplies purchased and a high price for output sold. To the extent that sector i is the principal source of sales and purchases for establishments within some sector j, and organizations within sector i are coordinated so as to negotiate as a single buyer/consumer, these alternatives are absent and sector i poses a severe market constraint for sector j.

This understanding of market constraint is obviously consistent with the resource dependence perspective. As would be expected, cooptive interorganizational relations are predicted by market constraint so conceived. To the extent that sector i poses a market constraint for obtaining profits in manufacturing sector j, organizations in the two sectors tend to be connected by three types of directorate ties simultaneously: (1) ownership ties, firms in sector j owning an establishment in sector i; (2) direct interlock ties, firms in sector j having interlocked directorates with other firms that own establishments in sector i; and (3) indirect financial interlock ties, firms in sector j having interlocked directorates with financial institutions that in turn have interlocked directorates with firms owning establishments in sector i. These three types of interorganizational relations through corporate boards of directors have the potential to coopt sources of market constraint (Burt, 1980a, forthcoming: Chapter 3). That they tend to occur together with the most severe market constraints on corporate profits certainly gives them the appearance of being used with cooptive intent (Burt et al., 1980; Burt, forthcoming: Chapter 4).

The empirical adequacy of alternative concepts of constraint poses a basic question for the resource dependence perspective on organizational behavior: How important is it to understand constraint in terms of the structure of resource relations rather than equating constraint with the strength of a resource relation? The structure of resource relations is emphasized in the network model of structural autonomy, and the concept of constraint in this model has some appealing features. When applied to organizations and markets, the constraint posed by sector i for sector j is the profit margin in sector j attributable to buying and selling with sector i. It is also the profit margin foregone in sector j by failing to coopt sector i (see Burt, 1982: Equation 7.5, forthcoming: Equations 2.10ff.). In other words, constraint has a precise theoretical meaning. Moreover, this theoretical meaning has substantive merit in the sense that low profit margins in fact occur in sectors confronted with severe market constraint as defined by the model and cooptive directorate ties occur as a function of severe market constraint defined by the model.

This does not mean that the persons responsible for creating and maintaining cooptive relations are accurate in perceiving the market constraints confronting them. It is much simpler to understand constraint solely in terms of a resource relation's strength, and empirical evidence can be mustered to advocate such an understanding. Available research within the resource dependence perspective shows that the likelihood of cooptive relations between two corporate actors increases with the strength of the resource relations between them. If relational strength alone predicts cooptive relations, then perhaps relational strength alone defines constraint as perceived and that perception is the stimulus for cooptive relations. The directors of an organization operating within a highly competitive market might be so insecure about their survival that they strive to coopt all of their suppliers and consumers in order to reduce some of the uncertainty in their profits. It is not impossible, in other words, to envision cooptive relations maintained solely as a function of resource relation strength, regardless of actual constraints on profits. Further, it is not impossible that the success of structural autonomy constraint in predicting cooptive directorate ties merely reflects the fact that the intensity of buying and selling between two sectors is a component in the structural autonomy constraint they pose for one another's profits.

Data on manufacturing sectors in the 1967 American economy can be used to show that this possibility did not occur in fact. The persons responsible for cooptive directorate ties among large American firms in 1967 were quite accurate in perceiving sources of market constraint on their profits. The likelihood of directorate ties increased in a systematic way with the market conditions proposed in the structural autonomy model to be conditions of constraint—conditions demonstrated to have a negative effect on profits.

Data

Three types of data are required in order to demonstrate this point: data on the strength of resource relations, data on sector oligopoly, and data on cooptive relations. I shall consider data on relations between sectors of the American economy. For each of 20 two-digit manufacturing industries defined by the Standard Industrial Classification for 1967, let z_{ji} be the proportion of extraindustry sales and purchases transacted with organizations in some sector i where z_{ji} is based on the aggregate input-output table for the 1967 American economy. In other words, z_{ji} is a measure of the extent to which industry establishments transacted all of their extraindustry buying and selling with establishments in sector i. Data for computing these percentage measures are listed elsewhere (Burt, forthcoming: Appendix, based on U.S. Department of Commerce, 1974). Also given there are measures taken from census data released by the Commerce Department regarding the extent to which sector i was dominated by a small number of large firms so as to constitute an oligopoly. The score for sector i, y_i, measures the extent to which all sales from the sector were made by a small number of large establishments (see U.S. Department of Commerce, 1971). For the purposes here, I make a crude distinction between sectors that were competitive (y_i low) versus those that were oligopolistic (y_i high). This liberal definition of oligopoly is in keeping with the approximate nature of the data available and ensures a sufficient number of oligopolistic sectors to illustrate the structural autonomy market constraint effect.[1] Also given in the above reference are frequencies with which sample establishments in any one of the 20 two-digit industries were connected in 1967 by each of three types of cooptive directorate ties to establishments in each of 43 other nonfinancial sectors.[2] Establishments in an industry could have been connected–through corporate boards of directors–to establishments in some other sector in one, or all, of three ways. The same firm could have owned an establishment in the industry and another in the sector. This would have constituted an ownership tie between industry and sector. A director on the board of a firm in the industry could have been on the board of a different firm in the sector. This would have been a direct interlock tie between industry and sector. These interlocking directorates also defined indirect interlock ties. A firm in the industry could have interlocked with a bank or insurance company which in turn interlocked with a firm in the sector. This would have constituted an indirect financial interlock tie between industry and sector. More generally, the strongest cooptive directorate tie would have been the simultaneous presence of all three types of ties as a multiplex cooptive relation (see Burt, 1980a, forthcoming: Chapter 3). Let w_{ji} be the number of establishments in industry j connected to sector i where each industry establishment has an ownership tie, direct interlock ties, and indirect financial interlock ties to sector establishment(s). Given establishments in 20 industries buying and selling with establishments in 43 other nonfinancial sectors, there are 860 transactions defined by these data. For each transaction, there is a resource relation (z_{ji}, the proportion of extraindustry sales and purchases transacted with sector i), sector oligopoly (y_i, competitive versus oligopolistic, 0 versus 1, respectively), and a cooptive relation (w_{ji}, the number of sampled establishments in industry j that had all three types of directorate ties to sector i).[3]

Market Conditions for Directorate Ties

The structural autonomy concept of constraint predicts that the likelihood of cooptive directorate ties between industry j and sector i increases to the extent that two market conditions simultaneously characterize buying and selling between industry and sector establishments: (1) A high proportion of industry sales and purchases are transacted with the sector–that is, z_{ji} is high, and (2) the sector is oligopolistic in the sense of being dominated by a small number of large firms–that is, y_i equals 1 rather than 0. To the extent that z_{ji} and y_i are high simultaneously, sector i posed a severe market constraint in 1967 for profits in industry j and cooptive directorate ties are expected between industry and sector establishments. Put another way, highly competitive sectors (y_i equal to 0) posed no constraint for profits and so should not have been the object of competitive directorate ties–regardless of the extent to which they were a source of industry sales and purchases. This is precisely what occurred.

One illustration of this point is obtained by regressing the strength of cooptive relations over the strength of corresponding resource relations–holding constant differences in sector oligopoly. The following results are obtained across all 860 transactions when w_{ji} is regressed over z_{ji}, y_i, and their interaction (routine t tests for null hypotheses are given in parentheses):

$$\widehat{w_{ji}} = .23 + .94(z_{ji}) + .47(y_i) + 14.36(z_{ji}y_i)$$
$$\qquad\qquad (1.1) \qquad (6.1) \qquad (10.2)$$

which accounts for 28 percent of the variation in multiplex directorate ties ($R^2 = .28$). Similar results are obtained if the cooptive relation is measured as the proportion of sampled industry establishments with complete multiplex ties to sector i:

$$\widehat{w_{ji}/n_j} = .02 + .10(z_{ji}) + .05(y_i) + 1.08(z_{ji}y_i)$$
$$\qquad\qquad (1.3) \qquad (7.4) \qquad (8.1)$$

where n_j is the number of establishments sampled from industry j and routine t tests are given in parentheses.[4] This second equation accounts for 25 percent of the variation in proportionate cooptive relations ($R^2 = .25$ for the dependent variable w_{ji}/n_j).

From these results, I infer a strong interaction effect between resource relation strength (z_{ji}) and sector oligopoly (y_i) in determining cooptive relations between industry and sector. The direct effect of extensive buying and selling with a sector (the effect of transactions with a non-oligopoly) was negligible, as indicated by the respective t tests of 1.1 and 1.3, which provide no basis for rejecting the null hypothesis. In other words, the expected number of multiplex directorate ties between industry j and sector i when sector i is highly competitive is $\widehat{w_{ji}} = .23 + .94(z_{ji})$, and the proportion of industry establishments with such ties to the competitive sector is $\widehat{w_{ji}/n_j} = .02 + .10(z_{ji})$. The strength of the industry-sector cooptive relation increased with the strength of the industry-sector resource relation, but the increase can be attributed to random error in sampling directorate ties. In contrast, the expected number of multiplex directorate ties when sector i is oligopolistic is $\widehat{w_{ji}} = .70 + 15.30(z_{ji})$, and the proportion of industry establishments with such ties to the oligopolistic sector is $\widehat{w_{ji}/n_j} = .07 + 1.18(z_{ji})$.[5] The strength of the industry-sector cooptive relation increased in a significant way with the strength of the corresponding resource relation. The t tests for sector oligopoly effects in the above regression equations are significant at well beyond the .001 level of confidence.[6] It was when an industry relied on a sector for extensive sales and purchases *and* the sector was oligopolistic that cooptive directorate ties were most likely between industry and sector.[7]

A more intimate feel for the interaction effect can be obtained from Figure 11.1, where bar graphs indicate the strength of cooptive relations typical of different combinations of market conditions. The height of each bar in Figure 11.1 indicates the percentage of sampled establishments in industry j that had complete multiplex directorate ties to sector i (that is, 100 times w_{ji}/n_j for specified market conditions. Market conditions are distinguished in terms of sector oligopoly (y_i low versus high) and five categories of resource relation strength (z_{ji} equal to .00, .01, .02 to .04, .05 to .09, and .10 or more).[8]

The observed association between resource relation strength and cooptive relation strength is illustrated by the dotted bars. They show that cooptive directorate ties were increasingly likely with increasingly intense buying and selling between industry and sector. About 2 percent of industry establishments had multiplex directorate ties to sectors in which they conducted no buying and selling. With a mere 1 percent of their extraindustry buying and selling being transacted with a sector, the mean percentage increases to 5 percent. The percentage of industry establishments with multiplex directorate ties to a sector increases further to 10 percent, 14 percent, and 20 percent with increasingly strong resource relations to the sector (.02 to .04, .05 to .09, and .10 or more, respec-

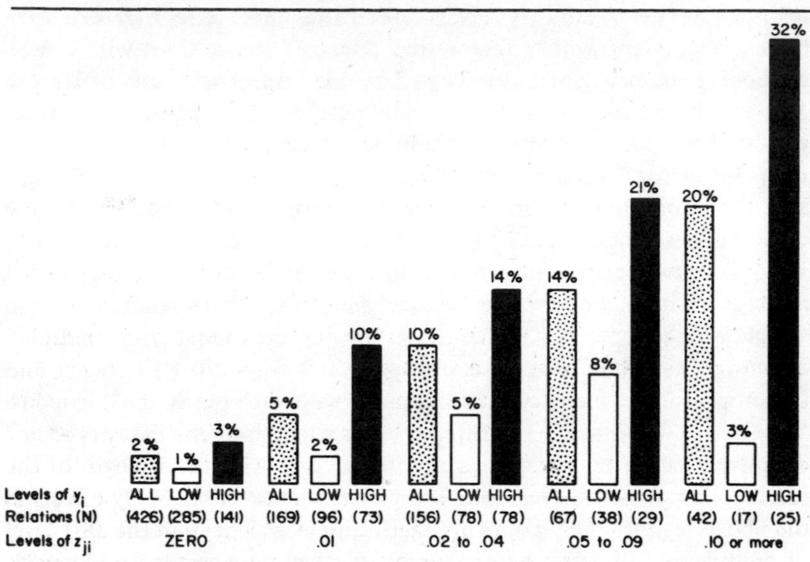

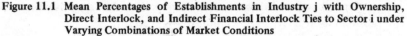

Figure 11.1 Mean Percentages of Establishments in Industry j with Ownership, Direct Interlock, and Indirect Financial Interlock Ties to Sector i under Varying Combinations of Market Conditions

tively). In short, the often-reported association between resource relation strength and cooptive relation strength is apparent in these data.

The importance of sector oligopoly is illustrated by the white and dark bars in Figure 11.1. The white bars refer to relatively competitive sectors and the dark bars refer to relatively oligopolistic sectors. Note that within each category of buying and selling intensity, the dark bar is higher than the white bar. The difference is small when there is no buying and selling between industry and sector; 1 percent of industry establishments had multiplex ties to competitive sectors, and 3 percent had such ties to oligopolistic sectors. The difference between competitive and oligopolistic sectors increases quickly after that. With the smallest fraction of extra-industry buying and selling being transacted with some sector (that is, $.00 < z_{ji} < .015$), 2 percent of industry establishments had multiplex directorate ties to the sector if it was competitive, and 10 percent had such ties if the sector was oligopolistic. These respective percentages increase to 5 percent and 14 percent if 2 to 4 percent of extraindustry transactions were conducted with the sector, and to 8 percent and 21 percent if 5 to 9 percent of extraindustry transactions were conducted with the sector.

TABLE 11.1 Cooptive Directorate Ties Observed Under Different Combinations of Market Conditions

Market Conditions		*Cooptive Directorate Ties*		
Proportion of Extraindustry Buying/Selling with Sector (z_{ji})	*Sector Oligopoly* (y_i)	*Null*	*Mixed*	*Complete Multiplex*
none	low	101	113	71
	high	19	71	51
.01	low	10	29	57
	high	0	11	62
.02-.04	low	5	26	47
	high	1	11	66
.05-.09	low	4	9	25
	high	0	0	29
.10 or more	low	3	6	8
	highe	0	1	24

NOTE: The three categories of cooptive directorate ties refer to the complete absence of all three types of ties (null), the occurrence of one or two, but not all three, types of ties (mixed), and the occurrence of all three types of ties simultaneously (complete multiplex). The varying market conditions are distinguished in Figure 11.1 and discussed in the text.

When z_{ji} was .10 or more, then 3 percent of industry establishments had multiplex ties to sector i if the sector was competitive, while 32 percent had such ties to the sector if it was oligopolistic. In short, there was a clear tendency for industry establishments to have ownership, direct interlock, and indirect financial interlock ties simultaneously to oligopolistic sectors with which they conducted an extensive proportion of extraindustry buying and selling. In comparison, competitive sectors were all but ignored, regardless of the extent to which they were sources of industry purchases or sales.

The point illustrated with Figure 11.1 can be made more formally with the frequencies in Table 11.1, where rows distinguish the market conditions distinguished in Figure 11.1 and columns distinguish three categories of cooptive relation strength between industry j and sector i: null relations (the complete absence of all three types of directorate ties between industry and sector), mixed relations (the presence of one or two types of directorate ties, but not all three), and complete multiplex (the presence of all three types of directorate ties between industry and sector).

The categories of cooptive relation strength are contingent on both resource relation strength and sector oligopoly. The null hypothesis that the five categories of buying and selling and the two categories of sector oligopoly are independent of the three cooptive relation categories can be rejected at well beyond the .001 level of confidence (likelihood ratio chi square of 286.9 with 18 degrees of freedom). Neither sector oligopoly nor the extent of extraindustry buying and selling with the sector can be ignored. The null hypothesis that the three cooptive relation categories are independent of sector oligopoly–given the five categories of buying and selling–can be rejected at well beyond the .001 level of confidence (with a chi square of 88.6 and 10 degrees of freedom). Similarly, the null hypothesis that the three cooptive relation categories are independent of the five categories of buying and selling–given sector oligopoly–can be rejected at well beyond the .001 level of confidence (with a chi square of 207.0 and 16 degrees of freedom). Finally, the null hypothesis that there are no three-way interactions among categories of cooptive directorate ties, sector oligopoly, and buying and selling can be rejected at the .001 level of confidence (with a 26.4 chi square and 8 degrees of freedom).

More specifically, directorate ties were more likely with oligopolistic sectors than with competitive sectors. The observed number of complete multiplex relations to competitive sectors is, on average, half the number expected from extraindustry buying and selling. The observed number to oligopolistic sectors is, on average, twice the number expected from extraindustry buying and selling with the sector. This tendency is significant at well beyond the .001 level of confidence, given its 5.6 unit normal test statistic.[9] The tendency is illustrated in Figure 11.1 by the fact that within each category of buying and selling with a sector, the white bar (competitive sectors) is lower than the dotted bar (sectors on average), which is lower than the dark bar (oligopolistic sectors).

Conclusion

These results have a clear implication for organizational research within the resource dependence perspective. The constraints organizations strategically manage are defined more by the structure of resource relations in their environments than the strength of their resource relations to specific actors in their environments. Systematic errors in predicting cooptive relations can be expected if constraint is equated with the strength of a resource relation. Cooptive directorate ties between sectors of the 1967 American economy did increase with the intensity of buying and selling between the sectors. However, the frequency of directorate ties expected from buying and selling alone is consistently greater than the observed frequency of such ties to competitive sectors (dotted versus white bars in Figure 11.1) and consistently less than the observed frequency of such ties to oligopolistic sectors (dotted versus dark bars in Figure 11.1). In other words, the market constraints that cooptive directorate ties were patterned to manage are the constraints defined by the structural autonomy model and demonstrated to have had a negative effect on corporate profits. Competitive suppliers and consumers posed no threat to a firm's profits and were not the object of cooptive directorate ties. Oligopolistic suppliers and consumers could have posed a threat and were the object of cooptive ties. The bottom line here is that across varying intensities of resource dependence, cooptive relations can be expected to occur as a function of both the intensity of resource exchange and the structure of relations among the actors with whom resources are exchanged.

NOTES

1. This liberal definition of oligopoly weakens empirical support for the market constraint effect implied by the structural autonomy model, since relatively competitive sectors are being treated as if they were oligopolistic. In other words, sectors that could not impose a constraint on industry profits are being treated as if they could. Of 44 nonfinancial sectors, 18 (or 41 percent) are coded as oligopolistic and accordingly have the potential to constrain profits in industries buying or selling with them. The criterion level of y_i used to dichotomize sectors as competitive versus oligopolistic is based on the distribution of the y_i across different sectors and the distribution of directorate ties among competitors within manufacturing industries. The mean value of y_i across the 44 nonfinancial sectors considered is .221 (roughly indicating that the four largest firms in the typical sector accounted for 22 percent of all sector sales), but industries with higher scores than this contained very few interlock ties among competitors, giving them the appearance of being highly competitive. The highest frequencies of intraindustry directorate ties were observed in industries with values of y_i greater than .28, so sectors over this criterion are coded as relatively oligopolistic in order to illustrate the market constraint effect on directorate ties. Not all sectors over this criterion had extensive directorate ties, as is clear from the analysis, but the most frequent ties occurred in industries over this criterion (for example, see Burt, 1982: Figure 8.2, forthcoming: Figure 4.3, for illustrative graphs of intraindustry directorate ties and values of y_i).

2. These frequencies are based on a sample of 152 firms representative of large firms involved in American manufacturing. Directorate ties between sectors of the economy were computed from connections among the 414 establishments these firms owned in diverse economic sectors and the 2903 persons serving as directors of these firms in 1967. These data are taken from *Fortune* and *Poor's* for 1967. Details

concerning the sampling design and computation of directorate tie frequencies can be found in several places (for example, Burt, 1980a, forthcoming: Chapter 3; Burt et al., 1980).

3. The conclusions reached here with complete multiplex directorate ties are also reached if cooptive relations are measured in terms of each type of directorate tie. For the purposes of this chapter, I have only presented results for the strongest of cooptive directorate ties: the complete multiplex ties.

4. I have presented the proportion measure w_{ji}/n_j in the text because it is easily interpreted. This proportion does not consider the number of establishments sampled from sector i for two reasons: (1) the sample was drawn to represent the manner in which firms in manufacturing industries reached across economic sectors generally with directorate ties, and (2) an industry establishment need not have coopted every sector establishment in order to have circumvented market constraint from the sector. All that would have been needed were ties to selected trade partners in the sector to ensure access to sales and purchase transactions and access to information on business activities within the sector. These points are elaborated elsewhere (Burt, forthcoming: Chapter 3).

5. The effects in these equations are summed coefficients in the ordinary least squares regression equations above. If sector i is an oligopoly, y_i equals 1 and the regression equations can be stated as:

$$\widehat{w_{ji}} = .23 + .94(z_{ji}) + .47 + 14.36(z_{ji})$$

$$\widehat{w_{ji}/n_j} = .02 + .10(z_{ji}) + .05 + 1.08(z_{ji})$$

and summing effects in these equations gives the relation between cooptive relations and z_{ji} reported in the text for oligopolistic sectors.

6. More important than the absolute significance of these effects is their significance relative to the significance of the direct effect of z_{ji} on cooptive directorate ties. The direct effect of z_{ji} is negligible, while the direct and interaction effects of sector oligopoly are quite strong. The significance of both effects is probably overstated by routine statistical inference, however, because the w_{ji}'s do not constitute 860 independent observations. They are based on a much smaller number of firms and establishments. In the absence of appropriate test statistics here, I have reported routine statistical tests. This means that the relative significance of effects is much more meaningful than their absolute significance.

7. It is worth noting that this conclusion is true if effects are limited to relations among manufacturing industries alone. Of the 44 nonfinancial sectors being considered, 21 are manufacturing industries. Since large firms involved in manufacturing have been sampled and oligopoly tended to be higher in manufacturing industries than in nonmanufacturing sectors, it might seem that the results in the text merely reflect a separation between manufacturing and nonmanufacturing sectors. This is not the case. If the two regression equations in the text are estimated from only the 400 transactions between manufacturing industries, the direct effect of resource relation strength is negligible (t tests of .04 and .05, respectively, for z_{ji}'s direct effect on w_{ji} and w_{ji}/n_j). The effects of sector oligopoly are quite strong. The effects of the dummy variable y_i on w_{ji} and w_{ji}/n_j have t tests of 4.4 and 5.8, respectively. The interaction effects of $z_{ji}y_i$ on the same two measures of cooptive relation strength have t tests of 4.5 and 3.6, respectively. Sector oligopoly cannot be ignored as a determinant of cooptive directorate ties.

8. Distinctions among categories of z_{ji} are based on substantive and/or analytical considerations. There is a qualitative difference between the complete absence of buying and selling (z_{ji} equal to zero) and a very small amount of buying and selling (z_{ji} nonzero). Cooptive relations are more frequent when z_{ji} equals a mere .01 than when it is completely zero (see Figure 11.1). I have distinguished a category of no buying and selling (z_{ji} equal to zero) from a category of very little buying and selling (z_{ji} greater than zero but less than .015 defines the .01 category in Figure 11.1). While it would be analytically advantageous to have many categories across increasing values of z_{ji}, few relations are available. Values of z_{ji} range from zero up to .56; however, the distribution is highly skewed, with many industries having no transactions with many sectors and very few having extensive transactions with a single sector (note the Ns under the dotted bars in Figure 11.1). All values of z_{ji} greater than .09 have been grouped together as a category of strong resource relations because (1) there are very few relations within small intervals of z_{ji} greater than .09, (2) the frequency of cooptive relations was consistently high past the .09 criterion for z_{ji}, and (3) all z_{ji} greater than .09 correspond to especially severe market constraint in the detailed analysis of these data (Burt, forthcoming: Appendix).

9. This effect, and the chi-square statistics discussed above, are based on log-linear models of the frequencies in Table 11.1. Where f_{ijk}^{ZYW} is the observed number of industry-to-sector relations at level i of buying and selling (i equal to one of the five categories of z_{ji}), level j of sector oligopoly (j equal to competitive or oligopolistic), and level k of the three-category cooptive relations (k equal to null, mixed, or complete multiplex), four marginal effects and four interaction effects are defined by the table (see, for example, Goodman, 1970):

$$f_{ijk}^{ZYW} = [\gamma \gamma_i^Z \gamma_j^Y \gamma_k^W] \gamma_{ij}^{ZY} \gamma_{ik}^{ZW} \gamma_{jk}^{YW} \gamma_{ijk}^{ZYW}$$

where marginal effects are in brackets and the tendency for complete multiplex directorate ties to have occurred with oligopolistic sectors—holding constant the intensity of buying and selling with the sectors—is given by γ_{23}^{YW}. After adding .5 to the tabulated frequencies in order to eliminate zeros, γ_{23}^{YW} has an estimated value of 1.91 with a unit normal test statistic of 5.58. This means that there was a .52 tendency for complete multiplex ties to have occurred with competitive sectors ($1/\gamma_{23}^{YW}$)—holding constant the intensity of buying and selling with the sectors.

The likelihood ratio chi-square statistics reported in the text have been generated by forcing specific effects in the above model to be negligible (equal to 1) and attempting to describe the frequencies in Table 11.1 with the simplified model. The null hypothesis that cooptive relations were independent of sector oligopoly and buying/selling assesses the fit of the marginal parameters (in brackets) and γ_{ij}^{ZY}. In other words, γ_{ik}^{ZW}, γ_{jk}^{YW}, and γ_{ijk}^{ZYW} are forced to equal 1. The null hypothesis that sector oligopoly is independent of cooptive relations, given buying/selling, was tested by forcing γ_{jk}^{YW} and γ_{ijk}^{ZYW} to equal 1. The null hypothesis that buying/selling is independent of cooptive relations, given sector oligopoly, was tested by forcing γ_{ik}^{ZW} and γ_{ijk}^{ZYW} to equal 1. Finally, the null hypothesis of no third-order interaction was tested by forcing the γ_{ijk}^{ZYW} effects to equal 1. As discussed in the text, all of these null hypotheses are rejected.

12

Modes of Resource Allocation

Corporate Contributions to Nonprofit Organizations

JOSEPH GALASKIEWICZ

This chapter focuses on unilateral transfer payments (Boulding, 1962), or donative transfers that business corporations make to private nonprofit charity organizations (NPOs).[1] The sociological literature that focuses on interorganizational relations has examined primarily exchange transactions (see Laumann et al., 1978). In contrast, I will focus on a class of interorganizational transactions in which one actor—the corporate donor—receives no direct reciprocated benefit from another—the nonprofit donee—for the transfer of control over some scarce resource, such as money, facilities, personnel, or property.

Interorganizational transactions of this kind are not common, even between corporations and nonprofit organizations, and are seldom, if ever, the principal means to allocate resources in any type of economy (Kennett, 1980: 185). According to IRS data, in 1970 only 20 percent of the corporations that earned a profit took a charitable deduction on their federal income tax forms (Harriss, 1977: 1789), and only 6 percent gave contributions over $500 (Vasquez, 1977: 1843). This finding is corroborated by the Conference Board (Troy, 1980: 3), which estimates for 1978 that only 25 to 30 percent of all the corporations in the United

AUTHOR'S NOTE: Funding for this research has been provided by the National Science Foundation (SES 800-8570) and the Program on Nonprofit Organizations, Yale University. The chapter has benefited greatly from discussions with Edward O.

States made contributions.[2] On the donee's end, in 1979 corporate philanthropy accounted for only 5.3 percent of total philanthropic giving in the United States (American Association of Fund-Raising Counsel, 1980: 22-23). If we consider that philanthropy accounted for roughly one-third of charities' total budgets, we see that corporate giving plays a very small part in supporting nonprofit organizations.[3] Still, the American Association of Fund-Raising Counsel (1980) estimates that in 1979 business corporations gave $2.3 billion to private nonprofit organizations.

The discussion in this chapter focuses on the transfer payment itself and the institutions that have arisen around it. Essentially, I will view the corporate donor as the purchaser or buyer of a service, the charitable organization as the vendor or seller of a service, and the individual client, patient, student, spectator, and the like as the consumer of the service (see also Hansmann, 1980). Most important, the actor who buys the service is not the one who consumes it. I will assume that the structure of this transaction, as here defined, qualifies it as a unilateral transfer payment or donative transfer. The goal of this chapter is to identify the problems and costs surrounding this type of economic transaction and to explore the possible ways that donors and donees could solve these problems and reduce these costs (compare Williamson, 1975).

The chapter purposely will not consider motives for giving. The problems surrounding the transaction have very little to do with motives. Whether the donor is engaging in a long-term "social contract" with generations past and future (McKean, 1975), has interdependent utility functions with those it serves (Hochman and Rodgers, 1969), or is interested in accruing the respect and esteem of significant others (Ermann, 1978; Baker and Shillingburg, 1977), the transactional problems are essentially the same.

Nor will this chapter consider functions or consequences of philanthropy, since these also are unrelated to the transactional problems. On the one hand, philanthropy could result in income redistribution where those who are wealthy either give money directly to the poor or buy services that would help to increase the poor's earning capacity. On the other hand, philanthropy could result in the provision of more collective goods that the community as a whole could share. Third, philanthropy

---

Laumann, Scott Boorman, and Paul D. Reynolds. I would like to thank John Delany, Wayne Kobbervig, David Knoke, Peter V. Marsden, Patti Mullaney, and Asha Rangan for their thoughtful comments on drafts and Jeanne-Marie Rohland and Lisa Thornquist for typing the manuscript. The issues explored in this chapter will be presented more fully in the author's forthcoming monograph *The Purveyors of Prestige,* to be published by Academic Press in 1983.

could benefit only certain status groups that, for one reason or another, the corporate donor seeks to support. Regardless of the consequences, however, I believe that the transactional problems are similar.

Donative Transfers: Characteristics and Problems

My goal is to highlight the special problems that surround donative transfers. I am not going to draw any analogies between transactions that take place among self-interested economic actors in a for-profit marketplace and economic transactions among altruistic actors in a nonprofit marketplace. On the contrary, I will focus on the uniqueness of the donative transfer. The circumstances surrounding donative transfers from a corporate donor to a nonprofit charity are much different from circumstances surrounding transactions between a buyer and seller in a simple commodities market. Economists have noted these differences in detail (Arrow, 1975; Kennett, 1980; Vickrey, 1962). This chapter will focus in particular on the uncertainty that surrounds many donative transfers.

Uncertainty Surrounding Price

One source of uncertainty is the grant request that prospective donees quote interested donors. Price elasticity, fluctuation in the dollar amount requested by the donee as payment for the service, is not a function of market-related forces (such as supply and demand), but rather depends on forces at work within the NPO itself. NPOs are expected to quote to the donor a "price" that is always "at cost." NPOs are not expected to adjust the amount of the grant request to market conditions; there is no economic incentive to do so. The nondistribution constraint, which prohibits a nonprofit organization from distributing its net earnings to individuals who exercise control over it, is the institutional guarantee ensuring prospective donors that the quotation does not embody a "profit" factor (Hansmann, 1980).

Still, grant requests from different nonprofits often vary greatly, even though these organizations promise to provide essentially the same service. It is also common for prospective donors and donees to negotiate the amount of a grant request with donees, lowering the request if the donor balks too much.

One factor that may contribute to the instability of grant requests is competition for power and prestige among professional staff within the nonprofit organization. Staff may be motivated to "pad" proposals by norms within the NPO. If a staff member is able to secure large amounts of money from donors, his or her own prestige, power, and working conditions in the NPO may be enhanced (for example, he or she may receive released time from normal duties). This, in turn, is tolerated by the organization because expanding budgets are often taken as a signal of the organization's legitimacy (Drucker, 1973) and because through expropriation of overhead costs, pet projects that would not be funded by donors can be supported. This enables the NPO to expand into new service areas without having to find new donors to finance these ventures.

The problem for the donor is that it does not know how much a grant request is inflated by factors extraneous to the service provided. Should it assume that such costs are part of doing business with an NPO? Should it try to "chew" the donee down? It is a difficult issue for the donor to decide, and it introduces considerable uncertainty and distrust into the transaction.

Uncertainty Surrounding Consumer Demand

A second dilemma for donors is to establish the level of consumer (student, patient, audience, and so on) demand for the donee's services. What is the guarantee that there is a clientele or need for the service a nonprofit offers? Should donors simply trust NPOs to tell them that there is? Private firms can point to sales and the exchange value of goods and services. Demand for goods and services in the for-profit sector is established by the fact the customers are willing to pay for them with their own dollars. The demand for the goods and services the public sector produces is established by the citizens' willingness to pay for them with their votes. Nonprofits may have "body counts" that they can parade before potential contributors as indicators of need, but essentially NPOs have no reliable means by which to establish the demand for their products or their services. On the one hand, large "body counts" may simply reflect the free-rider problem—that people will exploit an opportunity to get something for nothing or at reduced costs (such as public radio or public TV). On the other hand, low utilization may reflect the fact that people really do not know what is good for them (for example, exposure to experimental theater). Again, an element of uncertainty is introduced into the transaction.

Uncertainty Surrounding Consumption

Even worse, once a donor makes a contribution, it is difficult to hold the recipient accountable or even to know if the funds were spent as intended.[4] There is seldom anything even approaching a contract. Granted, few market transactions among business firms entail a written contract (see Macaulay, 1963), but when a person purchases a commodity for himself or herself, he or she has a pretty good idea whether it was a wise or foolish decision (see Hansmann, 1980: 853). In contrast, when one voluntarily pays for a service that another consumes, there is likely to be a great deal of uncertainty. The consumer knows whether he or she is satisfied, but the buyer does not. Hansmann argues that the nondistribution constraint should alleviate some of the donor's anxiety; at least the donor knows that the NPO is not skimming a profit as the funds flow through its hands. But even without a profit motive, nonprofits can provide services different from those the donor would prefer. For example, professional norms could easily motivate this response. Staff could feel that donors really do not know what the client needs most and that it is their professional responsibility to reorder priorities, even though this goes against the wishes of the donor. Unless they make special efforts, donors do not know for sure how their contribution dollars are spent.

Coping with Problems of Uncertainty on an Organizational Level

Individual donees have tried to help prospective donors solve these problems of uncertainty by developing a set of marketing strategies. By this I mean the orchestration of campaigns to project certain images of the nonprofit organization to prospective donors. Some of these strategies are more effective than others. I will review only one here.

The most common strategy for an NPO to improve its credibility and trustworthiness is to signal or market its prestige. If donors are skeptical of the costs NPOs quote them or are unsure that the service will be delivered as expected, donees can develop external referents that will signal the "integrity" of the staff, the "quality" of the services, and the "extraordinary accomplishments" of the organization. As Thompson (1967: 33) pointed out, prestige is an important resource. "To the extent that an environmental element finds it prestigious to exchange with an organization, the organization has gained a measure of power over that element without making any commitments." The donor may still have doubts, but the benefits of associating with "excellence" overcome its squeamishness.

For example, Perrow (1961) demonstrated how NPOs can use prestige in his study of a voluntary hospital. By creating and maintaining a favorable image before its public, the hospital was better able to control its dependency on others. If a prospective donor or opinion maker could be convinced that the institution was a respected, "class" operation, economic and political resources were made readily available. If a nonprofit's image is an important incentive for its potential supporter, the organization has to maintain an "artsy" interior design and the sovereignty of its professionals, as well as high performance standards.

Nevertheless, the heavy emphasis on prestige can lead to serious problems for the nonprofit. Kamens (1977) has shown that being overly concerned with prestige and reputation can result in goal displacement. Lee (1971) noted that pressures to maintain organizational prestige can seriously strain NPO budgets. Finally, Perrow (1961: 341) summarized the pitfalls in store for organizations that are overly concerned about their prestige. First, "the production of indirect indexes of intrinsic qualities may take precedence over maintaining the quality of goods and services. Second, resources may be diverted from activities supporting official goals to those which produce and market extrinsic characteristics. And, third, multiple dependencies may interfere with the marketing of either intrinsic or extrinsic referents and may create conflicts within the organization and/or between the organization and its target group." This third problem seems to be most important, as nonprofits find themselves needing both the recognition and the esteem of the professional community and donors. As Perrow correctly foresaw, the pressures to please both audiences can tear a nonprofit apart (see, for example, Zolberg, 1974).

Coping with Problems of Uncertainty on an Interorganizational Level

Individualistic marketing strategies are only one response to uncertainty. Alternatively, donors and donees can come together and incorporate a brokerage that would assume the responsibility of aggregating funds from donors and disbursing them to donees. In the United States the Community Chest, United Fund, and United Way have historically played this role for donors and charitable organizations. In Minneapolis-St. Paul I have also found separate brokerages for private colleges (Minnesota Private College Fund) and cultural organizations (St. Paul-Ramsey Arts and Science Council). From historical documents it appears that large-scale fund drives of the sort with which I am concerned became common just after World War I (Harriss, 1977: 1791).[5]

Brokerages have many advantages, at least in theory. First, a brokerage relieves donors of the difficult task of evaluating the demand function of every charity that asks them for a contribution; second, it performs auditing and monitoring functions that assure the donors the donee is providing what they paid for. As Susan Rose-Ackerman (1980: 325-326) argues, "in the absence of a United Fund, [donors] must either spend time finding out about charities, rely on charities to provide information as part of their fund-raising efforts, or simply remain uninformed. A United Fund . . . [reduces] solicitation costs and permits donors to delegate a difficult resource allocation task to someone else," who ensures that the funds are being spent for the stated purposes.

A third advantage of the brokerage is that it solves a serious free-rider problem. A disincentive for philanthropy is that the donor's gift is usually too small to affect the donee significantly. Unless nonprofit organizations were to remain very small, donors who give directly to NPOs might never have the sense that their dollars mean much. A brokerage can help solve this dilemma for donors. As long as the brokerage is a trusted fiduciary, the donor can join its small donation with others' and thus be assured that its philanthropy will have an impact. Of course, the problem here is that ideally there should be several brokerages, mirroring the pluralism in the donor community. This, though, is typically not the case; and the United Way usually operates as a virtual monopoly (Smith, 1978).

There are other advantages to a brokerage (see Rose-Ackerman, 1980). Donors are promised that member donees will not solicit them for additional funds. Avoiding solicitations is an important incentive for firms. The differential visibility of nonprofits is neutralized. Some nonprofit organizations are more in the "limelight" than others, either because of the nature of their activities or their ideologies. Visibility can both help and hurt when fund raising, and funding through a brokerage supposedly neutralizes this. Finally, with united giving there should be more specialization among nonprofits, less duplication of services, and less competition. With input boundaries stabilized, organizations need not maintain a "diversified portfolio" to attract different corporate donors. The activities of the organization can be more specialized, since it only needs to impress one donor (the brokerage), rather than several.

Coping with Problems of Uncertainty Through Donor Peer and Reference Groups

In a more speculative vein, staffs of prospective donors could use their peer groups and their reference groups as sources of information to aid them in evaluating and recommending grant requests. Corporations may not always act autonomously in making grant decisions. The staffs, which do the research and make recommendations on grant requests to contribution committees or company executives, could rely on networks of friends (strong ties) and acquaintances (weak ties) to supply them with definitions, norms, priorities, and, in a limited number of cases, specific tidbits of information that could be used to help them recommend or reject grant requests more confidently. I will first discuss how peer groups of staff can help overcome problems of uncertainty, and then I will discuss the role of their reference groups.

Peer Group Ties

Bolnick (1975) suggests that the staffs of donor institutions may be greatly influenced by their group memberships as they search for ways to overcome the uncertainty surrounding charitable contributions. He agrees with Sherif (1936) that "individuals in ambiguous situations are inclined to depend on one another for clues or suggestions about the course of action to take," and to carry over this effect of group consensus to behavior outside the group (see also Asch, 1951). Obviously the impact of group norms on decision making varies, depending on "the amount of interaction within the group, the familiarity among group members (depending on group size and group history), the homogeneity of opinion within the group, the salience of the issue in question, and cohesiveness, or attractiveness to the members of the group" (Bolnick, 1975: 206).

Bolnick cautions that not every group member's opinion holds equal weight. Within groups, subjective status relationships emerge. A leadership role develops wherein some individual assumes or takes the responsibility for prescribing norms for the rest of the group. Bolnick reviews in detail the characteristics of group leaders and the factors that contribute to their success, and I will not repeat his discussion here. However, I do find his discussion of leadership useful and suspect that as decision making becomes even more uncertain, leaders' opinions will carry more and more weight.

If Bolnick is correct, we should find peer groups or "brainstorming" groups among the staffs of different firms who are responsible for corporate contributions. Such groups will meet formally or informally as often as once a week or as seldom as two or three times a year. These meetings would provide staffs of different corporations with the opportunity to meet one another and trade inside information on their respective giving programs and on donees.

It is theoretically possible that group definitions that identify "worthy" and "unworthy" nonprofits and community needs would emerge from these peer groups. Crosbie (1975: 432) defines beliefs in these definitions as informational conformity. In a context of uncertainty, people often try to devise a sense of what is valid or correct by checking their standards and beliefs against those of fellow group members. Informational conformity occurs when people revise their standards and beliefs in the direction of others (Nixon, 1979: 118). It is possible that these definitions, in turn, influence allocative decisions, especially where decision makers have little else to go on.

An interesting question is whether or not these peer groups would extend beyond the organizational contexts in which they are formed and include members of the nonprofit sector as well. This probably depends on the career routes of the staff members. Staff members who have worked only in the business community are not likely to have personal friends among professionals in the nonprofit community unless they have done a great deal of volunteer work. Staff members who worked in the nonprofit community and later moved into the corporate sector are more likely to include nonprofit outsiders in their peer networks. Indeed, this may have been why they were hired. While the maintenance of these cross-sector or boundary-spanning acquaintances may impede the socialization of newcomers into corporate roles and, to a certain extent, keep them marginal to the firm, it ensures that the firm has firsthand information on the donee community and a sense of its priorities.

Reference Group Ties

Bolnick (1975: 211-215) further suggests that "an individual may be motivated . . . by identification with certain persons or groups, whether or not these relationships involve direct contact. . . . Reference groups serve two functions for the individual–first as sources of norms for behavior and attitudes, and second as sources of social comparison. For the latter function, an individual is likely to refer himself to status groups which are neither far above nor far below his own, and will very likely refer heavily to groups of which he is a member." But for normative references, "the individual chooses a normative reference group so that . . . he can feel himself part of a more favored group." Because higher-status groups often have high salience and because one's aspirations often anticipate upward mobility, "individuals identify with advantaged groups and thereby gain gratification, especially in a society where mobility is perceived or is stressed." In practical terms this means that "every editor, politician, broker, capitalist, employer, clergyman, or judge has a following with whom his opinion has weight. He in turn is likely to have his own authorities. The anatomy of collective opinion shows it to be organized from centers and subcenters, forming a kind of intellectual feudal system" (Bolnick, 1975: 214). Bolnick goes on to cite various studies that have shown the impact of reference groups and opinion leaders on behavior (see, for example, Merton, 1957; Eisenstadt, 1968; Katz and Lazarsfeld, 1955).

I suspect that the reference groups of staff members among the elite of the community are as important as their peer groups in helping them to sort out their priorities and overcome the uncertainty that surrounds contributions. However, the communication between the reference group and the staff members is not likely to be as direct as that between the peer group and staff members. The elites of the community are unlikely to have networks of primary or "strong" group ties that extend throughout the community and into the company (see Merton, 1957). It is more probable that elite opinion is voiced through the local community press (Janowitz, 1952). Through editorials, letters to the editor, and selective reporting of news stories by editors, the opinions of elites can be communicated to the community. The press can act as a vehicle to articulate elite goals and priorities and to communicate them to others.

Alternatively, elite opinions can be communicated through secondary or "weak" group ties to contributions staff (see Granovetter, 1973). In the Granovetterian world, individuals are related through a combination of strong and weak ties, and, paradoxically, the integration of this world may well depend more on the latter than the former. In his seminal work, Granovetter discusses the weak-tie hypothesis as it relates to such varied phenomena as diffusion, social mobility, political organization, and social cohesion in general. I believe that its application to reference group theory and decision making under conditions of uncertainty is straightforward. Elites, of the type referred to above, are quite often employed in large bureaucratic organizations, perform boundary-spanning functions for their respective organizations, and are more likely to participate in citywide voluntary associations than the ordinary citizen. While such secondary group memberships may or may not be rich in strong ties, they do provide members of the elite with a host of weak-tie opportunities. Minimal involvement with several different groups allows elite members to act as bridges and to communicate to several sectors of the community at once.

In sum, I have identified two alternative ways corporate staff members can overcome the uncertainty that surrounds a donative transfer. When in doubt, staff members can fall back on peer groups and reference groups to help them decide to recommend or reject a grant request. Curiously, I suspect that in most instances peer groups or reference groups do not provide the actual tidbits of information that a staff member needs. For example, these groups would probably have difficulty verifying the capacity of a particular organization to provide a particular service or to evaluate a particular grant request. I would not expect that these groups provide consultant services for donors. Such services are available from "support groups" or "consultants" in the community on a fee basis. Rather, peer groups and reference groups provide general impressions of "what's going on" or "track records." Reliance on them is then a satisficing strategy (Simon, 1957). By relying on vague prescriptions and generalized impressions, a donor has enough "gut feeling" to go on. As in most institutional solutions to complex problems, there is a tradeoff. Giving governed by group definitions or norms is economical; however, donors must forfeit specificity.[6]

The Success and Failure of Coping Methods

Thus far I have described several different ways donors can overcome the problems of uncertainty surrounding donative transfers. The questions I now pose are: Under what conditions will one set of strategies be employed rather than another? When will prospective donees invest heavily in market signaling and pursue atomistic marketing strategies to overcome problems of uncertainty? When will brokerages be successful? When will staffs of corporate donors turn to peer or reference groups for direction? To put it another way, when will donees be unable to use marketing strategies? When will brokerages be unsuccessful? When will corporate staff be unable to rely on peer groups or reference groups for direction?

When Marketing Fails

H1: Marketing, as a solution to the problems of uncertainty surrounding donative transfers, is likely to fail where the donee population is highly specialized and domains are clearly demarcated.

It is rational for a nonprofit to mount a campaign to highlight its trustworthiness or the demand for its service if there is little else to distinguish it from another organization. I suspect that external referents of prestige produce the most benefits for an organization when there is little else that a donor could use to judge the merits of one organization against those of another. In other words, marketing should be most cost-effective if two or more organizations compete in the same niche, that is, serve the same clientele with the same service. However, if NPOs provide a unique service to a well-identified market segment, marketing strategies should yield few additional benefits to an organization. If there is no competition for clients and every organization is "doing its own thing," then it should be enough for NPOs simply to communicate what they do to donors. Building up an image or using prestige does not seem necessary. It only wastes resources.[7]

When Brokerages Fail

H2: Brokerages, as a solution to the problems of uncertainty surrounding donative transfers, are likely to fail as they get larger or as their decision making becomes highly centralized.

Just as marketing strategies can fail, so also can brokerages. The weakness of consolidated giving can be traced to the loss of power that individuals experience when they invest resources in any corporate actor, whether it be a family unit, business organization, nation-state, or brokerage. However, I suspect that the loss of power, and thus potential failure, may be even more pronounced in brokerages.

Coleman (1973b: 4-5) states that the loss of control that individual investors experience is a function of the size of the corporate actor. Individuals will forfeit control over their resources to a corporate actor if they expect to realize a greater benefit than would be possible if they were to retain control over the resources themselves. The problem occurs when the corporate actor becomes too large; people come to have less and less control over it, and they become uneasy about this. It is not that the investor does not trust the corporate actor to pay off on the benefits promised; rather, the uneasiness seems to be rooted in some deep-seated psychological need for control over situations in which one has an interest (Coleman, 1973b: 8). Thus, on the basis of size alone, larger brokerages are more likely to fail than smaller brokerages.[8]

The probability of brokerage failure is even greater if power is concentrated in an oligarchical elite. Coleman describes the situation of a very simply structured social organization, in which decision making is by majority vote, each participant contributes an equal amount of resources, and no special powers have been delegated to an elite. Obviously, in the real world, one seldom finds such a corporate group, and the threat to the power of individual participants is usually much greater than Coleman suggests. Elites often come to dominate decision making in organizations (see Michels, 1949). In the case of oligarchy, I expect that both donors and donees would be distraught, for their control would be even less there than in the "democratic" organization that Coleman describes. There is no reason to expect that brokerages are immune to the "iron law of oligarchy." Decision making on allocation of funds could be subsumed as a "staff function." If this happens, I suspect that both donors and donees will find the situation intolerable and the brokerage will fail, just as any highly centralized corporate actor will fail.

Yet, given the nature of the benefits donors and donees expect to reap, the likelihood of brokerage failure seems to me to be greater than other types of corporate failure, regardless of group size or the degree of oligarchical control. The motive behind investing in brokerages is to reduce transaction costs. Both donors and donees are enticed by this benefit. Yet it is very difficult, if not impossible, to calculate how much a broker saves in transaction costs. How much time did a brokerage save the firm last year? How much anxiety did it alleviate? These are not tangible benefits, like an investor's return on equity, that can be easily quantified. Because benefits are difficult to calculate, members may be less tolerant of losing control over the corporate group and more willing to withdraw, even if the brokerage is not too large and decision making is still democratic.

Given the discussion thus far, we must wonder why brokerages as corporate actors have been as popular and successful as they have. Following Coleman (1973b), I offer several suggestions. First, the event over which the brokerage has control, giving away trivial amounts of a company's earnings to local charities, may be of little interest to business donors. As Coleman argues, loss of control is only acutely felt if a participant has a strong interest in the event over which the corporate actor has control, and contributions are not a priority item on the agenda of most corporate officers. However, if contributions do become important, I expect more corporate donors will "go it alone." Ermann's (1978) recent study of corporate giving to the Public Broadcasting System and Burt's (1981) research linking contributions to a firm's position in the marketplace provide some support for this hypothesis.

Second, there may be no alternative sources to which charities can turn. A donee cannot believably threaten to withdraw from a brokerage if there is not another way for it to secure funds from donors. If donees can turn to two or three alternative brokerages or independent donors, then they can effectively mount a threat. If they cannot, then there is little to stop the brokerage from punishing the rebels and cutting their allocations. Recent research efforts by Pfeffer and Leong (1977) and Provan et al.

(1980) couch this discussion in terms of power dependency and provide some support for the argument in studies of allocation decision making within the United Way.

When Peer Groups Fail

H3: Peer group opinion, as a solution to the problems of uncertainty surrounding contributions decisions, is likely to fail where there is little overlap in the pattern of disbursements among donors.

Peer groups are likely to fail, in the sense of being unable to provide reliable definitions for staff people, when their memberships have few or no contribution areas in common. On a general level the thesis is very simple. To be effective opinion makers, peer groups must be able to come to some agreement on shared definitions, norms, and priorities. If participants have information and opinions for which others have no use, this is very unlikely.

White et al.'s (1976) and Burt's (1976) work on structural equivalence in relational systems provides the theoretical backdrop for my argument. Essentially, the objective interests of the various staff members are defined by their firms' positions in the role structure of corporate philanthropic giving. To restate in simpler terms, a staff member is mostly interested in activity areas that his or her firm supports with contributions. The staff member will have an interest in, or be concerned about, only that segment of the nonprofit world to which his or her company is currently giving money.

My hypothesis states that peer groups whose members have the same objective interests are likely to succeed in working out useful definitions, norms, and priorities, while groups whose members have different objective interests are likely to fail. If peer groups include staff members who are involved in supporting different types of nonprofit organizations, members may soon find themselves bored with, or at least indifferent to, one another's opinions and anecdotes. If the individuals are personally attracted to one another or derive ego satisfaction from playing out their roles as representatives of their firms, then members may continue to attend. However, I think it unlikely that definitions, norms, and priorities would emerge from group interaction.

When Elite Reference Groups Fail

H4: Elite reference group opinion, as a solution to the problems of uncertainty surrounding donative transfers, is likely to fail where there are few weak-tie linkages between the elite and donor agents.

Elite reference groups can fail to provide generalized definitions, norms, and priorities just as peer groups can fail. One problem is the nature of social prescriptions that emanate from such groups. I shall discuss this only briefly. But even if this problem is solved, the effectiveness of elite reference group opinion depends to a great extent on the structure of the interface between the elite and staff members in corporations.

One problem with the opinions of a reference group is that these opinions often cannot be associated with particular individuals. I argued that one relevant reference group for the set of corporate donors is the elite of the community, that class of individuals occupying key decision making positions in community institutions. Moreover, I argued that staff are more interested in the opinions of judges, corporate executives, political chieftains, and cultural gatekeepers in general than in the opinions of a particular judge, executive, or politician. To borrow an analogy from Martindale (1981: 415), the reference group is akin to the "generalized other" of Mead. These definitions, norms, and priorities are often a set of unattached opinions. It is important to remember that just as there is no one individual who could be identified as a person's generalized other, so also there is rarely a set of individuals who could be identified as one's reference group.

This, however, presents serious problems for empirical sociologists who want to take reference group theory seriously. The researcher has a difficult time in operationalizing and assessing the impact of reference group opinions on corporate donor agents. I expect that agents would be sensitive to the opinions of the community elite, but there are few methodological guidelines that would enable me to recover these opinions. Are there members of the elite who epitomize elite opinion? Who is the prototypical elite member? Should we take a random sample of elite members and ask them their opinions? If so, what are the criteria for membership in the elite?

Methodological problems aside, it is unlikely that elite reference groups can supply useful definitions if there are few weak-tie linkages between the elite and the staff of a corporation. It is important to remember that both the elite and staff people are heterogeneous lots. A community's elite includes corporate VIPs, journalists, physicians, jurists, artists, governmental officials, and educators. Furthermore, staff members have very different personal backgrounds. Some are aging executives; others are young with previous employment in the nonprofit sector. Staff members also come from different types of firms in different industries. Therefore, we cannot assume that the elite has dense weak ties, let alone strong ties, to a cross-section of staff members in the donor community. As Laumann and Pappi (1976: 225) showed in their study of Altneustadt, different members of the elite are closer, in terms of interaction and advocacy, to some population subgroups than others. To the extent that staff members are not equally close to all elite members, they will be exposed to only a segment of elite opinion. If they adopt the opinions of the elite members they encounter at Kiwanis Club meetings or chamber of commerce luncheons (in all likelihood the "downtown business" elite), their allocation decisions will only partially reflect the opinions of the more inclusive elite that, I assume, staff members prefer to take into account.

A great deal, then, depends on the organizational settings in which both community elites and staff members circulate. I suspect that members of the elite communicate elite opinion as they perform boundary-spanning roles for their employers or for their voluntary associations. They themselves act as the weak ties between elite opinion and corporate staff members. If organizational roles expose the elite to staff members, then the staff will have access to elite opinion. If such roles do not provide that exposure, then elite reference group opinion fails.[9]

Summary and Conclusion

The purpose of this chapter has been to explore the various problems that surround donative transfers of resources from business corporations to nonprofit charitable organizations. The discussion highlighted the uncertainty that surrounds these transactions. It is apparent that trust is a crucial element in such transactions, since there are so many points at which donees could act opportunistically (see Williamson, 1975).

Trust, however, is not always enough, and donors and donees have created institutions that reduce transaction costs by helping donors to overcome some of the uncertainty that plagues donative transfers. These institutions include marketing strategies that donees use to establish their prestige; brokerages where a new corporate actor is created to collect donations from business donors and then disburse them to needy charitable organizations; peer groups involving donor staff members where definitions, norms, and priorities are negotiated that, in turn, help staff members make their own recommendations; and elite reference groups that supply corporate staff with general guidelines on funding priorities and community needs.

I suspect that empirical investigation will find that all four institutional arrangements are operative in most communities. Nevertheless, I have outlined the circumstances in which I suspect that each of the strategies would fail. Marketing should not prove cost-effective where charitable organizations are highly specialized and operate in clearly defined domains. Brokerages should fail as they become larger and/or as their decision making becomes more centralized. Peer group opinion should prove unreliable where staff are evaluating and recommending very different types of grant requests. Finally, elite reference group opinion should fail where there are few weak ties between the community elite and staff members responsible for corporate contributions.

The chapter has purposely avoided a number of policy-related issues that surround corporate philanthropic giving. If a larger proportion of income transfers and/or public goods come to be provided by or through unilateral transfer payments, there will likely be new legislation to regulate individual and corporate philanthropy. My hope is that legislators would be mindful of the important differences between transactions that take place in the nonprofit donative marketplace and transactions that take place in the for-profit commodities market. Economists have had very little to say about resource allocation in an economy of donative transfers, and serious inquiry into this aspect of the economy has only just begun (see Weisbrod, 1975). Just as social scientists had to develop a new set of concepts and models to understand the emerging role of the government in the post-New Deal economy, perhaps social science ought to be scrutinizing donative transfers as they become a more significant factor in the Reagan economy of the 1980s.

This chapter is intended to raise questions and to stimulate interest. Sociologists have been studying, for years now, public and private nonprofit organizations (Zald, 1970; Selznick, 1949) and their interorganizational relations (Levine and White, 1961; Aldrich, 1976; Hall et al., 1977; D. Rogers, 1974; Galaskiewicz, 1979), yet many questions still remain unanswered. In this chapter I have given considerable attention to the micro-level processes that surround the donative transfer, focusing on the management of uncertainty. From this I have expanded the discussion to formulate propositions on the macro level. This sort of "bottoms up" approach to theory building has great promise, and, I believe, can yield useful results. Its usefulness, however, can only be assessed after close theoretical scrutiny and rigorous empirical study.

NOTES

1. The nonprofit organization discussed in this chapter is the public charity. Public charities and private foundations have a special legal status, for only contributions to these types of nonprofit organizations are tax-deductible. The Internal Revenue Service stipulates that tax-deductible nonprofit organizations be corporations and any community chest, fund, or foundation, "organized and operated

exclusively for religious, charitable, scientific, testing for public safety, literary, or education purposes, or for the prevention of cruelty to children or animals" (26 Code of Federal Regulations, Section 1, 501[c] [3]-1).

In fact, a wide range of organizations come under this title, including (but not exclusively) YMCAs, theaters, universities, orphanages, teenage crisis centers, hospitals, day-care centers, senior citizen recreation centers, amateur baseball leagues, management support groups, museums, community organizations, environmental groups, legal aid clinics, radio stations, newspapers, and summer camps. There are also a number of "charitable" organizations that are not involved in any charitable activities per se but that are appendages to other organizations. For example, the educational arm of the American Citizens Concerned for Life (a pro-life lobbying group) qualifies as a public charity, as well as the educational arm of the American Libertarian Party. Furthermore, funds appended to voluntary associations or public facilities to receive private donations can qualify as public charities. A number of public policy study groups have also received public charity status. For an extended discussion of the legal restrictions on nonprofit organizations, see Treusch and Sugarman (1979), Hopkins (1979), and Oleck (1979).

2. The bulk of contributions to nonprofits is made by the largest firms. The Conference Board notes that for 1974, the 2 percent of the companies holding 72 percent of business assets accounted for 57 percent of the contributions made in that year. The Conference Board suggests that smaller corporations may write off their contributions as business expenses (Troy, 1980: 4).

3. The estimate that philanthropy accounts for one-third of charities' budgets is probably very generous. The Theatre Communications Group (1978) estimated that private sources accounted for only 21.3 percent of nonprofit theater income in 1977; the American Symphony Orchestra League (private communication) estimates that private sources accounted for 23.9 percent of nonprofit professional orchestra budgets in 1977; and the National Center for Educational Statistics (1980: 156) estimates that private sources accounted for only 9.9 percent of all private four-year college and university income in 1978. For a sample of nonprofit organizations in Philadelphia, Reiner and Wolpert (1981) found private sources accounting for 30.3 percent of total income in 1978.

4. Harris and Klepper (1977: 1773), in their interviews with representatives of 417 corporations, verify that corporate donors have very imprecise ways in which to assess how their contributions were used by donees. Officers, in fact, said that they would be willing to give more if only they knew that their contributions did any good. See also Moskowitz (1977: 1830) for a discussion of these issues.

5. To get some perspective on the United Way, we should remember that only a small proportion of all philanthropy goes through this brokerage. J. Cook (1979: 45), in an article for *Forbes,* notes that the United Way in 1978 raised only $1.3 billion out of the $9 billion given to charities and the $35 billion given to all philanthropic activities, including religion, education, culture, and the arts (Rose-Ackerman, 1980: F-10).

6. The schemes I have described are not the only means that corporate donors have used to make contributions to nonprofit organizations. For example, matching gifts are common. In this scheme, the donor delegates the responsibility for "checking out" prospective donees to third parties. If the third parties, usually employees, believe that their interests will be served by an NPO, the corporate donor matches the gift. Another strategy is to provide funds for vouchers. Donors can make contribu-

tions, for example, to a nonprofit "coordinating arts organization," which, in turn, dispenses vouchers to different population subgroups in the community. These vouchers are to be used as discount coupons for theaters, orchestras, and dance performances. The performing arts group then can "cash them in" to the coordinating unit for its "donation."

Both alternatives are appealing to corporate donors for several reasons. First, neither alternative requires that donors search out or check up on prospective donees. Employees or members of the public do this for them. Second, neither holds the donor directly responsible for contributions decisions. Someone else is deciding where the money should go. Finally, both alternatives are compatible with a free market ideology. The nonprofits that can "sell themselves" to mass markets will be subsidized, and those that cannot will wither away. We should keep in mind, however, that neither alternative solves the problems of uncertainty surrounding a donative transfer. Both schemes just pass the responsibility of making the donation to other parties.

7. One could argue that without a profit incentive there is little to discourage NPO administrators and staff from idly marketing themselves, even if no additional funds are forthcoming. The trappings of prestige (carpeted offices, the latest lab equipment, a new auditorium, free travel to conferences, flexible hours, and so on) are tempting to NPO staff and administrators, especially if they have tenure. Over time, these accoutrements can come to be considered as essential for goal atttainment and are legitimated by "professional norms."

8. For another view of the loss of control that donors incur when giving through brokerages, see Fisher (1977).

9. Cibola, as described by Schulze (1961), would be a case in which, I expect, elite reference group opinion would fail. In this town I suspect that staff would have access to the opinions of the political elite but not those of the economic elite. While the organizational roles of political leaders put them in touch with the citizenry on a day-to-day basis, the organizational roles of the economic leaders did not. It is not that Cibola's businesspeople were more apathetic; it is just that their more cosmopolitan roles did not expose them to locals. To the extent that staff members lack access to the economic elite, it would be difficult for them to be informed as to its opinions.

13

The Social Organization of National Policy Domains

An Exploration of Some Structural Hypotheses

DAVID KNOKE and EDWARD O. LAUMANN

We propose a method for studying a neglected aspect of national policy-making: the initiation and advocacy of national policy proposals, or agenda-setting. While an extensive literature has accumulated on the "proximate decision makers" in the federal executive and legislative branches, much less is known about the more distal actors, such as private corporations, trade associations, foundations, and public interest groups, and the processes by which they exert influence on governmental authorities. To redress this imbalance, we ask a fundamental question: How does the social organization of relations among the elite actors constituting a national policy domain affect the process by which policy proposals are generated and put on the national policy agenda? Although we develop a general framework for analyzing the structure and process of national policy domains, our current research investigates two specific domains: health and energy. Because data collection was still going on at the time this chapter was written, our results must be presented in later publica-

AUTHORS' NOTE: Authors' names appear in alphabetical order to reflect equal contributions. Writing was supported by a National Science Foundation grant (SES-8015529) and by an NIMH research scientist development award (KP2MH00131) to

tions. We will, however, illustrate various concepts and principles here by reference to these two substantive policy domains.

Policy Domains

In Parsons's (1951: 19) succinct definition, a *social system* is a "plurality of actors interacting on the basis of a shared symbol system." Membership in any social system under analysis is substantively defined by a criterion of mutual relevance and common fate that stipulates the basis on which members are to take each other into account in their actions. That is, the basis of their mutual relevance to one another or their common orientations to some shared reference point (such as the production of coal for market) serves to mediate their interdependence (Laumann et al., 1982). Simply put, a *policy domain* is the substantive focus of concern of policy initiatives and debate. More formally, a policy domain is a subsystem identified by specifying a substantively defined criterion of mutual relevance or common orientation among a set of consequential actors concerned with formulating, advocating, and selecting courses of action (that is, policy options) that are intended to resolve the delimited substantive problems in question. Once this substantive criterion is specified, the researcher is in a position to define the core set of actors who are oriented to this criterion of relevance. Note that this criterion may change over time and even across the set of actors, transforming the definition of what is meant by a particular policy domain with consequent implications for the delimitation of its actor membership.

To illustrate the point, we might construe a health matter today as referring to any phenomenon affecting the physiological, psychological, or health-related social well-being of an individual or group of individuals. Such a construction reflects a much more inclusive definition of health-related issues, since it encompasses mental health issues, than would generally have been accepted by major actors in the policy domain even thirty years ago. A *national* health policy domain asserts the further restriction that the relevant health policy options include only those currently considered permissible to be undertaken by federal government organizations or nonpublic organizations with nationally oriented clienteles. Similarly, a national energy policy domain is delineated by the

---

Knoke. We thank Joseph Galaskiewicz, Bernard McMullen, Peter V. Marsden, David Prensky, Nancy Reaven, and Lynn Robinson for their useful suggestions on early versions of this chapter.

set of all policy options involving the production and allocation of physical power resources that are seriously considered by the federal government and the major private organizations with national markets or supporters.

The active participants in a policy domain include all consequential organizations that have responsibility for directing, coordinating, or otherwise controlling the creation and distribution of domain values (symbolic or material) pertaining to the subsystem's primary function or to externalities that are thereby engendered. An organization's consequentiality in a particular domain is established by the extent to which its actions are taken regularly into account in the actions of other domain participants. Of particular significance is the set of organizations that occupies the dominant structural positions in the subsystem from which influence over collective decision making can be exercised. This set comprises the elite or core organizations of the policy domain.

Delineating Domain Membership

For all practical purposes, the members of a national policy domain are complex formal organizations–such as corporations, confederations, commissions, and committees–rather than natural persons acting in their own right. But such corporate bodies rarely are wholly engaged in policy direction for a given subsystem. Only certain organizational components, particularly those at the executive level, participate in a domain.

We have already noted that the basic analytic criterion determining whether an organization belongs to a subsystem's policy domain is the standard of relevance or fate whereby actors take each other into account in their actions (Laumann et al., 1982). This mutual relevance criterion effectively excludes from the domain any actors whose actions or potential actions are inconsequential in shaping binding collective decisions for the subsystem. Actors with trivial capacities to affect the actions of domain policymakers thus may be safely ignored as peripheral to the actions of the elite. Mere inaction, however, is an insufficient clue to marginality, since some consequential actors can have their interests taken into account through the anticipated reactions of other core members, without needing to exert themselves overtly.

The boundaries between actors in the policy domain and the more peripheral members of a subsystem are never rigidly drawn. On the contrary, entry or exit from membership in a policy domain is a continuing collective social construction by the domain actors. Membership is the outcome of continuous negotiations between the consequential actors currently forming the elite, who seek to impose their preferred definitions and requirements for inclusion, and various excluded nonelite actors, who seek the right to participate in collective decision making for the subsystem as a whole.

The specific steps we followed to identify the core actors in the health and the energy domains are too detailed to present comprehensively in this chapter. In brief, they involve counting the frequency of occurrences in national news media, appearances at congressional hearings, and participation in lobbying and court cases, and a final scrutiny of the list by a panel of expert insiders. The result of applying these empirical criteria for domain membership was to identify some 200 energy organizations and 175 health organizations as the elite set among which informant interviews were to be conducted.

Structural Relations

The social structure of a policy domain refers to those stable, recurrent patterns of relationships that link consequential actors to each other and to the larger social system. Research on social networks during the past decade indicates that social structure may be usefully conceptualized in terms of the multiple types of ties among system members, the patterning of which, in turn, may be used to identify a subsystem's fundamental social positions and the roles performed by particular organizations.

Contemporary treatments of social networks view the *positions* in a system of social relations as "jointly occupied" by empirical actors (Burt, 1976, 1977a, 1977c; Sailer, 1978). The two prevailing techniques for identifying social positions are structural equivalence and subgroup cohesion. In the approach using the criterion of structural equivalence, two or more actors jointly occupy a structurally equivalent position to the extent that they have similar patterns of ties with other system actors, regardless of their direct ties to each other. The criterion of subgroup cohesion, on the other hand, aggregates only those actors who maintain dense mutual interactions either as "cliques" (maximally connected subsets) or "social circles" (highly overlapping cliques; see Alba and Moore, 1978). Although important conceptual and methodological differences exist between the two approaches, Burt (1978) has pointed out that the clique approach is a special case of the more general approach of structural equivalence.

Research on interorganizational relations and local community political systems suggests that three generic relationships are especially significant in identifying social structure, namely, information transmission, resource transactions, and boundary penetration.

1. *Information Transmission.* Over the course of their research on local communities, Laumann and his colleagues have increasingly emphasized the flow of information about community affairs among elite actors as the primary social network for the resolution of issues (Laumann and Pappi, 1976; Laumann et al., 1977; Galaskiewicz, 1979; Laumann et al., 1982). Extrapolating this perspective to the national level, the social structure of a national policy domain is primarily determined by the network of access to trustworthy and timely information about policy matters. The greater the variety of information and the more diverse the sources that a consequential actor can tap, the better situated the actor is to anticipate and to respond to policy events that can affect its interests.

2. *Resource Transactions.* The resource dependence model of interorganizational relations (Aldrich and Pfeffer, 1976; Benson, 1975; Cook, 1977) begins with the commonplace observation that no organization is capable of generating internally all the resources necessary to sustain itself. Major sources of essential resources, especially information, money, and authority, typically are controlled by other formal organizations. In choosing exchange partners, organizational managers try to minimize the loss of autonomy, which might lead to a takeover by the dominant partner. But supply and demand conditions, resource essentiality (Jacobs, 1974), availability of alternative partners, and other factors can conspire to force some organizations into dependent positions. In this model, an organization's power and influence in a system is a function of its position or location in the overall resource exchange networks generated out of dyadic resource exchanges (see Knoke, 1982).

3. *Boundary Penetration.* The third type of actor-to-actor linkage involves relationships serving both instrumental and solidarity-maintenance functions through the shared use of personnel. The more important examples of this mode of coordination include common membership in commissions or confederations of organizations (such as a peak trade association); ad hoc coalitions to pursue limited political objectives; joint operations in research, development, or production (such as a consortium to build a gas pipeline); and shared board directorships. These practices vary along dimensions of superordination-subordination, formalization, duration, and purpose.

The Policy Process

What does an elite subsystem oriented to a particular policy domain do when it attempts to influence national policy?

Here we shall be primarily concerned with accounting for the policy development process and only secondarily with the activities of particular consequential organizations, although the behaviors of the latter are intrinsic to the process.

Broadly following the sequence of events outlined in Smelser's (1963) model of social change, we suggest that the paradigmatic policy process begins with the perception of some disruption or malfunction in the ongoing operations of a subsystem. Various actors propose alternative interpretations of the nature of the problem and the need for collective action to deal with it. In discussing the problem, policy domain actors communicate their preferred ways for dealing with the problem to one another, to nonelite audiences, and to governing actors with the authority to make binding decisions for the subsystem. Domain actors or coalitions of actors attempt to influence the authorities to place the issue on the governmental agenda for resolution. When an issue reaches the agenda, actors mobilize in an effort to influence the outcome of a concrete issue event, which may be part of a larger event scenario. The policy cycle is closed when the authorities select one option to deal with the precipitating policy problem. If implementation of the policy option fails to alleviate the original condition or triggers additional problems, the cycle may commence again, perhaps activating other domain actors' participation in the process.

We should stress here that we most certainly do not conceive of this process as an approximation of the rational actor model of decision making so beloved by organizational theorists (compare Allison, 1971). We find much more suggestive the characteristics of the organizational decision-making process proposed by March and Olsen (1976), which stresses the fundamental ambiguities of choice at every stage as actors try to decide what to do. Characteristic ambiguities are inherent in an actor's identification of the problem, definition of the objectives it wants to achieve, and determination of the procedures whereby it proposes to accomplish them. The chief feature of this perspective to which we must pay attention is the time-dependent nature of the various actors' searches for problems and solutions. Note, further, that policy processes do not occur in a vacuum, but evolve simultaneously with many others, at various stages of completion, that compete for the scarce attention of domain members. This multiplicity of competing activities places significant constraints on any given policy cycle and must somehow be taken into account in the empirical analysis. The following sections elaborate key features of the approach that inform our empirical analysis.

Problem Recognition

The typical policy process starts when one or more actors label some condition as a problem or *issue* and draw the attention of other actors to the problem. The organization itself may be directly experiencing strains in its operations, or it may respond to difficulties encountered by other actors (including nonelites and participants in other subsystems) that are drawn to its attention—for example, by customer complaints or criticism in the mass media. The important point is that a subsystem condition does not become a domain issue until it is recognized as a strain problem by a consequential actor in the policy domain. Nonmembers, including academic observers, cannot meaningfully assert that a subsystem's "objective" conditions are policy issues if they are ignored by such domain actors. Indeed, one criterion of membership in a domain is the willingness of other core actors to accept an organization's assertions about what constitutes an issue.

Problem recognition is clearly a subjective conceptual process by consequential organizations or, more precisely, by their agents in policy-making roles. Just as we emphasized that membership is a collective social construction of reality, so we argue that the recognition of conditions as policy problems is a continuously constructed social phenomenon, as, indeed, is the entire policy process. Subsequent conditions may stimulate participants' retrospective reinterpretations of earlier activities as having greater or lesser relevance for a problem. Problem recognition thus takes on the flavor of a constantly modified "story," one having a beginning, middle, and end but which, like the old newspapers in Orwell's *1984,* is subject to perpetual revision as suits the needs of actors to make sense of their world and their actions toward it.

Whether an "objective" condition will be labeled and accepted by other domain actors as a legitimate policy issue for subsystem action depends on the result of negotiations among domain members (see Hermann, 1969; Lyles and Mitroff, 1980; Billings et al., 1980). Problem recognition may be highly uncertain when conditions depart markedly from past experience or have traditionally been the province of other subsystems. For example, a major problem for the energy domain actors during the 1970s was disagreement among themselves as to the root of the "energy crisis"—a real depletion of resources or an artificial imbalance created by governmental interference in the marketplace. Differing beliefs about the nature of the problem clearly affect the types of actors who become involved and the policy alternatives that they champion.

Option Generation

Empirically, the generation of policy options or alternatives may occur simultaneously with issue recognition, but in the proposed analytic model, option generation is a subsequent step. Indeed, in some real cases we may find that the organizations first drawing attention to an issue are not the same actors who subsequently propose various policy options or solutions aimed at eliminating or reducing the strain problem and restoring the subsystem to a new equilibrium.

A *policy option* is the empirical unit act in the policy process. It consists of a statement made by a policy domain actor that advocates that a specific action be taken, either by that actor or some other authoritative actor, with regard to a socially perceived issue. Most policy options can be cast in the form: "Organization A proposes that authority B undertake action X for reason Y." For example, in 1974 the Association of American Railroads concluded that the Nuclear Regulatory Commission Safety Standards for casks used to ship nuclear wastes by rail were too low and, therefore, that the Interstate Commerce Commission should change the conditions under which nuclear waste shipments are made.

A domain actor communicates–both to a target organization and to other core actors, as well as to a larger nonelite "attentive public"–its preferred policy option with regard to a specific subsystem problem or issue. Other actors, either differently interpreting the defining problems or perceiving that actor A's proposed alternative might be disadvantageous for themselves or others they care about, offer alternatives to cope with the problem. To illustrate, following the 1979 accident at the Three Mile Island nuclear power plant, some actors proposed a moratorium on new plant construction, others advocated shutting down existing plants as well, and the industry actors wanted to continue operations while tightening safety procedures.

The solutions proffered by domain actors may seldom be arrived at by the ideal-typical search procedures of an abstract rational actor who systematically scans all alternatives and selects one that maximizes utility. Rather, organizational option generation may more often resemble solutions in search of issues. Organizational routines and standard operating procedures dispose actors toward a stock set of solutions that can be applied across a wide range of problems (see March and Olsen, 1976).

Agenda Placement

Recognition of strain problems and communication of policy options among domain members are necessary for issues to reach the "systematic agenda" (Cobb and Elder, 1972: 82), where the subsystem elites become aware that a condition exists requiring authoritative resolution. If the problem can be dealt with only by some component of the federal government, the next step in the policy process is to place the issue on the "governmental agenda." An *agenda* is a formal calendar or docket that specifies the order and time at which matters are to be considered before a final selection is made among the available policy options. The governmental agenda is almost always smaller and more difficult for an issue to reach than is the subsystem agenda. Despite the enormous size and specialization of the federal government, there are more problems from the full range of subsystems seeking the attention of executives, legislators, and regulators than can possibly be seriously entertained in a given period. Advancement onto the governmental agenda typically requires actions by proponents of an issue alternative to increase the salience and political importance of the issue to gatekeeping authorities, particularly by mobilizing politically relevant resources, including coalitions with other actors, to influence authoritative decision makers. In the process of reaching the stage of formal consideration by authorities, an issue's policy options may have undergone considerable modification and reduction as proponents and opponents negotiate over terms. This process we refer to as *winnowing* the alternatives in preparation for moving the issue onto the agenda.

Events and Scenarios

When an issue reaches a national policy domain's agenda, its subsequent progress can be analyzed in terms of discrete events. An *event* occurs when a concrete proposal for authoritative action is placed before a decision-making body, such as the Congress or a federal regulatory agency. An event is typically concerned with a pro-or-con decision about a single policy option as the solution to an issue. Those actors who favor and those who oppose the particular proposal may be observed marshaling their forces to try to influence the decision outcome. Such variables as the timing of activation, the influence tactics used, and cooperative and competitive interactions among mobilized actors can be investigated. Of particular interest in our research is how the domain social structure determines the time at which core actors become involved in particular types of events.

To illustrate a single event in the energy domain: On February 22, 1978, the House Interior Committee reported out a bill to promote the development of coal slurry pipelines. Such pipelines would pump a mixture of crushed coal and water from mines to the users, often over hundreds of miles. Around this event the following actors were mobilized: the coal industry, electric utilities, and construction trade unions, who favored the bill's passage; the railroads, who opposed development because it would cost them lucrative coal-hauling business; and environmental groups and farmers, who opposed the project on the grounds that it would deplete scarce water resources. By asking these organizations' spokespeople about their organizations' actions before and after the committee reported out the bill, we will be able to reconstruct the pattern of activation on this event and relate it to the social organization in this sector of the national energy domain.

Discrete events can be concatenated into larger event *scenarios* that may span considerable time, revealing changing configurations of actors and patterns of action. Events can be chained together because they share some logical similarities, exhibit some temporal proximity and succession, or display some causal connections. To continue the illustration, coal slurry pipeline bills were brought before Congress at least three times during the Carter administration but were never passed. At a higher level of abstraction, these coal slurry pipeline events can be included in a scenario called "coal industry development" that also includes events pertaining to strip mining control and reclamation, railroad deregulation, and utility air pollution standards. The ability to aggregate discrete events into more encompassing equivalence classes gives the researcher greater flexibility in trying to understand how the social organization of a policy domain affects the policymaking process.

Authoritative Decision

We will say little in this chapter about this final stage in the policy process. Political scientists have exhaustively studied the procedures by which laws and regulations are authorized, primarily from an institutional perspective that stresses the motives and interests of proximate decision makers (such as senators' desires for reelection). In contrast, our research brings a distinct sociological perspective to bear on the selection of outcomes, emphasizing how the social organization of timely and trustworthy information flow from interested core actors to the proximate authorities defines and constrains the nature of the policy debate and its outcome. We do not deny the existence, and frequently substantial importance, of processes internal to the legislative and executive decision-making organizations, but our primary focus is on the contribution of social structural variation in policy domains to an understanding of ultimate policy decisions.

Research Hypotheses

The social structure of policy domains serves as the main independent variable in explaining variations in the policy process. For present purposes, information transmission, or the communication pattern, will be treated as the primary relationship among consequential actors defining a domain's social structure. Information is a prerequisite for recognizing the existence of a subsystem problem requiring collective action. In addition, information is essential in developing policy options and in persuading authorities that one's policy preferences should be adopted.

In the hypotheses below, the *preexisting communication structure* is the pattern of information transmission among domain actors existing before communication about a specific event. In empirical terms, uncovering the communication pattern of a domain necessitates asking actors to identify the usual or typical partners to whom they send and from whom they receive various kinds of information about subsystem matters. The researcher then reconstructs the communication structure by aggregating these routine dyadic exchanges of information.

The structure of communication within a national policy domain imposes constraints on policy development. Particular configurations of communication channels place limits on the recognition of subsystem conditions as problems, the sequence and timing of actor participation in issues, the nature of the policy options generated by the domain, the way that agenda placement occurs, the mobilization of actors around issue events, and the selection of outcomes by the authorities. To hypothesize about the effects of domain structure on the policy process, we must understand the various ways communication structures can differ from each other.

The remainder of this chapter explores hypotheses concerning the ways in which four dimensions of domain social organization—centralization of the preexisting communication structure, polarization on event-specific structures, the constitutional bases for organizational decision making, and the equality of resource distribution—affect the various components of the policy process.

Centralization

Centralization of the preexisting communication structure is the degree to which control over information transmission is concentrated among positions. In more centrally organized domains, positions are tightly integrated into the communication network, and one or more positions act as the central focus for the receipt and transmittal of domain-relevant information. Centralization refers only to the formal configuration of communication linkages, without regard to aspects of the actors' attributes, resources, or policy preferences. Four ideal-typical communication patterns arrayed along the centralization continuum are:

(1) complete fragmentation: no interpositional communication channels are present;

(2) localized: only short-linked connections occur between positions, with many disconnected subsets, resulting in an overall "balkanized" or compartmentalized pattern in which some positions cannot communicate with others;
(3) chain-linked: most positions in the domain are reachable through a series of indirect connections, with some positions serving as information "brokers", or transmitters, between more distant positions; and
(4) hierarchical: one or more central positions direct the two-way flow of information to peripheral positions that are not laterally linked.

We now offer a selective set of hypotheses about the relationship of domain centralization to the basic features of the policy process. These propositions are presented as *ceteris paribus* relationships, and one of the main objectives of empirical research will be to assess their validity after controlling for other factors that may be important. Our centralization hypotheses include the following:

C.1. The more centralized a domain's communication structure, the fewer the number of subsystem conditions recognized as issues per unit of time.

C.2. The more centralized a domain's communication structure, the smaller the number of policy options generated and the fewer the positions involved in generating policy options for a given issue.

C.3. The more centralized the communication structure, the more rapidly are policy options winnowed and the shorter the time required for an issue to reach the governmental agenda.

C.4. The more centralized a domain's communication structure, the more likely are the authorities to select that policy option preferred by the central position.

Polarization

We now consider how the social structure that emerges on a specific event contributes to explaining variation in the policy process. Once the subsystem actors label some condition as a problem, generate their set of policy options for that issue, and bring an option up for decision by an authoritative body, a unique but transitory social structure is activated. That *event-specific structure* is constructed from two components:

(1) the pattern of preexisting communication among the domain actors, as described in the preceding section; and
(2) the policy preferences held by the domain actors involved in the concrete issue event in question.

At the analytic level, any issue has at least two policy options, which can be labeled the "pro" and "con" alternatives. Empirical events may, of course, attract many alternative proposals, but the treatment here is best developed in simple dichotomous form.

Together, the preexisting communication structure and the actors' policy preferences on the specific event suffice to identify the formation of a *collective actor.* A collective actor is the set of all domain organizations that are in direct or indirect communication with each other and that prefer the same policy outcome for a given event. A collective actor is thus "the maximal opportunity structure for coalition formation on a given issue" (Laumann and Marsden, 1979: 717).

In an event-specific social structure, the collective actors are the nodes and the communication channels between them constitute the structural relations of interest. The basic dimension along which event-specific structures vary is called the *polarization dimension.* Laumann et al. (1977: 606-613) discussed two fundamental forms found along this dimension, the bargaining and the oppositional models. In an oppositional structure, opponents on a specific issue event are only indirectly linked by communication channels that connect them to neutral, or less partisan, "brokers." Although preferences are likely to be adamantly held, at least the framework for controversy resolution has been erected in this type of structure. In the bargaining structure, opposing collective actors have direct, unmediated contact with each other, which should facilitate the negotiation of outcomes by "compromise and trading of concessions on the points at issue" (Laumann et al., 1977: 608).

The following are representative hypotheses concerning the relation of polarization of event-specific structures to the key aspects of the policy process:

P.1. The less centralized a domain's preexisting communication structure, the more likely is a polarized structure to emerge on a specific event.

P.2. The more often domain actors generate policy options that are instrumental rather than consummatory, the less likely is a polarized structure to emerge on a specific event.

P.3. The more polarized the specific event structure, the longer the time required for alternatives to be winnowed and for the event to reach the government agenda.

P.4. The more polarized the specific event structure, the longer the time required before authorities will make a definitive decision.

P.5. The more powerful the collective actor advocating a policy option for a specific event, the more likely are the authorities to select that option as the definitive outcome.

Constitutional Basis

The consequential organizational actors in a national policy domain may be described by many characteristics: size (number of employees or members), resources (annual budgets), scope of operations (international, regional), technology (materials versus people processing), and so on. For understanding the policy process, however, one of the most important attributes is the organization's *constitutional basis* for making collective decisions. Three ideal-typical patterns may be distinguished:

(1) *governmental organization:* an actor possessing legitimate public authority to make binding decisions for some aspect of the subsystem, either (a) an elected collegial body, such as a congressional committee, in which a division of interest is to be expected, or (b) a more unitary body, such as an executive agency headed by a politically appointed director;
(2) *confederated organization:* an assembly of organizations or individuals in which the constituents retain substantial power for autonomous decision making and action; and
(3) *monocephalic organization:* a nongovernmental actor in which the authority to make binding decisions about its posture toward the outside world has been relinquished by participants to a central unit.

Governmental actors, such as congressional committees (Senate Energy and Natural Resources, House Ways and Means), cabinet departments (State, Interior), and independent establishments (Environmental Protection Agency, National Transportation Safety Board), are familiar entities that need no discussion here. The distinction between confederated and monocephalic actors turns on the question of which positions within the organization have ultimate authority to commit the collectivity to a policy preference. In confederated organizations—such as peak trade associations (National Association of Manufacturers) and most professional societies (American Medical Association)—the member units retain substantial veto power over decisions made by an executive unit. In many confederations, serious and enduring cleavages within the membership may prevent the collectivity from taking a stand on an issue. By contrast, for monocephalic organizations—such as most private corporations (General Motors) and interest groups (Common Cause)—the real capacity to commit the collectivity to action resides fully in a board of directors or managers, despite the fiction of stockholder or membership control. Monocephalic organizations, as the name implies, can more readily reach policy decisions and pursue collective actions without having to consult lower-level participants.

Some hypotheses about the relationship of the actors' constitutional bases to the policy process are the following:

B.1. Monocephalic organizations are the quickest to become involved in the recognition of problems and the generation of policy options, while confederated organizations are the slowest to act.

B.2. The more centralized a domain's communication structure, the more likely that the central positions will be occupied by monocephalic or governmental actors and that the periphery will consist of confederated actors.

B.3. When the domain's central positions are occupied predominately by monocephalic organizations, the policy options favored by these actors are more likely to survive the winnowing process and advance to the governmental agenda.

B.4. The more that a domain is polarized across specific event structures, the more often will collective actors be dominated by monocephalic organizations.

B.5. When monocephalic organizations predominate in central positions and collective actors, the authorities are more likely to select as definitive policies those options favored by such organizations.

Resource Distribution

In the collective decision-making model that informs our perspective on national policy domains, resource transactions between actors with interests in the outcome of events underlie the authoritative decision-making process. The list of resources useful for influencing policy is potentially long, and we will not restate catalogues available elsewhere (see Clark, 1968; Laumann and Pappi, 1976), nor will we develop research hypotheses involving different types of resources. Instead, we use a generic resource category to refer to any "attribute, circumstance, or possession that increases the ability of its holder to influence a person or group" (M. Rogers, 1974: 1425).

As we are developing hypotheses mainly about the relationships among domain properties, the relevant dimension of resource variation is not the aggregate amount of resources but rather their distribution among the positions and collective actors of the domain. Our expectations are based on the assumption that more evenly spread resources permit more actors to engage in scrutinizing the subsystem for the presence of problems. But equal resource distribution is detrimental to the rapid development of issues, particularly the option generation, winnowing, agenda placement, and definitive selection phases. Resources concentrated in fewer hands enable the possessors to move quickly toward their policy objectives without having to spend much time and effort mobilizing and coordinating the activities of many participants and without experiencing extensive delays created by opposing actors who control sufficient resources to block the policy development process.

Here is the final sample of hypotheses, pertaining to the relationships between resources and the policy process:

R.1. The more equal the distribution of resources among positions in a domain, the larger the number of actors involved in problem recognition and in option generation for issues.

R.2. The more equal the distribution of resources among positions in a domain, the more likely are opposing collective actors to be formed on specific events.

R.3. The more equal the distribution of resources among positions, the less rapidly will the options be winnowed and the less rapidly will the issue reach the governmental agenda.

R.4. The more equal the resource distribution, the longer the time before authorities will make a definitive choice among the policy options.

Conclusion

This chapter has presented the basic structural framework for a model of national policy domains. We emphasized relationships among comparatively static elements and various basic components of the collective decision-making model. Such structural analysis is an essential first step in understanding the policy process, but it is incomplete by itself. The dynamic elements, particularly the temporal patterns of organizational activation and participation in events and the significance of event concatenations for the unfolding of decisions in real time, remain to be developed in subsequent articles that will use the structural framework presented here as a starting point.

We have presented only a handful of many testable propositions that could be developed using the structural framework of this chapter. A proper test of many of these hypotheses that are stated at the domain level requires data from a large number of policy domains that exhibit wide variation in their social organization. Unfortunately, the costs of replicating a detailed analysis of social structure and event participation in large numbers of domains are prohibitive. Our alternative is the pilot project now underway, which examines the policy process in the national energy and health domains. We believe that these two subsystems display sufficiently divergent social structures and agenda-setting processes for a reasonable evaluation of the theoretical model to be possible.

IV.

Network Analysis and Structural Sociology

The two commentaries in this part provide assessments of the other contributions to this collection and of the network approach to studying social structure. Blau's chapter contrasts the structuralism represented by the preceding chapters with other approaches to structural analysis. He argues that network analysts must be wary of narrow technical studies that analyze structure in social relations in isolation from antecedent or consequent variables; he states that the contingent propositions necessary for the development of structural theory can only be developed by relating the structural descriptions produced by a network analysis to explanatory and response variables. Aldrich, from the perspective of a population ecologist of organizations, reviews the chapters in Part III, giving special attention to the ways they deal with the origins and persistence of social networks. Aldrich's discussion states that social network analysis has achieved the objective of providing explicit descriptions of social structure. It also suggests that efforts in the future be devoted to advancing understanding of the difficult problems of conceptualizing and analyzing structural change and transformation.

14

Structural Sociology and Network Analysis

An Overview

PETER M. BLAU

The chapters in this volume, diverse as they are, represent a distinct version of structural analysis that has developed quite recently, jointly with network analysis, primarily in the United Kingdom and the United States. To be sure, all of us sociologists are, to paraphrase Davis (1959), structuralists in the broadest sense of the term. But to use a concept so broadly robs it of all its scientific meaning and discriminating power. Davis was wrong: We are not all functionalists, although all of us study the interrelations of parts in a larger social whole, because functionalism not only implies such interdependence but also refers to the fact that the various parts make positive contributions to the whole and thereby produce equilibrium, adjustment, and order. These assumptions many of us do not make. Similarly, not all of us are structuralists unless we mean by the term "structuralism" merely the interdependence of elements in a larger social system.

There are, however, several types of structural analysis that are quite different from the one illustrated by the sociological orientation of the chapters here. The theory of Marx—particularly what has come to be known as "the late Marx"—is a structural theory, which explains other aspects of society—religion, politics, family, folkways, mores—in terms of its infrastructure, which entails notably productive forces, people's relations of production, and the resulting class structure. Whereas Marx's theory has some similarity to functionalism, as has often been noted (for example, Lipset, 1975), his focus is on conflict, exploitation, and contradictions, not on order, adjustment, and integration as in functionalism. A second type, in sharp contrast to Marx's theoretical approach, is Parsons's structural-functionalism. Parsons explains such objective conditions as people's class differences and their relations and interactions with one another ultimately by the values and norms that most people in a society share and that orient their behavior and hence govern social life and institutions. Structure in this scheme pertains to the interrelated institutional subsystems of value and normative orientations that develop and become increasingly differentiated in order to satisfy the four basic functional requirements any social system or subsystem must meet.

However, it is a third kind of structuralism that is nowadays most often meant by the term, namely, Lévi-Strauss's. For him and his followers, "deep structure" is a fundamental, unconscious characteristic of the human mind that underlies all empirically observable social phenomena, be they kinship arrangements or myths. The deep structure finds diverse expressions in various cultures–different kinship systems, different mythologies–yet it alone can satisfactorily explain these culturally specific, empirically observable phenomena. Whereas British structuralists considered the observed kinship patterns (for example, the kinship structure), these patterns were an epiphenomenon for Lévi-Strauss, to be explained by an underlying universal structure. This scheme was influenced by the linguistic structuralism of Saussure and Jakobson.

The structural analysis found in this book differs from all three of these more famous types of structuralism. (A partial exception is the chapter by Knoke and Laumann, which does use Parsons's scheme.) In purely formal terms, it is more similar to Marx's than to Parsons's or Lévi-Strauss's, but only because it also centers attention on objective positions and relations rather than beliefs or mental constructs; none of the chapters reveals any Marxist ideological slant. (Indeed, I do not even know which authors, if any, are sympathetic to Marxism.) What is the difference? One way to answer the question is to start with Parsons's own definitions of social structure and culture.

Parsons repeatedly stressed the distinction between culture and social system or structure. A joint article with Kroeber presents the most explicit analysis of this distinction (Kroeber and Parsons, 1958). In a subsequent summary, Parsons (1961: 34) defines the two concepts in the following words: Social structure refers to "the conditions involved in the interaction of actual human individuals who constitute concrete collectivities with determinate memberships. . . . [Culture refers to] 'patterns' of meaning, e.g., of values, of norms, of organized knowledge and beliefs, of expressive 'forms.' " In other words, social structure is composed of people's relations manifested in their interaction and, by implication, the roles and positions involved in and conditioning these relations, whereas culture comprises the common values and norms, meanings, and symbols. Since Parsons himself consistently analyzes and explains patterns of social relations in terms of the underlying value orientations governing them, his theory of social structure is actually a cultural theory, as others have also indicated (see Wallace, 1981: 213).

The approach to structural analysis of most, and perhaps all, the authors in this book, on the other hand, focuses precisely on social structure, as distinguished from culture by Parsons. It assumes that social life, including its cultural manifestation, is rooted in the structure of social positions and relations and must be explained by analyzing these patterns or distributions of positions and these networks or rates of relations in groups and societies. Some chapters examine the connections between social positions and social relations; some, those between different aspects of social positions or between social relations and the processes underlying them. Others investigate how structural and network conditions affect cultural factors, such as the diffusion of innovation in the spread of youth culture (for instance, Granovetter), political attitudes (Erickson), or policy issues (Knoke and Laumann). Thus, weak ties play an important role in the diffusion of subcultures, Granovetter points out, because they often link different groups and cliques that otherwise would be insulated from one another.

To understand the dynamics of social structure requires knowledge of the social processes involved in implementing social change. Social structures change if the distribution of resources or that of people changes, and both of these altered distributions are the result of social processes. Social exchange is a process that changes the distribution of resources, and social mobility is a process that changes the distribution of people among groups or strata. Several chapters are concerned with these processes. Cook examines the connections between network analysis and exchange processes, and Marsden constructs a refined theoretical model of how power accrues to central positions with access to multiple suppliers in exchange networks. The influence of the class structure for social mobility is studied in two chapters, those by Breiger and by Moore and Alba. Children of business owners have a much better chance than others to move into the elite, Moore and Alba find, but once there, their advantaged origins do not seem to influence their chances of becoming well integrated within the elite. Lin shows in a path diagram that weak ties help people find better jobs primarily because people tend to have weak ties with persons of superior status and persons of superior status are most likely to have access to better jobs. (I say "primarily," though Lin says "only," because the direct path in his Figure 6.2b from tie weakness to job, controlling contact status, looks marginally significant to me. It seems plausible that a person's weak ties are with more diverse others, even if they are not of higher status, and this increases the chances of finding a good job.)

Structural and network analysts are sometimes accused of being too formalistic and ignoring the substantive content of their subject matter. This is quite correct, but it is not a criticism. It is necessary to abstract from the specific contents, which are the subject matter of various specialized disciplines, the form of social relations, and distributions of positions. We are concerned with the proportion of isolates in a group and not with whether they are Jack and Jim or Jill and Joan. The work of physicians in a hospital is very different from that of the faculty in a university. But a study of the division of labor ignores these differences in task content and simply ascertains how much diversity among individuals there is in the two places. The religion of the people of Spain and that of those in Sweden is not the same. But structural analysis is concerned with religious heterogeneity (a formal property of the structure), not with the content of religious ideas, and both these countries are very homogeneous compared to the religiously much more heterogeneous United States. Indeed, it is possible to go one step further in abstraction and talk about heterogeneity as such, regardless of whether religious or ethnic or political heterogeneity is involved (which implies that the theorems so formulated must be corroborated by tests of all forms of heterogeneity).

Two chapters deal with heterogeneity, Rytina's and Kadushin's. Rytina shows that heterogeneity (in the three respects he examines) promotes intermarriage, as my theory (1977b) predicted. But what is particularly interesting about his analysis is that he shows that a tautological set of propositions can be instructive and testable. The rate of intermarriage in an SMSA depends (positively) on heterogeneity and (negatively) on ingroup salience. Since salience is defined in terms of the two other variables, the preceding sentence states a tautology. Accordingly, the two metric coefficients are one, and R^2 is also one. But the standardized coefficients vary and indicate the relative strength of various influences. For instance, heterogeneity with respect to mother tongue influences (mother tongue) intermarriage more than educational heterogeneity does (educational) intermarriage. To be sure, this is simply the result of differences in the variances of heterogeneity and salience, but this makes it no less real. Moreover, if it should have turned out that heterogeneity exerts no significant influence and only salience affects intermarriage, it would have falsified the theoretical prediction I had made. Kadushin studies how the social density of friendship groups reduces the mental stress of Vietnam War veterans. In his concluding comments, he suggests that in heterogeneous big cities, only a homogeneous friendship group—fellow Vietnam veterans—can provide the social support that reduces mental stresses; but in more homogeneous small towns, any closely knit friendship group, whether mostly veterans or not, can. If such an interaction effect between size of place and social density were documented empirically, it would mean that some common experience is important to furnish stress-reducing social support. In homogeneous towns, there will be many such experiences people share, making veteran status relatively unimportant; in heterogeneous cities, where there are fewer such common experiences, the shared war experience assumes increasing significance.

The focus on the study of the structure of social positions and the structure of social relations raises the question of which of the two are the starting points or most primitive concepts. Do we first analyze social relations and distinguish positions on the basis of differences in patterns of relations, or do we start by categorizing people by social position to examine the patterns of relations among them? On the one hand, a sociogram or sociomatrix of relations between persons is generated, and people are classified as occupying the same role or position either on the basis of having direct links and thus constituting subgroups, as in graph theory (Harary et al., 1965), or on the basis of having the same or similar links to other persons and thus being structurally equivalent, as in block-models (White et al., 1976). On the other hand, people are classified by their attributes into categories of social position—for example, occupational strata or ethnic groups—to generate a square matrix, and the entries in the cells are the rates of social relations of a given kind between persons occupying two positions (with in-group rates in the diagonal), such as social contacts or marriage. Implicit in the first procedure is the causal assumption that people's social relations delineate their roles and define their positions in the group, whereas the second procedure implicitly assumes that differences in attributes and positions affect people's social relations. Both are undoubtedly sometimes true. However, the first assumption is probably most justified in studies of small, recently formed groups, while the second is justified in studies of established communities and societies, where social positions have become crystallized. Appropriately, therefore, the first procedure is generally used in microsociological investigations and the second in macrosociological inquiries. However, the first procedure can be adapted for macrosociological study by entering into the rows and columns of the matrix not persons but collectivities–organizations, industries, communities, or entire societies–and entering into the cells not rates of interpersonal relations but rates of interorganizational or international connections, such as interlocking directorates (Burt, 1979) or export and import trade relations (Breiger, 1981c). Burt's study here treats market transactions between industries, and implicitly between the major corporations representing the industries, in this manner.

An interesting combination of the two procedures is used in Breiger's chapter on occupational mobility. He defines class, in accordance with Weber, as comprising all those economic positions that do not differ in their chances of social mobility, and he asks what combination of occupations would yield a class structure that can explain the empirically observed patterns of mobility in a British sample. He starts with an eight-category origin-destination matrix of British men and uses the observed mobility entries to combine the eight categories into a smaller number of occupational classes. The criterion for doing so is that within a submatrix of mobility relations among occupations combined into pairs of classes, origins and destinations are independent. He derives a three-class model from the literature, and his analysis shows that this model fits the mobility data quite well; that is, origin and destination are unrelated for occupations assigned to pairs of classes, but are related between classes. As noted by Breiger and by Goodman's comment on Breiger's discussion, Goodman (1981) published a paper that addresses the same problem but uses a different procedure and criterion for combining occupational groups into broader classes. Goodman combines two (or more) categories of a mobility matrix only if the entire array of numbers in the two columns and the entire array in the two rows are homogeneous, that is, statistically independent. Substantively, this homogeneity implies that the chances to reach any occupational destination do not differ for the two origins and the chances to come from any origin do not differ for the two destinations.

Structural analysis centers attention on emergent properties that characterize groups and larger collectivities as a whole and cannot be used to describe their individual members (except, of course, as characteristics of their social environment). The simplest of these, though by no means the least important, is the collectivity's size, the number of its members. Three other kinds of emergent properties are of major importance. One is the network or pattern of social relations–for example, the proportion of isolates in a group or the rate of racial intermarriage in a city. Another is the composition of the collectivity, notably if conceptualized in formal terms, as illustrated by the degree of religious heterogeneity (not the nature of people's religion) or the extent of income inequality. A final type of emergent property is the degree to which various kinds of differences among people intersect—for instance, whether ethnic and economic differences are closely related or largely independent, or whether different races live together in the same neighborhoods or are segregated into different ones.

The objective of structural analysis is to advance systematic sociological theories that can explain empirical observations and that are falsifiable. There is a danger that the refined methods that network analysis, in particular, has developed will lead to sterile descriptive studies. Factor analysis can illustrate the point by analogy. Although it is a technique that can be most useful in research, factor analysis lends itself to pedestrian studies that merely report the dimensions underlying a set of items without relating these factors to anything else and hence without testing or even exploring contingent propositions, which are the very building blocks of theory. Similarly, there is a danger that blockmodeling, a useful technique, is employed simply to describe the structure of social positions in a group, without relating these to any conditions producing this structure or any of its consequences. Such sheer description does not advance social science, just as conceptual analysis does not, until it develops contingent propositions about empirically observable relationships between concepts. However, most studies in this volume report empirical research or theoretical models that do deal with the influences of some structural conditions on others. By providing some knowledge about contingent propositions, these chapters may well contribute to the arduous task of developing rigorous structural theory in sociology.

15

The Origins and Persistence of Social Networks

A Comment

HOWARD ALDRICH

Social network analysis has struggled for three decades to earn a place alongside other modes of social analysis. More often treated as a method for displaying data than as a substantive approach, network analysis may actually have suffered from the ease with which investigators coopt its concepts. Since the early 1970s, a sustained effort by dedicated network analysts has generated a substantial number of empirical studies, from which theorists have extracted some very useful generalizations and propositions. However, as Wellman (1982a) notes, "its substantive achievements have been less notable to date than its critique of other sociological approaches. Its most significant substantive achievements have been in *posing new intellectual questions* and *showing new ways to describe social structures.*" We might well ask, what more could one expect of any social science field?

The five chapters I have been asked to comment on demonstrate that one *can* expect more from social network analysis. Recent network literature has forced sociologists to take notice of the fact that although they have talked about *social structure* for decades, they really have not faced up to the task of what a true structural analysis would look like. Social structures have a pervasive effect on almost all phenomena of interest to sociologists, affecting the social distribution of resources and the terms on which they are available. Social network analysis provides a framework within which we can study the processes whereby "resources are gained or mobilized–such as exchange, dependency, competition and coalition–and the social systems that develop through these processes" (Wellman, 1982a).

A successful social analysis, therefore, cannot take social structures as given, but rather must be able to account for their origins and their persistence. In my critique, I will first show that networks can usefully be conceived as structures of recurrent transactions, permitting us to apply the powerful conceptual scheme of transaction analysis (Williamson, 1975, 1981). Using the transaction cost approach, I show that a few underlying themes run through all the papers, illuminating their differences. Next I examine what these chapters have to say about the origins and boundedness of networks, paying particular attention to the origins of broker roles. Finally, I ask what the five chapters have to say about the persistence of networks.

Networks as Structures of Recurrent Transactions

All social behavior involves interaction between actors with partially convergent and partially divergent interests. Some of these interactions are recurring and are connected to other interactions. To the extent that a fairly stable pattern prevails, we speak of interaction within networks of relations.

Two of these chapters (Cook's and Marsden's) explicitly approach the study of network via the smallest interaction unit–a transaction. The other three chapters are less explicit about their unit of analysis, but their concepts and propositions draw heavily upon the implicit concept of a transaction.

The Transaction Cost Approach

The contributions and limitations of these chapters are very clearly evident when examined from the perspective of transaction cost analysis, embedded within the population ecology perspective (Aldrich, 1979; Hannan and Freeman, 1977). The population ecology model explains organizational change (and change in other types of social units) by examining the distribution of resources in environments and the terms on which they are available. The transaction cost approach focuses on the specific selection pressures driving organizational change in competitive environments. Use of a transaction cost approach does not constitute reductionism, as the ultimate explanation for the structuring of transactions is based on the constraining effect of *external* conditions on social actors.

Two assumptions are made about social behavior: Actors operate within the constraints of bounded rationality, and much of human behavior is driven by opportunism. Most actors are intendedly rational, but textbook rationality is denied them because of a host of limitations. Cognitive deficiencies and peculiarities, limits on information availability, and sheer limits to information processing preclude most actors from making optimal choices, where "optimal choice" is defined as the one that would be made by an omniscient being. Information search costs, in particular, lead most actors to choose satisfactory, rather than optimal, alternatives. Such behavior is also complicated by the tendency of other actors to behave opportunistically, pursuing their own self-interest at the expense of other parties. In short, actors tend to lie, cheat, and steal to further their own ends. Information is withheld or distorted, preferences are concealed, and a variety of other deceptions are practiced.

Given bounded rationality and opportunism, transactions with other actors are always problematic and potentially quite costly. Given a resource-scarce environment, actors will be under pressure to find ways to economize on transaction costs. Williamson (1981) hypothesized that three dimensions to transactions are particularly important in affecting the type of relationship established: the frequency of the transaction, uncertainty surrounding the transaction, and the level of transaction-specific investments. The more frequently an actor enters into transactions with specific other actors, the greater the pressure to find an economical way to handle the relationship. One-time events are not worth bothering about, and indeed would not be legitimately described in terms of the language of relationships. Uncertainty clouds transactions, with bounded rationality and opportunism requiring actors to expend more resources than they might prefer, given their gains from the transaction. In the language of population ecology, transaction structures that reduce uncertainty will have a selective advantage over those that do not.

Transaction-specific investments refer to the resources actors invest in a relationship to keep it going. As Swanson (1971) pointed out, purely self-seeking behavior destroys rather than sustains relationships. If relationships benefiting actors are to persist, the actors must invest some resources in maintaining the relationships themselves.

Examination of the five chapters, using the above scheme, reveals the difficulty investigators have in constructing explanatory, rather than descriptive, network schemes.

Frequency. Clearly, without recurring transactions, an investigator would have no basis for analyzing connections between actors in terms of social network imagery. The only chapter to make this explicit is Cook's, which defines exchange relations as opportunities for exchange resulting in transactions between the same parties over time. Burt's chapter contains a surrogate measure of interaction frequency, as he measured the intensity of relations by the proportion of required resources obtained from a sector by an industry. The other three chapters are silent on this issue, although Knoke and Laumann, and Galaskiewicz describe their structure in implicitly evolutionary terms.

Uncertainty. Degree of uncertainty in interorganizational relations is explicitly the central issue in Knoke and Laumann and also in Galaskiewicz, and it is implicit in the other chapters. Galaskiewicz identifies a number of areas of uncertainty. First, uncertainty surrounds the actual size of a gift in terms of price, consumer demand, and consumer satisfaction. Second, his account of the conditions under which various interorganizational relationships fail contains an implicit theory of the conditions under which such relationships are used. The theory contains two factors: the level of competition in the donee population and the extent of interlocking in the donor population. Competition is increased, and uncertainty heightened, when there is high domain overlap among donees and there are many donees competing for resources in the community. These sources of uncertainty lead to marketing strategies and the use of brokers. On the donor's side, interlocks among donors, in the form of staff meetings and weak ties between organizational elites, reduce uncertainty within donor organizations and thus enable staff members to decide on which donees receive grants.

In Burt's analysis, uncertainty in a firm's supply of sources is increased when it deals with concentrated or oligopolistic sources of supply. As coordination increases between organizations supplying the firm with resources, firms seek mechanisms to coopt these organizations and thus reduce uncertainty.

In Cook's and Marsden's analyses, conflict of interest between actors is explicitly assumed. In these negatively connected networks, uncertainty is heightened by opportunism as well as by bounded rationality. In Knoke and Laumann's analysis, uncertainty is rampant. After presenting a very rationalistic model, based on Smelser (1963), they quickly abandon it in favor of the garbage-can model of March and Olsen (1976). In the garbage-can model, everything is up for grabs: who participates, which problems are addressed, which solutions are attempted, and the access structure that brings these three elements together. Indeed, Knoke and Laumann succeed so well in describing the uncertainty surrounding decision making in national policy domains that I wondered whether any a priori predictions were possible.

Transaction-Specific Investments. As a group, the chapters appear to underplay the costs of maintaining particular relationships. Connections, even in positively connected networks, are not maintained free of cost. In a personal network, consider the investments an actor makes to maintain links to friends and acquaintances: There are letters to write and phone calls to make, gifts to be sent on special occasions, evenings or perhaps weekends taken up with sociable interaction, and, for really close friends, the need always to be "on call." Interorganizational relations require similar investments, *unless* the transaction is a one-time affair. However, in that case it would not make sense to think of such a transaction as part of a social network, as no connection has been established.

Cook, in her laboratory research, has dealt with transaction-specific investments under the rubric of commitment to the same partner in interaction over time. She and Richard Emerson (1978) explicitly stated that commitment was operationalized as persistence in a particular line of behavior, rather than in terms of attitudes or values, since they wanted to leave that an open question. Cook's experiments involved exchange networks in which transactions were relatively concurrent and involved on-the-spot negotiations. She noted, however, that other kinds of exchanges imply a longer-term commitment, as in reciprocal gift-giving, in which there is not mutual negotiation over the terms of trade, but rather a much more generalized exchange throughout a community of actors. Generalized exchange depends very heavily on trust and within-group solidarity, which are forms of investment in relationships.

Burt's chapter treats transaction-specific investments as an outcome of organizational responses to intensive and uncertain relations between organizations and sectors. Cooptation through ownership and direct or indirect director linkages represent a commitment to a relationship, which then must be sustained. For example, in the case of direct or indirect director interlocks, the firm will have to release executives from their firm-specific tasks periodically so they can attend board meetings and board subcommittee meetings, which can be quite time-consuming. Galaskiewicz argues that brokerages allow donor organizations to escape establishing direct relations with donees that might drain the organization's resources. However, the impulse to avoid making transaction-specific investments was not treated as a major factor in donors' choices of transfer payment mechanisms.

Marsden includes transaction costs in his model, but these occur for each transaction, rather than being incurred as a cost of maintaining the relationship itself. His model posits a cost to subordinate actors in dealing with the dominant position and a cost involved in using brokers for transactions with a third party. The great virtue of Marsden's formal modeling of network structure is that transaction-specific investments can easily be incorporated by positing a fractional resource decrement for each relationship per unit of time.

Summary. Evaluating the five chapters by the extent to which they incorporate transaction cost considerations reveals considerable similarity among them. Even though frequency of interaction is obviously a key dimension of relations between actors, only one chapter explicitly includes a measurement of frequency. All five chapters treat the management of uncertainty as a key problem, with several chapters explicitly identifying specific sources of uncertainty. What is missing in this group is greater concern for the cost of maintaining relationships, although I do not doubt that all authors would readily assent to the importance of transaction-specific investments.

Origins and Boundaries of Networks

The unit of analysis in network studies is often problematic. Many investigators argue that although data may be collected at the level of dyadic relationships, their true unit of analysis is the network, rather than the actors or relationships constituting it. Critics then raise the thorny issue of how such a network is bounded. Within bounded networks, brokerage roles play an important part in resource allocation, as several of the chapters argue. Are these roles the result of strategic behavior by individual actors, or is there something about the structure of networks that generates brokerage roles? The population ecology perspective sheds some light on both issues.

Bounding Networks

Transactions can be studied whether or not they are in networks. Presumably, however, transactions within networks are influenced by properties of the field of relations surrounding them. Moreover, without the assumption of a bounded system of social actors, a network unit of analysis is problematic.

Locating Boundaries. Boundaries to resource exchange networks are critical in these chapters, some authors recognizing the problem and others having the luxury of defining it away. What is the justification for including a set of positions in the same social network? Why would the actors identified in an analysis remain in their locations long enough to be characterized as part of a social network?

Boundary identification is most straightforward when the positions investigated are roles within an organization, community (Galaskiewicz), interorganizational system (Burt), or national system (Knoke and Laumann). In these cases, roles are defined in custom and tradition. Actors move into positions that carry historical precedence, and analysts need only act as sensitive ethnographers to gain a good idea of how to locate boundaries.

Boundaries become problematic when actors come together for solely "purposive action" that is *not* collective. In this case, what reason do we have to expect dyadic transactions to cohere into networks? The transaction cost model leads us to expect that infrequent transactions, with low transaction-specific investments, will *not* become enduring features of social systems. Networks, in other words, emerge when actors begin making transaction-specific investments of sufficient magnitude to commit themselves to relations. Boundaries can then be defined in relational rather than categorical terms, following the suggestions of White et al. (1976) or Alba (1973).

Cook and Marsden avoid the problem of boundaries by coercing subjects into a network and simulating a stable network, respectively. Burt examines the commitments organizations apparently are making to organizations in other sectors. These commitments (or cooptive relations, as he calls them) were explained by high-frequency and important transactions occurring between industries and sectors. No evidence is offered for stability in these relations, given the cross-sectional nature of the data, but the dependent variable has the presumption of stability built into it.

Working within a community context, Galaskiewicz examines transactions occurring directly between two parties and others taking place indirectly, through brokers. As he discusses failed transactions, he obviously takes the existence of relations as problematic. The requirements of logical symmetry would seem to necessitate his asking why such relations are established in the first place. As I indicated earlier, his chapter does contain a two-factor theory, explaining which kinds of transactions will occur under different environmental conditions.

Knoke and Laumann achieve a viable object of analysis by assuming intercommunication occurred between interested parties regarding a target policy. The boundaries of the policy domains they discuss are highly permeable, and they make matters more difficult for themselves by arguing that organizations taking no visible actions within the domain can still be included, because active participants are influenced by their perceptions of what the inactive participants would desire. They define centralization of the preexisting communication structure as the degree to which control over information transmission is concentrated among positions, and they distinguish four ideal-typical communication patterns. The first two patterns—complete fragmentation and nearly localized communication—would seem to prohibit the possibility of a national policy domain, since by definition there would not be communication between the interested actors. Only under conditions of chain-linked or hierarchical communication would one expect a national policy domain worth studying to emerge. I suspect that they will have to take an intercommunicating set of actors as given and concentrate their empirical analysis on the other hypotheses.

In long-standing communities or groups, the transaction cost approach may well break down. In these contexts, actors may have ties with those whom they would actually like to ignore or ties they would like to break. The structure of role relationships within which actors are implicated may prevent such instrumental behavior. For example, in Knoke and Laumann's policy domains, it is possible that some ties simply come with the territory. An actor occupying an important position on the national political stage may have obligations to other actors, whether or not such transactions make sense for that actor's own self-interest.

Broker Roles

Only Burt's chapter omits broker roles from consideration, suggesting that the other authors feel that broker roles are an important concept in network analyses. They take the broker role as given, but I will show that the population ecology approach is easily extended to cover the origins of such roles.

Origins of Broker Roles in Networks. From the population ecology perspective and the transaction cost approach to selection pressures, intermediary or broker roles are a natural result of actors' attempts to minimize transaction costs. Such positions exist because of their function of linking actors having complementary interests, transferring information, and

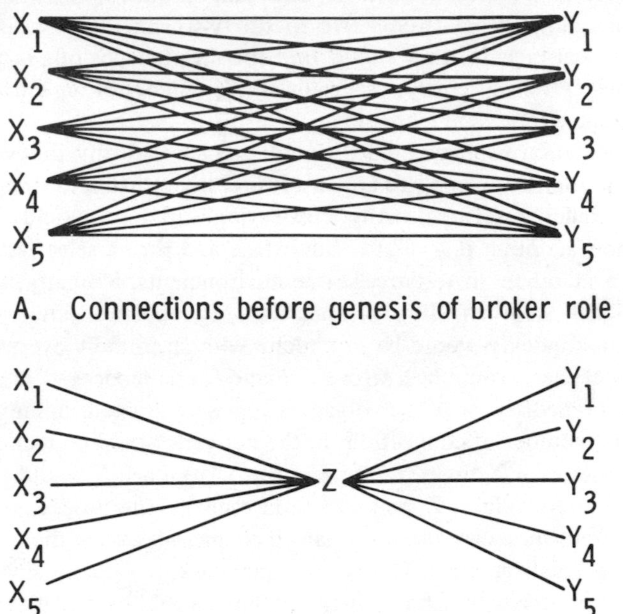

Figure 15.1 The Emergence of Broker Roles in Social Networks

otherwise facilitating the interests of actors not directly connected to one another.

Consider an example of a population divided into two major types of organizations, X and Y (such as buyers and sellers), where some method of interorganizational communication is desired by the organizations in both sets. Communication is possible if all organizations of one type are directly joined to all organizations of the other type, creating a fairly complex set of relations. The total number of relations in the population would total X times Y, assuming a link is established in each direction. If there were five organizations of each type, the total number of links would be twenty-five (see Figure 15.1a).

Each new organization added to each subpopulation would increase the number of required links linearly. If another X is added, five more links are created, and if yet another is added, an additional five connections are needed. If an organization were added to each subpopulation, the increase in links would be exponential. If one pair is added, the number of connections jumps from twenty-five to thirty-six. In a large population, large individual organizations would find the maintenance of a large set of connections extremely costly, especially if the number of organizations in both subpopulations were increasing.

The population ecology model would predict that any innovation or random variation happening to create a less costly solution to the problem would be quickly selected. Any cost-saving variation would give the organization adopting it a relative advantage and thus a selective survival prospect over others in resource-scarce environments. Similarly, any new organizational form enabling organizations to communicate with one another more quickly would be in a niche with an initially overwhelming advantage, as there would be a strong demand for its services.

If an intermediary or broker organization were created, linking the Xs and Ys, the number of connections in the network would be reduced to X plus Y, rather than X times Y (see Figure 15.1b). Each X would have one link to the intermediary, Z, and so would each Y. The process of sorting out the various messages and information channels between the Xs and Ys would be internalized by Z. This is a complex task, but Z specializes in the role of broker and only a fraction of the links would be active at any one time. The selective advantages of a broker role would be greatest when the population of Xs and Ys is sufficiently heterogeneous to rule out using stereotypes of the others in its operations. (If all Xs were alike, then any given Y would need only a single link to an X to get all of the other information it needed.)

More than one intermediary or broker would surely arise, as the selective advantages in this niche are substantial. Note that a broker is not positively selected on the basis of its contribution to joint X-Y survival, but rather because of its obvious appeal to Xs and Ys as a method of cutting their own costs. The broker survives in its niche because those organizations using it have a selective advantage over others that do not, and their survival, in turn, allows a broker to survive. Once introduced into a population, we would expect this function to persist, and the concept of the broker would be carried by the culture, passed on via imitation and tradition.

Broker roles will thus arise in communities of actors with a common fate because of exposure to similar environmental contingencies. No "altruism" need be assumed—all parties benefit from the existence of broker roles. The role, of course, can be played badly or well, and variation in broker behavior partially reflects other actors' problems with bounded rationality and opportunism. But there will be limits to variation in broker behavior if the network of connections is not fixed, permitting actors to move between brokers. Fixed connections would only be expected under a common authority structure, which means mostly *within* organizations rather than between them.

Limits on Exploitative Behavior. Given the powerful adaptive advantage broker roles would give an evolving population or community, they are quite common and, more important, invested with cultural norms and values. Indeed, they are probably more subject to social control and regulation than any other role (either by self-regulation or community regulation). But one-off transactions would be another matter.

Imagine a person walking up to you on the street corner and offering to get something for you wholesale. Is he a broker? In pure structural terms (on paper) he may *look* like one, but he is not—"trust" is missing. The person has not approached you in a role-appropriate context. Trust, in this context, does not mean consensus on ultimate values or objectives, but rather that the person has a stake in preserving his or her reputation as an "honorable broker." Marsden's insightful discussion lists three conditions affecting central actors' use of exploitative behavior in the broker role: Is exploitation in the broker's self-interest, is the network positively or negatively connected, and does the broker control some resources unique to his or her position that are not available *via* the channels he or she brokers? To this list we must obviously add the questions of whether the network is stable or changing and whether we are discussing a person in a broker role, defined by custom and tradition, or a person in a temporarily advantageous position who has made no transaction-specific investments in that position as broker.

Persistence of Networks

As a final issue, one thing that intrigued me about these chapters was the manner in which the issue of network persistence was passed over rather lightly. Knoke and Laumann were the only authors to discuss explicitly the degree to which actors and connections in the networks they studied were stable. Burt, because of cross-sectional data, was not able to address this question, and Cook and Marsden excluded persistence as an issue because they wished to focus on the effects of centrality with actors and connections held constant. Galaskiewicz dealt with the persistence issue by discussing the conditions under which specific kinds of interorganizational relations failed.

Accounting for Persistence

As Cook and Emerson (1978: 728) note, economic exchange theory assumes that exchange partners develop no loyalties or long-standing commitments to one another. "By contrast, reinforcement psychology and much of sociology and social anthropology tend to take the existence of longitudinal commitments as theoretically expected." The thrust of my comments to this point has been that persistence depends on the investments actors have in relationships. As Burt notes in his chapter, resource dependence (or lack of viable alternatives) is a powerful force toward maintaining a relationship with another actor. Knoke and Laumann's model suggests an organizational basis for network persistence, as they distinguish between confederated and unitary organizations, on their "constitutional basis" dimension. Unitary (or monocephalic) organizations are able to make enduring commitments to relationships, whereas such commitments are problematic for confederated organizations. However, to the extent that the staffs in confederated organizations are less tightly controlled by single-minded CEOs, they are free to persist in relationships long after the transaction justification is gone (Wood, 1972; Michels, 1949).

Effects of Network Persistence

Most of the five chapters reviewed here evince some concern for the ability of actors to exploit their positions and networks via strategic moves. Such exploitation may not be tolerated in relations that are recurring, rather than one-off. Frequent transactions, in which investments have been made, are less likely to lend themselves to grossly exploitative behavior, unless heavy coercive pressures are applied; or, rather, substantial exploitation in persisting relationships would be accounted for not through network position but through more general theories of power and domination.

A number of the chapters also make reference to the fact that networks eventually shape and transform the interests of actors, thus ultimately bringing about their own transformation. Networks affect interests because they give positions access to solutions that were not there before and also pose problems that were not recognized previously. Knoke and Laumann's discussion, although not their original model, demonstrates this characteristic of networks very well.

In considering the issue of persistence, we are left with a number of questions that these authors will, I am sure, follow up. Why would actors remain in disadvantaged network positions? Why not maneuver out of them, via coalitions, withdrawal, or other strategies? Rigidity of one's network position would only be predicted in a totally closed system, and it is difficult to imagine such scenarios outside of the laboratory. Could it be that real, totally negatively connected networks are not very stable? The central actors in positively connected networks are kept there by others' contributions and trust. In negatively connected networks, centrally located actors must fight to stay there. As Cook and Emerson (1978) note, most networks are probably combinations of positive and negative connections.

Conclusion

I have tried to show how the population ecology perspective, together with the transaction cost approach to selection pressures, sheds light on the origins and persistence of network structures. Taking account of transactions' frequency and uncertainty and the level of transaction-specific investments provides a framework within which the stability of relations is a central issue. Using the example of broker roles, which figure prominently in several of these chapters, I illustrated the population ecology model's power in explaining the genesis of network positions.

Social network concepts, applied in describing existing social structures, are very powerful analytic tools. Most social theories, however, are ultimately concerned with social change and the conditions under which it occurs. Network analysts have shown themselves adept at characterizing structures in the cross-section, but integrating structural analysis with change processes has proved a more daunting task. These five chapters demonstrate the potential and the limitations of such an integration, even though that was not their primary concern.

Bibliography

ABELSON, R. P. (1979) "Social clusters and opinion clusters." Pp. 239-256 in P. W. Holland and S. Leinhardt (eds.), Perspectives on Social Network Research. New York: Academic Press.

ALBA, R. D. (1981) "Taking stock of network analysis: A decade's results." Pp. 39-74 in S. B. Bacharach (ed.), Perspectives in Organizational Research. Greenwich, CT: JAI Press.

ALBA, R. D. (1973) "A graph-theoretic definition of a sociometric clique." Journal of Mathematical Sociology 3: 113-126.

ALBA, R. D. and C. KADUSHIN (1976) "The intersection of social circles: A new measure of social proximity in networks." Sociological Methods and Research 5: 77-102.

ALBA, R. D. and G. MOORE (1978) "Elite social circles." Sociological Methods and Research 7: 167-188.

ALDRICH, H. (1979) Organizations and Environments. Englewood Cliffs, NJ: Prentice-Hall.

ALDRICH, H. (1976) "Resource dependence and interorganizational relations: Relations between local employment services offices and social service sector organizations." Administration and Society 7: 419-454.

ALDRICH, H. and J. PFEFFER (1976) "Environments of organizations." Annual Review of Sociology 2: 79-106.

ALDRICH, H. and J. WEISS (1981) "Differentiation within the United States capitalist class: Workforce size and income differences." American Sociological Review 46: 279-290.

ALLISON, G. (1971) Essence of Decision: Explaining the Cuban Missile Crisis. Boston: Little, Brown.

American Association of Fund-Raising Counsel (1980) Giving USA. New York: Author.

American Psychiatric Association (1980) Diagnostic and Statistical Manual III. Washington, DC: Author.

ANDERSON, B. and M. L. CARLOS (1976) "What is social network theory?" Pp. 27-51 in T. Burns and W. Buckley (eds.), Power and Control. London: Sage.

ANTONUCCI, T. and J. BORNSTEIN (n.d.) "Changes in informal social support systems." Unpublished paper, Survey Research Center, University of Michigan.

ARROW, K. J. (1975) "Gifts and exchange." Pp. 13-28 in E. S. Phelps (ed.), Altruism, Morality, and Economic Theory. New York: Russell Sage Foundation.

ASCH, S. E. (1951) "Effects of group pressure upon the modification and distortion of judgments." Pp. 171-190 in H. Guetzkow (ed.), Groups, Leadership, and Men. Pittsburgh: Carnegie Press.

ATTEWELL, P. and R. FITZGERALD (1980) "Comparing stratification theories." American Sociological Review 45: 325-328.

BAKER, R. P. and J. E. SHILLINGBURG (1977) "Corporate charitable contributions." Research Papers, Commission on Private Philanthropy and Public Needs. Washington, DC: Department of the Treasury.

BALTZELL, E. D. (1964) The Protestant Establishment: Aristocracy and Caste in America. New York: Vintage.

BALTZELL, E. D. (1958) Philadelphia Gentlemen: The Making of a National Upper Class. New York: Free Press.

BARNES, J. A. (1972) Social Networks. Reading, MA: Addison-Wesley.

BARNES, J. A. (1969) "Networks and political process." Pp. 51-76 in J. C. Mitchell (ed.), Social Networks in Urban Situations. Manchester, England: Manchester University Press.

BARTON, A. H. (1974) "Consensus and conflict among American leaders." Public Opinion Quarterly 38: 507-530.

BARTON, A. H. and D. W. PARSONS (1977) "Measuring belief system structure." Public Opinion Quarterly 41: 159-180.

BAVELAS, A. (1950) "Communication patterns in task-oriented groups." Journal of the Acoustical Society of America 57: 271-282.

BAVELAS, A. (1948) "A mathematical model for group structure." Human Organization 7: 16-30.

BEARDEN, J., W. ATWOOD, P. FREITAG, C. HENDRICKS, B. MINTZ, and M. SCHWARTZ (1975) "The nature and extent of bank centrality in corporate networks." Presented at the annual meetings of the American Sociological Association, San Francisco, August.

BEAUCHAMP, M. A. (1965) "An improved index of centrality." Behavioral Science 10: 161-163.

BÉLAND, F. (1978) "La Réduction de catégories dans les tableaux de contingence: les hypothèses d'indépendance régionale." Ph.D. dissertation, Department of Sociology, Université Laval.

BÉLAND, F. and J. FORTIER (1981) "The reduction of categories of variables in contingency table analysis: A model." Unpublished paper.

BELL, D. (1973) The Coming of Post-Industrial Society. New York: Basic Books.

BENDER, T. (1978) Community and Social Change in America. New Brunswick, NJ: Rutgers University Press.

BENNETT, W. L. (1975) The Political Mind and the Political Environment. Lexington, MA: D. C. Heath.

BENSON, J. K. (1975) "The interorganizational network as a political economy." Administrative Science Quarterly 20: 229-249.

BERGE, C. (1962) The Theory of Graphs. New York: John Wiley.

BERKMAN, L. F. and S. L. SYME (1979) "Social networks, host resistance, and mortality: A nine-year followup study of Alameda County residents." American Journal of Epidemiology 109: 186-204.

BERKOWITZ, L. and L. R. DANIELS (1963) "Responsibility and dependency." Journal of Abnormal and Social Psychology 66: 429-436.

BERKOWITZ, S. D. (1982) An Introduction to Structural Analysis. Toronto: Butterworths.

BERNARD, H. R., P. D. KILLWORTH, and L. SAILER (1981) "Summary of research on informant accuracy in network data and on the reverse small world problem." Connections 4: 11-25.

BILLINGS, R. S., T. W. MILBURN, and M. L. SCHAALMAN (1980) "A model of crisis perception: A theoretical and empirical analysis." Administrative Science Quarterly 25: 300-316.

BISHOP, G. F., A. J. TUCHFARBER, R. W. OLDENDICK, and S. E. BENNETT (1979) "Questions about question wording: A rejoinder to revisiting mass belief system revisited." American Political Science Review 73: 187-192.

BISHOP, Y.M.M., S. E. FIENBERG, and P. W. HOLLAND (1975) Discrete Multivariate Analysis: Theory and Practice. Cambridge, MA: MIT Press.

BLAU, J. (1980) "When weak ties are structured." Unpublished paper, Department of Sociology, State University of New York at Albany.

BLAU, P. M. (1981) "Diverse views of social structure and their common denominator." Pp. 1-23 in P. M. Blau and R. K. Merton (eds.), Continuities in Structural Inquiry. Beverly Hills, CA: Sage.

BLAU, P. M. (1977a) Inequality and Heterogeneity. New York: Free Press.

BLAU, P. M. (1977b) "A macrosociological theory of social structure." American Journal of Sociology 83: 26-54.

BLAU, P. M. [ed.] (1975) Approaches to the Study of Social Structure. New York: Free Press.

BLAU, P. M. (1974) "Parameters of social structure." American Sociological Review 39: 615-635.

BLAU, P. M. (1964) Exchange and Power in Social Life. New York: John Wiley.

BLAU, P. M. and O. D. DUNCAN (1967) The American Occupational Structure. New York: John Wiley.

BLUMBERG, P. M. and P. W. PAUL (1975) "Continuities and discontinuities in upper-class marriages." Journal of Marriage and the Family 37: 63-77.

BOISSEVAIN, J. (1974) Friends of Friends: Networks, Manipulators and Coalitions. Oxford: Blackwell.

BOISSEVAIN, J. and J. C. MITCHELL [eds.] (1973) Network Analysis: Studies in Human Interaction. The Hague: Mouton.

BOLNICK, B. R. (1975) "Toward a behavioral theory of philanthropic activity." Pp. 197-224 in E. S. Phelps (ed.), Altruism, Morality, and Economic Theory. New York: Russell Sage Foundation.

BOORMAN, S. A. (1975) "A combinatorial optimization model for transmission of job information through contact networks." Bell Journal of Economics 6: 216-249.

BOORMAN, S. A. and H. C. WHITE (1976) "Social structure from multiple networks: II. Role structures." American Journal of Sociology 81: 1384-1446.

BOOTH, A., D. R. JOHNSON, and J. N. EDWARDS (1980a) "Reply to Gove and Hughes." American Sociological Review 45: 870-873.

BOOTH, A., D. R. JOHNSON, and J. N. EDWARDS (1980b) "In pursuit of pathology: The effects of human crowding." American Sociological Review 45: 873-870.

BOTT, E. (1971) Family and Social Network (2nd ed.). London: Tavistock.

BOTTOMORE, T. B. (1964) Elites and Society. Baltimore: Penguin.

BOULANGER, G. (1981) "Conditions affecting the appearance and maintenance of traumatic stress reactions among Vietnam veterans." Ph.D. dissertation, Department of Psychology, Columbia University.

BOULDING, K. E. (1962) "Notes on a theory of philanthropy." Pp. 57-71 in F. G. Dickinson (ed.), Philanthropy and Public Policy. New York: National Bureau of Economic Research.

BREIGER, R. L. (1981a) "Comment on Paul W. Holland and Samuel Leinhardt, 'An exponential family of probability distributions for directed graphs.' " Journal of the American Statistical Association 76: 51-53.

BREIGER, R. L. (1981b) "The social class structure of occupational mobility." American Journal of Sociology 87: 578-611.

BREIGER, R. L. (1981c) "Structures of economic interdependence among nations." Pp. 353-380 in P. M. Blau and R. K. Merton (eds.), Continuities in Structural Inquiry. Beverly Hills, CA: Sage.

BREIGER, R. L. (1979) "Toward an operational theory of community elite structures." Quality and Quantity 13: 21-57.

BREIGER, R. L. and P. PATTISON (1978) "The joint role structure of two communities' elites." Sociological Methods and Research 7: 213-226.

BRYM, R. J. (1978) The Jewish Intelligentsia and Russian Marxism. London: Macmillan.

BURT, R. S. (forthcoming) Corporate Profits and Cooptation: Networks of Market Constraints and Directorate Ties in the American Economy. New York: Academic Press.

BURT, R. S. (1982) Toward a Structural Theory of Action: Network Models of Stratification, Perception, and Action. New York: Academic Press.

BURT, R. S. (1981) "A note on corporate philanthropy." Presented at the Albany Conference on Contributions of Networks Analysis to Structural Sociology, Albany, New York, April.

BURT, R. S. (1980a) "Cooptive corporate actor networks: A reconsideration of interlocking directorates involving American manufacturing." Administrative Science Quarterly 25: 557-582.

BURT, R. S. (1980b) "Autonomy in a social topology." American Journal of Sociology 85: 892-925.

BURT, R. S. (1980c) "Models of network structure." Annual Review of Sociology 6: 79-141.

BURT, R. S. (1979) "A structural theory of interlocking corporate directorates." Social Networks 1: 415-435.

BURT, R. S. (1978) "Cohesion versus structural equivalence as a basis for network subgroups." Sociological Methods and Research 7: 189-212.

BURT, R. S. (1977a) "Positions in multiple network systems. Part One: A general conception of stratification and prestige in a system of actors cast as a social topology." Social Forces 56: 106-131.

BURT, R. S. (1977b) "Power in a social topology." Pp. 251-334 in R. J. Liebert and A. W. Imershein (eds.), Power, Paradigms and Community Research. Beverly Hills, CA: Sage.

BURT, R. S. (1977c) "Positions in multiple network systems. Part Two: Stratification and prestige among elite decision-makers in the community of Altneustadt." Social Forces 56: 551-575.

BURT, R. S. (1977d) "Power in a social topology." Social Science Research 6: 1-83.

BURT, R. S. (1976) "Positions in networks." Social Forces 55: 93-122.

BURT, R. S. (1975) "Corporate society: A time series analysis of network structure." Social Science Research 4: 271-328.

BURT, R. S., K. P. CHRISTMAN, and H. C. KILBURN (1980) "Testing a structural theory of corporate cooptation: Interorganizational directorate ties as a strategy for avoiding market constraints on profits." American Sociological Review 45: 821-841.

BURT, R. S. and M. J. MINOR [eds.] (1982) Applied Network Analysis. Beverly Hills, CA: Sage.

BUSACKER, R. and T. SAATZ (1965) Finite Graphs and Networks: An Introduction with Applications. New York: McGraw-Hill.

CARTWRIGHT, D. (1968) "The nature of group cohesiveness." Pp. 91-107 in D. Cartwright and A. Zander (eds.), Group Dynamics. New York: Harper & Row.

CAULKINS, D. (1980) "Community, subculture and organizational networks in western Norway." Presented at the First World Congress of IVAR/VOIR, Brussels, June.

CHADWICK-JONES, J. K. (1976) Social Exchange Theory: Its Structure and Influence in Social Psychology. London: Academic Press.

CHUBIN, D. (1976) "The conceptualization of scientific specialties." Sociological Quarterly 17: 448-476.

CLARK, T. N. (1968) Community Structure and Decision-Making: Comparative Analyses. San Francisco: Chandler.

CLOGG, C. C. (1981) "Latent structure models of mobility." American Journal of Sociology 86: 836-868.

COATES, D. B. et al. (1970) Yorklea Social Environment Survey Research Report. Toronto: Clarke Institute of Psychiatry, Community Studies Section.

COBB, R. W. and C. D. ELDER (1972) Participation in American Politics: The Dynamics of Agenda-Building. Baltimore: Johns Hopkins Press.

COLEMAN, J. S. (1977) "Social action systems." Pp. 11-50 in K. Szaniawski (ed.), Problems of Formalization in the Social Sciences. Wroclaw: Polskiej Akademii Nauk.

COLEMAN, J. S. (1974) Power and the Structure of Society. New York: Norton.

COLEMAN, J. S. (1973a) The Mathematics of Collective Action. Chicago: Aldine.

COLEMAN, J. S. (1973b) "Loss of power." American Sociological Review 38: 1-17.

COLEMAN, J. S. (1972) "Systems of social exchange." Journal of Mathematical Sociology 2: 145-163.

COLEMAN, J. S. (1964) Introduction to Mathematical Sociology. New York: Free Press.

COLEMAN, J. S. (1958) "Relational analysis: The study of social organization with survey methods." Human Organization 17: 28-36.

COLEMAN, J. S. (1957) Community Conflict. New York: Free Press.

COLEMAN, J. S., E. KATZ, and H. MENZEL (1966) Medical Innovation: A Diffusion Study. Indianapolis: Bobbs-Merrill.

COLLINS, H. (1974) "The TEA set: Tacit knowledge and scientific networks." Science Studies 4: 165-186.

COLLINS, R. (1975) Conflict Sociology. New York: Academic Press.

CONVERSE, P. (1964) "The nature of belief systems in mass publics." Pp. 206-261 in D. E. Apter (ed.), Ideology and Discontent. New York: Free Press.

COOK, J. (1979) "Is charity obsolete?" Forbes 123: 45-51.

COOK, K. S. (1979) "Exchange, power and equity." Didactic seminar presented at the annual meetings of the American Sociological Association, Boston, August.

COOK, K. S. (1977) "Exchange and power in networks of interorganizational relations." Sociological Quarterly 18: 62-82.

COOK, K. S. and R. M. EMERSON (1978) "Power, equity and commitment in exchange networks." American Sociological Review 43: 721-739.

COOK, K. S. and R. M. EMERSON (1977) "Design of a computerized laboratory for the experimental analysis of social interaction." Technical report, Institute for Sociological Research, University of Washington.

COOK, K. S. and R. M. EMERSON with M. R. GILLMORE and T. YAMAGISHI (forthcoming) The Structure of Social Exchange. New York: Academic Press.

COOK, K. S., R. M. EMERSON, M. R. GILLMORE, and T. YAMAGISHI (1980) "Power and positional centrality in exchange networks." Technical Report, Institute for Sociological Research, University of Washington.

COOK, K. S., M. R. GILLMORE, and J. LITTLE (1980) "Power, dependency and collective action in exchange networks." Technical Report, Institute for Sociological Research, University of Washington.

COSER, R. (1975) "The complexity of roles as seedbed of individual autonomy." Pp. 237-263 in L. Coser (ed.), The Idea of Social Structure: Essays in Honor of Robert Merton. New York: Harcourt Brace Jovanovich.

CRAVEN, P. and B. WELLMAN (1973) "The network city." Sociological Inquiry 43: 57-88.

CROSBIE, P. V. (1975) Interaction in Small Groups. New York: Macmillan.

CRUMP (LEIGHTON), B. (1977) "The portability of urban ties." Presented at the annual meetings of the American Sociological Association, Chicago, September.

DAVIS, K. (1959) "The myth of functional analysis as a special method in sociology and anthropology." American Sociological Review 24: 757-772.

DEAN, A. and N. LIN (1977) "The stress-buffering role of social support: Problems and prospects for systematic investigation." Journal of Nervous and Mental Disease 65: 403-417.

DELANY, J. (1980) "Aspects of donative resource allocation and the efficiency of social networks: Simulation models of job vacancy information transfers through personal contacts." Ph.D. dissertation, Department of Sociology, Yale University.

DOHRENWEND, B. P. (1979) "Stressful life events and psychopathology: Some issues of theory and method." Pp. 1-15 in J. E. Barrett, R. M. Rose, and G. L. Klerman (eds.), Stress and Mental Disorder. New York: Raven Press.

DOHRENWEND, B. P. and B. S. DOHRENWEND (1974) "Social and cultural influences in psychopathology." Annual Review of Psychology 25: 417-453.

DOHRENWEND, B. P. and the Social Psychiatry Research Unit (1977) "Appendix I to the measurement of psychopathology in the community: Problems and procedures, the psychiatric epidemiology research interview: A report on twenty-two scales." Unpublished memo dated February 7, Department of Psychiatry, Columbia University.

DOMHOFF, G. W. (1979) The Powers That Be: Processes of Ruling Class Domination in America. New York: Vintage.

DOMHOFF, G. W. [ed.] (1975) New Directions in Power Structure Research. Special issue of The Insurgent Sociologist, Vol. 5.

DOMHOFF, G. W. (1971) The Higher Circles: The Governing Class in America. New York: Vintage.

DOMHOFF, G. W. (1967) Who Rules America? Englewood Cliffs, NJ: Prentice-Hall.

DRUCKER, P. (1973) "Managing the public service institution." The Public Interest 33: 43-60.

DUNCAN, O. D. (1979) "How destination depends on origin in the occupational mobility table." American Journal of Sociology 84: 793-803.

DURKHEIM, E. (1902/1960) The Division of Labor in Society (2nd ed.; trans. G. Simpson). New York: Free Press.

DURKHEIM, E. (1897/1951) Suicide (trans. J. A. Spaulding and G. Simpson, ed. G. Simpson). New York: Free Press.

DYE, T. R. (1979) Who's Running America: The Carter Years. Englewood Cliffs, NJ: Prentice-Hall.

East York, Borough of (1976) The Golden Years of East York. Toronto: Centennial College Press.

EDWARDS, A. M. (1943) Comparative Occupational Statistics for the United States, 1870 to 1940. Washington, DC: Government Printing Office.

EISENSTADT, S. N. (1968) "Studies of reference group behavior." Pp. 413-429 in H. H. Hyman and E. Singer (eds.), Readings in Reference Group Theory and Research. New York: Free Press.

EISENSTADT, S. N. and L. RONIGER (1980) "Patron-client relations as a model of structuring social exchange." Comparative Studies in Society and History 22: 42-77.

EKEH, P. (1974) Social Exchange Theory: The Two Traditions. Cambridge, MA: Harvard University Press.

EL-ANSARY, A. and L. W. STERN (1972) "Power measurement in the distribution channel." Journal of Marketing Research 9: 47-52.

EMERSON, R. M. (1982) "Charismatic kingship in Baltistan." In A. Ahmed (ed.), Pakistan Society: Problems of Ethnic Diversity and Nationhood.

EMERSON, R. M. (1981) "Social exchange theory." Pp. 30-65 in M. Rosenberg and R. H. Turner (eds.), Social Psychology: Sociological Perspectives. New York: Basic Books.

EMERSON, R. M. (1976) "Social exchange theory." Annual Review of Sociology 2: 335-362.

EMERSON, R. M. (1972a) "Exchange theory, Part I: A psychological basis for social exchange." Pp. 38-57 in J. Berger, M. Zelditch, and B. Anderson (eds.), Sociological Theories in Progress (Vol. 2). Boston: Houghton Mifflin.

EMERSON, R. M. (1972b) "Exchange theory, Part II: Exchange relations and networks." Pp. 58-87 in J. Berger, M. Zelditch, and B. Anderson (eds.), Sociological Theories in Progress (Vol. 2). Boston: Houghton Mifflin.

EMERSON, R. M. (1962) "Power-dependence relations." American Sociological Review 27: 31-40.

ENSEL, W. M. (1979) "Sex, social ties and status attainment." Ph.D. dissertation, Department of Sociology, State University of New York at Albany.

ERICKSEN, E. and W. YANCEY (1980) "Class, sector and income determination." Unpublished paper, Department of Sociology, Temple University.

ERICKSEN, E. and W. YANCEY (1977) "The locus of strong ties." Unpublished paper, Department of Sociology, Temple University.

ERICKSON, B. H. (forthcoming) "The relational basis of attitudes." In S. D. Berkowitz and B. Wellman (eds.), Structural Approaches to Sociology. Cambridge, England: Cambridge University Press.

ERMANN, M. D. (1978) "The operative goals of corporate philanthropy: Contributions to the Public Broadcasting Service, 1972-1976." Social Problems 25: 504-514.

FARARO, T. J. (1973) Mathematical Sociology. New York: John Wiley.

FARIS, R.E.L. and H. W. DURHAM (1939/1965) Mental Disorders in Urban Areas. Chicago: University of Chicago Press.

FEATHERMAN, D. L. and R. M. HAUSER (1978) Opportunity and Change. New York: Academic Press.

FELD, S. (1981) "The focused organization of social ties." American Journal of Sociology 86: 1015-1035.

FELD, S. (1977) "A reconceptualization of the problem of collective decisions." Journal of Mathematical Sociology 5: 257-271.

FESTINGER, L. (1954) "A theory of social comparison processes." Human Relations 7: 117-140.

FESTINGER, L., S. SCHACTER, and K. BACK (1950) Social Pressures in Informal Groups. New York: Harper & Row.

FINE, G. and S. KLEINMAN (1979) "Rethinking subculture: An interactionist analysis." American Journal of Sociology 85: 1-20.

FINE, M., G. ROTHBART, and S. SUDMAN (1979) "On finding the needle in a haystack: Multiplicity sampling procedures." Presented at the annual meetings of the American Association for Public Opinion Research, Buck Hill Falls, Pennsylvania, June.

FISCHER, C. S. (1982) To Dwell Among Friends: Personal Networks in Town and City. Chicago: University of Chicago Press.

FISCHER, C. S. (1976) The Urban Experience. New York: Harcourt Brace Jovanovich.

FISCHER, C. S. (1975a) "Toward a subcultural theory of urbanism." American Journal of Sociology 80: 1319-1341.

FISCHER, C. S. (1975b) "The study of urban community and personality." Annual Review of Sociology 1: 67-89.

FISCHER, C. S., R. M. JACKSON, C. A. STUEVE, K. GERSON, and L. McCALLISTER JONES with M. BALDASSARE (1977) Networks and Places. New York: Free Press.

FISHER, F. M. (1977) "On donor sovereignty and united charities." American Economic Review 67: 632-638.

FRANK, O. (1981) "A survey of statistical methods for graph analysis." Pp. 110-155 in S. Leinhardt (ed.), Sociological Methodology 1981. San Francisco: Jossey-Bass.

FREEMAN, L. C. (1979) "Centrality in social networks: I. Conceptual clarification." Social Networks 1: 215-239.

FREEMAN, L. C. (1978) "Segregation in social networks." Sociological Methods and Research 6: 411-429.

FREEMAN, L. C. (1977) "A set of measures of centrality based on betweenness." Sociometry 40: 35-41.

FREEMAN, L. C., D. ROEDER, and R. R. MULHOLLAND (1980) "Centrality in social networks: II. Experimental results." Social Networks 2: 119-141.

FREUD, S. (1930/1962) Civilization and Its Discontents (trans., ed. J. Strachey). New York: Norton.

FRIEDKIN, N. E. (1981) "The development of structure in random networks: An analysis of the effects of increasing network density on five measures of structure." Social Networks 3: 41-52.

FRIEDKIN, N. E. (1980) "A test of the structural features of Granovetter's 'Strength of Weak Ties' theory." Social Networks 2: 411-422.

GALASKIEWICZ, J. (1979) Exchange Networks and Community Politics. Beverly Hills, CA: Sage.

GANS, H. (1962) The Urban Villagers. New York: Free Press.

GATES, A. S., H. STEVENS, and B. WELLMAN (1973) "What makes a good neighbor?" Presented at the annual meetings of the American Sociological Association, New York, August.

GIDDENS, A. (1973) The Class Structure of the Advanced Societies. New York: Harper & Row.

GILLIES, M. and B. WELLMAN (1968) "East York: A profile." Toronto: Clarke Institute of Psychiatry, Community Studies Section.

GLASS, D. V. (1954) Social Mobility in Britain. London: Routledge & Kegan Paul.

GOLDHAMMER, H. and A. MARSHALL (1955) Psychosis and Civilization: Two Studies in the Frequency of Mental Disorder. New York: Free Press.

GOODMAN, L. A. (1981) "Criteria for determining whether certain categories in a cross-classification table should be combined, with special reference to occupational categories in an occupational mobility table." American Journal of Sociology 87: 612-650.

GOODMAN, L. A. (1979) "Simple models for the analysis of association in cross-classifications having ordered categories." Journal of the American Statistical Association 74: 537-552.

GOODMAN, L. A. (1972) "Some multiplicative models for the analysis of cross-classified data." Pp. 649-696 in L. LeCam, J. Neyman, and E. L. Scott (eds.), Proceedings of the Sixth Berkeley Symposium on Mathematical Statistics and Probability. Berkeley: University of California Press.

GOODMAN, L. A. (1970) "The multivariate analysis of qualitative data: Interactions among multiple classifications." Journal of the American Statistical Association 65: 226-256.

GOODMAN, L. A. (1969) "How to ransack mobility tables and other kinds of cross-classification tables." American Journal of Sociology 75: 1-39.

GOODMAN, L. A. (1968) "The analysis of cross-classified data: Independence, quasi-independence, and interactions in contingency tables with or without missing entries." Journal of the American Statistical Association 63: 1091-1131.

GORE, S. (1980) "Stress buffering functions of social support: An appraisal and clarification of a research model." Pp. 202-222 in B. S. Dohrenwend and B. P. Dohrenwend (eds.), Life Stress and Illness. New York: Neale Watson.

GORE, S., L. I. PEARLIN, and C. SCHOOLER (1979) "Comment." Journal of Health and Social Behavior 20: 201-203.

GORZ, A. (1968) Strategy for Labor: A Radical Proposal. Boston: Beacon Press.

GOTTLIEB, B. H. (1981) "Preventive interventions involving social networks and social support." Pp. 201-232 in B. H. Gottlieb (ed.), Social Networks and Social Support. Beverly Hills, CA: Sage.

GOVE, W. R. and M. HUGHES (1980a) "The effects of crowding found in the Toronto study: Some methodological and empirical questions." American Sociological Review 45: 864-870.

GOVE, W. R. and M. HUGHES (1980b) "In pursuit of preconceptions: A reply to the claim of Booth and his colleagues that household crowding is not an important variable." American Sociological Review 45: 878-886.

GRANOVETTER, M. S. (1976) "Network sampling: Some first steps." American Journal of Sociology 81: 1287-1303.

GRANOVETTER, M. S. (1974) Getting a Job: A Study of Contacts and Careers. Cambridge, MA: Harvard University Press.

GRANOVETTER, M. S. (1973) "The strength of weak ties." American Journal of Sociology 78: 1360-1380.

HALBERSTAM, D. (1972) The Best and the Brightest. New York: Random House.

HALL, R., J. CLARK, P. GIORDANO, P. JOHNSON, and M. VAN ROEKEL (1977) "Patterns of interorganizational relationships." Administrative Science Quarterly 22: 457-474.

HALLER, M. and R. W. HODGE (1981) "Class and status as dimensions of career mobility: Some insights from the Austrian case." Zeitschrift fuer Soziologie 10: 133-150.

HALLINAN, M. (1974) The Structure of Positive Sentiment. New York: Elsevier.

HAMMER, M. (1981) "Impact of social networks on health and disease." Presented at the annual meetings of the American Association for the Advancement of Science, Toronto, January.

HANNAN, M. and J. FREEMAN (1977) "The population ecology of organizations." American Journal of Sociology 82: 929-964.

HANSMANN, H. B. (1980) "The role of nonprofit enterprise." Yale Law Review 89: 835-901.

HARARY, F., R. Z. NORMAN, and D. CARTWRIGHT (1965) Structural Models: An Introduction to the Theory of Directed Graphs. New York: John Wiley.

HARRIS, J. and A. KLEPPER (1977) "Corporate philanthropic public service activities." Pp. 1741-1788 in Research Papers, Commission on Private Philanthropy and Public Needs. Washington, DC: Department of the Treasury.

HARRISS, C. L. (1977) "Corporate giving: Rationale, issues, and opportunities." Pp. 1789-1825 in Research Papers, Commission on Private Philanthropy and Public Needs. Washington, DC: Department of the Treasury.

HARTIGAN, J. A. (1980) "Using mobility data to develop occupational classifications: Exploratory exercises." Pp. 411-418 in A. R. Miller, D. J. Treiman, P. S. Cain, and P. A. Roos (eds.), Work, Jobs and Occupations: A Critical Review of the Dictionary of Occupational Titles. Washington, DC: National Academy Press.

HAUSER, R. M. (1979) "Some exploratory methods for modeling mobility tables and other cross-classified data." Pp. 413-458 in K. F. Schuessler (ed.), Sociological Methodology 1980. San Francisco: Jossey-Bass.

HAUSER, R. M. (1978) "A structural model of the mobility table." Social Forces 56: 919-953.

HEATH, A. (1976) Rational Choice and Social Exchange. Cambridge, England: Cambridge University Press.

HENDERSON, S. (1977) "The social network, support and neurosis: The function of attachment in adult life." British Journal of Psychiatry 131: 185-191.

HERMANN, C. F. (1969) Crisis in Foreign Policy: A Simulation Analysis. Indianapolis: Bobbs-Merrill.

HOCHMAN, H. M. and J. D. RODGERS (1969) "Pareto optimal redistribution." American Economic Review 59: 542-557.

HOLLAND, P. W. and S. LEINHARDT (1981) "Rejoinder to comments on 'An exponential family of probability distributions for directed graphs.' " Journal of the American Statistical Association 76: 62-65.

HOMANS, G. C. (1950) The Human Group. New York: Harcourt Brace Jovanovich.

HOPE, K. (1981a) "Trends in the openness of British society in the present century." Pp. 127-170 in D. J. Treiman and R. V. Robinson (eds.), Research in Social Stratification and Mobility, 1981. Greenwich, CT: JAI Press.

HOPE, K. (1981b) "Class closure in the United States and Europe." Unpublished paper, Nuffield College, Oxford.

HOPE, K. (1981c) "Vertical mobility in Britain: A structured analysis." Sociology 15: 14-55.

HOPKINS, B. R. (1979) The Law of Tax-Exempt Organizations. New York: John Wiley.

HOROWITZ, A. (1978) "Family, kin and friend networks in psychiatric help-seeking." Social Science and Medicine 12: 297-304.

HOWARD, L. (1974) "Industrialization and community in Chotangapur." Ph.D. dissertation, Department of Sociology, Harvard University.

HUBER, J. (1980) "Ransacking mobility tables." Contemporary Sociology 9: 5-8.

INKELES, A. and D. H. SMITH (1974) Becoming Modern: Individual Change in Six Developing Countries. Cambridge, MA: Harvard University Press.

JACOBS, D. (1974) "Dependency and vulnerability: An exchange approach to the control of organizations." Administrative Science Quarterly 19: 45-59.

JACOBS, J. (1961) The Death and Life of Great American Cities. New York: Random House.

JANOWITZ, M. (1952) The Community Press in an Urban Setting: The Social Elements of Urbanism. Chicago: University of Chicago Press.

KADUSHIN, C. (1974) The American Intellectual Elite. Boston: Little, Brown.

KADUSHIN, C. (1968) "Power, influence, and social circles: A new methodology for studying opinion makers." American Sociological Review 33: 685-698.

KADUSHIN, C. (1966) "The friends and supporters of psychotherapy: On social circles in urban life." American Sociological Review 31: 786-802.

KAMENS, D. (1977) "Legitimating myths and educational organization: The relationship between organizational ideology and formal structure." American Sociological Review 42: 208-219.

KANTER, R. (1977a) Men and Women of the Corporation. New York: Basic Books.

KANTER, R. (1977b) "Some effects of proportions on group life." American Journal of Sociology 82: 965-990.

KAPFERER, B. (1976) Transaction and Meaning: Direction in the Anthropology of Exchange and Symbolic Behavior. Commonwealth Essays in Social Anthropology (Vol. 1). Philadelphia: Institute for the Study of Human Issues.

KAPFERER, B. (1973) "Social networks and conjugal roles in urban Zambia: Towards a reformulation of the Bott hypothesis." Pp. 83-110 in J. Boissevain and J. C. Mitchell (eds.), Network Analysis: Studies in Human Interaction. The Hague: Mouton.

KAPFERER, B. (1972) Strategy and Transaction in an African Factory. Manchester, England: Manchester University Press.

KARWEIT, N., S. HANSELL, and M. RICKS (1979) "The conditions for peer associations in schools." Report No. 282, Center for Social Organization of Schools, Johns Hopkins University.

KATZ, F. E. (1958) "Occupational contact networks." Social Forces 37: 52-55.

KATZ, E. and P. LAZARSFELD (1955) Personal Influence. New York: Free Press.

KELLER, S. (1963) Beyond the Ruling Class: Strategic Elites in Modern Society. New York: Random House.

KENNETT, D. A. (1980) "Altruism and economic behavior I and II." American Journal of Economics and Sociology 39: 183-198, 337-353.

KIRSH, S. (1981) "Emotional support systems of working-class women." Ph.D. dissertation, Department of Educational Theory, University of Toronto.

KNOKE, D. (1982) "Organizational sponsorship of social influence associations." Presented at the Second Sun Belt Social Network Conference, Tampa, Florida, February.

KOMORITA, S. and J. M. CHERTKOFF (1978) "A bargaining theory of coalition formation." Sociometry 40: 351-361.

KOMORITA, S. and T. M. TUMONIS (1980) "Extensions of some descriptive theories of coalition formation." Journal of Personality and Social Psychology 39: 256-268.

KORNHAUSER, W. (1968) "Mass society." International Encyclopedia of the Social Sciences (Vol. 10). New York: Macmillan.

KRITZER, H. M. (1978) "Ideology and American political elites." Public Opinion Quarterly 42: 484-502.

KROEBER, A. L. and T. PARSONS (1958) "The concept of culture and social system." American Sociological Review 23: 582-583.

LANGLOIS, S. (1977) "Les réseaux personnels et la diffusion des informations sur les emplois." Recherches Sociographiques 2: 213-245.

LaROCCA, J. M., J. S. HOUSE, and J.R.P. FRENCH, Jr. (1980) "Social support, occupational stress and health." Journal of Health and Social Behavior 21: 202-217.

LAUMANN, E. O. (1979) "Network analysis in large social systems: Some theoretical and methodological problems." Pp. 379-423 in P. W. Holland and S. Leinhardt (eds.), Perspectives on Social Network Research. New York: Academic Press.

LAUMANN, E. O. (1973) Bonds of Pluralism: The Form and Substance of Urban Social Networks. New York: John Wiley.

LAUMANN, E. O., (1966) Prestige and Association in an Urban Community. Indianapolis: Bobbs-Merrill.

LAUMANN, E. O., J. GALASKIEWICZ, and P. V. MARSDEN (1978) "Community structure as interorganizational linkages." Annual Review of Sociology 4: 455-484.

LAUMANN, E. O. and P. V. MARSDEN (1979) "The analysis of oppositional structures in political elites: Identifying collective actors." American Sociological Review 44: 713-732.

LAUMANN, E. O., P. V. MARSDEN, and J. GALASKIEWICZ (1977) "Community influence structures: Replication and extension of a network approach." American Journal of Sociology 83: 594-631.

LAUMANN, E. O., P. V. MARSDEN, and D. PRENSKY (1982) "The boundary specification problem in network analysis." In R. S. Burt and M. J. Minor (eds.), Applied Network Analysis. Beverly Hills, CA: Sage.

LAUMANN, E. O. and F. U. PAPPI (1976) Networks of Collective Action: A Perspective on Community Influence Systems. New York: Academic Press.

LAUMANN, E. O. and F. U. PAPPI (1973) "New directions in the study of community elites." American Sociological Review 38: 212-230.

LAWLER, E. J. (1975) "An experimental study of factors affecting the mobilization of revolutionary coalitions." Sociometry 38: 163-179.

LAZARSFELD, P. F. and R. K. MERTON (1954) "Friendship as a social process: A substantive and methodological analysis." Pp. 18-56 in M. Berger, T. Abel, and C. Page (eds.), Freedom and Control in Modern Society. New York: Van Nostrand.

LEE, M. L. (1971) "A conspicuous production theory of hospital behavior." Southern Economic Journal 38: 48-59.

LEIGHTON, B. and B. WELLMAN (1978) "Interview schedule/aide-memoire: East York social networks project–phase IV." Resource Paper No. 1, Centre for Urban and Community Studies, University of Toronto.

LEIBENSTEIN, H. (1976) Beyond Economic Man. Cambridge, MA: Harvard University Press.

LEINHARDT, S. [ed.] (1977) Social Networks: A Developing Paradigm. New York: Academic Press.

LÉVI-STRAUSS, C. (1969) Elementary Structures of Kinship. Boston: Beacon Press.

LEVINE, S. and P. WHITE (1961) "Exchange as a conceptual framework for the study of interorganizational relationships." Administrative Science Quarterly 5: 583-601.

LIN, N., P. W. DAYTON, and P. GREENWALD (1978) "Analyzing the instrumental use of relations in the context of social structure." Sociological Methods and Research 7: 149-166.

LIN, N., P. W. DAYTON, and P. GREENWALD (1977) "The Urban Communication Network and Social Stratification." Pp. 55-72 in B. Ruben (ed.), Communication Yearbook I. New Brunswick, NJ: Transaction Books.

LIN, N. and M. DUMIN (1982) "Access to occupational resources through social ties." Presented at the annual meetings of the American Sociological Association, San Francisco, September.

LIN, N., W. M. ENSEL, and J. C. VAUGHN (1981) "Social resources and strength of ties: Structural factors in occupational status attainment." American Sociological Review 46: 393-405.

LIN, N., R. S. SIMEONE, W. M. ENSEL, and W. KUO (1979) "Social support, stressful life events and illness." Journal of Health and Social Behavior 20: 108-119.

LIN, N., J. C. VAUGHN, and W. M. ENSEL (1981) "Social resources and occupational status attainment." Social Forces 60: 1163-1181.

LIPSET, S. M. (1975) "Social structure and social change." Pp. 172-209 in P. M. Blau (ed.), Approaches to the Study of Social Structure. New York: Free Press.

LOMNITZ, L. (1977) Networks and Marginality. New York: Academic Press.

LORRAIN, F. and H. C. WHITE (1971) "Structural equivalence of individuals in social networks." Journal of Mathematical Sociology 1: 49-80.

LUTTBEG, N. R. (1968) "The structures of beliefs among leaders and the public." Public Opinion Quarterly 32: 398-409.

LYLES, M. A. and I. I. MITROFF (1980) "Organizational problem formulation: An empirical study." Administrative Science Quarterly 25: 102-119.

MACAULAY, S. (1963) "Non-contractual relations in business: A preliminary study." American Sociological Review 28: 55-67.

MALINOWSKI, B. (1922) Argonauts of the Western Pacific. London: Routledge & Kegan Paul.

MARCH, J. G. and J. P. OLSEN (1976) Ambiguity and Choice in Organizations. Bergen, Norway: Universitetsforlaget.

MARSDEN, P. V. (forthcoming) "Restricted access in networks and models of power." American Journal of Sociology 88.

MARSDEN, P. V. (1981) "Introducing influence processes into a system of collective decisions." American Journal of Sociology 86: 1203-1235.

MARSDEN, P. V. (1979) "Community leadership and social structure: Bargaining and opposition." Ph.D. dissertation, Department of Sociology, University of Chicago.

MARSDEN, P. V. and E. O. LAUMANN (1977) "Collective action in a community elite: Exchange, influence resources, and issue resolution." Pp. 199-250 in R. J. Liebert and A. W. Imershein (eds.), Power, Paradigms, and Community Research. London: Sage.

MARTINDALE, D. (1981) The Nature and Types of Sociological Theory (2nd ed.). Boston: Houghton Mifflin.

MARX, K. (1844/1972) "Economic and philosophic manuscripts of 1844." Pp. 66-125 in R. C. Tucker (ed.), The Marx-Engels Reader. New York: Norton.

MATTHEWS, D. R. (1960) U.S. Senators and Their World. Chapel Hill: University of North Carolina Press.

MAYER, P. with I. MAYER (1974) Townsmen or Tribesmen (2nd ed.). Cape Town, South Africa: Oxford University Press.

McALLISTER, L. and C. S. FISCHER (1978) "A procedure for surveying personal networks." Sociological Methods and Research 7: 131-148.

McCLELLAND, D. C. and D. G. WINTER (1969) Motivating Economic Achievement. New York: Free Press.

McCLOSKY, H., P. J. HOFFMAN, and R. O'HARA (1960) "Issue conflict and consensus among party leaders and followers." American Political Science Review 54: 406-427.

McKEAN, R. N. (1975) "Economics of trust, altruism, and corporate responsibility." Pp. 29-44 in E. S. Phelps (ed.), Altruism, Morality, and Economic Theory. New York: Russell Sage Foundation.

MERTON, R. K. (1957) Social Theory and Social Structure. New York: Free Press.

MICHELS, R. (1949) Political Parties: A Sociological Study of the Oligarchical Tendencies of Modern Democracy. New York: Free Press.

MILGRAM, S. (1967) "The small world problem." Psychology Today 22: 61-67.

MILLER, S. M. (1960) "Comparative social mobility." Current Sociology 9: 1-89.

MILLS, C. W. (1956) The Power Elite. New York: Oxford University Press.

MINTZ, B. (1975) "The President's Cabinet 1897-1972: A contribution to the power structure debate." Insurgent Sociologist 5: 131-148.

MITCHELL, J. C. (1974) "Social Networks." Annual Review of Anthropology 3: 279-299.

MITCHELL, J. C. (1969) "The concept and use of social networks." Pp. 1-50 in J. C. Mitchell (ed.), Social Networks in Urban Situations. Manchester, England: Manchester University Press.

MITNICK, B. M. (1975) "The theory of agency: A framework." Working Paper Series, School of Public Administration, Ohio State University.

MOLM, L. and J. WIGGINS (1979) "A behavioral analysis of the dynamics of social exchange in the dyad." Social Forces 57: 1157-1179.

MOORE, G. (1979) "The structure of a national elite network." American Sociological Review 44: 673-692.

MORENO, J. L. (1934) Who Shall Survive? Washington, DC: Nervous and Mental Disease Publishing Company.

MORGAN, L. H. (1877/1964) Ancient Society (ed. L. White). Cambridge, MA: Belknap.

MOSKOWITZ, M. (1977) "Corporate charitable contributions and corporate social responsibility." Pp. 1827-1838 in Research Papers, Commission on Private Philanthropy and Public Needs. Washington, DC: Department of the Treasury.

MOXLEY, R. L. and N. F. MOXLEY (1974) "Determining point-centrality in uncontrived social networks." Sociometry 37: 122-130.

MUELLER, C. M. and C. M. JUDD (1981) "Belief constraint and belief consensus: Toward an analysis of social movement ideologies." Social Forces 60: 182-187.

MUKHERJEE, R. and J. R. HALL (1954) "A note on the analysis of data on social mobility." Pp. 218-241 in D. V. Glass (ed.), Social Mobility in Britain. London: Routledge & Kegan Paul.

MURRAY, S., J. RANKIN, and D. MAGILL (1981) "Strong ties and job information." Sociology of Work and Occupations 8: 119-136.

National Center for Educational Statistics (1980) The Condition of Education, 1978. Washington, DC: Government Printing Office.

NEIMEIJER, R. (1973) "Some applications of the notion of density." Pp. 45-64 in J. Boissevain and J. C. Mitchell (eds.), Network Analysis: Studies in Human Interaction. The Hague: Mouton.

NIE, N. H., S. VERBA, and J. R. PETROCIK (1976) The Changing American Voter. Cambridge, MA: Harvard University Press.

NIEMINEN, U. J. (1974) "On centrality in a graph." Scandinavian Journal of Psychology 15: 322-336.

NIEMINEN, U. J. (1973) "On the centrality of a directed graph." Social Science Research 2: 371-378.

NIXON, H. L. (1979) The Small Group. Englewood Cliffs, NJ: Prentice-Hall.

NYSTROM, P. C. and W. H. STARBUCK (1981) Handbook of Organizational Design, Volume 1: Adapting Organizations to Their Environments. New York: Oxford University Press.

OLECK, H. L. (1979) Non-profit Corporations, Organizations, and Associations (3rd ed.). Englewood Cliffs, NJ: Prentice-Hall.

OLIVER, P. (1980) "Rewards and punishments as selective incentives for collective action: Theoretical investigations." American Journal of Sociology 85: 1356-1375.

OLSON, M. (1965) The Logic of Collective Action. Cambridge, MA: Harvard University Press.

PAPPI, F. U. (1981) "The petite bourgeoisie and the new middle class: Differentiation or homogenisation of the middle strata in Germany." Pp. 105-120 in F.

Bechhofer and B. Elliott (eds.), The Petite Bourgeoisie: Comparative Studies of the Uneasy Stratum. London: Macmillan.

PARK, R. E. (1916/1969) "The city: Suggestions for investigation of human behavior in the urban environment." Pp. 91-130 in R. Sennett (ed.), Classic Essays on the Culture of Cities. New York: Appleton-Century-Crofts.

PARSONS, T. (1961) "An outline of the social system." Pp. 30-79 in T. Parsons, E. Shils, K. D. Naegele, and J. R. Pitts (eds.), Theories of Society. New York: Free Press.

PARSONS, T. (1951) The Social System. New York: Free Press.

PAYNE, G., G. FORD, and C. ROBERTSON (1977) "A reappraisal of social mobility in Britain." Sociology 11: 289-310.

PEARLIN, L. I. and C. SCHOOLER (1978) "The structure of coping." Journal of Health and Social Behavior 19: 2-21.

PERROW, C. (1961) "Organizational prestige: Some functions and dysfunctions." American Journal of Sociology 66: 335-341.

PFEFFER, J. and A. LEONG (1977) "Resource allocation in United Funds: Examination of power and dependence." Social Forces 55: 775-790.

PFEFFER, J. and G. SALANCIK (1978) The External Control of Organizations: A Resource Dependence Perspective. New York: Harper & Row.

PILISUK, M. and C. FROLAND (1978) "Kinship, social networks, social support, and health." Social Science and Medicine 128: 273-280.

POLSBY, N. W. (1980) Community Power and Political Theory: A Further Look at Problems of Evidence and Inference. New Haven, CT: Yale University Press.

POOL, I. (1980) "Comment on Mark Granovetter's 'The strength of weak ties: A network theory revisited.' " Presented at the Annual Meetings of the International Communications Association, Acapulco, May.

POOL, I. and M. KOCHEN (1978) "Contacts and influence." Social Networks 1: 5-51.

PREWITT, K. and A. STONE (1973) The Ruling Elites: Elite Theory, Power and American Democracy. New York: Harper & Row.

PROVAN, K., J. M. BEYER, and C. KRUYTBOSCH (1980) "Environmental linkages and power in resource-dependence relations between organizations." Administrative Science Quarterly 25: 200-225.

PUTNAM, R. D. (1976) The Comparative Study of Political Elites. Englewood Cliffs, NJ: Prentice-Hall.

PUTNAM, R. D., R. LEONARDI, and R. Y. NANETTI (1979) "Attitude stability among Italian elites." American Political Science Review 73: 463-494.

REINER, T. A. and J. WOLPERT (1981) "The non-profit sector in the metropolitan economy." Economic Geography 57: 23-33.

REISS, A. J. with O. D. DUNCAN, P. K. HATT, and C. C. NORTH (1961) Occupations and Social Status. New York: Free Press.

RIKER, W. H. (1962) The Theory of Political Coalitions. New Haven, CT: Yale University Press.

ROBERTS, B. R. (1973) Organizing Strangers: Poor Families in Guatemala City. Austin: University of Texas Press.

ROBINS, L. N., D. M. DAVID, and D. W. GOODWIN (1971) "Drug use by U.S. Army enlisted men in Vietnam: A follow-up on their return home." American Journal of Epidemiology 99: 235-249.

ROBINSON, R. and J. KELLEY (1979) "Class as conceived by Marx and Dahrendorf: Effects on income inequality and politics in the United States and Great Britain." American Sociological Review 44: 38-58.

ROGERS, D. (1974) "Sociometric analysis of interorganizational relations: Application of theory and measurement." Rural Sociology 39: 487-503.

ROGERS, E. (1979) "Network analysis of the diffusion of innovations." Pp. 137-164 in P. W. Holland and S. Leinhardt (eds.), Perspectives on Social Network Research. New York: Academic Press.

ROGERS, E. and D. L. KINCAID (1981) Communication Networks: Toward a New Paradigm for Research. New York: Free Press.

ROGERS, M. F. (1974) "Instrumental and infra-resources: The bases of power." American Journal of Sociology 79: 1418-1433.

ROGOFF, N. (1953/1979) Recent Trends in Occupational Mobility. New York: Arno Press.

ROSENBAUM, J. E. (1979) "Organizational career mobility: Promotion chances in a corporation during periods of growth and contraction." American Journal of Sociology 85: 21-48.

ROSENBAUM, J. E. (1981) "Careers in a corporate hierarchy: A longitudinal analysis of earnings and level attainments." Pp. 95-124 in D. J. Treiman and R. V. Robinson (eds.), Research in Social Stratification and Mobility, 1981. Greenwich, CT: JAI Press.

ROSE-ACKERMAN, S. (1980) "United Charities: An Economic Analysis." Public Policy 28: 323-350.

ROSSI, P. H. (1966) "Research strategies in measuring peer group influence." Pp. 190-214 in T. M. Newcomb and E. K. Wilson (eds.), College Peer Groups. Chicago: Aldine.

RUBIN, J. Z. and B. R. BROWN (1975) The Social Psychology of Bargaining and Negotiation. New York: Academic Press.

RYTINA, S. (1980a) "Differentiation reconsidered." Ph.D. dissertation, Department of Sociology, University of Michigan.

RYTINA, S. (1980b) "Contacts and complexity: Networks and differentiation on a macro scale." Unpublished paper, Department of Sociology, State University of New York at Albany.

RYTINA, S. and D. MORGAN (1982) "The arithmetic of social relations." American Journal of Sociology 88: 88-113.

SABIDUSSI, G. (1966) "The centrality index of a graph." Psychometrika 31: 581-603.

SAILER, L. D. (1978) "Structural equivalence: Meaning and definition, computation and application." Social Networks 1: 73-90.

SARTORI, G. (1969) "Politics, ideology, and belief systems." American Political Science Review 63: 398-411.

SAVAGE, I. R. and K. A. DEUTSCH (1960) "A statistical model of the gross analysis of transaction flows." Econometrica 28: 551-572.

SCHELLING, T. (1978) Micromotives and Macrobehavior. New York: Norton.

SCHMIDT, S. M. and T. A. KOCHAN (1977) "Interorganizational relationships: Patterns and motivations." Administrative Science Quarterly 22: 220-234.

SCHOOLER, C. (1976) "Serfdom's legacy: An ethnic continuum." American Journal of Sociology 81: 1265-1286.

SCHULZE, R. (1961) "The bifurcation of power in a satellite city." Pp. 19-80 in M. Janowitz (ed.), Community Political Systems. New York: Free Press.

SCOTT, J. and L. TILLY (1975) "Women's work and the family in nineteenth-century Europe." Comparative Studies in Society and History 17: 36-64.

SELZNICK, P. (1949) TVA and the Grass Roots: A Study in the Sociology of Formal Organizations. New York: Harper & Row.

SHERIF, M. (1936) Psychology of Social Norms. New York: Harper's.

SHERIF, M., O. J. HARVEY, B. J. WHITE, W. R. HOOD, and C. W. SHERIF (1961) Intergroup Conflict and Cooperation: The Robbers Cave Experiment. Norman: University of Oklahoma Book Exchange.

SHORTER, E. (1973) "Female emancipation, birth control, and fertility in European history." American Historical Review 78: 605-640.

SHULMAN, N. (1976) "Network analysis: A new addition to an old bag of tricks." Acta Sociologica 19: 307-323.

SHULMAN, N. (1972) "Urban social networks." Ph.D. dissertation, Department of Sociology, University of Toronto.

SIMMEL, G. (1955a) Conflict (trans. K. H. Wolff). New York: Free Press.

SIMMEL, G. (1922/1955b) The Web of Group Affiliations (trans. R. Bendix). New York: Free Press.

SIMMEL, G. (1950a) "The metropolis and mental life." Pp. 409-424 in K. Wolff (ed., trans.), The Sociology of Georg Simmel. New York: Free Press.

SIMMEL, G. (1950b) The Sociology of Georg Simmel (trans., ed. K. Wolff). New York: Free Press.

SIMON, H. (1957) Models of Man. New York: John Wiley.

SIRKEN, M. E. (1970) "Household surveys with multiplicity." Journal of the American Statistical Association 65: 257-266.

SMELSER, N. J. (1963) Theory of Collective Behavior. New York: Free Press.

SMITH, D. H. (1978) "United Way is the name, monopoly is the game." Business and Society Review 25: 30-35.

SMITH, E.R.A.N. (1980) "The levels of conceptualization: False measures of ideological sophistication." American Political Science Review 74: 685-696.

SØRENSEN, A. B. (1977) "The structure of inequality and the process of attainment." American Sociological Review 42: 965-978.

SOROKIN, P. A. (1927) Social Mobility. New York: Harper & Brothers.

SPILERMAN, S. (1977) "Careers, labor market structure, and socioeconomic achievement." American Journal of Sociology 83: 551-593.

SROLE, L. (1980) "Mental health in New York." The Sciences 16: 20-29.

SROLE, L., T. S. LANGNER, S. T. MICHAEL, P. KIRKPATRICK, M. K. OPLER, and T.A.C. RENNIE (1975) Mental Health in the Metropolis (Rev. and enlarged ed.). New York: Harper & Row.

STACK, C. (1974) All Our Kin. New York: Harper & Row.

STAR, S. A. (1950) "The screening of psychoneurotics in the army: Technical development of tests." Pp. 486-547 in S. A. Stouffer, L. Guttman, E. A. Suchman, P. F. Lazarsfeld, S. A. Star, and J. A. Clausen (eds.), Measurement and Prediction. Princeton: Princeton University Press.

STEINBERG, L. (1980) "Preexisting social ties and conflict group formation." Presented at the annual meetings of the American Sociological Association, New York, August.

STEINBERG, S. (1974) The Academic Melting Pot. New York: McGraw-Hill.

STEWMAN, S. (1975) "Two Markov models of open system occupational mobility: Conceptualizations and empirical tests." American Sociological Review 40: 298-321.

SULLIVAN, J. L., J. E. PIERESON, G. E. MARCUS, and S. FELDMAN (1979) "The more things change, the more they stay the same: The stability of mass belief systems." American Political Science Review 73: 176-186.

SULS, J. M. and R. L. MILLER [eds.] (1977) Social Comparison Processes. New York: Hemisphere.

SWANSON, G. E. (1971) "An organizational analysis of collectives." American Sociological Review 36: 607-623.

TESSER, A. (1971) "Evaluative and structural similarity of attitudes as determinants of interpersonal attraction." Journal of Personality and Social Psychology 18: 92-96.

Theatre Communications Group (1978) TCG Survey 76-77. New York: Author.

THOMPSON, J. D. (1967) Organizations in Action. New York: McGraw-Hill.

TILLY, C. (1974) "Introduction." Pp. 1-35 in C. Tilly (ed.), An Urban World. Boston: Little, Brown.

TOENNIES, F. (1887/1963) Community and Society (trans., ed. C. P. Loomis). New York: Harper & Row.

TOLSDORF, C. (1976) "Social networks, support and coping: An exploratory study." Family Process 15: 407-417.

TREUSCH, P. E. and N. A. SUGARMAN (1979) Tax-exempt Charitable Organizations. Philadelphia: American Law Institute.

TROUWBORST, A. (1973) "Two types of partial networks in Burundi." Pp. 111-123 in J. Boissevain and J. C. Mitchell (eds.), Network Analysis: Studies in Human Interaction. The Hague: Mouton.

TROY, K. (1980) Annual Survey of Corporate Contributions, 1980 Edition. New York: The Conference Board.

TYREE, A. (1973) "Mobility ratios and association in mobility tables." Population Studies 27: 577-588.

U.S. Department of Commerce (1974) "Input-output structure of the U.S. economy: 1967." Survey of Current Business 54: 24-55.

U.S. Department of Commerce (1971) 1967 Census of Manufactures, Concentration Ratios in Manufacturing. Washington, DC: Government Printing Office.

VANNEMAN, R. (1977) "The occupational composition of American classes: Results from cluster analysis." American Journal of Sociology 82: 783-807.

VASQUEZ, T. (1977) "Corporate giving measures." Pp. 1839-1852 in Research Papers, Commission on Private Philanthropy and Public Needs. Washington, DC: Department of the Treasury.

VEBLEN, T. (1904) The Theory of Business Enterprise. New York: New American Library.

VERBRUGGE, L. M. (1978) "Peers as recruiters: Family planning communications of West Malaysian acceptors." Journal of Health and Social Behavior 19: 51-68.

VERBRUGGE, L. M. (1977) "The structure of adult friendship choices." Social Forces 56: 576-597.

VICKREY, W. S. (1962) "One economist's view of philanthropy." Pp. 31-56 in F. G. Dickinson (ed.), Philanthropy and Public Policy. New York: National Bureau of Economic Research.

Vietnam Era Research Project (1979) Working Papers. New York: Center for Policy Research.

WALKER, G. (1977) "Social networks and territory in a commuter village, Bond Head, Ontario." Canadian Geographer 21: 329-350.

WALLACE, W. L. (1981) "Hierarchic structure in social phenomena." Pp. 191-234 in P. M. Blau and R. K. Merton (eds.), Continuities in Structural Inquiry. London: Sage.

WALLACE, W. L. (1966) Student Culture: Social Structure and Continuity in a Liberal Arts College. Chicago: Aldine.

WARREN, D. I. (1976) Neighborhood and Community Contexts in Help Seeking, Problem Coping and Mental Health: Data Analysis Monograph. Ann Arbor: University of Michigan, Program in Community Effectiveness.

WARREN, R. (1978) The Community in America (3rd ed.). Chicago: Rand-McNally.

WEBER, M. (1922/1978) "Status Groups and Classes." Pp. 302-307 in G. Roth and C. Wittich (eds.), Economy and Society. Berkeley: University of California Press.

WEBER, M. (1922/1957) The Theory of Social and Economic Organization (ed. T. Parsons). New York: Free Press.

WEIMANN, G. (1980) "Conversation networks as communication networks." Abstract of Ph.D. dissertation, University of Haifa, Israel.

WEISBROD, B. A. (1975) "Toward a theory of the voluntary non-profit sector in a three-sector economy." Pp. 171-195 in E. S. Phelps (ed.), Altruism, Morality, and Economic Theory. New York: Russell Sage Foundation.

WEISSBERG, R. (1976) "Consensual attitudes and attitude structure." Public Opinion Quarterly 40: 349-359.

WELCH, M. S. (1980) Networking: The Great New Way for Women to Get Ahead. New York: Harcourt Brace Jovanovich.

WELLMAN, B. (1982a) "Network analysis: From metaphor and method to theory and substance." Sociological Theory 1.

WELLMAN, B. (1982b) "Studying personal communities in East York." Research Paper No. 182, Centre for Urban and Community Studies, University of Toronto.

WELLMAN, B. (1981) "Applying network analysis to the study of support." Pp. 171-200 in B. H. Gottlieb (ed.), Social Networks and Social Support. Beverly Hills, CA: Sage.

WELLMAN, B. (1979) "The community question: The intimate networks of East Yorkers." American Journal of Sociology 84: 1201-1231.

WELLMAN, B. (1968) Community Ties and Mental Health. Toronto: Clarke Institute of Psychiatry, Community Studies Section.

WELLMAN, B., P. CRAVEN, M. WHITAKER, H. STEVENS, A. SHORTER, S. DUTOIT, and H. BAKKER (1973) "Community ties and support systems." Pp. 152-167 in L. S. Bourne, R. D. MacKinnon, and J. W. Simmons (eds.), The Form of Cities in Central Canada. Toronto: University of Toronto Press.

WELLMAN, B. and B. LEIGHTON (1979) "Networks, neighborhoods and communities." Urban Affairs Quarterly 15: 363-390.

WHITE, H. C. (1970) Chains of Opportunity: System Models of Mobility in Organizations. Cambridge, MA: Harvard University Press.

WHITE, H. C., S. A. BOORMAN, and R. L. BREIGER (1976) "Social structure from multiple networks: I. Blockmodels of roles and positions." American Journal of Sociology 81: 730-780.

WHITE, H. C. and R. L. BREIGER (1975) "Pattern across networks." Transaction 12: 68-73.

WHITTEN, N. E. and A. W. WOLFE (1973) "Network analysis." Pp. 717-746 in J. J. Honigman (ed.), The Handbook of Social and Cultural Anthropology. Chicago: Rand McNally.

WHYTE, W. F. (1955) Street Corner Society. Chicago: University of Chicago Press.

WILLIAMSON, O. E. (1981) "The economics of organization: The transaction cost approach." American Journal of Sociology 87: 548-577.

WILLIAMSON, O. E. (1975) Markets and Hierarchies: Analysis and Antitrust Implications. New York: Free Press.

WIRTH, L. (1938) "Urbanism as a way of life." American Journal of Sociology 44: 3-24.

WOLFE, A. W. (1978) "The rise of network thinking in anthropology." Social Networks 1: 53-64.

WOOD, J. R. (1972) "Unanticipated consequences of organizational coalitions." Social Forces 50: 512-521.

WRIGHT, E. O. (1980) "Class and occupation." Theory and Society 9: 177-214.

WRIGHT, E. O. (1979) Class Structure and Income Determination. New York: Academic Press.

WRIGHT, E. O. (1978) Class, Crisis and the State. London: New Left Books.

WRIGHT, E. O. and L. PERRONE (1977) "Marxist class categories and income inequality." American Sociological Review 42: 32-55.

YAMAGISHI, T. (1981) "Two approaches to defining positions in networks." Technical Report, Department of Sociology, University of Washington.

YAMAGISHI, T., K. S. COOK, and R. M. EMERSON (1981) "The simulation of social exchange in networks." Technical Report, Department of Sociology, University of Washington.

YAMAGUCHI, K. (1982) "The structure of intergenerational occupational mobility: Generality and specificity in resources, channels and barriers." American Journal of Sociology 88.

ZALD, M. (1970) Organizational Change: The Political Economy of the YMCA. Chicago: University of Chicago Press.

ZOLBERG, V. (1974) "The Art Institute of Chicago: The sociology of a cultural organization." Ph.D. dissertation, Department of Sociology, University of Chicago.

About the Contributors

RICHARD D. ALBA is Associate Professor of Sociology and Director of the Center for Social and Demographic Analysis at the State University of New York at Albany. He is currently working on a book on Italian Americans, a strategic group for assessing the state of ethnicity in America.

HOWARD ALDRICH is Professor of Sociology at the University of North Carolina at Chapel Hill. His book, *Organizations and Environments* (Prentice-Hall, 1979) is now in its second printing and is the vehicle through which he hopes to spread the message concerning the population ecology perspective on organizations. He is currently working on a study of producers' cooperatives (with Robert Stern) and an observational study of chief executive officers (with Lance Kurke); he is also analyzing data from a panel study of Asian and white shopkeepers in English cities.

PETER M. BLAU is Quetelet Professor of Sociology at Columbia University and Distinguished Professor of Sociology at the State University of New York at Albany. His present research involves a study on intermarriage within the 125 largest U.S. standard metropolitan statistical areas, designed to test the theory outlined in his book *Inequality and Heterogeneity* (Free Press, 1977).

RONALD L. BREIGER is Professor of Sociology at Cornell University and a faculty research associate at the Cornell Institute for Social and Economic Research. He is engaged in comparative studies of social class, mobility, and community elites, studies of the evolution of role structure, and the further development of network theory and models for the aggregation of social categories.

RONALD S. BURT is Associate Professor of Sociology at Columbia University. His interest is in the general development of structural sociology.

KAREN S. COOK is Associate Professor of Sociology at the University of Washington. She is engaged in experimental research on social exchange. This research analyzes both equity and power processes within exchange networks.

BONNIE H. ERICKSON is Associate Professor of Sociology at the University of Toronto. She is currently studying an urban voluntary association of several hundred duplicate bridge players in Ottawa-Hull (with T. A. Nosanchuk). Among other things, this study is concerned with the *in situ* operation of social comparison processes and the effect of activities and social relationships on the well-being of the aged.

JOSEPH GALASKIEWICZ is Associate Professor of Sociology at the University of Minnesota, Minneapolis. He is currently conducting research on corporate philanthropy and the voluntary support of nonprofit organizations in the Minneapolis-St. Paul metropolitan area. He is the author of *Exchange Networks and Community Politics* (Sage, 1979).

LEO A. GOODMAN is Charles L. Hutchinson Distinguished Service Professor of Sociology and Statistics at the University of Chicago and a faculty research associate at the Population Research Center of the University. He is developing mathematical models and statistical methods for the analysis of social processes. His article in *Sociological Methodology 1981* (Jossey-Bass) provides an overall view of the main ways in which log-linear models and corresponding statistical methods can be applied.

MARK GRANOVETTER is Associate Professor of Sociology at the State University of New York at Stony Brook. He is currently writing a monograph on threshold models of collective behavior and continuing to explore the connections between economic and sociological theory.

CHARLES KADUSHIN is Professor of Sociology and Psychology in the Graduate School and University Center, City University of New York. His current interests involve the study of social networks as applied to the sociology of Vietnam veterans, the sociology of Post Traumatic Stress Reaction, and the sociology of intellectuals.

DAVID KNOKE is Professor of Sociology at Indiana University. His main interest is in political sociology, with an emphasis on voluntary associations, interorganizational networks, and other forms of collective action.

He is studying the social organization of the national energy and health policy domains (with Edward O. Laumann).

EDWARD O. LAUMANN is Professor and Chair of the Department of Sociology at the University of Chicago and editor of the *American Journal of Sociology*. He has recently completed a book on the sociology of the legal profession (with John P. Heinz) and is in the middle of a study of the social organization of the national policy domains of health and energy (with David Knoke).

NAN LIN is Professor of Sociology at the State University of New York at Albany. His current interest is in the development of a theory on social resources and social actions. He is examining the theory with data regarding access to social resources in the occupational structure and the effect of social resources and social support on mental health.

PETER V. MARSDEN is Assistant Professor of Sociology at the University of North Carolina at Chapel Hill. His interests include stratification, formal organizations, and network analysis.

GWEN MOORE is Visiting Assistant Professor of Sociology at the State University of New York at Albany. She is currently at work on a cross-national study of elite social structure and a study of gender, networks, and managerial careers in the New York State government administration.

STEVE RYTINA is Assistant Professor of Sociology at Harvard University. He is working on further models of the effects of structure on contact, focusing most recently on implications of inequality for intermarriage (with Peter Blau, Terry Blum, and Joseph Schwartz). He is also examining cognitive models of equity judgments for housework (with Glenna Spitze).

BARRY WELLMAN is Professor of Sociology, Director of the Structural Analysis Programme, and a faculty research associate at the Centre for Urban and Community Studies at the University of Toronto. He coordinates the 400-member International Network for Social Network Analysis and edits its journal, *Connections.* His principal interest is in analyzing the effects of such large-scale phenomena as bureaucratization and capitalism on the structure and content of urban social networks.